Praise for *Eleanor Powell: Born to Dance*

"This book is a loving and faithful tribute to one of Hollywood's great dance icons. Well written and thoroughly researched, it will be indispensable for anyone interested in Eleanor Powell and the art of tap."—Brian Harker, author of *Sportin' Life: John W. Bubbles, an American Classic*

"What a unique treasure trove this long-awaited biography is for film buffs, students of the dance, and of course, fans of the ever-fascinating MGM musical! An inspiring story, too. This wonderful book is a not-to-be-missed keepsake and a celebration of the truly one-of-a-kind Powell."—Michael Troyan, author of *MGM: Hollywood's Greatest Backlot*

"Eleanor Powell was arguably one of the best female dancers in an era that included Rita Hayworth, Ginger Rogers, and Ann Miller. Unlike most of her contemporaries, she usually danced solo, though her partners included Fred Astaire, George Murphy, Buddy Ebsen, and—surprisingly, one of her most enjoyable—Gracie Allen. After reading *Born to Dance*, I want to go back and watch every one of her films. It's about time someone wrote a biography of Powell, and after this book, there is no reason for anyone to write another!" —Eve Golden, author of *Strictly Dynamite: The Sensational Life of Lupe Velez*

"In Paula Broussard and Lisa Royère, Eleanor Powell has the biographers she deserves. Their *Eleanor Powell: Born to Dance* is a warmhearted account of Powell's ascent from childhood poverty to international stardom, a journey reliant on both Powell's immense talent and her relentless perfectionism. The authors combine vivid descriptions of Powell's fabulous tap-dance sequences with behind-the-scenes accounts of the painful physical and emotional costs she endured to achieve them."—Sydney Ladensohn Stern, author of *The Brothers Mankiewicz: Hope, Heartbreak, and Hollywood Classics*

"Eleanor Powell was without a doubt the premier tap-dancing film star of all time. Her legendary performances graced such MGM motion pictures as *Born to Dance* and *Rosalie*, and her 'Begin the Beguine' number with Fred Astaire in *Broadway Melody of 1940* will never be duplicated. . . . Powell has long deserved a good biography. Her life and career should never be forgotten." —Stephen Michael Shearer, author of *Patricia Neal: An Unquiet Life*

Eleanor Powell

ELEANOR POWELL

BORN TO DANCE

PAULA BROUSSARD AND LISA ROYÈRE

UNIVERSITY PRESS OF KENTUCKY

Published by the University Press of Kentucky
Scholarly publisher for the Commonwealth,
serving Bellarmine University, Berea College, Centre
College of Kentucky, Eastern Kentucky University,
The Filson Historical Society, Georgetown College,
Kentucky Historical Society, Kentucky State University,
Morehead State University, Murray State University,
Northern Kentucky University, Spalding University,
Transylvania University, University of Kentucky,
University of Louisville, University of Pikeville, and
Western Kentucky University.
All rights reserved.

Editorial and Sales Offices: The University Press of Kentucky
663 South Limestone Street, Lexington, Kentucky 40508-4008
www.kentuckypress.com

Cataloging-in-Publication data available from the Library of Congress

ISBN 978-0-8131-9788-3 (hardcover)
ISBN 978-0-8131-9789-0 (epub)
ISBN 978-0-8131-9790-6 (pdf)

This book is printed on acid-free paper meeting
the requirements of the American National Standard
for Permanence in Paper for Printed Library Materials.

Manufactured in the United States of America.

Member of the Association
of University Presses

For Ellie

Contents

CONTENTS

Preface

Writing the story of a life is a complex and unique journey filled with lush valleys of information, arid flatlands devoid of knowledge, and towering mountains of discovery. Coupled with these ups and downs, the writing of this book also spanned a full year during the COVID-19 pandemic, a trying season of unprecedented isolation. I was especially thankful for this project, as I never felt completely isolated—I spent it wholeheartedly with Eleanor Powell. Following the sinuous trail of Eleanor's life across each decade of the twentieth century, I was buoyed and consoled by her history as well as that of America—an intense experience perhaps only researchers can relate to. The road was also marked by new friendships, the sharing of treasured recollections, and the discovery of many unknown nuggets of details. But while unexpected findings abounded, what was most surprising were the eerie nudges and random appearance of serendipitous gifts of information that kept reminding us we were heading on the right path and assured us we were spending our time on the right project.

Throughout the writing, our challenge remained how to relentlessly search out and present to the world "Ellie Powell" behind the mask of "Eleanor Powell." As a private person who guarded many avenues of her life, she carefully selected the high points and pinnacles of her career that were shared in interviews and talks. It was the heartbreaking low points that were meticulously packed away and shielded from public view. Naturally, these were the most elusive, but also the most important to present a balanced portrait of this amazing woman. When many were unearthed, they were also the ones which best illuminated her courage, strength, and faith.

On the corkboard above my desk, I keep a photo of the worn and battered undersoles of the pair of Ellie's tap shoes gifted to Lisa. These shoes date from Eleanor's Las Vegas comeback and represent the result of a year of painful perseverance after finally closing the book on a sixteen-year tumultuous marriage. Just like her life, they were an instrument of wonderful rhythms, inspiring music and love. Hidden from view, the soles took all the wear and tear as the polished upper shoe flashed the glamour. The nicks, scrapes, and gouges on those soles are a daily reminder that hard work, on both the inside and out, produces the unforgettable melody that remains of our lives. The joyful and triumphant rhythm of Ellie's life resonated through the writing of each page of this book. It is my supreme wish that readers hear it loud and clear and that, just like her dances, it inspires them with every beat.

Paula Broussard

Stepping back into a project begun forty years ago was certainly no easy task, but how rewarding it has been to finally bring it to completion! Originally inspired by our intense admiration of a woman who was peerless in her field, yet all but ignored by film and dance historians, we set out to rectify this grave error. At the time, we were teenagers with a lot of spunk and very little experience, but we learned to research well—and that laid a vital foundation to our present-day project.

Along the way, we got to know our subject intimately, discovering that the private "Ellie" was every bit as exceptional as the dancer "Eleanor." From the first night I met her at the Gary Theatre in 1974, I felt an immediate connection, and over the next year, our friendship deepened. She was warm and genuine, and whatever she saw in the young girl I was, she poured herself into me in a special way, giving me the love, strength, and encouragement of a mother to her "adopted" daughter. From sharing deep thoughts to a lighthearted tap step with Paula and me in her kitchen, I will forever treasure these memories.

After Ellie's death, I found it too painful to continue the project. I moved to France in 1985, where I spent the next twenty-five years raising my family. Without Paula's nudging during the height of the pandemic, I doubt that I would have ever done anything with the boxes of research, carefully conserved over the years (lugged overseas and back). Completing this project has been a dream come true, and we have both felt Ellie's presence every step of the way.

Not having a life steeped in scandal as many stars of her day, Eleanor often felt her story would be of little interest to others. Having lived with her up close again over the past year, we strongly disagree. Hers is a good life—a life of joy, love, tenacity, faith, and dedication. We are proud to tell her story.

Lisa Royère

Prologue

8:30 p.m., February 28, 1961
Sahara Hotel, Las Vegas

Eleanor Powell stared long and hard at her reflection in her dressing room mirror. She was about to step back in front of a live audience for the first time in twelve years. Tracing the lines that gave evidence of her forty-eight years, she shifted her gaze to the photo of her teenage son, propped against her mirror as a constant reminder of how proud she was of him. But though the press would believe she was chided into a comeback to win his dare, she was actually doing this for herself. Her catastrophic sixteen-year marriage had taken a hard toll, and she had spent a full year to rebuild her body and broken spirit to get to this place. As she had told the press, "It took a lot of glue to put me back together." The real secrets? Her faith, her son, and her love of dance. The secret to her joy had always been that simple.

She heard the orchestra launch into the overture and stood to put on the last piece of her costume, a white brocade jacket with a high, arched collar that framed her face. With a gentle grin, the lines melted, and a hint of the little girl from Springfield looked back at her from the mirror. She opened the door, letting the opening strains of the overture wash over her. A stagehand was instantly by her side, guiding her as they navigated a path through a myriad of extra sets toward the stage. The murmurs of the audience grew louder as Eleanor and the stagehand stopped at the fold of the curtain where she would make her entrance. "Knock 'em dead, Ellie!" he said. She met his gaze and blew him a kiss.

The energy of the packed house was so electric, the curtain vibrated when she touched it. Beads and sequins on her costume shimmered in the dim light as she adjusted her wig, testing for snugness. But the extras didn't matter at all. Because she knew as soon as she stepped onto the stage, the rhythm of her feet would take over. She could do this. She closed her eyes and inhaled deeply, then threw a glance upward and linked herself with the forces of God. As her introduction echoed through the room, she released her grip from the curtain, and took a step out into the waiting spotlight.

Overture

(1912–1927)

1

First Steps

The girl who was to become film's most celebrated female tap dancer hurried into the world completely unprepared for her close-up—with no eyebrows, fingernails, or hair. Like an unprotected pearl, she was cocooned in an incubator for the first weeks of her life. Her mother, Blanche Helen Torrey Powell of Springfield, Massachusetts, was just three days shy of her seventeenth birthday. Brimming with youthful innocence, she had been unprepared for the flattery and charms of the handsome captain of the school soccer team, seventeen-year-old Clarence "Sonny" Powell. Photographs show him confident and secure in his own allure, posing with his teammates on the steps of Springfield's Technical High School or lounging in his rowboat with a casual glint in his eye that likely made all the teen girls swoon. His calculated boyish charm melted both Blanche's heart and her defenses. At her age, even in 1912, it was impossible to be immune to a flash of that lazy smile.

When a shocked Blanche found herself pregnant, her parents marched with indignation down the street to the Powell home, where a heated conference ensued. On August 29, 1912, the two mothers accompanied their children to the nearby city of Hartford, Connecticut, away from the prying eyes of Springfield locals, for a rushed marriage before the justice of the peace. Reluctantly married and with a child on the way, Blanche's young husband had in no way abandoned that gleam in his eye. Barely three months into the marriage, he contracted a venereal disease that doctors feared could threaten Blanche and the baby. A subsequent examination induced premature labor, and tiny, bald Eleanor Torrey Powell made her appearance with all the pomp and drama befitting a future dancing star, two months early on November 21, 1912.

Baby Eleanor had landed in a prime location that boasted a centuries-old pedigree that dated back to colonial days. Springfield's prominent location at the crossroads of New England prompted George Washington to build the US National Armory in the city, establishing it as a major arms-building center. Attracting skilled artisans and metalworkers, the armory made America's first muskets and rifles. It soon became the "Silicon Valley" of the early arms world and provided needed jobs for a hefty portion of the city residents.

By the time of Eleanor's birth, Springfield had evolved into a thriving city with a population of approximately ninety-five thousand, and the 130-year-old armory and neighboring Smith and Wesson plant were still the major employers in the region. Downtown was a bustling hub of horse-drawn wagons, trolleys, and early motor cars, all vying for the right-of-way down Main Street. The city's thousands of colorful Victorian homes gave its tree-lined streets a bucolic, storybook quality. The majestic Court Square Theatre had hosted live dramatic productions since 1892. Set to open in 1913 was Poli's Palace, the largest and most lavish theater in town. Silent films and lively vaudeville shows would soon be a mainstay. It was a fortunate place to grow up.

Eleanor's toddler years reflected her upbringing by her practical but loving mother and grandparents, all products of an old New England family. Hardworking and sensible, Blanche's paternal side stretched back centuries to the early English settlers in Plymouth, Massachusetts. One of the first to emigrate from England was clothier James Torrey, born in 1612 in the village of St. Nicholas in Somerset. Bequeathed "thirty pounds at sixteen [years of age] and one silver spoon when he is one-and-twenty"[1] on his father's passing, he came to Massachusetts in 1637. He was described as a "man of great usefulness and respectability,"[2] a description that might well fit all the subsequent Torreys. Harold Torrey, Blanche's father, was born in Weymouth, Massachusetts, where Torrey Street bears the family name. He came to Springfield at age four and, after high school, worked as an office boy at the local newspaper before he landed a job at Smith and Wesson.

On Blanche's maternal side, ancestors came from a French-Canadian line, François (anglicized to Francis) from St. Lambert, just opposite Montreal and across the bank of the St. Lawrence River. Eleanor's great-grandfather, blacksmith Vétile François, emigrated from Canada as a teen in 1854, settled in Northampton, Massachusetts, and was naturalized in 1872. While Eleanor's discipline and relentless dedication to her craft would usually be attributed to her New England ancestors, her natural penchant for rhythm and dance (what her ebullient and plainspoken great-aunt Hattie would call "the hell in her feet") was said to originate from her French side. Though Vétile had strict rules that his nine children (eight daughters and one son) were not allowed out after dark, he reportedly loved to dance so much that he opened his Northampton home to regular parties. He would put all the furniture outside, sand down the floors, and invite neighbors and friends over to dance until the early hours of the morning.

The Powell lineage, reportedly dating to an ancestor on the Mayflower by way of Plymouth, also had deep roots in early American stock. Eleanor's paternal grandfather, Benjamin Lewis Powell, came from generations of farmers in Greene County, New York, near the Catskill region, where Washington Irving's gothic tales "The Legend of Sleepy Hollow" and "Rip Van Winkle" take place. He married Eleanor's grandmother, Ina Vesta Gardner, in 1886, and they settled in her hometown of Springfield. There, he started an eavestroughing business. But because Eleanor had no childhood contact with her father or his family, she knew little of previous generations. Nevertheless, Eleanor was proud of her New England heritage and never lost sight of the strong values that served as a solid anchor throughout her life.

In 1912, Clarence's father ran the family eavestroughing business, Benjamin Powell & Sons, and Clarence was destined to follow in the family trade. There was, however, no future for Blanche with Clarence. The marriage was solely to save the family from the shame of a child born out of wedlock, and Clarence had already moved on to other conquests. His family made no effort to welcome Blanche or the baby; the unexpected teen pregnancy was looked upon as an unfortunate setback to their son's promising future. After Eleanor's birth, eighteen-year-old Clarence lived alone in rented rooms next door to his parents' home. On November 19, 1913, while Eleanor was still too young to remember a father, a divorce was granted on the grounds of "cruel and abusive treatment,"[3] and Blanche was given full custody of the baby, affectionately called "Ellie."

The teen and her small daughter lived with Blanche's parents, Harold and Susie Torrey, in a modest home at 175 Allen Street (just two blocks from the home of Clarence Powell), which they shared with Harold's brother, Frank, and his wife, Mary. Despite limited funds and space, the Torreys welcomed the new baby. A two-story, four-bedroom Victorian-style home with a large front and backyard, the Allen Street house was a snug fit for six people. To augment the meager salary Harold earned at a gun shop, in 1910 they had taken in a boarder, twenty-three-year-old Galen Atherton, who worked at the shop alongside Harold. He became a part of the family and even accompanied the Torreys each August to Atlantic City to visit Susie's sister Cora and her family.

Forced into adulthood, Blanche urgently needed to contribute to the household income. During World War I, she worked at the armory, the sole woman putting bullets in the belts that would be sent to soldiers. She later took any job she could—bank teller, waitress, and chambermaid.

Galen, eight years Blanche's senior, was a stocky, solidly built young man, just five feet, four and a half inches tall. He and Blanche came to an understanding, and they were married on January 3, 1916, in Bridgeport, Connecticut. They set up housekeeping with three-year-old Eleanor in a small apartment at 40 High Street in Springfield. Good with his hands, Galen now worked at Hendee Manufacturing Company, the makers of the Indian Motocycle brand.[4]

While Blanche was starting her new life with Galen, Clarence's life also shifted in a new direction. On June 1, 1917, Clarence married Cassandra Johnston. An article in the local newspaper noted that "they received many gifts of silver, cut glass, linen, and china" and that they would set up a household nearby after their return from a honeymoon motor trip around New York state—a stark contrast to his marriage to Blanche.[5]

Galen, Blanche, and Eleanor shared a traditional family life for a time, but this took a turn when Galen was drafted into military service in May 1918. His previous experience as a gunsmith was in great demand in the artillery division at Camp Hancock, a large training camp in Georgia. Although he attempted to get his call deferred, his claim was denied. During his absence, Blanche and Eleanor moved in with the Torreys in Stratford, Connecticut. There, Eleanor began her schooling.

Having been told that her own father died of pneumonia when she was a baby, now, with Galen's absence, Eleanor experienced the loss of a father for the second time in her young life. Galen served until June 21, 1919. After his discharge, instead of returning home to Blanche and his stepdaughter, he decided to move in with his brother's family. He never filed for divorce, and it is unknown whether Blanche ever saw him again.

Her Torrey family attempted to fill the gap. Eleanor now came to rely on Harold Torrey, who stepped in as a father figure to his "Ding," as he affectionately called her. As Harold was the family's main source of income, the household moved wherever his work took him. They were even found briefly in Amherst, Massachusetts, where Eleanor earned her first mention in the press when she danced with other schoolchildren as a flower in an elaborate May Day festival put on by the local church.

A reserved and serious child, Eleanor struggled to adapt. She grew so shy that when anyone approached, she would grab her mother's skirts and hide rather than greet them. Concerned friends remarked on Eleanor's extreme shyness. Blanche worried about her little girl who seemed so unlike the Torreys—all so outspoken and confident. "She was the only one in the family who was ever bashful," Blanche later commented. "She couldn't bear meeting strangers or come into a room where there were grownups."[6] Finally, someone suggested dancing lessons. Blanche followed the advice and made a decision that would change her daughter's life.

Six-year-old Eleanor was enrolled in a beginner class at a local studio. Brought by her grandmother on the first day, a bashful Eleanor took in the large room. Her eyes welled with tears as she quietly joined the group of little girls. The teacher nodded to the pianist, and the lovely strains of Edward McDowell's "To a Water Lily" filled the room. As the teacher began leading the group in lyrical arm movements, Eleanor felt a glorious stirring inside. She was completely transported. For the entire first class, the pupils concentrated only on basic ballet arm positions, never moving their feet at all.

Her grandmother sensed that the music sparked something unique inside the little girl. So, the family continued to scrape together the one dollar for each lesson, in the hopes that these classes would eventually give the child self-confidence. Luckily, it was dancing class that had been recommended to her mother, or she might never have stepped foot inside a studio. "Now, if there'd been Girl Scouts or group therapy, she would have taken me there. But there was a dancing school and my going there had nothing to do with me wanting to [dance] or having big talent or anything," Eleanor later explained.[7]

By the end of March 1921, the family had returned to Springfield and Eleanor, now eight years old, was enrolled at the Eastern Avenue School. The following month, they relocated to 47 Thompson Street, and she began attending the Tapley School. Over the next three years, this pattern would be repeated; ultimately, Eleanor changed schools seven times over a four-year period.

Meanwhile, the solitary child grew like a wild weed, with knobby knees and spindly little legs. Though she loved school, the constant moves made consistent learning and steady friendships difficult. Gangly from growth spurts and ashamed of her crooked teeth, she was in awe of little girls with pretty faces. She longed to wake up looking like them. With the frankness of a New Englander, her grandmother observed, "You are not too attractive. I sure hope you develop a personality."[8]

But dance had already begun to transform Eleanor, now enrolled at the prominent H.P. Lane School of Dance in Springfield. There, "the spirit and atmosphere is [sic] delightful and learning to dance becomes a pleasure," their advertisements claimed. She dove headlong into this new love and poured her heart into ballet and toe dance classes. She made her first theatrical appearance at nine years old alongside other Lane students in an afternoon benefit for the Daughters of Veterans on February 28, 1922, at the Court Square Theatre in Springfield. "The general high grade of work which the young dancers showed was worthy of note and was deeply appreciated, as shown by the applause which was given the artists by the more than 1,000 attending," the press reported.[9]

Three months later, Eleanor appeared at the Springfield Auditorium in the Lane studio's annual May Festival recital, dancing in the "Up to the Minute" section of an original ballet and as a snowflake in "Fête Day in Iceland," touted as "the most spectacular number . . . entirely of toe dancing . . . the biggest thing ever attempted by the classes."[10] The earnest little girl delighted in all the trappings of the beautiful world of ballet. An early photograph shows her bedecked in her full-skirted, white snowflake costume, perched shakily atop a pair of ill-fitting pointe shoes. However, Eleanor did not stay with H.P. Lane. By fall of 1922, she was enrolled in the Ralph MacKernan School of Dance, the school she would always credit with her early training.

Eleanor eagerly joined the classes in the airy upstairs studios on Worthington Street in downtown Springfield, not far from where Blanche worked. Run in partnership by Ralph and his dancer wife, Alice, the studio held large annual recitals for their students. MacKernan also recruited some of his advanced dancers for a pro group, "The Originalities," who performed on the vaudeville bill at the local theater. Just thirty years old, the tall and slender MacKernan had been teaching for over ten years. He had a unique talent for encouragement and took great pride in the studio's success. Notwithstanding its modest stature as a small dance school, the MacKernan studio produced a surprising number of students who went on to a career on the stage, one of the most noted being Broadway dancer and choreographer Robert Alton.

In addition to dance class, Eleanor also enjoyed school. Despite the constant moving throughout her early childhood, she was a serious student and loved reading. She liked to play basketball and was gifted with excellent hand–eye coordination. On Saturdays, she enjoyed the freedom of the open air and often navigated her bicycle down State Street or to a nearby field of violets, where she could lose herself in the sea of purple flowers. Springfield's lush and wooded Forest Park, which bordered a wealthy stretch of stately Victorian homes, proved another favorite place to visit. On Sundays, the Torrey family regularly attended church. Eleanor was very proud of the little Bible she received for perfect Sunday School attendance.

Whenever the family could afford it, they went to the big theaters to see silent films and a live vaudeville show. A matinee at Poli's Palace was an exciting adventure. Eleanor eagerly joined the children gathered round the saltwater taffy vendor in front of the theater who sold the candy for a nickel a bag. Taffy in hand, she would stare in awe at the photos of the film stars on display. Their glamour seemed completely unattainable.

In 1980, dancer John Bubbles told an interviewer a tale of one of his vaudeville performances in New England. He remembered Blanche brought a very young Eleanor backstage and asked him to teach her daughter a step. Buck and Bubbles were indeed on the bill at Poli's Palace twice in Springfield during Eleanor's childhood, but no meeting could be verified.

While living on Newbury Street and attending Liberty School, Eleanor made a special friend. Gabriella Bonfitto hailed from a large, Italian immigrant family. While Blanche worked, after school the two girls would do their homework in the kitchen as Gabriella's mother, Josephine, kept them fueled with hearty food. Participating in the joy and warmth of this traditional Italian family was a novel experience for the only child.

The Torreys actively embraced Eleanor's growing love for dance. They turned a small back room into a practice space with a ballet barre she could use between lessons. She constantly rehearsed her class routines at home and worked to perfect each difficult move. When a loud thump would interrupt a conversation with visitors at home, Blanche would just shrug and tell them it was Eleanor practicing a leap or a jump. The eager student was also diligent about keeping her grades up. She knew that her mother would have reason to pause her dancing lessons if she fell behind at school or misbehaved. It was something she couldn't bear.

Eleanor continued at the MacKernan studio every Friday and Saturday. Even as an awkward little girl with knobby knees, Eleanor's talent was evident. "I picked her out of McKernan's [sic] dance class as a kid who really had it," dancer Billy Austin later recalled. A Springfield local who had gone on to Broadway and then returned for an appearance at the Poli, Austin was asked by MacKernan to take a look at the students. "I said I'd pick that kid over there with the crooked teeth and the spindly legs as the one who would make it."[11]

MacKernan nurtured Eleanor's natural aptitude for dance. With her limber back, she excelled at both acrobatics and ballet. In the school recital, she exhibited her talent in an exotic "Oriental" routine to a popular tune of the day, "Japanese Sandman." "I did this number," she recalled, "standing on my head, doing splits, turning round and so forth. Very slow. Big deal!"[12]

Soon, Eleanor was helping MacKernan and Alice teach the younger students as an arrangement to aid with tuition. Her weekly lessons increased with each passing year, until she was spending all her free time at the studio. She was even given charge of the "baby" class, which she loved. Eleanor eagerly pitched in around the studio; MacKernan found her endearing and would take her with him around town for errands and walks. She was thrilled to be an active helper and looked up to her teacher with awe. MacKernan had so much confidence in young Eleanor that he once asked her to replace him at a teaching date in Connecticut when he was ill. Even as a child, she managed a successful class. In trusting her with his youngest students, MacKernan had not only boosted her confidence but also helped her use dance as a bridge off the island of her intense shyness.

Eleanor continued school and dance lessons in Springfield. By 1924, her grandparents had settled in Atlantic City, where they joined Susie's sister Cora. In May of that year, Eleanor left Springfield before the end of the school year to go to the seaside town, and she and Blanche spent the summer with the Torreys.

Back in Springfield in the fall, Blanche and eleven-year-old Eleanor took up residence at the Morrison Hotel, where Blanche worked as a chambermaid. The job didn't pay much but included free housing. To lighten her mother's workload, Eleanor would hurry home after school and empty all the wastebaskets in the hotel rooms. Her busy life was divided among MacKernan's, her schoolwork, and helping Blanche, but clearly the muse of dance already held a firm grip on her heart.

2

Atlantic City

A tlantic City in 1925 was at the height of its popularity as a vacation destination for New Yorkers, who flocked to its beaches during the hot summer months. One could hop on a train, and in just a few hours, go from steamy downtown Manhattan to the balmy seaside resort. Famous for its mile-long Boardwalk teeming with tourists, it attracted fashionable flappers who flirted with men in jaunty straw hats and summer suits, as well as elegant senior citizens who strolled with parasols. Some enjoyed the view while they were pushed leisurely along by attendants in three-wheeled rolling chairs; others swam in the ocean or played on the beaches. America's Favorite Playground was also home to the Inter-City Bathing Beauty Contest, later renamed the Miss America Pageant. With Prohibition in full swing, it became a place where a blind eye was turned on certain illegal activities.

In June of that year, the sun, crowds, and steady work that came along with that again brought Blanche and Eleanor to spend the summer with the Torreys at their new home on Arctic Avenue. In stark contrast with the quiet neighborhoods of Springfield, the Torrey house was just a few blocks from the lively Boardwalk. Blanche brought her daughter warily into this high-spirited domain.

When the sun set, Jazz-Age frolickers on the beach moved indoors to the dance floors of supper clubs and the gaming tables of swanky nightclubs. There were dozens, such as the Garden Pier Ballroom, with weekend dancing to Barney Zeeman's Kentucky Cardinals of Philadelphia, and the Golden Inn, with Alec and His Smart Alec Band. Then, there was the top of the line, Martin's, frequented by all the celebrities down for the weekend from New York.

More than twelve hundred hotels lined the Boardwalk. Blanche quickly found work as a waitress in the Canary Tea Room of the Ambassador Hotel, one of the most prestigious of the resort. While her mother carried tea and sandwiches to the hungry tourists, Eleanor happily planted herself on the beach just across the street, where she turned cartwheels and practiced acrobatics learned at MacKernan's. Full of pluck and energy, she had developed such a variety and skill that a crowd would often gather around her to watch. Young Johnny Weissmuller was working as a lifeguard there that summer with fellow Olympic competitor Stubby Kruger. Weissmuller was charged with keeping an eye on the busy beach on the very day a dark-haired middle-aged man spotted Eleanor practicing on the crowded stretch of sand. Intrigued, the man paused to watch. Weissmuller recognized him immediately. To Eleanor, he was just another curious onlooker.

Gus Edwards was a well-known songwriter and producer, who specialized in kiddie revues. His keen eye had already started youngsters like Groucho Marx, Eddie Cantor, and George Jessel on the early path to stardom. Eleanor's raw talent was clear. "You're pretty good," he told her. "I'd like to have you work over in the Grill at the Ambassador Hotel." Not used to strange men approaching her, Eleanor initially hesitated when he asked to speak with her mother. Later, Edwards met Blanche at the hotel and showed her the modest dinner venue. Eleanor pleaded with her mother to let her perform. It was a simple dinner show with no drinking, so Blanche finally relented. Eleanor was ecstatic. At seven dollars a night for three shows a week, she now earned more than Blanche.

Eleanor grasped this new opportunity with gusto. Student recitals had introduced her to the tantalizing sensation of stepping out onto a stage and inhaling the great energy of the audience. Onstage she was no longer a spindly-legged ugly duckling, but a beautiful lyrical dancer, doing what she loved best. And, instead of adulation, it was a pure love of dance that motivated her. "I'd rather dance than eat," she used to say.

Eleanor made her solo debut at the Ambassador's Pompeiian Grill in the home-sewn costume her grandmother had made for MacKernan's recital—short burnt orange velvet pants with rhinestones, a matching top, and fitted cap. She reprised her recital routine to "Japanese Sandman," appearing on the bill with headliners Leota and Lola Lane.

By August, Edwards had paired Eleanor with another young dancer, Dorothy Warfield, and advertised the act as "Duo Dancing by the Dot and El Sisters (Dolly Warfield and Eleanor Powell)." A publicity photo shows the girls posing side-by-side with one leg extended, both dressed in ladies' dresses and capes edged in fur. The show's summer theme was a Round-the-World Cruise, this "port of call" being "The Land of King Tut." The recent discovery of King Tut's tomb had made this a popular topic. A local newspaper wrote: "Two of Atlantic City's most talented grammar school pupils will dance tonight at the Pompeiian Grill . . . when a night in Egypt will be staged. Miss Dorothy Warfield and Miss Eleanor Powell . . . are so clever that they have been asked to dance the second time in the Grill. Little Miss Warfield will do her 'Cymbal Dance' and her young partner her interpretation of the 'Orientale.'"[1] By the end of summer, Eleanor, gaining in popularity, was invited to dance on the Ambassador float for the big parade that coincided annually with the Miss America pageant. Newspapers deemed her performance "a big hit."[2]

In the fall, Blanche and Eleanor returned to Springfield and the Morrison Hotel. Eleanor settled into her academic routine at State Street School and continued her dance training at Ralph MacKernan's. The excitement of a summer in the spotlight had further fueled her love for dance. MacKernan's spring recital would be the last time Eleanor performed with the studio.

Blanche, having heard nothing from Galen Atherton in the six years since he was discharged from duty, finally filed for divorce in March 1926, citing desertion. On May 26, she was again officially a single woman.

Eleanor left Springfield for good in June 1926. She and Blanche moved permanently to Atlantic City, where Eleanor enrolled in the Brighton School. Gus Edwards had invited her back onto the bill at the Pompeiian Grill, and the talented youngster's local fame began to grow.

On June 25, 1926, newspaper ads proclaimed the "Inauguration of the Summer Season" at the Ambassador with the flowery verbiage of the era: "Tonight, we sail from Pier 61 on the Panama Pacific Liner *Mongolia*. Eleanor Powell, Terpsichorean Exponent."[3] Taking a brief break from the fictitious SS *Mongolia* the following week, Eleanor was one of the featured dancers at the Ambassador Recreation Club's June Frolic, also held in the Pompeiian Grill. The press praised her "delightful dances" and reminded readers of her successful appearance the preceding year in the pageant parade.

As the summer progressed, the theme took another international turn as the SS *Mongolia* "docked in Havana," which gave Eleanor the opportunity to perform in a brand-new style. "Miss Eleanor Powell . . . will dance the Spanish Fandango garbed in a mantilla. She will also lead the guests in a Cuban Dansant, the national dance of Cuba."[4]

Her performance vocabulary and her reputation increased by the week as the little dancer delighted in a wide variety of styles and themes. The thirteen-year-old knew next to nothing about the dances of distant Asia or Cuba, but her creativity easily met the challenge. In August, she was booked by a local sorority to perform a Charleston exhibition and acrobatic waltz as part of a show for their annual dance at the new Hotel President. For the first time, her photo appeared in the newspaper. She proudly wore the little burnt orange velvet costume and posed in a graceful lunge, her youthful face fixed in a serious gaze. The caption described her as "Eleanor Powell, popular member of the younger social set of the resort."[5]

The more she performed, the less time she had for childhood fun and freedom. As she walked to the hotel on weekends, she often passed groups of children playing and felt a twinge of regret that she couldn't join them. She soon adapted to the new routine, and her free time was rich with family activities. Because she worked on Saturday nights, she slept till noon on Sunday. After a late breakfast, Eleanor and her grandmother sat around the radio. Her grandmother fondly remembered following a serial story about a little boy who ran away to join the circus. Late afternoons she spent reading; she particularly enjoyed O. O. McIntyre's descriptive column, A Day in New York, which wove tales of people and places in daily life. One caught her fancy—a sentimental story of falling leaves that never failed to make her cry. She cut it out and read it over and over. In the evening, the family would sing together. Though the Torreys were never well-off, their activities were comforting and happy, and they grounded Eleanor in the nurturing circle of a loving family. These solid roots grew deep and provided a foundation for years to come.

Later that summer, Benny Davis from the Silver Slipper nightclub contacted Edwards looking for a quick replacement for modern dancer Evan Burrows Fontaine, who was ill. "Take the kid," Edwards said. Eleanor figured it was because she was the least important. Though only an emergency replacement, a headliner spot was a big step up. The move from the family supper club to a real nightclub also meant a more discerning audience.

The Silver Slipper Supper Club, located at Boardwalk and Kentucky Avenue, was advertised as "The Rendezvous of the Elite" with "High-Class Entertainment."[6] That summer, raucous hostess Texas Guinan even brought her whole show down from New York, including George Raft ("Foremost Exponent of the Charleston"), then billed as "Georgie" in his pre–"Hollywood gangster" days. It was the height of the Jazz Age, and the audiences appreciated class acts and a good time.

Davis' wife, vocalist and dancer Dorothy Gumpert, helped Eleanor add some upscale glamour and maturity to her onstage look. Eleanor now wore a purple chiffon midriff top with one long sleeve and a jeweled strap across the opposite bare shoulder. The bottom half consisted of matching purple shorts with long panels that formed an open skirt; the outfit allowed her freedom in her acrobatic moves and showed off her signature high kicks. A jeweled belt matched the shoulder strap, and a snug cap topped off the ensemble. But the ultimate new addition to her performance was a five-foot cerise ostrich feather fan that she wielded as a dramatic accent to her acrobatics. It was the first time she would use a prop in her choreography. Gumpert also applied makeup to Eleanor, another first. Her lips were painted in a deep red bow shape, her cheeks were brightened with rouge, and her eyes were lined in deep shadow much like the silent film stars of the day.

Eleanor represented the Silver Slipper on September 1, in a contest hosted by Benny Davis at the Follies Bergère; her mastery of the trendy Black Bottom dance earned her the top prize. Instead of the usual, high-energy version performed by originator Ann Pennington, Eleanor slowed the tempo way down, making it "hot," as Blanche described it. Audiences loved it. As the winner, she received two tickets to the upcoming heavyweight championship fight between boxers Jack Dempsey and Gene Tunney in Philadelphia. Unfortunately, the club's cunning headwaiter managed to talk the young girl out of the coveted prize.

Eleanor filled in at the Silver Slipper for a few weeks in early September before she graduated to the even swankier Café Martin. Run by Henri Martin, the nightclub was a high-end gathering spot for performers like Jack Benny, Al Jolson, and other noted vaudeville and radio stars. By mid-September at Café Martin, she was regularly advertised as a "top exponent" of the Black Bottom dance. Her local fame was continuing to grow.

As Eleanor was working steadily and keeping late hours, Blanche engaged a tutor to allow her to continue her studies during the school year. When summer arrived, the restaurants and nightclubs were again in full swing and, in May 1927, Eleanor was back dancing at Martin's. Now mistress of ceremonies, she was making seventy-five dollars a week. By this time, she had yet to perform a single tap step. She had seen tap dancers on the bill but felt no attraction at all for the loud, clunky dance style. Eleanor spurned the loathsome, flashy steps. She stuck to her more refined classical and acrobatic training with no thought of ever doing anything else.

Though only fourteen, Eleanor was rapidly outgrowing the local opportunities. Other performers advised her to set her sights on Broadway. People like Jack Benny and Eddie Cantor praised her and told her she should be in a show in New York. A decision had to be made about her future. Would she continue her education or pursue a career as a dancer in New York? "It took me just ten seconds to decide," Eleanor told a reporter in 1937. "Dancing was in my blood and by that time I would rather have starved at it than flourish at something else."[7]

Eleanor was also motivated by years of watching Blanche do menial jobs. She was determined to be successful enough that her mother would no longer need to work. She convinced Blanche to take the chance. They squirreled away as much of a nest egg as they could manage, and Blanche set a three-month limit. Her mother decreed that, if she didn't make it, it would be back to school for her.

In late fall 1927, Eleanor and Blanche left Atlantic City for New York with very little in hand except for their small savings, a few home-sewn costumes, and a lot of determination.

Act One

(1927–1935)

3

Broadway and the Joyful Noise

Eleanor arrived ready to conquer New York. But while her talents were singular and unique in the nightclubs of Atlantic City, in New York she was just one of the scores of young hopefuls who arrived weekly, looking to be cast in a show. Like pilgrims to a shrine, they streamed to New York from small towns and large, beckoned by the allure of the Broadway stage. When Eleanor and Blanche first laid eyes on the marquees of Broadway in October 1927, it was a glittering sight. In brilliant lights were the names of Fred and Adele Astaire in *Funny Face* at the Alvin Theatre, Eddie Cantor in the latest *Ziegfeld Follies* at the New Amsterdam, another Ziegfeld hit, *Rio Rita,* at the Ziegfeld Theatre, and Schwab and Mandel's *Good News* at the 46th Street Theatre. Awed by the dazzling array of talent, Eleanor and Blanche checked into a nearby hotel on Forty-Second Street and set about the daunting task of finding work.

"Years ago, you went door to door from producers to agents' offices and you made yourself known to them on a one-to-one basis," recalled actress Uta Hagen. "In the evening you had a bite and went to bed, then started again early the next morning."[1] Ever conscious that their small nest egg would not go far in New York, Eleanor and Blanche set about in the same fashion.

For the first year, there was the obstacle of Eleanor's age. Until she turned sixteen, when she would legally be permitted to perform in nightclubs and theaters, hiring her would be a risk to producers. While the rules barring underage performers were overlooked in many of the mob-controlled clubs, theatrical producers were not always as lucky.

An unconfirmed version of Eleanor's first few months in New York appeared in the press years later. In this tale of great irony and serendipity, she showed up at producer Florenz Ziegfeld's large call for dancers and show-girls for several upcoming shows. Eleanor was cast in the featured part of Mary in his show *Rosalie,* but in a stroke of bad luck, she was forced to bow out because she contracted measles. The part then went to actress/dancer Bobbe Arnst. Since vaccination for the highly contagious disease would not be developed for another thirty-five years, it was a rampant health problem at that time. This version also asserts that Eleanor passed the measles along to Ziegfeld. No early casting records or detailed documentation exist for the show, but the story paints a disheartening picture of her first days in New York.

She was, however, booked briefly at Peter's Blue Hour, a luxurious Fifty-Fourth Street club that was also host to a famous back-room speakeasy. It was the height of Prohibition, and police raided the known violators of the "dry law" regularly that year, often padlocking the door against customers. Work there was sporadic and just a brief way to tide her over until a better job appeared.

Eleanor finally landed a small spot in a show and earned her first mention in the trades. A *Variety* review places her at the Branford Theatre in Newark, New Jersey, on December 3, 1927, in a sprawling, jungle-themed vaudeville revue, with elaborate costumes, dramatic lighting effects, and a bevy of diverse performers. Overall, the praise was strong. "Harry Crull has again hit the bullseye with his show . . . it's a gem. . . . Eleanor Powell does some graceful acrobatics, and the girls sing the melody, working it up in musical comedy style."[2]

Bandleader Ben Bernie and songwriter Benny Davis had both told her to look them up when she got to the city. True to his word, Bernie booked her into his brand new "Club Intime," which opened on Forty-Ninth Street on December 13, 1927. Still performing lyrical acrobatics, Eleanor worked at the club for three weeks.

It had been an eye-opening three months. Though Eleanor had been fortunate enough to land some work, she and Blanche realized that it would require a constant hustle to assure any kind of regular income. They knew it was time to find an agent. Back in Atlantic City, everyone had recommended the William Morris Agency, the top of the line. They offered the most extensive coverage for performers in all fields of entertainment, including a second branch in Chicago and a newly opened branch office on the West Coast for Hollywood film work. In late December, Eleanor headed to the agency's headquarters on Broadway near Forty-Sixth Street. She approached the receptionist and boldly declared, "My name is Eleanor Powell, and I want to be in a Broadway show." "Oh, you do?" the bemused receptionist replied. As it was lunchtime, she called the only agent who was in the office to come and meet Eleanor. Impressed by her naive spunk, he decided to give her a chance. He was William "Billy" Grady, one of the leading agents of the day.

Grady set up an audition for Eleanor at Tom Nip's dance studio, but Eleanor was embarrassed when she arrived to find a class in session. The students agreed to take a brief pause while she danced. Grady was impressed enough to sign her.

Her first engagement was a part in *The Optimists,* which opened on January 30, 1928, at the Casino de Paris on the Century Roof at Sixty-Second Street and Central Park West.

The Optimists was described as "a musical comedy in twenty-four scenes." Among the cast were Luella Gear, George Hassell, Flora Le Breton, and dancer Evelyn de la Tour. Its producer, composer, and star was American-born ragtime musician Melville Gideon, who had produced five successful editions of the show in England, all known as *The Co-Optimists.* The Broadway version was made up of an all-American cast, with the exception of British master of ceremonies, George Hassell. The intimate show featured ten players doing ensemble work, all wearing identical costumes. The sets were simple, and there was no chorus, which reviewers attributed to the show's obvious lack of budget. Eleanor was featured in two numbers, "Lacquer Lady," "imagined by Melville Gideon, with aid from Eleanor Powell, George Hassell, and Richard Bold," and a solo number, "Eleanor Powell dances."

Eleanor was still trying to discern what appealed to sophisticated New York audiences, and reviewers gave her numbers mixed marks. "Eleanor Powell didn't belong, with a mediocre acrobatic specialty of the type below a general par of those seen on any cafe floor and in vaude,"[3] said one, while another was kinder: "Eleanor Powell's contribution is a dance with poses. I liked that."[4] After a mere twenty-four performances in New York, in March the cast headed out of town to Toronto and Pittsburgh for a brief road tour.

By the time she returned to New York and met again with Grady, the reality was becoming clear. While making the rounds of auditions, she was repeatedly told "we'll call you" when they discovered she didn't tap. Her balletic acrobatic style was appealing, but stage dance was changing. Tap dancing was the rage and Eleanor realized "anyone without taps was just out." Out of desperation, she took what little she knew of tap and worked it into her act. The attempt was just enough to get her booked into a week of vaudeville at the Fox Theatre in Washington, DC. Here, she received the first mention in a review as "Eleanor Powell, tap dancer" in late May 1928.

Back home after the brief run, on Grady's urging, she made a decision. As loathsome as she found the idea, she had to take the effort further and really learn to tap. A friend suggested Jack Donahue's brand-new school in New York.

In June 1928, Jack Donahue and John Boyle opened the Donahue-Boyle School of Stage Dancing, a "dance school with new ideas," which took up the entire sixteenth floor of the Gallo Theatre Building on West Fifty-Fourth Street, where they offered a variety of classes. Jack Donahue was currently starring on Broadway with Marilyn Miller in *Rosalie*. With a strong reputation for staging large, elaborately choreographed chorus lines, he was so well-known in the theatrical community that he didn't even need to teach his own classes. His name on the sign alone was enough to bring in students. Boyle, who later coached James Cagney in the dancing style of George M. Cohan, was said to be the New York dancing master with so much vocabulary under his belt that he could "trip for ten hours without repeating a step."[5] Having the "Jack Donahue-John Boyle Girls" billed on a show's poster meant audiences could count on quality tappers and stylish staging. With regular spots to fill in chorus lines, and with tap a necessary skill for every Broadway aspirant, many showed up to learn.

Eleanor paid thirty-five dollars for a series of ten lessons (over $500 by today's standards) and was placed in a beginner class taught by Boyle. Donahue also happened to be observing that day. To teach the students rhythm, Boyle started without any footwork. Seated in a room, they were told to beat out the counts on a table as a parade record was played. Then Boyle started teaching a dance. As the routine progressed, Eleanor fell behind. She had not even mastered the very first step. She felt a complete failure.

She decided that this new earthbound technique just wasn't for her. "I hated it. I loathed it. I was angry with myself. It was the first thing that had licked me."[6] On her mother's advice, she didn't go back the following week. She wanted to give up. But Donahue's trained eye had seen beyond the fumbled attempts, and he called and convinced her to return. On the next visit, to help ground her steps, he sat on the floor, took her ankles in his hands, and guided her in the precise execution of the basic tap steps.

At the next lesson, to further correct the aerial tendencies deeply instilled from her ballet training, Donahue outfitted her with a war surplus belt weighed down with heavy theater sandbags. The contraption worked. "I was riveted," she said. "That's why I dance so close to the ground . . . why I can tap without raising my foot even, because I was taught with this belt and these weights on me."[7]

Donahue remained with her for about forty-five minutes, then left her to practice and work out the new sensation alone. For hours, she diligently kept working. Then, just as when a difficult math problem suddenly becomes clear, she had a breakthrough. For the remainder of the series, Eleanor was up at the front of the class, demonstrating the routine for the other students. "That personal attention was all I needed," Eleanor said. "From then on, tapping was my love."[8]

Eleanor now rehearsed with a vengeance. Donahue gave her practice space in return for help with teaching classes. "I spent eight and ten-hour days just practicing and trying to improve on what Mr. Donahue had taught me," Eleanor recalled.

By late June, Grady had arranged a showcase at the Hotel Paramount's Grill with Eleanor and a few other new clients. To garner interest in the newcomers, he invited producers to watch the revue. Soon, producer Sammy Lee booked Eleanor for his new show *Cross My Heart*. For unknown reasons, the job never materialized, and Eleanor was not in the cast when it premiered two months later. Grady returned to his search. The challenge was to find just the right project. It would turn out to be a grueling wait. Offer after offer was turned down while Grady held out for the perfect match. He kept Eleanor practicing for seven lean months. Blanche got a waitress job to help out, but the two were still barely able to pay their hotel bill. Their funds were running so dangerously low that they survived only on the bowls of soup in the hotel dining room because they were served with large baskets of rolls they could fill up on. Confident that Eleanor was close to making her big break very soon, Blanche borrowed from everyone she knew. After she had exhausted all her possibilities, her Aunt Hattie stepped up with a larger loan to help tide them over for several more months.

Desperate for work, fifteen-year-old Eleanor feverishly continued her tap education, retraining her body and muscles in this new direction. Grady recommended new photos—ones that would give her more mature appeal—and sent her to one of the top theatrical photographers in Manhattan, John De Mirjian. Brothers John and Arto De Mirjian had been in business since the early 1920s. Their dramatic and alluring photos of showgirls adorned in little more than a skillfully draped yard of gauze, lace, or velvet had become a signature of the studio, filling the pages of souvenir programs for *Ziegfeld Follies, Earl Carroll's Vanities, George White's Scandals,* and the like. They were deemed a necessary calling card for chorus girls and dancers looking for work.

Several years earlier, in 1925, the studio was thrown into the nation's public eye when actress Louise Brooks sued to suppress the further distribution of nude photos John had taken of her in 1923. She had moved into film acting and felt the photos could be harmful to her career. At the time of her sitting, Brooks had found herself easily coaxed as her session segued into more daring photos after the standard portraits were taken. "I bear no animosity toward Mr. De Mirjian. He is nice and a real artist," Brooks recalled. "When I went to his studio . . . he made the photographs himself, instructing me to forget that there was a man in the room and to lose myself in an artistic thought. I did. I pictured myself in the Louvre trying to imitate various works of the old masters." She described the subtle progression of the session: "As the poses necessitated the gradual removal of the kimono I had brought with me, he very delicately replaced it with other drapes, which he hung about my body." Brooks stated that when the session was done, she "hurried into my own clothes and felt none the worse for my experience."[9]

Eleanor's experience with John De Mirjian was nearly identical. The photographer took numerous portrait shots, and soon the time came for the requisite "art" photographs. Though with her bobbed hair and bangs she was nearly a twin for Brooks, Eleanor could not have been more different from the free-spirited flapper actress. While the standard portraits from the session show a beautiful and confident young woman staring into the camera lens, a long strand of pearls placed across her shoulder, the draped nude pose shows a frightened small-town teenager. Uncomfortable that her job required her to show her body, she stares off in an uneasy gaze. Eleanor wears only dress heels and a thick loop of satin gracefully covering the front of her body.

Like many of the moments in her life she preferred to forget, Eleanor never spoke of the session. At just eight months into their New York adventure, Eleanor and Blanche were quickly learning how the theatrical world worked. In their eagerness to book Eleanor in a lavish Ziegfeld-like show, Grady and the men of the William Morris Agency were little concerned with whether they were placing an underage dancer in a vulnerable situation. The photo apparently made just one appearance in 1931 in an international publication. The experience represents a rite of passage that neither Eleanor nor Blanche felt they had the luxury to reject.

Finally, Grady landed Eleanor a small part in the musical *Follow Thru*, her first real Broadway show. She used the routine from Donahue's beginning tap class for her audition (to the show's "Button Up Your Overcoat"), as well as for her solo in the show. For the remainder of her career, it would be the only time she did not use her own choreography for a tap number.

Following tryouts in Cleveland and Detroit in mid-December through early January, *Follow Thru* opened at Chanin's 46th Street Theatre on Broadway on January 9, 1929. Sixteen-year-old Eleanor was cast in the small role of Molly in the tale of two women who compete for the affections of a man while trying to win a golf tournament. Produced by Lawrence Schwab and Frank Mandel, the show starred Jack Haley (later to play the iconic Tin Man in *The Wizard of Oz*), Zelma O'Neal, and Irene Delroy. The show's choreographer, Bobby Connolly, staged all dances except for Eleanor's solo.

Grady had made an excellent choice in landing Eleanor a spot in *Follow Thru*. Having just finished their successful show *Good News,* and with another currently running at the Imperial Theatre, *The New Moon,* Schwab and Mandel were the young "wonder producers" of the day. Nearly everything they produced turned to gold and *Follow Thru* was no exception. Reviewers loved it. "The dynamic Messrs. Schwab and Mandel, who broke all speed laws last season with their fast-stepping *Good News* have generated additional dance power in the sprightly-limbed cast of *Follow Thru*. . . . To the fetching lilts of [George 'Buddy'] DeSylva, [Lew] Brown, and [Ray] Henderson, Bobby Connolly projects his ideas of a dancing marathon."[10]

"One success never tread more joyously upon another's heels than *Follow Thru* tread upon the heels of the departed *Good News* at the 46th St. Theatre last night."[11] A *Variety* review raved, "It's a speed show chock full of entertainment, with everything in it a popular musical show should have. That's why it's a hit."[12]

Eleanor's solo received only brief but notable mentions: "The evening was filled with superb, lively dancing not only by a thoroughly drilled chorus but by a young lady in the very minor role of Molly, Eleanor Powell. Her scintillating tap numbers earned her several encores every night."[13] Well into the run, her photo appeared in a New York paper with the caption, "Eleanor Powell, sixteen-year-old buck dancer has been promised a good-sized part in the next Schwab-Mandel musical comedy. She is what is termed as a 'find' having been discovered during an audition at the Chanin Theatre."[14] The successful show ran nearly a year. It closed four days before Christmas, after 403 performances, and other companies played simultaneously in the fall in Chicago and Los Angeles.

Eleanor's thrilling success was overshadowed by a sad event. Shortly after the opening of the show, she sent tickets to Ralph MacKernan, looking forward to sharing her Broadway debut with her mentor. Tragically, MacKernan had recently fallen ill and died suddenly of grippe on February 26 at thirty-eight. His widow, Alice, attended alone and broke the news to Eleanor.

During the long run of the show, Eleanor took advantage of her accessibility to the theater to develop her ever-growing tap skills. In between shows on matinee days, she would lug her portable Victrola record player and a new collection of Fats Waller 78s to the empty stage to practice. These sessions, which became a staple in her Broadway days, allowed her to workshop choreography and perfect new steps.

Meanwhile, in Hollywood as well as on Broadway, the increasing popularity of talking film was wielding a strong influence on the world of dance. Sound in films had caused tap dance to skyrocket in popularity above other forms of dance. Audiences now enjoyed hearing dance as well as seeing it. The consensus was that "the country is going tap dance-wild."[15] An annoyed columnist wrote, "Wherever I go, uptown or downtown, or around the corner, there is an accompanying tap-tap-tap. It's been coming slowly for a couple of seasons, but at the moment it descends like a plague of clacking beetles."[16]

In August, the annual convention of the Dancing Masters of America met to discuss and debate dance styles. For the first time, they awarded titles to the best male and female tap dancers; to determine the winners, they stood under the stage so as to judge solely by sound. Eleanor won the honors along with Bill Robinson in 1929.

Wealthy high society rushed to add tap entertainment to their house parties. Whenever Eleanor had a schedule free of vaudeville dates, Grady booked her with Robinson (also handled by William Morris) for private events in the homes of wealthy Manhattanites, such as the Astors and the Vanderbilts. As a duo, they performed for one hundred dollars each. The king and queen of tap in New York, Robinson and Eleanor even dressed the part. "He'd come on in long tails, and I'd come on in a short pair—tails, but with shorts," Eleanor later recounted. But stepping inside the homes of the upper echelon proved to be a harsh introduction to the treatment of Black performers of the day. On arrival at the homes, while the hosts told Eleanor she could ride up the front elevator, Robinson had to use the back entrance. "In that case, I will ride with Mr. Robinson in the freight elevator," she replied.[17]

After one performance, the butler offered Eleanor something to drink. She said she would like a glass of water, if Mr. Robinson could have one also.

After they finished, Robinson broke his glass and offered to pay for it. "He knew no one was going to drink out of that glass after him," Eleanor recalled. "Most of the time it was a crystal glass, too, and they'd take his money."[18] The two developed a deep mutual respect and friendship that would last decades. Robinson paid Eleanor the ultimate compliment by teaching her his original choreography for his signature stair dance, the only dancer to whom he would ever teach the routine besides Shirley Temple.

The producers of *Follow Thru,* Schwab and Mandel, who in 1926 had brought the musical *Queen High* to Broadway, were now producing the same project as a musical film. Sound film was in its relative infancy and they were eager to capitalize on this newest form of musical entertainment. *Queen High* was the first of several musical films they planned, some of which would be shot later the same year in Hollywood.

While Eleanor's small part in *Follow Thru* would not be in the upcoming film version, the producers did include her in *Queen High,* marking her (uncredited) film debut. Eleanor dances with joyful abandon atop a table to a catchy ditty, "Brother, Just Laugh It Off," by Arthur Schwartz and Ralph Rainger with lyrics by Yip Harburg. Sung by nineteen-year-old Ginger Rogers, who had already made three film shorts and two feature films, the number was one of three new songs added to the film version.

Eleanor's short scene in the film was shot in one day at the Paramount Long Island Studio in Astoria, the center of New York silent film production throughout the 1920s. More than a hundred films were produced that decade, with many stars, such as the Marx Brothers, Gloria Swanson, Tallulah Bankhead, and Edward G. Robinson, making their first foray into talkies. For her first turn before the camera, Eleanor adapted her tap solo from *Follow Thru* (which in turn was based on the Jack Donahue class routine) for the dance in *Queen High.* This early glimpse shows her low-to-the-ground style, punctuated by flirtatious flourishes of her short skirt and an effortless high kick. Throwing her head back in a joyous smile, she already exudes an effervescent star quality.

Queen High, which also starred Frank Morgan, Charles Ruggles, and Stanley Smith, was released on August 9, 1930, to good reviews but with no mention of Eleanor's exuberant tapping. Considering it an insignificant debut, Eleanor never mentioned *Queen High* in any interviews, and neither did the carefully crafted publicity biographies that were later sent out to the press. It wasn't until film fans discovered the film in the late 1970s and recognized the lanky dancer with her signature smile that it was added to her list of credits.

In late March, Eleanor was booked for a unique two-week concert performance produced by Charles Dillingham, featuring Duke Ellington and his Cotton Club Orchestra and French singer Maurice Chevalier at Fulton Hall. The concerts ran for eighteen performances from March 30 through April 12, 1930. The evening was divided into two separate acts. The Ellington Orchestra, with tapper Ananias "Nyas" Berry (of the Berry Brothers), Henry Wetzel, and Eleanor were featured in the first act. The second act was entirely Maurice Chevalier.

In July 1930, she began rehearsals for a new show, *Fine and Dandy*. In her first supporting role, she won a prime spot as secretary to the star, zany comedian Joe Cook. Blanche was especially proud of Eleanor's good fortune and boasted of it in a letter to a Springfield friend. The first producing venture of Morris Green and Lewis Gensler, the show opened in Boston for tryouts in two different theaters starting on August 25, then moved to Newark before its Broadway opening at Erlanger's Theatre on September 23.

Directed by Morris Green and Frank McCoy, with a book by Donald Ogden Stewart and music and lyrics by Kay Swift and Paul James (the pen name of James Paul Warburg, Swift's then husband), the show would mark the first time a score had ever been written entirely by a woman (with the exception of the number "Mechanical Ballet"). Charles LeMaire, who had worked on numerous editions of the *Ziegfeld Follies,* was brought on board as costume designer. Dances were directed by Dave Gould. With the recent stock market crash and competition with the continual rise of the film musical, the show encountered funding problems shortly before opening and was saved only through Warburg's financial prowess. "Paul James simply took up his Jimmy Warburg side and came up with the necessary funds—aided by two of his best friends, Marshall Field and Averell Harriman, who had liked the musical in rehearsal,"[19] according to Swift's grandson-in-law, Nicholas Weber.

Fine and Dandy centered on the antics of Cook as Joe Squibb, who becomes general manager of the Fordyce Drop Forge and Tool factory after some deceitful wooing of the previous owner's widow. As Miss Hunter, Squibb's secretary, Eleanor appeared in three numbers: "Jig Hop," "Wedding Bells/Waltz Ballet" with the Merriel Abbott dancers, and her vocal debut "I'll

Hit a New High." Joining the packed house on opening night were such notables as George and Ira Gershwin, both close friends of Kay Swift, William
Demarest, Al Jolson, and Ruby Keeler. While Cook's antics rightfully dominated the show, given his multiple talents as juggler and tightrope walker, his
signature way of telling hilarious, nonsensical stories, and the creation of
Rube Goldberg–style contraptions, Eleanor received numerous mentions
and high praise. With skills that far surpassed those of other female dancers
of the 1920s and 1930s, Eleanor had single-handedly reset the standard for
tap. Even Cook noticed her intense dedication and commented to his friend,
actor Fred Stone, "There's a kid here who practices all day, every day." Stone
replied, "She'll be something."

Her unique blend of crisp footwork, syncopated rhythms, and buoyant
personality, embellished by her acrobatic moves, was fresh and new. "There
is a young lady by the name of Eleanor Powell who dances most amazingly
and is very nice to look at," wrote Edwin Stein.[20] "Miss Powell is a boyishly
bobbed stepper of notable skill and vigor; and the connoisseurs of dance arts
think she has something new to offer."[21]

During the Broadway run, a tragic loss marked the second time Eleanor
would lose a dance mentor in less than two years. Jack Donahue died of a
heart attack at the age of thirty-eight on October 1, 1930, just sixteen months
after he and Johnny Boyle had given Eleanor her first tap lessons.

Closing after eight months on May 2, 1931, the New York run lasted for
255 performances, ranking among the top shows of 1930. After Broadway,
the company continued on for a two-month stretch in Chicago; then during
a short hiatus, Eleanor was booked for a few weeks of vaudeville. She first
appeared in *The Four Seasons* at Paramount Theatre in Times Square with
Jesse Crawford and the Paramount Concert Orchestra. The following week,
she was in a brand-new revue at Brooklyn's Paramount Theatre, *Happy Days*.
On March 27, Eleanor made a special promotional appearance as one of the
stars of *Fine and Dandy* at the grand opening of Ohringer's Department Store
at Broadway and Thirty-Ninth Street alongside Bill Robinson (then starring
in *Brown Buddies*) and several other dancing stars of current Broadway
musicals.

Eleanor rejoined *Fine and Dandy* on September 26, 1931, as the show
packed up the entire original cast and company of 125 and went on tour to
Newark, Washington, DC, Ithaca, Scranton, and Springfield, Massachusetts.
"So lavish is the entertainment that four baggage cars are required to transport
the scenery, silks, satins, and equipment that are utilized."[22] Strong notices

continued to follow the performances, with Eleanor meriting special mention. Cook "has gathered a capable cast, including Eleanor Powell, by far the best tap dancer I have seen this season," wrote New Jersey reporter James O'Neill. "The audience was fully cognizant of her skill and gave her as good a hand as Cook himself. For the girl, who also appears to be something of a ballet dancer, too, fairly exudes 'It.'"[23] And another: "Eleanor Powell flashes a handsome smile, a pair of lithesome feet, and a manner of dancing which is original."[24] An Ithaca reporter mentioned, "The most capable support for the comedian came from Miss Powell, whose dancing was superb and brought forth the only encore of the evening."[25]

Most memorable for Eleanor, however, were the two nights at the Court Square Theatre in Springfield, where reviewers lauded the return of their hometown girl. "*Fine and Dandy* [is] filled with comedian's old inventions— then there is Eleanor Powell, who can dance." Critic Louise Mace was impressed by Eleanor's technique: "Eleanor Powell trips away with the individual honors through her fast and vigorous interpretation of the rhumba and agile toe manipulations."[26] Eleanor had come far since the last time she had appeared on this stage as a Lane School student.

The final two weeks of 1931 brought Eleanor back to the vaudeville stage; she moved back and forth over subsequent weekends between Paramount Theatres in New York and Brooklyn with alternating crooner headliners Bing Crosby and Russ Columbo. Onstage with Crosby, she teamed with him for a duet of "Goodnight, Sweetheart." Also on the bill were the ballroom dance team Veloz and Yolanda, Lillian Roth, the singing Mills Brothers, organist Jesse Crawford and his wife, Rubinoff and his orchestra, and singer/dancers Buck and Bubbles. Except for Bill Robinson, Eleanor rarely had the opportunity to interact with other tap dancers of the same caliber and technique, so when she landed on the same bill as Buck and Bubbles, she was ecstatic.

Fresh from a nearly five-month run of the *Ziegfeld Follies of 1931,* the Black performers Buck and Bubbles, Ford Lee "Buck" Washington and John W. "Bubbles" Sublett, who had been working together in a singing and dancing act since childhood, had worked their way up to headlining status on the Keith vaudeville circuit. Buck played piano and performed an eccentric style of dance; he would accompany Bubbles as the latter sang and executed an intricate tap solo. While both Bubbles and Bill Robinson were known for their crystal clear taps and rhythms, Robinson distinctively danced up on the toes with his unique wooden soles. Bubbles adapted a brand-new style of tap in 1922—rhythm tap—that used heel drops in a new way of accenting the beats. "I figured I'd cut the tempo," Bubbles explained. In reality, he added more intricacy to the rhythm. "In dancers' terminology, Bubbles changed from two-to-a-bar to four-to-a-bar, cutting the tempo in half giving himself twice as much time to add new inventions,"[27] wrote Marshall and Jean Stearns in *Jazz Dance: The Story of American Vernacular Dance.*

As she watched Bubbles from backstage during the Paramount run, Eleanor was entranced with his innovative style. So much so that, to study his foot and heel work as closely as possible, she lay on her stomach in the wings to see every nuance of his steps. With an average of five shows a day in theaters, she had a lot of opportunities to observe and learn. She found Bubbles a fantastic performer and he clearly appreciated her interest. "It got so that he was playing to me, not to the audience," Eleanor remembered.[28] When she would go on, she would do the same to him. In between shows, they would both jam down in the theater basement, a rare opportunity to trade steps with an equally masterful tapper. Three years earlier, Eleanor had been a rank beginner who hated tap; in that short time she had become the most skilled female tap dancer on Broadway. She had only just turned nineteen.

4

Gaining Traction

A two-page ad in *Variety* by the William Morris Agency listing Eleanor as one of their clients ushered in 1932. Her new agent, Johnny Hyde, kept her working consistently—an increasing challenge, given the impact of the Depression economy on the production of Broadway shows over the past two years. Hyde, then vice president with Abe Lastfogel, was one of the agency's top men.

Now, with Eleanor successfully on her way, Blanche had finally put waitressing behind her and could focus solely on supporting and advising her daughter. For the first time in nearly twenty years she could step back from the obligation of shouldering the financial burden.

As Broadway struggled to stay afloat with the reduction of available production money, so did its elder statesmen, most notably Florenz Ziegfeld. The *Follies of 1931,* in which Buck and Bubbles had appeared, would be his last *Follies*. Ziegfeld, along with many other producers who had readily bankrolled previous shows, had lost much of his fortune in the 1929 crash. In late 1931, a violent royalty dispute with producer George White left the musical team of Brown and Henderson without a producer for their latest show. They approached White's rival, Ziegfeld, who was interested but needed financing. Eddie Cantor was able to provide a loan of $100,000, but Ziegfeld still needed additional funds. He finally found it—from gangsters Dutch Schultz and Waxy Gordon. Despite serious health issues, Ziegfeld pushed forward with the project and put together a scaled-down version of his previously lavish productions. The story centered around an American waiter (Bert Lahr) who escapes to Mexico after police raid his speakeasy and then is coerced into becoming a bullfighter. Schultz and Gordon wanted to title the show *Laid in Mexico*; however, it was ultimately retitled *Hot-Cha!,* with their idea as a subtitle.

Gypsy Rose Lee, who was cast in a small role (under the name Rose Louise) as the Girl in the Compartment, reportedly got her part thanks to her friend Gordon. Fed up with burlesque life, she hoped to venture into musical theater. According to Lee's biographer Norman Frankel, mobster Gordon asked a favor of *Hot-Cha*'s songwriter Lew Brown. "How about using Gypsy in your show? She's as good looking as some of the other dames you got. Besides, she's a friend of mine."[1] Gypsy headed to the Ziegfeld Theatre the following day, displayed her legs, and got the job. Reportedly, Ziegfeld was a "leg man," as evidenced by his consistent choice of long-legged showgirl beauties. Gypsy was a perfect match. He must have also appreciated Eleanor's legs, but she was booked for the show without the help of a gangster friend. Film actor Buddy Rogers, in his stage debut, Lupe Velez, June Knight, and June MacCloy were the other headliners. Tryouts took place in Washington, DC, on February 15; on February 29, they moved to Pittsburgh for two weeks, where the entire company, including Ziegfeld, came down with the flu. The production team included Brown and Henderson (from *Follow Thru*), who provided music, costume designer Charles LeMaire (who had designed for *Fine and Dandy*), and dance director Bobby Connolly (also from *Follow Thru*). John Harkrider designed Eleanor's voluminous and flowing gold satin pajamas (he received complaints because they didn't show off her legs), as well as a vampy fringed gown for Lupe Velez.

The opening night crowd and critics at the National Theatre gave a rousing thumbs-up to the first act; but reviewers found that the second half of the show, with the sole exception of Eleanor's tap dance performed in front of the curtain, did little to match the first. Too ill to attend the opening, Ziegfeld watched the arrival of the crowd from his hotel room window just across the street. He was not well enough to see the show until three weeks later.[2]

Eleanor had just the one solo in the production, a standalone billed in the program simply as "Dance by Eleanor Powell." While it served merely as a novelty scene transition after the beginning of act two, it stopped the show at each performance. "But for the unexpected 'tapping' of Miss Eleanor Powell, who comes before the curtain in a sudden burst toward the end of the play and tears the audience wide open, there is less meat in the latter half than might suit the appetite of the usual Ziegfeld worshipper," wrote one reviewer. "Last night's audience, bolstered by the presence of Will Rogers . . . almost ripped the roof right off the National in its appreciation of one of the most happily contrived first acts ever conceived by man." Bert Lahr received high praise for his comic antics. "His rough and rugged clownings . . . prove that Mr. Ziegfeld was right when he tapped him as chief of his big comedians."[3]

The Broadway edition opened on March 8 at the Ziegfeld Theatre, at a time when most headlines were focused on the dramatic events unfolding after the Lindbergh baby kidnapping the week before. Despite good reviews for the majority of the show, behind-the-scenes drama plagued the run as severely as Ziegfeld's illness. While Lahr's boundless energy and gusto bolstered audiences, Velez was reported to be a difficult star, "frequently drunk, always erratic."[4]

As Ziegfeld's health worsened, the show's attendance also took a downturn, mostly due to the Depression. The opulence of Ziegfeld productions never wavered, no matter the reality of the economy. Top ticket prices on opening night were a whopping $16.50 (the equivalent of nearly $300 today), a luxury most could no longer afford. "Nineteen-thirty-two was the nadir of the Depression years. Everything was hitting bottom," theater critic Stanley Green observed.[5]

One member of the audience, Fred Astaire, was so impressed with the show that he made his way backstage to congratulate friend Bert Lahr, who introduced him to Eleanor. But even with celebrity interest in the show, box office receipts continued to lag. Ziegfeld continued to defend Velez' erratic performances, calling her "remarkable" as she only "had four days to get up in the part." He even went on to announce, through lengthy telegram correspondence with columnist Louella Parsons, that *Hot-Cha!* would be made into a film following the close of the production.

By May, the show's receipts had taken such a dive that it was impossible to continue without drastic measures. The cast was asked to accept a reduction in pay. Due to the difficulty in landing another show, all the cast members, with the exception of Buddy Rogers, accepted the pay cut on May 16. Rogers was replaced by Art Jarrett. But on May 23, after the show had run only twelve weeks, a notice was posted backstage: "It is with sincere regret that I am compelled to hereby give notice, in accordance with Equity contract conditions, that the *Hot-Cha!* company closes next Saturday, May 28. The terrific running expenses make it impossible for the show to play at prices possible for the public to pay during these depressing times."[6]

Negotiations were put in motion to move the show to the Globe Theatre on a rental basis. Eventually, the production was able to remain at the Ziegfeld Theatre until closing, and *Hot-Cha!* hung on for a few additional weeks. The show closed on June 18, 1932, after 119 performances.

Ziegfeld's flu had turned into bronchial pneumonia by the end of the Pittsburgh tryout, and his weakened condition had already affected his heart. His health declined steadily during the entire run of the show. He traveled to

California, where he planned to recuperate at Will Rogers' ranch near Pacific Palisades. When his condition worsened, he checked into Cedars of Lebanon Hospital. On July 22, Ziegfeld finally succumbed to his long illness.

Less than a week after *Hot-Cha!* closed, Eleanor was booked into a vaudeville revue at the Capitol Theatre, in a spectacle called *Yasha Bunchuk's Third Birthday Revue.* Orchestra leader Bunchuk, celebrating his third anniversary as conductor of the Capitol's Grand Orchestra, put together a show that was deemed better than the film it alternated with. "Vaughn DeLeath croons deliciously, Eleanor Powell dances divinely, the Three Sailors do their acrobatic dances with a share of quick wit," wrote critic Irene Thirer.[7] "This personable brunette . . . offers a rhythm tap dance which includes a top-spin tap, this feat being rewarded with a spontaneous reception."[8] Her now-signature "top-spin tap," a multiple pirouette in place punctuated by toe-tap accents as she turned, was an incredible feat that took Eleanor three years to perfect. She performed the turn so effortlessly and stopped so precisely that audiences were rightly amazed.

The following week, Eleanor was dancing in another vaudeville turn at the Ambassador Theatre in a show under master of ceremonies Dick Powell, and by July 22, it was back to the New York Paramount Theatre in a revue under fellow *Hot-Cha!* star Bert Lahr and Harry Richman. But while head-liners Lahr and Richman were touted in *Variety* as getting $9,500 between them, it was the nineteen-year-old tap dancer who upstaged them at every show. "Harry Richman and Bert Lahr . . . are forced to step aside by a girl who's inconspicuous in the billing, but who runs away with the show," *Variety* bragged. "She's Eleanor Powell, buck dancer . . . who nightly walked on at the Ziegfeld after *Hot Cha!* was practically over and proceeded to make everything look mild. . . . Attired in gold cloth pajamas, Miss Powell makes a nonchalant entrance that suggests anything but a walloping specialty will follow. She goes into . . . a series of simple-looking tricks mixed with shrewd showmanship. The audience didn't want Miss Powell to leave but gave in after an encore. When the company returned for bows after the finale, Miss Powell drew the big hand."[9]

The show went to the Brooklyn Paramount the following week, with Eddie Lowry taking over from Harry Richman as master of ceremonies; then Eleanor headed out of town for a week at the Fox Theatre in Philadelphia, where she headlined the bill as "Dancing Star of Ziegfeld's *Hot-Cha!*" The public was encouraged to "bring the kiddies" to enjoy the exciting foray into the jungles of Africa with the feature film *Congorilla.*

It was now back home to New York's palatial Cathedral of the Motion Picture, the Roxy Theatre, and the lavish stage production *Manhattan*, which was paired with Will Rogers' film *Down to Earth*. Built in 1927 on West Fiftieth Street near Times Square, the Roxy was the largest movie house in the world at that time. It could easily accommodate the large stage shows and full chorus lines of the Roxyettes, precursors to the Rockettes, and could hold an orchestra of 110 musicians in its rising pit. The *Manhattan* production had a "series of five song and dance tableaux resplendent in color and carrying out what might be the highest point in lighting effort reached by the Roxy for an entire program." The popular Roxyettes (thirty-two dancers) unabashedly performed in colorful Native American costuming (not politically correct today) in a section titled "The Wigwam." A finale, titled "Down to Earth" to correlate with the feature film, finally brought out Eleanor. "Eleanor Powell emerges from a New York skyline setting here for a solo tap, gracefully and entertainingly performed." Reviews noted, "Clad in gold cloth pyjamas, the girl crashed for the biggest applause spot in the closing." The critic applauded her effort further, stating, "She's a bet for any kind of show, clever and graceful with a figure that attracts."[10]

The following week at the Roxy found Eleanor in an all-new stage show. Structured much like the previous spectacle, it had five sections; each featured a different style and was either a solo or was backed by the Roxy ballet troupe or the Roxyettes. This week's version included Hal LeRoy. Just one year younger than Eleanor, the tall and lanky LeRoy had a clean rhythm tap and a slightly eccentric dance style. He began working on Broadway around the same time as Eleanor. Along with dancer Mitzi Mayfair, the trio had been dubbed "the kids of Broadway" due to their big talent and young age. In this case, LeRoy was the victim of poor staging: he had to sing right after he had performed an energetic number. *Variety* commented, "So instead of singing, the LeRoy kid has to gasp it, which isn't his fault." Once again, Eleanor was placed in the finale against drawn drapes. The reviewer gave a curious opinion of her work, stating, "Miss Powell's eccentric buck work, upon closer analysis, seems based on a cleverly masked revival of an old-fashioned essence." His final observation seemed cast as an insult—"She dances like a man."[11]

Indeed, Eleanor's influences and mentors were male dancers; this was primarily due to the fact that so few female tap dancers were strongly skilled at that time. The female dancers of the day—white stage and film dancers Ann Pennington, Marilyn Miller, and Ruby Keeler, as well as Black female dancers such as the Whitman Sisters, Jeni LeGon, and Cora La Redd (who primarily performed in clubs like Smalls Paradise, the Cotton Club, and Connie's Inn)—were all strong, but few had the finesse, vocabulary of technique, and choreography that Eleanor possessed. Her confident style and strength, built from her early ballet and acrobatic training, went well beyond what was considered dainty and feminine.

A newly designed show was paired with the film *Chandu the Magician* the following week at the Roxy. As often proved the case with the revolving door of headliners and supporting acts who were integrated into the existing stables of the Roxyettes and the Roxy ballet corps, decisions about the show were made with very little rehearsal. This week, it was Eleanor whose number fell victim to poor judgment. Her upbeat dance was unfortunately sandwiched between the slow, choreographed descent of the Roxyettes down a wide set of stairs onstage and a lyrical number by the beautiful ballroom team of Veloz and Yolanda. It was entirely the wrong setting for her dance.

After bouncing from theater to theater and being placed randomly in shows with little rehearsal or thought to staging, it was a relief when in October, Eleanor was cast as a featured dancer in *George White's Music Hall Varieties,* a scaled-down and revamped version of the previous editions of *George White's Scandals*. In a valiant effort to meet the challenges of Depression-era financing, White did away with the former lavish look of his sets and staging. Relying instead on talent and music to carry the show, he described it as "a vaudeville entertainment in two acts and twenty-seven scenes." Top tickets were $2.50. With Eleanor alongside Harry Richman, Lili Damita, the Loomis Sisters, and, once again, Bert Lahr, the show previewed in Philadelphia on November 14, 1932, and then opened at the Casino Theatre on November 22, the day after Eleanor's twentieth birthday. (Lili Damita left the cast in December, and Willie and Eugene Howard and Tom Patricola were added in January 1933). Critics were lukewarm in their assessment of White's "experiment," lamenting that "it is not a variety show in the customary meaning of that term, and the passing of the Palace leaves a void on Broadway which will not immediately be filled." However, Eleanor's solos received their usual high marks. "There is a large dancing chorus, but among the supporting company it is the lanky Eleanor Powell, an excellent tap dancer, who stands out markedly."[12]

The scaled-down appearance of the production provoked much commentary. While it may not have provided the escapism many sought in Depression-era entertainment, some actually applauded the frugal approach. "The major difference seems to be that Mr. White has not squandered a fortune on scenery and costumes in this new piece. Black curtains take the place of magnificent sets, the performers working with nothing but themselves to entertain."[13]

A downside of working nightly on Broadway was the near impossibility of seeing other shows playing at the same time. But since Eleanor went on fairly early in the first act of the *Varieties* and didn't reappear until toward the end of the second, she would sometimes take advantage of her downtime to slip out and visit other productions nearby. A brisk five-minute walk would take her to the Music Box Theatre a few short blocks away, just in time to see the first act finale of her favorite show—the long-running Gershwin hit, *Of Thee I Sing*. The stage door manager, who had worked with her previously, was always happy to let her in so she could watch from the wings.

The *Varieties* closed after only forty-eight performances. Exchanging a run in a show for weeks of vaudeville over and over for years made for a grueling life for Eleanor. During the Depression, there was little choice but to accept work, if you were blessed enough to have it offered to you. Eleanor and Blanche recalled how desperate their situation had been back when they arrived in New York. By 1932, twelve million people were unemployed in the United States, which translated to about one out of every four households being without income. The visual evidence was stark. A shantytown of homeless people had even set up in the drained reservoir expanse in Central Park, not far from the wealthy homes where Eleanor had danced just a few years earlier with Bill Robinson. Soup kitchen lines stretched down many streets, and the devastated economy affected every aspect of life. Eleanor knew what people needed most during the Depression was entertainment.

◉　◉　◉

New York's entertainment landscape was changing. Movies were rapidly edging out vaudeville. The Palace, fabled theatrical mecca to all vaudevillian performers since it opened its doors in 1913, was converted into a movie house just as the new state-of-the-art Rockefeller entertainment center made its debut. Featuring a variety music hall, a movie theater, radio and recording studios, as well as a sixty-six-story office building, the center was touted as the place "where the arts meet science." Both theaters were wired for broadcasting, and in anticipation of the future, even early television options were being discussed.

The Radio City Music Hall, the first and largest of its theaters, opened on December 27, 1932. Built in just over a year at a cost of $7 million (the equivalent of $125 million today), it was truly a technological wonder for its time, featuring a hydraulic system that allowed different sections of the enormous stage to be raised and lowered. Seating nearly six thousand, it was the largest theater in the world. The complex also housed the new RKO Roxy Theatre, which opened two days later. Both theaters were connected by tunnels and had elaborate underground parking and a shuttle system.

Radio City Music Hall was originally intended as an international variety theater with a boarding school that would be free or at a nominal cost for talented students of the arts. The programming was to be a "pageant of the entire theatre . . . but excluding motion pictures."[14]

On opening night, a long line of eager attendees stretched far down Sixth Avenue, anxious to experience the very first show. On the bill were dancer Martha Graham and her company, the Tuskegee Institute Singers, a hundred-voice Black choir, contralto Vera Schwartz, ballerina Patricia Bowman, and a ballet corps of eighty. In addition, Ray Bolger was emcee, and there were the ninety-two tap-dancing Roxyettes, relocated from the original Roxy Theatre where Eleanor had recently performed. This elaborate first show, ambitious and experimental, dragged on until one o'clock in the morning. In the end, it tired the audience more than it entertained them. Management analyzed the unsuccessful debut and realized that audiences were less enthusiastic about this type of fare than the more plebeian offerings being presented at its sister theater.

The RKO Roxy, considerably smaller than the music hall, opened two days later and enjoyed immediate success as a movie house. Despite a seating capacity of thirty-seven hundred, the Roxy had been unable to accommodate the thousands of excited moviegoers. Within a week of the opening of Radio City Music Hall, it was announced that the bigger theater was going to "go popular," offering movies, a show, and a lower admission price that better fit the means of the Depression-era audiences. The new policy would now give more people the opportunity to spend a few hours in a lavish setting, a brief escape from the troubled times in which they were living.

The conversion of Radio City Music Hall into a movie house began in early January 1933. A special new seventy-by-forty-foot screen, the world's largest, was quickly installed, and the film *The Bitter Tea of General Yen* kicked off the new programming on January 11. The stage show was retained and featured an eclectic blend of opera, ballet, traditional song, and tap. Once again featured were Patricia Bowman and her corps de ballet, Ray Bolger, the

Tuskegee Institute singers, and of course the Roxyettes, popular carryovers from the opening night.

Eleanor was excited to be one of the first acts booked to perform at the spectacular new theater on January 26. Six times a day, she headlined the stage show, *Carnival,* which was paired with the third film to be shown in the venue, *State Fair,* starring Will Rogers and Janet Gaynor. The colorful and pageant-like *Carnival* featured thirty-two Roxyettes and a choral ensemble in "Dance of the Puppets," Patricia Bowman and the corps in the "Marionette Ballet," the Erno Rapee orchestra, singer John Pierce, and headliner Eleanor Powell with the ballet corps in the big finale number, "Merry-Go-Round."

Audiences marveled at the stunning use of the hydraulic stage that masterfully highlighted its different sections in motion throughout the presentation. Everything was designed with a dramatic build-up to the screening of the feature film. As a fitting overture, the orchestra began by playing carnival music from *I Pagliacci,* while a choral ensemble was raised on an elevated portion of the stage. The orchestra rose and traveled across the stage, while the ballet ensemble launched into the marionette number on another elevated portion of the stage in the background. Then, during a change of scenery, John Pierce sang while moving with the orchestra as it rolled back to its pit, revealing Eleanor onstage for her solo. The finale, "Merry-Go-Round," which acted as a prologue to the movie, showed the ballet and choral ensemble riding an enormous merry-go-round center stage, surrounded by the tapping Roxyettes. The chorus line would be a staple at Radio City Music Hall for years to come when the ensemble became famously known as the Rockettes. In a fitting conclusion to the spectacle, the merry-go-round revolved, the screen was lowered, and the picture faded in.

Cynical reviewer Mordaunt Hall from the *New York Times* found that "although there is too much dancing, it is all set forth so artistically that it is never tedious."[15] *Variety* praised the show for its colorful and rapid pace, and it gave a special mention to Eleanor, who "in beaded white pajamas, rivets attention single-handed by the effortless, fluid style of her easy taps."[16]

Crowds of sightseers and moviegoers from all walks of life flocked to the Rockefeller Center. On February 1, 1933, shortly before the close of Eleanor's first week, the music hall received a visit from the legendary Helen Keller, whose extraordinary life as a young girl without sight or hearing was depicted years later in the stage play and film, *The Miracle Worker.* Miss Keller was accompanied by her teacher, Anne Sullivan, and her secretary and companion, Polly Thompson, who acted as her interpreter for the occasion. With her innate sensibility, Miss Keller experienced the new theater entirely by touch, and not a detail escaped her. As she posed for photographs on the staircase beneath the mural on the north wall, a crowd of several hundred gathered to observe. With her fingertips, she carefully traced the carvings of the scantily clad dancing figures on the bronze entry doors and remarked, "It needs censoring. It's too seductive"; she also declared that Laurent's nude statue "Goose Girl" was "saucy."[17] As the tour continued, she was astonished by the cavernous size of the theater and showed a marked interest in its color scheme, questioning the dominant use of black. After the tour, Miss Keller attended the show. "She sat up front and put her hands on the railing of the stage so she could feel the vibrations I created by dancing," Eleanor recalled.[18] Keller marveled at the rhythmic sensations produced by Eleanor's taps. After the show, she and her entourage were welcomed backstage by the cast, where she made Eleanor's acquaintance by running her fingers over her face so she could "look" at her. Eleanor poignantly remembered this meeting as one of the most remarkable moments of her career. As Keller was leaving, Eleanor requested a photograph of her. Miss Keller, whose two very large pet dogs were well-known, wittily inscribed the photo with the message, "To Eleanor Powell—I'd gladly trade my two dogs for yours."

The following week both *State Fair* and *Carnival* moved over to the RKO Roxy; this annoyed critics, who were offended that the Roxy was relegated to second-run fare. They complained that the added intimacy of the venue only revealed the shortcomings of the stage show, instead of improving upon it. The audiences who packed the house for each show didn't seem to mind. The critics did, however, acknowledge Eleanor as the best individual element of the program and suggested that the measure of applause she received in comparison to the more classical numbers just might indicate that the public was tiring of a diet of highbrow fare forced upon them. The following week the film moved over to the RKO Palace, which had a new policy of showing only feature pictures, sans the stage show. A new trend was emerging, causing concern to stage performers who began to fear for their livelihood.

The week of February 8 found Eleanor back at Radio City Music Hall, this time in the stage show that introduced John Barrymore's new film, *Topaze*. Radio stars Amos 'n Andy opened the show with a skit, after which a newsreel was shown. Next were the resident Patricia Bowman and her ballet dancers, followed by York and King. In marked contrast to the elaborate productions that preceded him, soloist John Uppman provided a poignant moment when he sang the touching Depression-era ballad "Brother, Can

You Spare a Dime?" in front of moving images of people walking past an upscale restaurant on a crowded New York street. Next came the Roxyettes, whose elaborate number set the stage for Eleanor's solo. This time, instead of her white beaded pajamas, Eleanor dazzled in a silver fringed leotard, a silver high hat, and matching wrist gauntlets.

Eleanor ended up playing both theaters at the same time; she jumped fully costumed into a pair of slacks and ran across the complex after each show in order to make curtain for the next, doing up to eleven shows a day. Reporters quipped that she seemed to be making Radio City her permanent address, but with six shows a day at the Music Hall and five at the Roxy, this near-impossible feat would not be sustainable for long.

5

Traipsing the Boards

Eleanor and Blanche had now moved to a rented home in Crestwood, a forty-minute commute from downtown Manhattan. All the hard work put in over the previous three years had allowed them to squirrel away some savings, and they found a pleasant two-story Tudor house with a spacious front and backyard. The quaint neighborhood, in northeast Yonkers, today described as a "tidy 415-acre pocket of well-tended colonials, Tudors, and Victorian single-family homes,"[1] provided a quiet respite when they could actually spend time there. An exasperated Blanche lamented how little the home was enjoyed in those days, as Eleanor was constantly on the go, working and rehearsing. She had little time for real life. Her singular joy was found in dancing, fueled by an intense drive for perfectionism. "Dancing to me is some sort of a god, like a Buddha. It encompasses you, like jealousy. Very possessive," Eleanor recalled in later years. "I really didn't know what the outside world was all about."[2] Even when she had rare time off, she took the train into the city and spent the day rehearsing at a studio that offered a special rate of one dollar for a full-day rental.

Proud of the continued success of his protégé, Bill Robinson had sent her a holiday greeting telegram, saying, "Happy New Year! From a bum dancer to a good one. Signed, Bill Robinson."[3] In mid-February, she found herself once again booked for a show with George White. In an effort to continue his *Scandals* series yet still scale down production costs, White had put together a modified touring "tabloid" version of his eleventh edition of *George White's Scandals,* which had run on Broadway from 1931 to 1932. While that edition had starred Rudy Vallee, Ethel Merman, Ray Bolger, Everett Marshall, and Willie and Eugene Howard, only the Howards continued from that lineup. The show was falsely advertised as "the New York company." The weak economy inspired White's unusual move to book the tour not into regular theaters as stand-alone shows, but into movie theaters, where the shows ran two or three times per day, in slots similar to standard vaudeville. This allowed for much lower ticket prices, and in some cases, the show was actually offered free with the movie.

The national tour was a company of seventy-five. Eight were musicians who supplemented local bands in the pit. From the first performance in Ithaca, New York, it would be Eleanor's most intense tour schedule to date, with seventeen cities, some just one-nighters. Each performance day consisted of at least four shows, from ninety minutes to two hours apart. One-nighters often required packing up and getting on a train late at night after the show. Train delays were common, and one-night stands were often challenging to manage. Still, performers could sleep on the train and save the cost of a hotel. Life on the road in vaudeville was harsh and unpredictable, but the adage "the show must go on" prevailed. Blistered, taped-up feet were common for Eleanor, who still practiced constantly. Her shoes were not always the best fit and were not suited for long hours of dance.

Blanche traveled with Eleanor and shared every inconvenience of the one-night stands and week-long engagements throughout the country. Eleanor's feet were often so sore that Blanche had to massage them for an hour before she could go to sleep. By now an experienced vaudevillian, Eleanor traveled with a large steamer trunk that carried her costumes, makeup, portable Victrola record player with a stack of her favorite 78-rpm records, a rosin box (rosin is a sticky substance in rock form that dancers crush with their shoes to keep the soles from sliding on slippery surfaces), many pairs of shoes, and a small wooden tap board, along with her regular clothes and toiletries. Players in traveling revues were responsible for their own transportation and lodging from city to city and had to schedule tickets accordingly.

Eleanor was twenty years old and had little experience in anything but dancing; Blanche's expert help in navigating the quickest travel and best budget accommodations was very welcome on tours. Blanche was as skilled at management as Eleanor was at dance, and the two were a close team. With only a sixteen-year age difference, their bond was more akin to that of sisters than mother and daughter. But this period of Eleanor's life, in which everything of a practical nature was done for her, was both a blessing and a curse. Eleanor, relieved of all the practical duties, never truly learned how to navigate the everyday necessities of life. Their closely linked vision was focused simply on successfully getting through each day.

Though life on the road was at times a lonely existence, Eleanor's love of people led to an active social network backstage. Ever curious, she loved trading stories with the theater crews she befriended on the road. Her friends were the stagehands, theater staff, doormen, and backstage techs, whose stories she found more interesting than those of fellow performers. She met so many people while she was traveling that she started keeping a special notebook to help her recall their names on future visits. An avid letter writer, she would also correspond with many people she had met on her travels for decades to come.

White's confidence that this version of *Scandals* would be received well was cocky and bold in the unpredictable economy. The show had no real top names other than Willie and Eugene Howard, and their comedy routines were growing stale. This did not go unnoticed by critics. The remainder of the cast comprised the singing Loomis Sisters, also a holdover from the original production, Eleanor Powell, singer Ross MacClean, and the "famed" Scandals girls. The ninety-minute show contained most of the songs from the original 1931 production, all penned by Lew Brown and Ray Henderson— the Depression-era anthem, "Life Is Just a Bowl of Cherries," "This Is the Missus," "So I Married the Girl" (performed by Don Stewart and Eleanor, with Willie Howard in a baby buggy), "Ladies and Gentlemen, That's Love," "The Thrill Is Gone," "My Song," and the controversial "That's Why Darkies Were Born."

Early in the tour, reviews complained about the absence of the show's former headliners. "As seen here, the *Scandals* . . . were stripped, and I don't mean the chorus numbers. I mean the cast," a reporter in Ohio wrote. The critic noted a plethora of performers "who worked hard and honestly and may be big names soon, but at the moment are not in the top price class." It was true, and if the prices hadn't been so low, White might have had to deal with many angry ticket buyers. Despite the George White name, the show was considered barely a step above standard vaudeville fare. Unlike touring Broadway shows, it was presented multiple times a day. Ohio critic Edward Gloss moaned about how dated Willie and Eugene Howard's jokes and routines were: "Now, back when Willie and Eugene were building their acts, the numbers in this show were funny. They're still funny, but [with] the funniness of an oft-told joke." Gloss blamed the failure of touring shows on mistakes like this and scolded White and all New York producers, saying, "This must come to an end. . . . Look to your own job of sending out shows worth what you ask or send them at a price commensurate with what you have to sell."[4]

The show continued on from Cleveland, Ohio, to Fort Wayne, Indiana, but only after its scenery and costumes were briefly held hostage by an angry attorney, who was upset that White had not paid the full fee owed for securing an auditorium. After White agreed to make a down payment of $250 against the balance of $1,120, the attachment was released. The culprit was not a true inability to pay, but the repercussions of President Roosevelt's Emergency Banking Act and the subsequent four-day bank closure that caused a run on banks. One of the first acts of Roosevelt's New Deal, it was an effort to help restore confidence and stabilize the economy. But it wreaked havoc on theaters with live shows, causing them to lose paid dates and, thus, substantial income. By the time the bank holiday was over, theaters, at least those in Indiana, were finally open without problem. White offered newspaper readers two free tickets for buying cash want ads over two days; he used this sort of promotional collaboration with newspapers often during the tour.

Curiously, Indiana audiences seemed much more receptive to the show than those in Ohio, as reflected in the reviews. "Eleanore [sic] Powell, who makes even the most conventional tap dancing seem new and exhilarating, provoked a good many spontaneous bursts of applause," said a critic after opening night. "She has a sort of dash and swagger that really reaches the feminine performer, and her dancing is all the more effective for this bit of brashness."[5] Critic Walter Hickman, one of those who had to watch the show without a seat in the standing-room-only house, noted that over three thousand people in line were turned away.

Eleanor received some of the highest praise. "I want to call attention to the tap dancing of Eleanor Powell. When a girl can cause hundreds in an audience to whisper, 'She is wonderful,' then the verdict is best said. She has youth, showmanship, rhythm, and a pair of the best dancing feet in the business."[6] As the tour progressed, the accolades continued. "Eleanor Powell is the most vivacious dancer we have seen for years. Her whirls are even more astonishing than her dances."[7] "Eleanor Powell gets first dancing honors for her fine tap work, her remarkable muscular control, and her winning manner, whether she be singing or dancing."[8] "Miss Powell, who has the poise of a true comedienne . . . happens to be about the only tap dancer now extant who could compete, with any degree of assurance, with the one and only Bill Robinson."[9]

After a grueling four months, Eleanor's longest continuous time on the road with a show to date, the *Scandals* tour ended on June 22, 1933. Exhausted, Eleanor and Blanche returned home to Crestwood, but not for long. In just a few weeks, Eleanor was back in a shorter vaudeville run, this time just four cities, opening at the Paramount Theatre in New York along with the film *Her*

Bodyguard. She was third on the bill, again with the duo of Mr. and Mrs. Jesse Crawford on the twin organ consoles. Then, in Philadelphia, she was part of the *Going to Town* revue. Next, it was the Palace in Chicago and the RKO Downtown in Detroit with her *Hot-Cha!* and *Music Hall Varieties* co-star Bert Lahr and comedic impersonator Eddie Garr; *Variety* said Eleanor's performance showed audiences "what tap dancing is really all about."[10] All this touring and attention from the press attracted notice from one of the most legendary forces in entertainment.

It was only a matter of time before Eleanor's rising star would come to the attention of Billy Rose. In 1931, the diminutive theatrical impresario and lyricist had reworked a previous production, *Sweet and Low,* into a new show, *Crazy Quilt.* Casting his wife, Fanny Brice, as the headliner, along with Ted Healey and Phil Baker, clever Rose hyped the show into great success with ads featuring risqué photos of scantily clothed chorus girls. The hints of near nudity were merely exaggerated publicity, but by encouraging city officials along the road tour to "ban" the presentation, the brash and savvy salesman turned a relatively tame show into a hit. Now, in 1933, he sought to revive the same show, but this time without Brice. He booked Anita Page, Charles King, and suave sleight-of-hand artist Cardini to headline along with dancer Ann Pennington.

Following the recent trend of providing full shows as stage revues for movie houses, Rose announced his similar concept for *Crazy Quilt.* It was simply a pared-down version without an intermission, which enabled it to fit into the time constraints of a movie house stage show. Multiple performances with large seating capacities coupled with more affordable admission prices made for a profitable formula.

Several weeks into the tour, Pennington was relentlessly panned by critics. "Miss Pennington's dancing was so pitifully far removed from the bright and active hoofing of her heyday that almost any sort of substitution would have been welcomed, even Pat Rooney II, got up to resemble a dairymaid and doing an Irish clog," wrote theatrical columnist John Alden. The tiny Pennington, former star of the *Scandals* and *Ziegfeld Follies* and famous for her saucy rendition of the Black Bottom dance, was now forty years old. She was no longer the energetic soubrette of her prime. Rose decided to replace her with Eleanor. Alden humorously noted that he had previously been no fan of tap dancing—on the contrary, he had been "President of the local chapter of the Society for Protection of Audiences Against Tap Dancing"— but now that he had seen Eleanor in the recent *Scandals,* he no longer felt the position was necessary. "Miss Powell's smart dancing . . . changed all that. The Society was disbanded, and its members took up the weaving of fine old lace. Miss Powell adds at least fifty percent to the effectiveness of *Crazy Quilt* as entertainment."[11]

Eleanor was in familiar company. John Murray Anderson, who had recently produced the Radio City Music Hall shows, staged the production; Clark Robinson had been brought over from the Roxy Theatre to design sets; and Chester Hale, with whom she had also worked in her shows at the music hall, was the dance director.

Rose made a special trip to see her first night in the revue, and the audience response affirmed his decision. Billed fourth on posters and ads as "America's Foremost Tap Dancer," Eleanor performed one of the show's most popular songs, "The Wiggle of the World," a Tahitian-themed dance number. Critics agreed she enhanced the show greatly, declaring, "Powell dominates the evening and Rose's revue" and "Miss Powell's dancing is superb. It performs for the revue a service which its gaudy trappings and obviously beautiful girls could not easily accomplish alone."[12] She was increasingly being used for comedy sketches as well as songs, something that would strengthen her future casting options. "In the '*Scandals*' she proved she had a pleasant singing voice and a crisp and sure way with comedy roles," a critic noted.[13]

Though the reviews were excellent, the tour was arduous. Star Anita Page, booked mainly as eye candy, had a phenomenal sixteen costume changes per show, five shows per day, seven days a week. While she was never particularly a fan of tap dancing, she fondly remembered that she loved to watch Eleanor dance. "She was so graceful," Page remarked. "She did a tremendous job . . . what a trouper!"[14] Even though Fanny Brice was not performing in the show, she joined the tour when available and helped with costuming and makeup, doing whatever she could to help Rose's show be successful and run smoothly backstage.

Eleanor continued in *Crazy Quilt* until the show finally closed in January 1934. Though her billing had not improved, she was indisputably established as a tour de force in tap. Her singing and acting received positive reviews, and critics went to creative lengths to describe just how highly they thought of her. "She can touch her toe to the floor and make as much rhythm as fifty Albertina Rasch maidens all cavorting about the stage at the same moment,"

wrote one in Washington, DC. "You have only to observe one of those shuffling exits to be pinned to your chair with exuberance and be grateful for
such an outburst of well-timed craftsmanship."[15]

Even before *Crazy Quilt* closed, Billy Rose was already at work on his
next venture, anxious to keep money coming in. With an idea, but not enough
capital, Rose partnered with several figures of the organized crime world in
New York and accepted a proposition to oversee the opening and management of a new nightclub, the Casino de Paree, on their payroll for a thousand
dollars a month. The end of Prohibition, and hence, the end of lucrative illegal bootlegging, had caused New York's underworld to seek out new streams
of income, and nightclubs were always bankable with a savvy manager at the
helm. Seeking to establish his own reputation, separate from Brice, Rose
accepted the offer and set about creating a luxurious supper club with an
extravagant stage show. The club was located in the cavernous New Yorker
Theatre, originally the Gallo Opera House (the bottom floor of the same
building where Eleanor took her first tap lessons from Jack Donahue and
Johnny Boyle). Rose completely revamped the space, sparing no expense. He
removed the theater seats and installed a terraced floor filled with restaurant
seating; he also designed a stage that served as a dance floor between shows.

The glitzy Casino de Paree opened on December 14, 1933, while *Crazy
Quilt* was still touring. One columnist described the setting as "a sort of college boy's dream of what a night club ought to be," adding that it "is so gaudy
and loud and girly-girly, so aglitter with tinsel, so lavishly staged and bump-
tious with jazz, that it is more than absurd."[16] Bob Alton, another of Ralph
MacKernan's former pupils, staged the dances.

Boxer Max Baer emceed the gala opening event, performing a number
with a bevy of chorus girls from his film *The Prizefighter and the Lady*. Critics
said Rose ran the club "with a flair for magnificence"; they alluded to the
naughtiness of the place, describing Rose's chorus line as "fifty-odd girls
[that] are something *not* to write home about."[17] The club featured burlesque
dancer Hinda Wassau in her "almost" striptease at 2:00 a.m., and the upstairs
bar taunted passersby with nearly nude girls lounging seductively in large
glass fishbowls. Rose teasingly advertised fifty beautiful girls with forty-nine
costumes. On the walls of one section were nude drawings, each with the
head of a famous celebrity. The covers of the club's promotional flyer and
menu featured a topless chorine with a strategically draped strip of fabric.
Though ladies without escorts were not encouraged or even admitted at most
elegant clubs, those whose escorts preferred not to dance had a selection of

handsome gigolos provided by the club as dance partners, easily identified by the green carnations in their lapels and their personal numbers (names were not allowed). If a lady had enough dollar bills, she could dance with "Mr. Seven" all night.

However, not every aspect of the club was risqué. When *Crazy Quilt* ended its run, Rose wasted no time booking Eleanor. She started on February 6, 1934, and stayed for seventeen weeks. Eleanor performed in all three nightly shows at 7:45, midnight, and 2:00 a.m., closing the final show with her dance. Among others on the bill were British master magician Cardini (another popular holdover from *Crazy Quilt*), young dancer Hal LeRoy, singer Gertrude Niesen, and the dance team of Holland and June (Knight). Bill Robinson had taken over from Max Baer in January, but it is unclear whether he was still the host when Eleanor arrived on the bill a few weeks later. During Eleanor's long run at the club, it became a celebrity hotspot, with such notables as James Roosevelt, son of FDR, a regular attendee. He and his wife became fans of Eleanor's and would often invite her to sit at their table. Soon the club was amassing weekly profits of around $40,000.

But the crime bosses perceived that Rose's "magnificence" was taking too big a bite out of the profits. They thought he paid the top acts, like Eleanor, a little too well. He also spared no expense with the dinner service, employing gourmet chefs. The lavish decor was expensive to maintain. Rose provided his own original music for the revues; it was pricier than using existing songs but allowed him to maintain ownership of the music. The only low-priced item at the Casino de Paree was the cover charge of two dollars.

Business was going so well that in May 1934, Rose left on a European vacation for several months. Taking advantage of his absence, his bosses trimmed many of what they considered lavish expenditures and quickly raised the prices. Rose was livid when he returned at the end of August and found out that Eleanor, one of his biggest draws, along with several other of his hand-picked acts, had been fired in June.

Reportedly, Rose grabbed the columnist Walter Winchell as an unwilling cohort to meet with his bosses. When he cited his contract, which provided for decision-making control of the club, the weapon-wielding mobsters wise-cracked, "While you were in Europe, we shot out most of the clauses." Publicly, the lead financier Yarmi Stern stated simply, "We could not agree on certain policies and decided a change would be best."[18] Rose and Winchell left the meeting shaken. But Rose decided to pack up the scenery and costumes and place them in a secret storage location in New Jersey, where his gangster bosses couldn't easily locate them. In another risky move, he started litigation for $25,000 in back salary he figured he was owed, which the owners were unwilling to pay. In March, Stern had purchased the entire building in which the nightclub was located. While Stern had the option to continue the club if he chose, Rose had possession of the essentials related to the show.

Rose and his lawyer, Julian Abeles, contacted wealthy financier Bernard Baruch, whose top government connections gave him easy access to J. Edgar Hoover. Soon, FBI agents had the names of the mob bosses who had been in business with Rose, and Hoover's men informed them that their operations would be shut down if Rose was harmed. Thankfully for Rose, the truce was honored, but not until after Rose and Brice passed several nervous weeks at home with bodyguard protection. Ultimately, the club was stripped of Rose's name on all signage and publications, and the Casino de Paree continued to operate after some revamping of the show. After Rose left, the club's owners brought in Lew Brown as producer. It's not known whether Rose ever received his back pay, but he and Stern never spoke again after the incident.

Despite the tremendous attention and excellent pay, Eleanor and Blanche were happy to be out of the Casino de Paree environment. So far, Eleanor had been able to steer clear of the dubious world of mobsters and, thanks to the watchful eye of Blanche, men with singular intentions. Eleanor's wholesome demeanor throughout her teen years on Broadway had inspired many of her bosses to view her with a protective, fatherly eye. The theatrical world was full of men who objectified women, but the innocent teen and her mother had been lucky enough to encounter many who treated them with respect. "Gus Edwards discovered Eleanor when she was twelve, and ever since then, the wonderful men of show business have looked after and protected that girl," Blanche recalled. "Ben Bernie, George White, Flo Ziegfeld—when Eleanor was around, they saw to it that there was no cussing, no rough language." Now twenty-one, Eleanor, though mature in talent, was still an exuberant child at heart. Blanche turned a stern eye toward any men she felt might mistreat Eleanor, but, thankfully, that was rare. "Hers is really one of the strangest, most wonderful stories of all time: the men in show business were her collective father."[19]

Another friendly advisor and constant male supporter ever since her teen years in New York was dancer Bill Robinson. In his unique position as the undisputed King of Tap, Robinson had mentored and encouraged Eleanor from their very first meeting, recognizing her unique talents and her ethic of hard work. Greatly treasuring their friendship, he always wore a diamond stickpin in the shape of a dancing shoe that had been gifted to him by Eleanor.

During Eleanor's run at the Casino de Paree, fifty-six-year-old Robinson was dubbed the honorary Mayor of Harlem on February 26, in recognition of his long-standing charitable and philanthropic efforts in the community. Eleanor was invited to perform at the ceremony, along with two other Robinson protégés—the young Nicholas Brothers, Fayard and Harold. Honorees were chosen by the Locality Mayor's Association of New York for induction into the group. Robinson, the association's first Black honoree, was acknowledged before a crowd of over three hundred attendees of all races. In solemn acknowledgment of the horrific developments in Europe, one member, New York Judge William Greenspan, proclaimed that he "was sorry Hitler was not present to see the spirit of tolerance the gathering represented."[20]

Just as Blanche had breathed a sigh of relief that Eleanor had been relatively safe from romantic hounds, columns started buzzing with news of suitors, both real and imagined. One of the first to appear with regular mention was bandleader Abe Lyman, fifteen years her senior. Eleanor was listed as Lyman's "most attentive listener." It's not known when they met, but gossip-mongers already spoke of the two as "betrothed" by the time Eleanor was booked into a vaudeville gig with him on June 8. When a diamond ring appeared on her finger, it seemed confirmation of the engagement until Blanche stepped forward and told reporters that the ring was actually a twenty-first birthday present from her to her daughter. Eleanor took it all in stride and focused on her work, tolerating, but not encouraging Lyman's attention.

When the opportunity to be considered for an upcoming musical by Ray Henderson and Jack McGowan came her way, Eleanor was elated that she would have a role in addition to dancing. Henderson, the composer for *Scandals,* and McGowan were writing a new show for Harry Richman, *Say When,* and looking to fill spots in the cast. Many of the same people she had previously worked with would also be with the show, including costume designer Charles LeMaire. Eleanor was excited about this project, which could boost her career. She was in final discussions for the production when an equally interesting second offer came along in spring 1934 from the Shubert brothers, J.J. and Lee. This one would team her with dancer Ray Bolger as one of the headliners in the show *Life Begins at 8:40*. With her first commitment already in place for *Say When,* she reluctantly turned the Shuberts down.

In 1934, Vitaphone shorts were being produced almost every week at the Astoria Studios. Eleanor was listed in preproduction publicity for two in the two-reel Broadway Brevities series. The first, *The Winnah!,* with Arthur and Florence Lake, was released July 21. The short included a competition with competing tap soloists. The second, *No Contest,* with singer Ruth Etting, was released for preview on August 22. The story line included an international segment in which chorus girls performed various dances in costumes from different countries as featured singers introduced each segment on a rotating stage. While both films listed Eleanor as a participant in prerelease publicity, she is not visible on screen in either. They can be written off as mistakes on her list of credits.

The long-running gig at the Casino de Paree was behind her, and she was still waiting for further details on *Say When.* Eleanor went back to vaudeville. The booking with bandleader Lyman and his orchestra at the Capitol Theatre would bring in her highest vaudeville rate yet, $750 per week. She was sharing the bill for the first time with the sibling song and dance act, Vilma and Buddy Ebsen. The Ebsens, who had been on the vaudeville stage for about four years, had recently appeared in the *Ziegfeld Follies.* Buddy's loose, eccentric dance style and Vilma's sweet, wholesome demeanor had kept them steadily working the circuit. Their style was a good balance to Eleanor's sharp, clean rhythms and acrobatic moves. "The talented Eleanor Powell continues to uphold her reputation as the premiere female tap dancer in the country and Vilma and Buddy Ebsen . . . dance expertly together."[21] The following week the revue moved on to Loew's Valencia Theater with the same cast for a repeat of the show.

Eleanor joined the large entertainment line-up for the annual banquet of the International Circulation Manager's Association on June 20 and danced on a bill that included Bert Lahr, George Tapps, Cardini, Bill Robinson, Rudy Vallee, Helen Kane, Jimmy Savo, boxer Jack Dempsey, Gertrude Niesen, and the Hollywood Girls.

Word finally arrived from Jack McGowan that the book was ready and that the producers had plans to move forward with *Say When.* He called Eleanor in for a meeting to discuss the results of revisions to some of the parts. She had high hopes that this would prove to be a breakthrough role for her, one that finally allowed her to act as well as dance. But her hopes were dashed when McGowan instead informed her that the part had been revamped with much less dancing involved. Though they all loved Eleanor, the producers didn't have the same confidence in her acting ability. Their offer was rescinded. It was back to vaudeville once again.

On August 25, she started another week of vaudeville at the Loew's Century Theatre in the *Frolics of 1934* revue, finishing out the month with strong reviews. "One is amazed at the rhythm of her movements," wrote one critic. "Wearing blue sequin pajamas, . . . she seems to ripple and undulate from the middle downward continually, amazingly."[22]

Moving back to the Capitol Theatre at the beginning of September, paired with the Joan Crawford and Clark Gable movie *Chained*, she danced on a bill with Phil Spitalny and his All-Girl Orchestra. Newspapers noted that the upcoming vaudeville season would be strong, with Eleanor among the over two hundred performers who had already been booked by Loew's offices.

As a special highlight to the final week at the Capitol Theatre, Eleanor was paid a joint visit backstage by Ray Bolger, on a break from his show *Life Begins at 8:40*, and Bill Robinson. To the delight of the Chester Hale Girls, the three tappers went into a tap jam, conversing, as only tappers do, with a lively exchange of steps. It was an affirming reminder that dance is a universal language with no borders among hoofers. She finished out the month of September as part of the Ed Lowry revue with George Sidney at Loew's Metropolitan, Loew's Paradise, and Loew's Penn Theaters in Pittsburgh. Critics declared, "Eleanor Powell, the famous tap dancer, performed staccato miracles with her feet."[23] Moving on to Washington, DC, the revue played a week at the Loew's Fox, then continued to Baltimore, and finally ended in Jersey City. This was the final vaudeville date of Eleanor's career.

Her feet may have had the ability to perform miracles with their rhythm, but her career had reached a plateau. All the excellent reviews had yet to produce top billing, better opportunities to dance, or her personal dream—offers to go to Europe, where dancers and the legendary ballet companies were applauded and appreciated as artists. Though she wouldn't turn down chances to dance, the drudgery of long road tours was taking a toll.

One of Johnny Hyde's ongoing aims was to elevate Eleanor from the limbo position of featured dancer. They both agreed that unless she was offered lines and singing parts in addition to dancing, her career would stagnate. She was anxious to do more, but her singing voice was an obstacle. It was pleasant and expressive but did not have the volume needed for Broadway theaters in the days before amplification. She took singing lessons in an attempt to increase her vocal strength, but, as evidenced by the decision of the *Say When* producers, the theatrical community had little confidence in her ability to carry a full role.

Disappointed that they had been unable to sign Eleanor for *Life Begins at 8:40*, the Shubert brothers sent over a new offer. This time it was for *A*

Nautical Revue, currently being written by Raymond Knight. Eleanor was the first to be signed. Hyde made another valiant effort during further negotiations, stressing her stipulation for singing and acting, not just dancing. "She will have 'opportunity to speak lines and to sing,'" Stanley Joseloff (legal counsel to the Shuberts) stated in a letter to Shubert attaché Harry Kaufman. "I would recommend that this wording be retained unless she makes violent objections to it," Joseloff continued, adding that "it perhaps is better to do that with a person whose forte is dancing and whose singing and speaking ability are more ambition than fact."[24] His opinion was valued and held weight when figuring the details of Eleanor's contract. On November 8, 1934, she signed for a weekly salary of $650 with a projected start date of April 1, 1935. Since the Shuberts still had the rest of the cast to fill, it appeared she would have months of time on her hands with no performing opportunities of any real substance.

Soon after she signed the contract, George White offered Eleanor a small part in his upcoming film, *George White's 1935 Scandals.* Her immediate reaction wasn't excitement, but dread. It would mean going to Hollywood. To the little girl from Springfield, Hollywood seemed like a decadent place straight out of *The Great Gatsby.* She had heard stories about wild parties where people jumped fully clothed into swimming pools, and she was wary. She had observed similar atmospheres before: recently, at the Casino de Paree, back when she first arrived on Broadway in the late 1920s, and even, to some degree, as a child in Atlantic City. Still, her perception of what Hollywood was like topped them all. She was an attractive, vivacious twenty-one-year-old who didn't drink, smoke, or go out regularly to parties and nightclubs, and she didn't carouse with men. All she wanted to do was dance. If she went to Hollywood, how would she fit in?

Despite her recent offer from the Shuberts, jobs on Broadway were waning. Movies and musicals were the future, with many new opportunities for a dancer. She ultimately decided to accept the offer. It wasn't Europe, but it could open the door to new horizons. And Blanche would be by her side, as always. Confident that things would work out, as they usually did, they got their tickets to Los Angeles and prepared to set off across the country.

6

Westward Bound

On a rainy morning in November, the day before her twenty-second birthday, Eleanor and Blanche boarded the 20th Century Limited in New York, bound for Chicago, where they would transfer to the Santa Fe Chief for the two-day journey to Los Angeles. Her steamer trunk packed with her Victrola, heavy albums of Fats Waller 78s, her small tap mat, and an assortment of tap shoes, she was prepared to rehearse on the way. Pleased that Bill Robinson and his wife, Fannie, were on the same train, she felt better about her new venture. Robinson was also headed to Fox Studios, where he was about to make *The Little Colonel*, his first film with Shirley Temple. For Eleanor, having an old friend nearby would be comforting.

As they sped toward the coast, Eleanor, Blanche, Bill, Fannie, and some of the other passengers added a festive note to the trip by celebrating Eleanor's birthday on the train with, as Hemingway would later say, a "moveable feast." They sped past many of the towns she had played on her vaudeville tours, but soon they reached a part of the country she had never seen before. The landscape changed as they passed the flat heartland and moved into the arid desert of the West. She was in uncharted territory, in all senses of the word. They rolled into Los Angeles about 8:30 a.m. on November 22.

The Hollywood publicity machine had preceded her. Though she had earned a solid reputation on Broadway as the finest female tap dancer onstage, she was completely unknown to film audiences. Press releases, generated at the direction of George White in an effort to elevate her public stature, presented her as a New York–born tap dancer he had discovered in Europe. Ironically, Eleanor was touted as having danced at the casinos of Monte Carlo, even though she had never left the country. The only casino she had ever appeared in was the Casino de Paree in New York.

Eleanor and Blanche were greeted by beautiful clear skies, a vast change from the gray, chilly Novembers in New York. As they headed west and continued down a stretch of Pico Boulevard, buildings thinned out and large sections of open fields were dotted with oil pump towers. In 1934, large swaths of Los Angeles were still filled with citrus groves that thrived in the abundant sunny days.

Just a couple blocks from the studio, at Pico and Westwood, was California's first drive-in movie theater, which had opened only two months earlier. Eleanor reported to Fox "Movietone City," the campus built in 1926 on a large parcel of land between Pico and Santa Monica Boulevards in West Los Angeles. Known for its innovative Movietone sound-on-film process and one of the best-equipped studios of its time, Fox was now suffering woefully under the misdirection of its president, Winfield "Winnie" Sheehan. The studio was plagued with money troubles, still heavily in debt from loans taken to stay afloat during the Depression. Even the rapid ascendance in popularity of its newest little star, Shirley Temple (who had an uncredited bit part in the first film edition of *George White's Scandals*), was not enough to save the studio. Within six months, it would merge with 20th Century Studios, receive an overhaul in management, and become 20th Century-Fox.

As noted in the credits, George White had single-handedly "conceived, created, and directed" his first Hollywood version of the *Scandals* the year before. It starred Rudy Vallee, Jimmy Durante, Alice Faye, Cliff Edwards, and of course, George White. Although the film had been poorly received by the critics, the studio hoped that White, with a bit of movie-making experience under his belt, would not repeat his mistake. The trade papers were not optimistic but noted that one saving grace might be a young dancer from Broadway who could tap with the best of them—Eleanor Powell.

Eleanor arrived on the lot to be swiftly inducted into the Hollywood waiting game. But this was not the typical Hollywood set. White made up his own rules and ran the film shoot the same way he ran the rehearsals for his stage productions. Instead of the standard practice of beginning promptly at 9 a.m., White rarely started before midafternoon, by which time most of the cast members were well on their way to alcoholic oblivion. Everyone, except for Eleanor and Alice Faye, gathered in the property room, where they drank and swapped stories. Out on the set, the cameramen sat idle for hours. After reviewing the rushes from the previous day, White would call a dinner break around 6 p.m., then finally begin real production at 7 p.m. As word spread about the Broadway producer's unconventional style of filming, the press teasingly named his film set "George White's Night Club." On the best of days, White completed only two shots.

Nearly a month passed before Eleanor was finally called on to make some screen tests. White gave her instructions to go get made up. Following his vague directions to the makeup department, she spotted a queue of people next to a building marked "Makeup." She simply joined the line. Back on set, nobody seemed to notice that she was sporting the rich shade of brown applied to the extras playing Egyptians for another film. She proceeded to film her test.

Fortunately, Fox made multiple screen tests of Eleanor. When a colleague viewed one of them, he found her tap dancing so extraordinary that he excitedly notified Bill Robinson, who was in producer Buddy DeSylva's dressing room nearby, and suggested he take a look. "[Robinson] ambled over to look at the Powell screen tests while studio officials gurgled with enthusiasm over their 'find.' When the screen test began to run, Robinson began to laugh. 'She's been my tap dance pupil for five years,' he explained."[1] Robinson became a regular visitor to the set. In addition to giving tap lessons to some of the chorus girls, as well as to Alice Faye and James Dunn, he and Eleanor often met up to jam together.

Meanwhile, shooting progressed slowly. Co-star James Dunn, who struggled for years with alcoholism, was a major factor. Though he had just completed four films with Shirley Temple on the Fox lot that year, he was in a sad state. "He could only do two or three lines. They had to cut and come over to tell him his next two sentences to say," Eleanor later recounted. In her final scene, she dines with Dunn in a silent montage, while Alice Faye is also shown dining with her beau. Artificial food was set on the plates before them, and Eleanor watched in shocked silence as the drunken Dunn proceeded to eat it.

The thin backstage story was a mere pretext to show off the *Scandals* chorines in a setting reminiscent of White's stage shows. While traveling to Florida on vacation, George White (playing himself) stops off at a small town in Georgia, where he discovers Honey Walters (Alice Faye) and Eddie Taylor (James Dunn) singing in a local revue. White signs Honey for his upcoming *Scandals* in New York, but not before she and her Aunt Jane (Emma Dunn) convince White to hire Eddie as well. After the two join the show, success goes to their heads; Eddie falls for a dancer, Marilyn Collins (Eleanor), while Honey steps out with Daniels (Walter Johnson), both of whom had formerly walked out on George White's show. White is forced to fire Honey and Eddie as a result of their increasing unprofessionalism. Now, down on their luck and unable to find work, they are both dumped by their respective flirts.

White goes into a flurry of activity when kindly Aunt Jane shows up expecting to see the couple perform in the show. Not wanting to disappoint her, White finds and rehires them, and they sing and dance their way to a happy ending.

Cliff Edwards, Ned Sparks, and Lyda Roberti had supporting roles, and many newcomers to film were cast in uncredited roles (Benny Rubin, singer Kenny Baker) or in the chorus (Jane Wyman, Lynn Bari, June Lang, and Susan Fleming, among others). The most notable songs were "According to the Moonlight," sung by Faye, and "It's an Old Southern Custom," repeated endlessly throughout the film. The big production number, "Hunkadola," was sort of a poor man's "Carioca," complete with female dancers serving as jump ropes and other startling choreography.

Critics considered Eleanor's number to be the one showstopper of the film. Lowered to the nightclub dance floor on a seat held by giant bows, she makes her appearance exactly halfway through the movie, just in time to briefly rouse the audience from the plodding storyline. While tap dancers, most notably Ruby Keeler and Ginger Rogers, were in nearly every musical of the day, Eleanor's style, honed through her years on Broadway, was different from any other. Bill Robinson's influence in her solo is evident, but her mixture of joie de vivre, grace, and stunning tap turns was all her own. The trademark gestures and facial expressions that she had often employed on Broadway were utilized during the number to attract the attention of James Dunn's character, while her exiting strut added subtle humor.

Eleanor had a brand-new look for her Hollywood debut, exchanging the trademark Dutch Boy bob she wore as the "kid" of Broadway for a more feminine, up-to-date style with a center part and soft waves. Essential for her close-ups, her teeth were also straightened and capped. She wore the same black and white sequined pajamas designed by Charles LeMaire for her number in *George White's Music Hall Varieties*.

Eleanor's role was abbreviated at best, with minimal dialogue and no more than five minutes total screen time, including her dance number. In her first speaking role on screen, brief as it was, she plays with ease and confidence. Completely unimpressed by Hollywood, Eleanor and Blanche eagerly returned to New York.

Act Two

(1935–1943)

7

Taming the Lion

Metro-Goldwyn-Mayer Studios (MGM), located approximately five miles south of Hollywood in Culver City, was founded in 1924 and produced its first feature-length "all talking, all singing, all dancing" musical, *The Broadway Melody*, in 1929. The film won an Academy Award for best picture that year, prompting other studios to rush to explore the possibilities of the new technology. At Paramount, Ernst Lubitsch's first sound film, *The Love Parade* (1929), starring Jeanette MacDonald and Maurice Chevalier, kicked off a new trend of sophisticated European-inspired films with song. In 1933, at Warner Bros., Dick Powell and Ruby Keeler ushered in the Depression-era backstage musical with *42nd Street*. Director Busby Berkeley overcame the limitations of the early sound cameras with his innovative overhead shots, transforming dance numbers into kaleidoscopic works of art. Fred Astaire, on loan from RKO, did a brief guest spot that year in MGM's *Dancing Lady* (with Joan Crawford) before returning to his home studio to make his first appearance with Ginger Rogers in *Flying Down to Rio*. The resounding success of the film (and the dance duo) propelled Astaire to the forefront of Hollywood dancers.

Despite the initial success of *The Broadway Melody*, MGM was slow to find its niche in the genre and had since produced a string of unremarkable musical pictures. Eyeing the accomplishments of its rival studios, MGM mounted an effort to position itself as not just a competitor but a leader in the field by building and developing its own musical comedy stars. It was well on its way to establishing its dominance in the field of operetta with the acquisition of Jeanette MacDonald and the recent release of the high-budget film *The Merry Widow* (1934). But MGM was hard-pressed to find a dancing star of Astaire's caliber.

Sam Katz was heading a new musical unit, and *Broadway Melody of 1935* was to be the first production and their biggest musical effort yet.

John Considine Jr. would produce. Though not a true sequel, the film, eventually retitled *Broadway Melody of 1936,* maintained the general theme of backstage life as the linking thread.

The film had been in the planning stages since early 1934, but the project had suffered several setbacks before it finally got under way. In October, June Knight was engaged as the leading lady. MGM was unsuccessful in its attempt to again borrow Bing Crosby from Paramount, after his appearance in *Going Hollywood* the previous year, which left the project without a male star. The script had gone through sixteen writers before it was temporarily shelved. Now that it was back on the production schedule, casting had finally begun; Jack Benny was set to be the lead and Roy Del Ruth to direct. The studio was now on the hunt for dancers and interesting acts for featured spots in the film.

In December, *Daily Variety* announced the test of twelve-year-old Frances Garland, who was being considered for a featured part in the film. The youngest and most talented member of the Gumm Sisters trio (recently renamed the Garland Sisters), she had garnered attention at several local appearances, the latest at the Wilshire-Ebell Theatre earlier that month. Nothing came of the test, and it would be a year before young Frances would return to the studio as contract player Judy Garland.

When Fox amalgamated with 20th Century, screen tests of a variety of previously unsigned talent were made available to other studios. Searching for specialty acts, studio head Louis B. Mayer ran reel after reel of screen tests until finally one piqued his interest. Actor and screenwriter Sid Silvers, whom Eleanor knew from New York, was sitting with Mayer and recognized Eleanor when her Fox test came up. However, because this was one of the tests she had done with the dark "Egyptian" makeup, Mayer mistakenly took her for a Black dancer. Though he was impressed by her dancing, he felt he couldn't use her in a featured part. Silvers set him straight. "She's as white as I am," he said. "That's Eleanor Powell." Mayer decided to offer her a featured spot.

Overjoyed to get a call from MGM, her agent, Johnny Hyde, quickly let Eleanor know of the interest. At that time, the majority of William Morris' clients were stage performers, so inquiries from Hollywood provided a great opportunity for the agency to increase its business with the West Coast studios. However, after her less-than-stellar experience in Hollywood, Eleanor didn't share his excitement. When she returned to New York, she had gone to a midnight sneak preview of *George White's 1935 Scandals* at the Paramount Theatre with a few dancer friends. Thinking it would be fun to see her screen debut (not counting the quick glimpse of her in *Queen High*), they all settled in to watch. When her dance finally appeared on screen, she was mortified. The sound was one frame out of sync, which made her dance out of time with the taps. Disgusted, she decided she was finished with Hollywood. So, when MGM came calling, she turned them down.

Eleanor put the experience in the past and continued to dream of someday going to Europe. She did what she thought would be the quickest way to get MGM to back down. She asked for an exorbitant amount of money—a thousand dollars per week. Eleanor knew that was much more than her fellow "kids" of Broadway Hal LeRoy and Mitzi Mayfair were getting for their Hollywood work. When MGM agreed, she countered, asking for more money and an actual role in the film, something she had not had in *George White's 1935 Scandals*. "I might as well have said, 'I want a million dollars and my dressing room painted in gold,'" she said. But instead of the immediate rejection she expected, to her great surprise, they sent over a script.

Mayer's original idea was to have Eleanor play the role of Kitty Corbett, the part later given to Una Merkel, with a featured dance solo. It would place her opposite her old friend Sid Silvers, who was not only writing the film but also acting in it. In a move that frustrated Hyde, Eleanor finally upped her fee to $1,250, thinking this would silence them once and for all. MGM confirmed it was a go; they replied with an offer of one month's work and accepted her conditions. Again, Eleanor was shocked, but she realized she could hardly turn down such an opportunity. In mid-February, an announcement in the *Hollywood Reporter* confirmed she had been added to *Broadway Melody of 1935* as "dance talent." One month later, Blanche and Eleanor packed their bags and again headed west.

In the meantime, MGM continued to develop *Broadway Melody of 1935* as their lead musical project, considering various options. Production files dated March 16 indicate that costume designs for the "Broadway Rhythm" finale were requested for Technicolor. Due to the additional expense, by the time the number was shot in late June, the color segment was abandoned.

Casting moved forward. Engaged early on were Vilma and Buddy Ebsen. Actor Robert Wildhack, brought out from New York at Mayer's request, was set to do a comic specialty as a "snore expert" in the film. Dancers Jack Whiting and Paul Draper were also considered, but dancer Nick Long Jr. was ultimately engaged. Mayer was intrigued by a magician named Lamont, who made prop furniture and pianos disappear and reappear before the audience's eyes. Mayer liked the idea of this special effect and wanted to use it in the film. Eventually, this desire for a "magical" element was fulfilled by Thayer the Magician for the number "I've Got a Feelin' You're Foolin'." Floyd Thayer, inventor and fabricator of magical illusions for decades, was an expert in magic props. He regularly worked with Hollywood and was friendly with many top stars. During the number, flowers instantly bloom at the wave of a hand, tables pop up from the floor, and statues disappear into their bases, all part of the "Foolin'" theme.

Seeking established dance talent for the finale of the picture, they settled on an idea that first appears in studio production documents in early March—all the featured acts would perform in the elaborate "Broadway Rhythm" number, which would finish with King of Tap Bill Robinson paired with young tap dancer Jeni LeGon[1] and a full chorus line of Black dancers. Featuring Black talent so prominently in a big-budget feature would have been a highly unusual decision for a major motion picture studio at the time.

As befit Eleanor's new status as an MGM player under contract, even if with only a supporting role, she and Blanche were put up at the elegant Beverly Wilshire Hotel. Beverly Hills, at that time a small community with fewer than two thousand residents, was within a twenty-minute drive from the studio. Soon after they had settled in, it was time to visit her new studio home.

Eleanor first walked onto the MGM Lot in mid-March 1935. At that time, the studio was a sprawling 165-acre compound of six lots; the three largest contained sound stages and production offices. The other three included parking, transportation, the studio zoo, stables, and nursery. As Eleanor was becoming acquainted with studio life, discussions about the film continued. Still striving to find a dancing star to rival Fred Astaire, Mayer considered Eleanor's talents, but was wary about handing his new acquisition any further responsibility for this major undertaking. Nevertheless, he decided to take a closer look.

Directed to a rehearsal hall, Eleanor, Blanche, and Johnny Hyde joined Louis B. Mayer, Roy Del Ruth, Sam Katz, and Eddie Mannix (general manager and notorious scandal "fixer"). At the time, neither Eleanor nor Blanche knew who these executives were (other than Mayer). When they asked to see further demonstrations of Eleanor's dancing, she showed them some of her acrobatic and lyrical ballet work, as well as some work on pointe. After the group conferred privately, Mayer called her over and told her, with great officiousness, "I want to test you for the lead."

Eleanor shocked Mayer with her response. "Mr. Mayer, you can't do that. I don't know a thing about the camera." She proceeded to tout the charms and talents of actress June Knight, who was currently engaged as the lead and with whom she had worked in Ziegfeld's *Hot-Cha!* and at the Casino de Paree. Knight already had six films on her résumé. "She's glamorous, she's sexy, she sings, she's a good dancer," Eleanor said. She also mentioned Mayer's $3 million budget, adding again, "You can't do that." Stunned, Mayer replied, "Well, my dear child, you don't seem to realize that I run this studio, and if I want to make a test, I'm going to make a test." Eleanor responded, matter-of-factly, "Well, you're just wasting your time."[2]

Del Ruth handed Eleanor two scenes to prepare for a screen test on the following day. The scenes featured each of the dual roles of the part—the shy, small-town girl who shows up at the New York office of her high school beau turned producer, and, under masquerade, the flamboyant Parisian dancer, Mademoiselle Arlette, a persona invented to win his attention. Mayer, in his astuteness, recognized that the roles were, in fact, Eleanor's own two sides—the inner personality of the shy child and the confident and charismatic dancer she became when onstage. After studying the scenes, she explained as much to Del Ruth the next morning in his office. "They couldn't have found anything better than that part," she recalled.[3]

George Sidney, then just twenty-three, directed her test. Later, when the rushes were ready, Del Ruth was called from set to meet with Mayer, Katz, and Mannix. Eleanor retreated to her dressing room with Blanche as the conference ensued. She was now worried, despite her initial protests to Mayer, that she was about to be let go. After coming this far, she really didn't want to give up. She had also heard that, of all people, writer Jack McGowan was on the lot. Was he telling Mayer about the opinion of the *Say When* producers on Broadway and their lack of confidence in her acting abilities? During the torturous wait, she wondered why the discussion was taking so long.

In Mayer's office, strong opinions were indeed flying back and forth. Katz and Mannix felt that Eleanor's name next to Jack Benny's was not enough star power and suggested that it would be smarter to bring in someone with verified box office appeal, like Loretta Young. Dancing could be filmed with long shots, as had recently been done with *Reckless*. The original star, Joan Crawford (who could dance), had been replaced with Jean Harlow (who could not), to capitalize on Harlow's well-publicized romance with the film's leading man, William Powell. Harlow's vocals were dubbed by Virginia Merrill, and her dancing was doubled in long shots by dancer Betty Halsey. Despite all the effort, the film would be Harlow's lowest grossing film; it lost the studio $125,000, the equivalent of about $2.3 million today.

But the disappointing results of *Reckless* were not yet known, and a similar strategy was being suggested for *Broadway Melody of 1936*. Neither Eleanor nor her male co-star, young contract player Robert Taylor, were well-known, and management feared it was just too risky. But Del Ruth vehemently defended Eleanor, stating, "First, if you take this girl off the picture, I will walk off the picture immediately. Second, if she isn't a star overnight, I will direct any two pictures on this lot gratis. That's how much I believe in this girl."[4]

As Eleanor waited in her dressing room, Arthur Freed, the film's lyricist, came over and relayed the happenings of the meeting, swearing her to secrecy. At Del Ruth's recommendation, she had not seen the rushes, but she was flooded with gratitude when she heard about his unabashed praise and insistence that she be kept in the picture. "When I heard that, I would have walked through fire for that man!" she said.[5] What Freed didn't know was that a second person had also stepped up to defend Eleanor's place in the film—writer Jack McGowan. Unbeknownst to Eleanor, McGowan was the writer of the original *Broadway Melody* and was also working with Sid Silvers on the script for this film. Seeing the rushes reinforced McGowan's feeling that he had missed an opportunity by not using Eleanor in *Say When*. The lead role was now officially hers.

Eleanor signed a contract for the one picture on April 20, 1935, and production began on April 29. She was the newest member of MGM's stable of stars.

⊙ ⊙ ⊙

With Eleanor now under contract, MGM commenced the process that all their new actors underwent—they analyzed the newcomer from head to toe and then set about to correct, tweak, and adjust every part of her appearance. The full makeover was standard procedure, allowing the studio to present and promote their stars in the most glamorous light. Her hair was brightened to a light auburn tone so that it would photograph better in black and white, and her hairstyle was softened with layers and curls. Her crooked teeth had already been capped during her short time at Fox. Next, a special daily skin regimen was designed just for her, and violet-ray treatments were used to fade her freckles and smooth the texture of her skin. Her eyebrows were thinned and reshaped in the high, narrow arch popular in the day. Eleanor's eyes, one of her strongest features, were adorned with false eyelashes and special makeup to highlight their striking shade of blue. Finally, makeup artists studied her face and designed a technique to best contour her features for the camera.

Special leg exercises were prescribed to elongate the muscles in her thighs and calves, which were thick and toned from years of acrobatics and ballet. To lengthen the appearance of her legs, it was suggested she wear high heels on occasion. Wardrobe specialists gave her posture advice and prescribed padding, tucks, and details in the cut and tailoring of her clothing to correct or amplify certain curves. To accentuate her shoulders, designer Gilbert Adrian (known professionally as Adrian) would often use large collars or bows; the contrast made her hips appear slimmer. She was even coached on gesture and movement—every detail studied and refined to project a relaxed, yet polished, feminine style.

The newly refined Eleanor was now ready to be showcased at a few local events. In early April she performed at a benefit for Temple Israel at the Pantages Theatre in Hollywood, alongside Bill Robinson and Fats Waller. On May 10, she entertained at the Mayor's Benefit held on Stage 15 at the studio, on the same bill as dancer Jeni LeGon. She finished up the month with two additional benefits—one with Jeanette MacDonald and Nelson Eddy, and the second once again with Bill Robinson. Meanwhile, production was in full swing on *Broadway Melody of 1936*.

In the role of Irene Foster, Eleanor arrives in New York to ask her high school sweetheart, now producer, Bob Gordon (Robert Taylor) for a chance to audition for his new musical. Afraid that Broadway will spoil her innocence, he tells her to return to Albany. Aided by Gordon's secretary, Kitty (Una Merkel), gossip columnist Bert Keeler (Jack Benny), and his sidekick Snoop (Sid Silvers), she instead secretly takes on the identity of the fictitious Mademoiselle La Belle Arlette to get Gordon's attention. She surprises him in the final production number by revealing her true identity. Appearing first as the shy Irene Foster, she is later transformed into the extravagant, flirty alter ego, Mademoiselle Arlette, bedecked in a high platinum wig, furs, and exotic makeup. To complete the illusion, the studio brought in a French dialogue coach to aid her with the exaggerated French accent.

The film presented Eleanor in no fewer than four numbers of varying styles to highlight the versatility of its new star. In the first number Irene Foster is joined on the roof of her boardinghouse by her vaudevillian neighbors, played by Vilma and Buddy Ebsen in their film debut. The lively "Sing Before Breakfast" was the conception of music supervisor and arranger Roger Edens, who was developing a technique that would have songs emerge directly from the dialogue. Performed first as a trio, it branches into a solo dance for Eleanor, giving movie audiences their first glimpse of her athletic and personable style, fluid high kicks, and signature tap spins.

The magically staged fantasy number, "You Are My Lucky Star," finds Eleanor daydreaming in an empty theater. In her reverie, she imagines she is onstage, dancing on toe in a shimmering costume with the Albertina Rasch dancers. Though ballet was not Eleanor's forte, the ethereal beauty of the set infused the number with an enchanting quality that offset any imperfections. Filming under extreme conditions, Eleanor and the Rasch dancers worked hard to sustain the delicate illusion. As they danced for extended hours on pointe under the heat of the strong arc lights used in the 1930s, their feet, already swollen, blistered. After each take, the dancers would immediately rush to submerge their throbbing feet in buckets of ice water. Eleanor did not follow suit; her feet were so swollen that she feared she would never be able to put her shoes back on. By the end of the three long days required to film the ballet number, her feet were raw and bloody; she lost both big toenails. She was forced to don bedroom slippers and gingerly walk on her heels to the standby car.

When she filmed her numbers, Eleanor habitually avoided sitting between takes to keep from getting baggy stockings. The studio provided tall "leaning boards" for stars to rest against without disturbing their costumes. Eleanor rarely took advantage of them because she didn't want to lose momentum. Instead, she kept on dancing to the on-set orchestra as they jammed during breaks, riding the wave of her nervous energy until the next take.

Eleanor's singing voice in the film was dubbed by Marjorie Lane. "You Are My Lucky Star" became one of the most popular songs of the year. It was first recorded by Archie Bleyer and His Orchestra in June 1935, and Louis Armstrong gave the song his own special spin when he recorded it on October 3, 1935, just days before Eleanor recorded her version.

In her disguise, Mademoiselle Arlette is introduced, dancing to a swing piano version of "You Are My Lucky Star," which is played by Roger Edens in a rare cameo appearance. She follows with a flawlessly executed tacet (without music) solo in which the flamboyant Arlette shows off her intricate tap rhythms. With the exception of Bill Robinson, artists rarely featured long tacet sections in film. Like a solo by a virtuoso drummer, it required complete percussive precision, and Eleanor's display is a masterpiece. Her crisp tap arpeggios, performed effortlessly, continue to stump tap dancers today.

As Mademoiselle Arlette, Eleanor challenged the consensus that she had little sex appeal. "Everyone else at the studio thought she lacked femininity," Edens later remarked. "Still, she had a certain unusual quality that was very fresh and appealing, and she certainly could dance."[6]

Eleanor's numbers had been carefully paced through the film to progressively reveal her talents. By the time we reach the finale, "Eleanor Powell" as the studio's spectacular musical star is now fully unveiled to the public just as Irene is to Bob Gordon in the story. Here the Queen of Taps is shown in all her splendor. Edens' musical arrangement played a pivotal part in the buildup of her presentation. Popular radio singer Frances Langford introduces the number in her film debut. "I had the song "Broadway Rhythm" split up into five parts. . . . Powell came on in a slam-dunk finale. Everything built up to her. . . . Audiences went wild over it."[7] Dressed in sequined top hat and tails and backed by a line of similarly attired male chorus dancers, Eleanor dazzles in "Broadway Rhythm." Her syncopated rhythms, rapid traveling turns, graceful backbends, and tap pirouettes converge with the dynamic Freed and Brown score to establish her as MGM's ticket to musical dominance in the industry. Director Roy Del Ruth's firm stance on keeping her in the film was fully justified.

As she developed the choreography for this number, Eleanor had her first battle with the studio over her vision and requirements. She submitted her idea for the finale stage layout to art director Merrill Pye, who was in charge of musical presentation and designed the sets for all her dance numbers. A veteran with over a decade of design experience, Pye had been hired in 1926 at age twenty-four as part of the talented group overseen by Cedric Gibbons. As department head, Gibbons had the final say on productions handled by his team, but the skill of the MGM art directors was renowned in the industry.

When the time came to film "Broadway Rhythm," Eleanor discovered the set was ten feet shorter than she had expected, which required a dramatic adjustment in her choreography. It led to the first of many arguments with Pye. He had initially incorporated her specific requests into his design, but had been forced to make changes to meet the studio's budget. Pye and Eleanor both were frustrated with obstacles to their creativity, and neither was pleased with the situation.

In addition to dancing, Eleanor showed off her talent for mimicry in her spot-on impression of Katharine Hepburn from the film *Morning Glory*. Eleanor recalled the difficulty in shooting the scene. It took place just after the usually even-tempered director Roy Del Ruth had stormed off the set following an argument with a cameraman. Thirty minutes later, he returned and shooting resumed, but everyone was still on edge and uneasy, including Eleanor. After several unsuccessful takes, Eleanor told Del Ruth, "I just can't go on until you two make up." The gruff director and the cameraman begrudgingly complied. The tension instantly dissipated, and Eleanor completed the scene.

MGM's gamble with an unknown paid off. A favorite of critics and audiences alike, *Broadway Melody of 1936* was one of the highest grossing movies of the year. Edens felt it was the most successful musical since the birth of talkies. Dave Gould won an Oscar for Best Dance Direction for the production number "I've Got a Feelin' You're Foolin,'" winning out over "The Piccolino" from *Top Hat* and "Lullaby of Broadway" from *Gold Diggers of 1935,* among other nominees. The film was also nominated for Outstanding Production and Writing, Original Story. Most importantly, *Broadway Melody of 1936* made Eleanor Powell a star.

Critics dubbed her Astaire's female counterpart and were already hinting for them to be paired in a movie together. "A rangy and likeable girl with the most eloquent feet in show business. If she is not quite the distaff Fred Astaire, she is certainly the foremost candidate for that throne," declared Andre Sennwald of the *New York Times.* "Miss Powell's dazzling pedal arpeggios convert the sober art of tap-dancing into a giddy delight."[8] Her acting was found refreshing and true. "Miss Powell . . . plays with an engaging candor and straightforward charm that makes her an attractive screen personality."[9]

During her early days at MGM, Eleanor still felt like a starstruck fan when she encountered her idols on the lot. One of these was Joan Crawford; at work on her latest picture, *I Live My Life,* she passed Eleanor in the studio commissary one day. Eleanor jumped up from her table and grabbed her arm, saying, "Miss Crawford, I just have to tell you how much I admire your work."[10] Joan thanked her for her kind words, but as she walked away, Eleanor could see that Crawford hadn't recognized her. A few days later, the actress appeared on the set while Eleanor was filming a number. She called Eleanor over during a break and begged her forgiveness. She explained that she had seen the rushes of Eleanor's dances and was greatly looking forward to meeting her but hadn't realized who she was when she saw her in the commissary. Eleanor recognized Crawford's sincerity. Crawford, a dancer herself in her early films at MGM, was in awe of Eleanor's talent and became a frequent visitor to the set. Sometimes she would lie on her stomach to watch Eleanor dance, much as Eleanor had studied John Bubbles' steps.

As part of the process of induction into Hollywood life, Mayer invited Eleanor to one of the film industry's biggest affairs, the annual Mayfair Club dance. It was to be held at the Beverly Wilshire Hotel on May 4, 1935, and would be hosted by Fredric March. MGM's biggest stars would be present, and Mayer was eager to show off the newest member of the "family." Reluctant at first to accept Mayer's invitation, Eleanor finally agreed to accompany him. He took her to Adrian's and picked out a backless satin gown and ankle-length white fox cape. The evening of the event, Mayer sent her orchids and a young man from the studio to pick her up. Eleanor was surprised and felt some embarrassment and annoyance to find that this was the same man who had approached her frequently at the commissary and to whom she had regularly given the brush-off. At the event, MGM royalty awaited inside the glittering ballroom. Eleanor spotted stars like Norma Shearer, Jean Harlow, and Joan Crawford sipping cocktails. Soon she was seated at a table across from an odd man she didn't recognize. "He kept taking his paper hat, making little spitballs, dunking them in his glass of water and throwing them around the room so they landed on the women's bosoms," Eleanor remembered.[11] She found his childish behavior annoying. She later discovered the quirky man was millionaire Howard Hughes.

Just as Eleanor began to eat her dinner, Mayer approached her and said, "Miss Powell, aren't you going to ask me to dance?" Eleanor retorted, "Mr. Mayer, in my whole life I have never asked a gentleman to dance. And I don't intend to start now."[12] Mayer begrudgingly did his part, then proceeded to lecture her as they danced.

She found host Fredric March quite entertaining. The actor accidentally stepped on a woman's train and tore her dress off in back, almost to the hips. With exaggerated courtesy he bowed, handed the woman her train, and said, "Madame, permit me." The woman merely laughed it off, declaring that no one but Fredric March could amuse her in such a situation. March soon turned his attention to Eleanor. As they danced, his hand teasingly began straying lower and lower down her back. Stopping suddenly, he said, "Would you mind if I asked you a personal question? Are you wearing a girdle?" She shot him a stern look that quickly silenced him. "You want *just* to dance?" he asked, to which she replied, "Just dance." For years afterward, whenever they would meet, he would jokingly say, "Hi Ellie! Just dance! Just dance!"[13]

By 1:30 a.m. the party was waning, and Mayer and his guests moved on to the Clover Club, a well-known gambling spot on Sunset Boulevard. Ordering steak for everybody, Mayer mixed up his own spicy sauce and proceeded to spread it on each steak. Eleanor, who did not care for spicy seasonings, barely touched the steak and concentrated on her coffee instead. Mayer, suddenly very attentive, took something out of his pocket and dropped it into her cup. Convinced he was trying to drug her, she blurted, "What have you put in my coffee?" Mayer glibly explained that it was only saccharin, a sugar substitute he gave all his stars to keep them from gaining weight. She quickly reminded him that they had been regularly feeding her milkshakes on the set to help her keep her weight up.

Mayer finally prepared to escort Eleanor home. Despite his previous admonishments, she rebuffed him again. "No, Mr. Mayer, I'm very sorry, but where I come from . . . it's the fella that picks me up that brings me home."[14] Back in their rooms at the hotel, Blanche fixed scrambled eggs for her famished daughter. Eleanor, struggling to reconcile the marked contrast between her New England norms and casual Hollywood standards, wasn't ready to venture into the Hollywood party life again anytime soon.

On set, however, Eleanor was completely at ease. Her gregarious and fun-loving personality charmed those she worked with and lightened the mood, sometimes so excessively that it invited playful chiding. She laughed and joked in the makeup room, and every morning when she arrived on the set, she took the time to greet the gaffers, prop men, and electricians by name. As her time-consuming morning "love and kisses" routine continued, Roy Del Ruth would tap his watch and say, "OK, Ellie. Is it all right to get to work now?" Del Ruth, nicknamed Laughing Boy because of his habitual somber expression, had great fondness and respect for Eleanor since the day he had fought for her in Mayer's office. Eleanor was also fond of Del Ruth, and when she learned of his liking for molasses candy "kisses," as well as his enjoyment of practical jokes, she purchased several bags and hid out in wardrobe, where she sewed the candy into several long strings. When he left for the day, Del Ruth found his car elaborately draped with Eleanor's handiwork. The next morning when he took a seat in his director's chair and reached for his script, he found more kisses in the script pouch. "Now, just who has been playing these practical jokes on me?" Eleanor quickly glanced away innocently. "Don't look at me—I don't know anything about it!"[15]

As shooting progressed, the lighthearted fun and games began to sour. Originally scheduled to be completed by the end of May, shooting and production dragged on for nearly four months. Anxious to have Eleanor return to New York to begin rehearsals, the Shubert office was in constant contact with Hyde, Katz, and Del Ruth, pressing them for an expedited wrap date.

During a long phone conversation on July 8, Abe Lastfogel, treasurer of the William Morris Agency, pleaded with Katz and Del Ruth, explaining that Eleanor was needed in New York immediately. Katz and Del Ruth blamed the stalled production primarily on Eleanor's inexperience. "There have been further delays shooting due [to the] necessity [of] numerous takes to get [the] best possible results with Eleanor."[16] They were shooting seven days a week but predicted Eleanor would not be released until at least August 1.

By the time the finale number was being shot, Eleanor's foot condition had worsened. She sought relief from a local podiatrist, who took one look and declared the infection to be the worst he had seen in his seventeen years of practice. He prescribed a solution for bathing her feet at night, but because she still danced constantly the condition had little chance to improve. When the Shuberts continued to insist on Eleanor's immediate return, Blanche, in concern, penned a letter to Hyde that detailed Eleanor's extreme schedule of fifteen-hour days, seven days a week. She had not had a day off since May 30 until she collapsed on July 3, which finally forced MGM to release her for a few days. Hyde wrote Kaufman on July 8 to advise him that, considering an already exhausted Eleanor would be jumping straight into another demanding production, "it may be best for your interests to consider another artist for Eleanor's part." Hyde recommended that Eleanor be considered for a later show, adding, "I can offer no solution to this very disturbing situation and sincerely regret that you must suffer in this most unexpected disturbance to your plans."[17]

By late July, the situation was still at an impasse. Production on the film continued at a feverish pace, and the Shuberts ignored Hyde's recommendation and continued to demand Eleanor's presence. "Lee Shubert . . . began to chafe at the bit," the *Los Angeles Times* reported. "He swore, he sent wires, he threatened to sue. In a race against time, MGM went into high gear."[18] MGM made an attempt to pay off the Shuberts for Eleanor's services, but the brothers refused the studio's offer of $25,000.

Additional retakes were scheduled for early August. New personnel were brought in as Del Ruth had already started work on *Thanks a Million* at 20th Century-Fox. Screenwriter Joseph Mankiewicz, who was being groomed as a producer to lead a musical unit for MGM under Sam Katz, oversaw retakes on August 1 and 2.[19] The remaining retakes were shot under W. S. "Woody" Van Dyke. Eleanor and the rest of the cast were worn ragged with the extended push to meet deadlines on a production that was already drastically late in completion. For six straight weeks, she had no more than five hours of sleep a night. Eleanor got up at 5:30 a.m., dashed to the studio to be made up for the 7:00 a.m. call time, and then worked twelve to fourteen hours. Exhaustion and the ongoing pain of her injured feet made it a daily struggle to present her smiling, on-screen persona.

Ever conscious of the deep confidence placed in her and how much was riding on her successful performance, she continued to summon her strength from within. MGM utilized her remaining time in Hollywood to the very last minute. On the night before her return to New York, a final interview was scheduled, sandwiched in between two late-night portrait sessions. Eleanor showed the writer her bandaged feet, explaining, "I danced them off, trying to finish the picture so I could arrive in New York on schedule."[20] Thanks to her heroic efforts, no discomfort is apparent in the film.

The film completed, the studio held its breath as it tested the finished 110-minute product on sneak preview audiences in Southern California. Mayer was greatly pleased by the positive response to the film. Yet another preview, preceded by a special live radio broadcast with Jack Benny from the courtyard of Grauman's Chinese Theatre in Hollywood, was held on August 24, but without Eleanor (as a savvy marketing decision, this promotion was timed for the same week that Fred Astaire's newest film, *Top Hat,* opened). The final release version, after further trims, came to 102 minutes.

On August 15, after repeated delays to her release from the film, Eleanor left Los Angeles for New York by train. But four days of restful travel were not forthcoming. The Shuberts had arranged for a special private club car to be added to her train so that she could learn and rehearse the show's songs while en route.

8

Full Velocity

By the time Eleanor arrived in New York, the Shubert production, now titled *At Home Abroad: A Musical Holiday,* was already a week into rehearsals. Exhausted from intense months of shooting, tired from the cross-country trip, and still dealing with her aching feet, Eleanor asked for a day before coming to rehearsal. The Shubert brothers, especially Lee, who was solely handling this show, were not pleased that motion pictures had once again encroached on their territory. At that time, Broadway was feuding with motion picture studios, and any performers caught colluding with the enemy risked repercussions. Her request was refused, and she had just one hour to rush to the theater. The company was so large that rehearsals had to be split among three different theaters, the Masque, Majestic, and Shubert, to accommodate everyone. Eleanor arrived at her assigned location and was plunged into the first day's session, which lasted a grueling fourteen hours. With only two weeks to go before the show opened in previews, Eleanor settled in for a marathon of work.

MGM had been plagued with struggles throughout *Broadway Melody of 1936,* and *At Home Abroad* was also beset with challenges. J.J. Shubert expressed his dissatisfaction with the weakness of the book in a harsh note to the brothers' friend and attorney, William Klein, on August 2: "My dear Billy, I wish you would ask for a manuscript . . . of *At Home Abroad* and read it yourself. I read it and believe me when I tell you, there wasn't one outstanding thing in the play. . . . If you asked me to invest a five-cent piece in the proposition, I would absolutely refuse to do so. . . . My only hope is that it succeeds and gets over.—J.J. Shubert"

J.J. admitted he had not heard the music and conceded that the cast was "as good a cast as you can get," but he was not at all convinced of the show's potential for success. Thankfully, only Lee Shubert, or "Mr. Lee" as he was called by friends, was responsible for dealing directly with those working on

At Home Abroad. Soon, the book was fleshed out with additional sketches by Marc Connelly and Dion Titheradge.

The show opens to reveal a wealthy man in the throes of a vivid nightmare, acted out on stage by marionettes designed by Sue Hastings. The unique caricature puppets, which represented well-known celebrities of the day such as Shirley Temple, Eleanor Roosevelt, Huey Long, Greta Garbo, and Sally Rand, menace the man in the dream. When he wakes, the man decides to escape the United States and travel overseas. Each leg of his international trip prompts a new number in the revue; these are interspersed with projections of humorous "postcards" from the man and his wife along the way.

Comedienne Beatrice "Bea" Lillie, at the time one of Broadway's most popular actresses, headlined the show. With twenty years of performing behind her and a loyal following, Lillie commanded high respect. Songstress Ethel Waters, the first Black woman to integrate Broadway theater and the highest paid recording artist in the early 1920s, co-starred, also with top billing. Both names were above the title, but "Lillie" appeared above "Waters" in print and was slightly larger on the marquee. Next in billing, under the title, came comic Herb Williams and Eleanor. Reginald Gardiner, who had been working in André Charlot's revue in England, was brought over to make his American debut as a comic foil for Bea Lillie. Dancer Paul Haakon, who had as a teen performed in vaudeville with Eleanor in Atlantic City, Vera Allen, Eddie Foy Jr., and the singing group The Six Spirits of Rhythm filled the remainder of the bill. Actor John Payne, part of Roy Campbell's Continentals, served as understudy to Reginald Gardiner.

With a score by Arthur Schwartz and Howard Dietz, the show marked Vincente Minnelli's first directing job. Minnelli was also in charge of costumes and sets, the first time a director had handled all three jobs for a Broadway production. Fresh from the staff of the Radio City Music Hall, where he had designed sets and costumes, Minnelli had been hired by the Shubert brothers to produce three of their upcoming shows to raise the quality of their productions. "One person should do everything in musicals," he said, "then original ideas become untampered."[1] Ambitious and full of imagination, at just twenty-eight, Minnelli had already developed an innovative style recognized for its adventurous designs and lush colors. The international locales in the show proved to be a perfect match for his talents. Bea Lillie's numbers took her to the cosmopolitan settings of Paris, Tokyo, and Russia, while Ethel Waters traveled to exotic Africa and the West Indies. Britain and the Balkans were represented by Eleanor.

The tongue-in-cheek "That's Not Cricket" featured Eleanor, dressed in a dapper Eton boy uniform, with tie, vest, and trousers, with the twenty-four-girl chorus all in matching costumes, singing saucy lyrics in a proper British accent. In "Farewell My Lovely," the stage became giant binocular lenses, through which Eleanor was seen performing as an island dancing girl. "What a Wonderful World" and "The Number One Boy" partnered Eleanor and Eddie Foy Jr. "Got a Bran' New Suit" featured Eleanor and Ethel Waters in a dressing room scene, in which Waters played Eleanor's maid. This obligatory subservient role for a Black performer appearing alongside a white artist of the day was especially ironic considering the difference in their marquee stature. After Waters sang to Eleanor of her new beau, Eleanor replied with a song and dance. In "The Lady with the Tap," the Balkan number, Minnelli combined Eleanor's talents with an ambitious set; she played a spy who taps out a secret code.

The hundred-person show was set to preview in Boston on September 2 and then travel to the Forrest Theatre in Philadelphia, but the latter leg of the tryouts was ultimately canceled. Moving the bulky scenery and costumes to Boston along with crew and baggage proved to be a monumental feat that required eight train cars in total. The scenery was already on the way to Boston's Shubert Theatre when the company left New York on Friday, August 30; dress rehearsals were scheduled to begin immediately that night. The show had thirty scenes, and, by opening night, Minnelli and Howard Dietz were at odds about what trims to make. Each had been under the mistaken impression that he had total autonomy over decisions; however, on closer analysis, they discovered the sly Shuberts had given each of them exactly the same contract provisions. Dietz and Schwartz' 1932 song "Triplets," which later resurfaced in the 1953 film *The Bandwagon,* was one of Lillie's numbers that both agreed should be taken out before the Broadway opening. Also cut were "What a Wonderful World" and "The Number One Boy." A crucial topic of discussion was whether another of Eleanor's numbers, "The Lady with the Tap," would stay or be cut. An original idea conceived by Minnelli and the show's choreographer Gene Snyder, it was one of Minnelli's favorites, but Dietz was not fully convinced it was necessary. After a long debate, the number was kept but moved from the first act to the second. It would prove to be one of the most popular with the critics. *Variety* described it as a true "production and plenty" number, adding that the "two-story set and the girls backgrounding as soldiers give her a reason for a spy impersonation, and her dancing interprets the action." The critics praised the number as an "ideal blending of production and talent and one of the best things in the revue."[2]

As Minnelli and Dietz were busy pruning the show, Eleanor continued to rehearse her own routines, spending sometimes up to eighteen hours at the theater refining her steps. During preparations for the preview, a reporter from the *Boston Globe* found Eleanor in a coaching session with Eddie Foy Jr. The vaudeville veteran of the Seven Little Foys would go on to leave the show in December, but in the meantime he happily traded dance advice with Eleanor. After her session with Foy, she worked with the orchestra's drummer, marking the spot in her dance where he should add the percussive rolls for an accent. Entranced with Eleanor's energy, the reporter observed, "Her fingers are snapping, her eyes are aglow and her high, clear soprano voice rings out excitedly, 'That's it. Right there. Roll it.'"[3]

After the advance preview, reports spread about Eleanor's showstopping performance in *Broadway Melody of 1936*. The press approached her with inquiries about her Hollywood experience, much to the chagrin of the Broadway set. Eleanor elaborated to reporters about the lush treatment she had received from the studio, but she kept quiet at the theater, choosing instead to call her grandmother in Crestwood when she wanted to share updates about news from Mayer. And, just to keep MGM high on her list of priorities, the studio head regularly telephoned. That week he sent his congratulations on the preview, telling Eleanor, "You must be the happiest girl in the world."[4]

As Eleanor rehearsed, Minnelli dealt with more challenges. Due to scenery malfunctions and difficulties with the massive installation process, the opening had to be postponed for one day, and *At Home Abroad* made its Boston premiere on Tuesday, September 3.

Critics praised the ingenuity and style of the sets. They called Minnelli's work one "of outstanding beauty and novelty" and observed that he had "really brought something new to the staging of musical revues." Particularly notable, in the first act finale, the entire company climbs a mountain and disappears into the clouds. It was found to be stunningly effective.[5]

Critics agreed that the two leads masterfully dominated the show; however, it was Eleanor who truly astounded the audience. "Eleanor Powell . . . scored something that might conservatively be termed a sensational success," wrote the *Boston Globe*. The critic predicted that the show would be "one of the most memorable of the year."[6]

While Eleanor was still buoyant from the critics' praises, a knock on her dressing room door on the night of September 11 provided the most emotionally catastrophic event of her life to date. On the other side of the door was a man she had thought dead for her entire existence—her father,

Clarence "Sonny" Powell. Seeing that Eleanor was on the bill, he had come up to Boston from Springfield with his wife and contacted Blanche to ask if a meeting could be arranged. He was interested in finally meeting the daughter who had worked her way up to stardom and was unaware that she had never been told he was alive. It is not known if he had made any previous attempts to meet Eleanor, such as when she had appeared in Springfield at the Court Square Theatre in *Fine and Dandy* four years earlier, but it had been twenty-two years since Blanche had laid eyes on Sonny. In those two decades she had matured greatly from the naive teen she had once been. Now her daughter's savvy mother, manager, and loving friend, nothing meant more to her than Eleanor's well-being, and she didn't want to jeopardize that or cause her unnecessary hurt. Whether Sonny's pleading convinced her, or she just wanted to be rid of the secret, she decided to reveal the truth to her daughter. As arranged, he came backstage that night.

Eleanor rarely spoke about the event, saying only that when she opened the door and met her father for the first time, no rush of emotions flooded her. There was no overwhelming urge to take his hand or give him a tight hug. Eleanor, known to shower friends, family, and even new acquaintances with an abundance of affection, felt only emptiness for this man. Blanche and Eleanor turned down his invitation for dinner. It was clear there was no open path to pursue any kind of relationship. The realization that her mother had kept this painful secret inside her heart all these years was momentous, but she knew it had all been out of love for her.

The company returned to New York a few days later. Eleanor was at the pinnacle of her success; her film and her new show were scheduled to open across the street from each other on the same night. This dual premiere was fashioned to be Broadway's tribute to Eleanor Powell, but it precluded family and friends, not to mention the elite of the New York social scene, from attending both events. This, added to the concerns of local police about overwhelming traffic congestion, caused the plans to be reassessed, and the film premiere was moved one day forward.

On September 18, *Broadway Melody of 1936* opened at the Capitol Theatre with much accompanying fanfare, including a nationwide radio broadcast that featured the members of the cast. Eleanor, sitting in her dressing room at the Winter Garden Theatre, was thrilled to see her name in lights, twelve feet high, on the marquee across the way. Noticing the excitement surrounding the premiere, Lee Shubert laconically inquired about the commotion. When reminded that Eleanor, one of his own principals, was starring in the film, he feigned mild surprise. Still in rehearsals with the final adjustments for *At Home Abroad,* Eleanor was forced to divide her time, rushing from one theater to the next in order to fulfill both commitments.

◉   ◉   ◉

Broadway's elite gathered for the premiere of *At Home Abroad*. Intrigued by impressive advance reviews of Minnelli's audacious undertaking and anxious to cheer on their beloved Kid of the Street, stars poured into the theater. Among the producers, composers, and performers out front were Jimmy Durante, Sophie Tucker, Bert Lahr, George Burns and Gracie Allen, Ira Gershwin, Max Gordon, Lorenz Hart, Billy Rose, and of course, Howard Dietz, Arthur Schwartz, and Lee Shubert. Even with the Boston reviews virtually guaranteeing a hit, Minnelli was feeling the pressure. Weighed down by his responsibilities as director, set, and costume designer, he was now also contending with technical challenges. The stage at the Winter Garden was not as deep as the one at the Shubert Theatre in Boston; this caused some miscalculations that, in Minnelli's eyes, were magnified ten times over. He worried about missed lighting cues and feared the mistakes would be sorely evident to the audience.

Despite his concerns, critics heaped praise on the production. "Nothing quite so exhilarating as this has borne the Shubert seal before," said the *New York Times*.[7] Another wrote, "Eleanor Powell returns from her recent Hollywood endeavors to win new acclaim as the foremost feminine tap dancer in the land. . . . Miss Powell's descriptive number, 'The Lady with the Tap' is quite the most original thing of its kind that New York has seen."[8]

Good reviews did nothing to appease the Shuberts' animus toward MGM, and they remained embroiled in the contract dispute concerning their star. Eleanor, caught in the middle, thought it was Lee Shubert's personal choice not to adjust her billing status in order to capitalize on the film's obvious success. In reality, his hands were tied due to very specific billing requirements in the contracts of Bea Lillie and Ethel Waters. No matter what opinion the Shuberts had about Eleanor, her popularity was increasing with her movie-going fans; ever-larger crowds waited at the stage door after the show to "gape and thrill as the adored Eleanor swe[pt] out to her taxi."[9]

Opening night of *At Home Abroad* was memorable for another reason, completely unrelated to the show or her new film—Eleanor received a proposal of marriage from bandleader Abe Lyman. She had worked with Lyman in vaudeville before she went to Hollywood for the *Scandals* film, and rumors of romance had once swirled around the two. Now, whether due to her glamorous Hollywood makeover or her increasing fame, his interest in Eleanor was suddenly rekindled. She had little interest in pursuing a relationship, but, undaunted, Lyman sent a little box to her dressing room. After the show, she opened it and was shocked to find an engagement ring (which later she discovered was worth $5,000) accompanied by a note: "Congratulations, honey! We're engaged!" But Lyman himself was nowhere to be found and he did not reappear for nearly two weeks. Later, he put her on the spot when he publicly announced their engagement during an evening at the Hollywood Restaurant in New York. She was quick to set the record straight.

Eleanor soon became a sought-after commodity in a new field for her— radio. On October 5, she made a guest appearance on the *Shell Chateau* radio show alongside Milton Berle, Louis Armstrong, and host Walter Winchell. She performed her Katharine Hepburn imitation from *Broadway Melody of 1936* and sang and tapped to "You Are My Lucky Star." Her pleasant singing voice was well suited to radio, and her taps were clear and sharp, which allowed her dancing to be conveyed surprisingly well over the airwaves. *Variety* praised her performance, noting "what appeared to be a mediocre Broadway artist night fill-in program was made distinctive by the singing and magnetic tap dancing of Eleanor Powell. . . . Previous to Miss Powell's appearance, the program was stumbling along pretty ineffectually."[10]

The following Friday, October 11, she headed over to the RCA studios on West Twenty-Fourth Street to cut her first record for RCA Victor with Tommy Dorsey and His Orchestra. But upon arrival in Studio 2 to record her singing and tapping to "You Are My Lucky Star," she was dismayed to find a fully carpeted room. After an unfruitful mad dash to obtain a portable tap mat from any of the local dance studios, Eleanor went to the offices on the floor below to see if she could come up with anything suitable. With no other option available, she finally pointed to an office door. The solid wood would make the ideal surface. The technicians soon had the door off the hinges and brought it to the studio. It worked perfectly for the first part of the dance; however, Eleanor had planned to end by gradually fading out the taps, simulating a stage exit. At the time, sound recording techniques lacked the sophistication to produce this effect. "We improvised, using a rope, and what you hear is . . . a prop man slowly pulling me with the rope further and further from the orchestra to make the sound fade in the distance."[11] With this solution, they were able to record three songs that same day: "I've Got a Feelin'

You're Foolin'" and "You Are My Lucky Star" from *Broadway Melody of 1936* (released as two sides of a record on October 30, 1935) and "Got a Bran' New Suit" from *At Home Abroad* (released November 13, 1935). The following week, now in Studio 3 and equipped with a proper tap mat, they recorded two more songs from *At Home Abroad*: "That's Not Cricket" (released on November 13, 1935, on the flip side of "Got a Bran' New Suit") and "What a Wonderful World" (not released commercially at the time, it appeared later on a compilation album from the Tommy Dorsey sessions).

While in *At Home Abroad,* Eleanor was also under obligation to MGM to make a number of personal appearances. A live performance was announced at Loew's State at a screening of *Broadway Melody of 1936* on October 16. In the meantime, MGM was banking on the momentum created by the film's success. Accustomed to churning out new projects quickly after a hit, they could hardly wait for Eleanor to return to Hollywood. The writers were hard at work. *Variety* announced MGM's plans to star her in *Honolulu* with Robert Taylor and Buddy Ebsen, as well as in an additional untitled film.

To add to her already full schedule, on October 25, Eleanor began a series of appearances on a weekly radio program sponsored by Socony-Vacuum (Mobil Oil Company, whose logo was a red Pegasus). *The Flying Red Horse Tavern* aired on Friday nights at 8:00 p.m. The thirty-minute program, set in an imaginary tavern, had begun only three weeks earlier but was quickly revamped, and the only regulars retained were the Freddie Rich Orchestra and The King's Men male chorus. Anticipating the longevity of *At Home Abroad* and capitalizing on Eleanor's popularity, her contract was for thirty-nine weeks. Both the Shuberts and MGM took advantage of this opportunity to plug their respective vehicles. The recording studio was specially outfitted for Eleanor, with a tap mat and a microphone for her feet installed about a foot off the floor. On her first appearance she sang "Got a Bran' New Suit" and "I've Got a Feelin' You're Foolin'" in addition to "Broadway Rhythm," sung with the rest of the cast. Because the show ended at 8:30 p.m., curtain time for *At Home Abroad,* Eleanor had no break between shows. "I took a police escort down Broadway, did some quick-change work at the Winter Garden and put my costume on for the first number at ten minutes of nine."[12]

In addition to her own weekly show, Eleanor made two more guest appearances on radio, the first on the *Kraft Music Hall* on October 31 with the Paul Whiteman Orchestra. Again she performed "I've Got a Feelin' You're Foolin'," which Paul Whiteman erroneously introduced as "I've Got a Foolin' You're Feelin'."[13] Eleanor appeared two days later on the *Magic Key of RCA,* an hour-long broadcast on NBC with an eclectic lineup of performers from the classical music world as well as from Broadway drama and musicals. Near the end of the hour, Eleanor and Tommy Dorsey and His Orchestra energized the audience with a lively tap version of "You Are My Lucky Star." Eleanor ended the number with an enthusiastic "yeah!" and a laugh, topping off the high-brow entertainment of the evening.

After a two-week break from *The Flying Red Horse Tavern* at the beginning of November, Eleanor rejoined the show on November 15 along with new host, actor Osgood Perkins. Eleanor danced to "Sing Before Breakfast" and performed her Katharine Hepburn imitation from *Broadway Melody of 1936.* Nine-year-old rhythm tapper and seasoned vaudeville performer Teddy Hale made the first of several appearances as George Washington Lincoln Brown on the show, joining Eleanor in the number, "Truckin'." Young Hale went on to make his own mark in tap dance history before his untimely death at age thirty-three. *Variety,* in its review of this show, compared Eleanor once again to Fred Astaire, noting her "fair voice, pleasant personality, and fidgety feet."[14]

With performances at the Winter Garden, personal appearances, and rehearsals for her radio show, she and Blanche decided to take rooms at the nearby Park Central Hotel to save themselves the forty-minute commute from their home in Crestwood. Eleanor's busy schedule was beginning to take a toll on her health. At the end of November, she was forced to miss another two weeks on the radio show due to illness but she returned to her regular spot on December 6. She added to her repertoire with a representation of scenes from the play *Goodbye Again,* playing opposite Osgood Perkins. The announcement three days later that she would be performing scenes from *The Lake,* the play that had starred Katharine Hepburn, would indicate that her dramatic efforts were met with success. Eleanor thoroughly enjoyed the comfortable spontaneity she had with the studio audience during the live broadcasts. She felt as if she were "in the front room talking with the family,"[15] and her performances were relaxed and genuine.

The following week's show featured a Friday the thirteenth theme. Eleanor did a novel impression of Mae West, not just verbal but also portrayed in tap. In this episode, the role of George Washington Lincoln Brown was played by an uncredited young Harold Nicholas of the Nicholas Brothers, substituting for regular Teddy Hale.

December 14 marked the hundredth performance of *At Home Abroad.* A solid hit, the show had grossed $500,000 to date. MGM continued to announce new vehicles for Eleanor, until even they finally realized there were too many projects floating around. *Hats in the Air,* among those mentioned, was then shelved in favor of a new *Broadway Melody.*

Christmas and the New Year provided special occasions for celebration on *The Flying Red Horse Tavern.* For the remainder of her time on the show, Eleanor continued to sing and dance, perform scenes from plays, and promote her film and *At Home Abroad.*

On January 5, 1936, the cast of *At Home Abroad* performed a thirty-minute radio version of the show, with the show's lyricist Howard Dietz serving as master of ceremonies. The show had to be carefully orchestrated to accommodate the regular Sunday evening performance at the Winter Garden. Eleanor and Ethel Waters performed "Got a Bran' New Suit." Delayed by her performance onstage, Eleanor had only just arrived at the studio. When asked by the announcer what made her so late, she playfully responded, "I was truckin'!"[16]

Her January 18 performance was her last on *The Flying Red Horse Tavern.* In a Southern-themed show, she sang and danced to "Mandy" with The King's Men and performed with Osgood Perkins in a preview of the film *The Trail of the Lonesome Pine.*

At Home Abroad was scheduled to move to the Majestic Theater on Forty-Fourth Street on January 20, in order to allow *Ziegfeld Follies of 1936* to take over the Winter Garden. Because *The Follies* had special stage requirements that could only be fulfilled there, the condition had been written into the original agreement with the Shuberts. After the company finished their shows on January 19, everyone prepped to make the shift to the new venue.

⊙ ⊙ ⊙

At Home Abroad continued to thrive, but Eleanor did not. Since September, she had lost nearly sixteen pounds. A few months earlier, her physician, Dr. Ernesto Lopez, had warned her to slow down and take better care of herself. Instead she had done the opposite: the grueling schedule of her film work had been immediately followed by *At Home Abroad,* ongoing personal appearances, and radio work.

Eleanor's feet were in serious condition, suffering from abscesses and several lost toenails. They had become so swollen that she spent most of her time in house slippers and only put on regular shoes to perform. Every night as her daughter slept, Blanche would diligently apply a special treatment to her feet.

Eleanor was at the highest point of her career, but Blanche greatly feared her daughter was headed in a dangerous direction. On January 22, Eleanor was to report early to the theater for the matinee, but she could barely summon enough strength to get out of bed. As she feebly attempted to get dressed, she fainted. There simply was not an ounce of strength left in her body. Blanche immediately called Dr. Lopez, who rushed into the city from Crestwood.

The news was sobering. The doctor found that Eleanor had a functional heart murmur (athletic heart) and a variety of other conditions that were contributing to her extreme fatigue and vertigo. In his medical report, he noted that she was "exceedingly nervous and excitable" and that she had severe anemia and a high level of stress. "The signs of nervous collapse are obvious."[17] Fortunately, it wasn't a permanent condition. He gave her a sedative to help her sleep that night and recommended an indefinite period of complete rest. On Dr. Lopez' orders, Eleanor was taken to the Westchester Medical Center, a private sanitorium in Yonkers, near her home in Crestwood. Eleanor's understudy, Marjorie Gayle, was prepped to fill in.

The Shuberts, however, were not ready to relinquish one of their stars. The ongoing contract dispute made them suspicious of their usually energetic workhorse who had never before missed a single performance. Eleanor was important to the show and losing her would prove a definite blow at the box office. They sent over their personal physician for a second opinion. On January 23, Dr. Louis Morton told the press that "while Miss Powell is suffering from fatigue, she would 'probably' return to the show on Monday."[18] In a clear effort to discount Dr. Lopez' diagnosis of extreme exhaustion, Morton's letter to the Shuberts downplayed her condition. "Her heart sounds are clear and regular. No evidence of any murmurs present."[19] He added that her tired state was "aggravated by the onset of her menstrual period," and concluded that "several days rest and proper diet" should restore her to health. Fortunately, blaming Eleanor's condition on a strong case of PMS was discounted as a viable diagnosis, and Blanche vehemently vetoed the Shuberts' attempt to force her daughter to return to work without the thorough rest she obviously needed.

The Shuberts were in talks with Ruby Keeler to replace Eleanor, but Mitzi Mayfair ultimately landed the part. No sooner had Eleanor settled into the sanitorium than the press latched onto the story, relentlessly in search of a sensational reason for her absence.

"Backstage intrigue, brewed in a teapot of prima donna jealousies, stilled the twinkling toes of Eleanor Powell last night," wrote reporter Edna Ferguson in the New York *Daily News*.[20] Ferguson went on to imply that Eleanor's newfound movie success, as well as her prominence in the *At Home Abroad* reviews, had made cast members Bea Lillie and Ethel Waters jealous. Lillie and Waters had reportedly intimidated and belittled Eleanor, and Waters had tried to upstage her in their number together. "Eleanor got the cold shoulder backstage and in the wings," she wrote. "The nerves can't take it."[21]

The inflammatory and dramatic story was simply not true. Blanche flatly denied the gossip, referring to a kind telegram Eleanor had just received from Bea Lillie. Not one to give in to gossip or backbiting, Eleanor never admitted to any type of jealousy or bullying from either star. Even so, the story caused serious repercussions for Ethel Waters. "As a result of . . . this article, I have been deluged with vile letters threatening to hiss me in the theater and promising me physical violence," Waters wrote to the *Daily News*.[22] When word reached Eleanor, she quickly made an effort to squelch the gossip; she asserted that the reports of backstage troubles were untrue and that it made her feel sicker to hear them. Her telegram to Waters was published for the public to see: "My dear Ethel: No statement nor article such as the malicious one appearing in today's *Daily News* could possibly express a greater untruth or misstatement of facts. Your friendship, cooperation, and help is something I have always appreciated, and I will be happy to get back to work as quickly as the doctors will permit, which I hope will be in a few days. Sincerely, Eleanor Powell."[23]

Eleanor was not to return to *At Home Abroad*. After weeks went by with little improvement in her health, the Shuberts finally released her from her obligations by transferring her contract to the William Morris Agency for $25,000. MGM reimbursed the agency, happy that their star was finally at liberty.

Though she was still recuperating under the doctor's care, MGM churned out notices to the press about her impending return to work, stating she was due to report to the studio by mid-March. Her next project was to be *Yours and Mine* with Buddy Ebsen, a film originally meant for British dancer Jessie Matthews and again penned by Jack McGowan and Sid Silvers.

Eleanor was eventually able to return home to Crestwood, where she enjoyed rare time with her family. About this time, the press began to mention a new member of the Powell/Torrey household—a twelve-year-old girl named Betty Meyer. Although more of an age to be a younger sister to Eleanor, Betty, newly dubbed "Eleanor's adopted daughter," was a somewhat mysterious figure. In a 1935 article, Blanche told reporter Harmony Haynes that Betty had been brought into the household as a baby when Eleanor was ten years old. The child had been abandoned by her mother and, because her father was unable to take care of her, Harold and Susie had taken her in. She stayed on when the Torreys moved to Crestwood with Eleanor and Blanche, and later traveled west with the family when they all moved to Beverly Hills. After Betty reportedly exhibited an interest in design, Eleanor expressed plans to send her off to Paris to study in a few years. No photos of Betty were ever shown and, after 1936, she disappeared from all articles. No explanation of her later absence in the household was ever given. The vague and contradictory statements about Betty have never been clarified. Her true identity and what became of her remain a mystery.

In those restful months in Crestwood, for the first time in years, Eleanor had time to nurture domestic pastimes like gardening, needlework, and cooking. She enjoyed being with her grandparents, learned to drive, and got her driver's license. She developed an interest in ornithology and was often seen by locals birdwatching in the early morning hours on the banks of the Bronx River. Neighbors on her block remembered the resonating sound of her taps as she practiced. Finally, the havoc that exhaustion had played on her system started to subside, and her energy returned.

9

Born to Dance

Focused on her recovery, Eleanor was unaware that her next movie was undergoing development drama. It had begun in the weeks prior to her breakdown. In July 1935, MGM had signed Cole Porter to write the score of an as yet to be decided musical picture. Fresh from his highly successful show, *Anything Goes,* Porter was living comfortably off the royalties but was nevertheless eager to make his first extended trip to Hollywood.

On December 20, 1935, Porter met with producer Sam Katz to set in motion the project that would eventually become *Born to Dance*. Porter's diary recounts that Katz, who "could not have been more charming," had promised that "unlike other productions . . . my picture would not be the result of havoc." Cole Porter's first encounter with Katz and writers Jack McGowan and Sid Silvers did little to reassure him. The meeting produced only a vague idea for a musical envisioned for Clark Gable and Jean Harlow, whom Katz felt would be great box office draws. By January 6, that idea had already been scrapped: "It was dangerous to have two principal leads who could not sing, play in a musical."[1]

A bemused Porter sat through another unfruitful meeting where they presented a myriad of equally unacceptable ideas. The conference concluded with McGowan's suggestion that Porter write an opening song to be used as inspiration and that he and Silvers "try to think of a story within a reasonable time."

Though Porter had heard many Hollywood tales from colleagues, the slow progress and lackadaisical approach to these meetings still surprised him. Katz and Porter continued to meet over the month of January, but it wasn't until countless unusable ideas had been knocked around and discarded that Porter finally suggested to Katz "a Cinderella story . . . with Eleanor Powell." Delighted with the idea, Katz sent the writers off to flesh out a storyline tailored to her specific talents. Silvers and McGowan suggested an old concept they had previously worked on with Buddy DeSylva that involved two sailors and the hostess of a lonely hearts club. If DeSylva would sell his share of rights to the story, it could work.

As Eleanor continued to recover, the conferences carried on in full swing. In early March, she suffered a relapse. She had lost another two pounds and, in her weakened condition, had barely managed to fight off pneumonia. MGM was forced to update her new contract starting date to April 1, and then later to sometime in May because of her slow progress.

Eleanor's return journey to Hollywood conveniently coincided with the maiden voyage of the luxurious Super Chief. This new 3,600-horsepower locomotive of the Santa Fe Line was eloquently lauded as "the six-car conqueror of time and distance." Eleanor departed from New York and transferred to the Super Chief in Chicago. She and Ida Cantor (wife of Eddie) were part of the celebrity passenger group promoting the first trip, which left on May 12. Across the country, crowds packed the stations in anticipation of the train's arrival, many hoping to get a glimpse of Eleanor. Reporters dubbed her "the queen of the inaugural run." In tiny Streator, Illinois, just eighty miles west of Chicago, where the train made a brief inspection stop, more than a thousand people packed the platform and "managed to get a glimpse of Eleanor Powell, famous tap dancer."[2] In Albuquerque on May 13, the press reported that "a large crowd gathered around the coach where Eleanor Powell, famous tap dancer of stage and screen, sat at a window. Miss Powell acknowledged friendly shouts and handclappings with smiles and pressed a bouquet of flowers against her face."[3] When she and Blanche stepped off the train at Union Station in Los Angeles, a beaming Eleanor was photographed and ceremoniously greeted with two dozen roses. In response to reporters' questions, Eleanor declared, "First I want to go home and put on some slacks and try out a dance I originated on the train. Next, I'd like to spend a few days at the beach getting tan, and then I'll be all ready to start rehearsing for the new picture."[4]

Contrary to her desire for a little respite, she reported to the studio on May 14, 1936. In actuality, her MGM duties had begun the moment she stepped on the train in Chicago. As she warmly greeted the familiar crew and production personnel who had worked long days and nights with her on *Broadway Melody of 1936,* it was like returning home to a very large, if slightly dysfunctional, family.

Concerned about Eleanor's health, Blanche had vowed to put a stop to the harsh working conditions she had endured during the previous film, which had set the dangerous downward spiral in motion. "She isn't going to wolf her lunch and dance all night in rehearsals," Blanche promised a New York reporter the week before they left for Hollywood.[5] To prevent blisters caused by ill-fitting shoes, Blanche began to break in Eleanor's dance shoes before she passed them along to her so that they would be more comfortable to wear. Blanche said she couldn't even watch the film without noticing her daughter's battered feet on screen.

Anxious to settle into a home of their own, Eleanor and Blanche rented a Tudor-style house from Marion Davies at 727 North Bedford Drive in Beverly Hills. The peaceful neighborhood was about a twenty-minute commute from the studio. With five bedrooms and baths, in addition to servants' quarters, it was a welcome change from their hotel accommodations at the Beverly Wilshire.

The studio's publicity machine was already in motion, linking her romantically with singer Nelson Eddy, whose recent operetta films with Jeanette MacDonald were among MGM's biggest moneymakers. The two were friends, but both denied rumors of romance. Next, gossip swirled when she began keeping company with John Payne, who had been signed to a film contract by Samuel Goldwyn while appearing in *At Home Abroad*. Though the two had reconnected when Eleanor arrived back in Hollywood, they enjoyed only a friendship. Eleanor and Payne spent time swapping Hollywood stories and reminiscing over dinner about their Broadway days. She enjoyed keeping company with the handsome men who flocked around her in Hollywood, but Eleanor still guarded her heart. She had no intention of being distracted from her career.

At Mayer's direction, Eleanor started vocal lessons with Dr. Mario Marafioti. The Italian physician, a friend of the famed singer Enrico Caruso, was now a vocal coach for the studio. Mayer ordered, "Whenever Miss Powell has time, she is to take lessons for a full hour."[6] New MGM players also regularly met with drama coach Lillian Burns. Burns, married to director George Sidney, had a reputation for recognizing and nurturing acting talent; she often brought little-known contract players with untapped abilities to Mayer's attention. While Eleanor exhibited remarkable verve and personality when she danced, her performance in *Broadway Melody of 1936* displayed only passable acting skills. But her time on radio performing scenes and comedy sketches with Osgood Perkins had significantly improved her ability to deliver her lines with authority. Though she still projected a natural aura of naïveté, the added experience helped her to relax and have fun with her scenes, in the same way she had fun with her dancing.

Upon her return, Eleanor found she was no longer the only one tap dancing on the lot. Tap dance had made a splash on Broadway in the late 1920s, and, now, tap in sound films had propelled the dance's popularity across the country. "Hollywood is being swept by a dance craze," claimed one reporter.[7] Dance director Dave Gould now held regular tap classes for MGM's roster of contract players, whether or not they were booked for musicals. "Since Eleanor Powell came on the lot and made a hit, Gould's classes have multiplied," another article boasted. "Some tap for fun, some tap for work, and some just because everybody else is tapping."[8] Inspired by the success of Shirley Temple, Ruby Keeler, Fred Astaire, and Ginger Rogers and by Eleanor's overnight screen sensation, young tap students with pushy stage mothers were packing the dance studios. "La Powell, it seems, has been the answer to a dancing master's dream," another reporter wrote. "Ever since the magnetic Eleanor tapped her way to stage and screen stardom, the tap factories have been running day and night."[9]

With tap overtaking ballroom and ballet as a necessary tool for MGM players, Eleanor used her newfound clout to convince the studio to bring on Black dancer Willie Covan as a tap coach on the lot. Covan, who toured the vaudeville circuit for years with his family act, The Four Covans, was a master technician as well as choreographer. A fixture at MGM through the 1950s, he taught and staged dances for stars such as Mae West, Shirley Temple, Debbie Reynolds, and Ann Miller.

As Eleanor readjusted to life at MGM, *Born to Dance* was finally taking shape: Katz had bought out Buddy DeSylva's rights and McGowan and Silvers finalized the story. Jack Cummings, Mayer's nephew, had been assigned as producer of *Born to Dance* in the first of a three-film probationary period (he had been assistant producer on two prior films). Katz repeatedly argued that a battleship scene, with "one ship covered with boys, and one covered with girls," would make a fine production number. However, Cummings preferred a more unusual submarine setting.[10]

Singer Allan Jones was set to star opposite Eleanor, with Sid Silvers playing opposite Una Merkel. Frances Langford would play a haughty socialite (the role was later changed to "temperamental star Lucy James"). Buddy Ebsen was cast as the third sailor, to play alongside newcomer Judy Garland.

Garland had been at MGM since October 1935 but had sat idle for much of the time; the studio was unsure how to use this young teen with the mature voice. Garland had a major supporter, however—Louis B. Mayer's influential assistant Ida Koverman. This enterprising woman wielded strong control in casting and recruiting talent for the studio and had taken Garland under her wing. Although Koverman had been urging Mayer for months to utilize Garland's talents in a notable capacity, by July 1936 Garland had made only one short (*Every Sunday*) with another young girl under contract, Deanna Durbin. Durbin was subsequently let go, but the studio kept Garland. *Born to Dance* would give Garland her first featured role since she was put under contract. However, further discussions edged both Jones and Garland out of the cast. Jones' recent performance in Universal's *Show Boat* had convinced Katz he was wrong for the part. Frances Langford replaced Garland in the role of Peppy Turner. Sultry blonde actress Virginia Bruce would now play Lucy James.

Young contract player James Stewart was being tried in various genres to see what fit him best; at Porter's urging, he landed the lead opposite Eleanor. He was neither a singer nor a dancer, but Porter and Katz both thought that his boyish charm was a suitable draw. Porter, though married, was a known homosexual, and there were rumors that he was smitten with Stewart. When Mayer learned that Porter had invited Stewart to his home for a private singing audition, he was livid. At a time when any appearance of an "inappropriate relationship" would hurt a career, he was adamant: "Keep him at his piano, writing at home and off the set as much as possible. And for God's sake, don't let Jimmy Stewart go over to his house again . . . and he is not to see him alone!"[11]

With the question of the male lead settled, Mayer set about introducing Stewart to Eleanor. After searching the studio, Mayer finally located her; she was rehearsing acrobatic moves alone on an empty sound stage. Sweaty, grimy, and with her hair tucked snugly under a homemade stocking cap, she was mortified when Mayer approached her with the handsome actor at his side. "Eleanor, this will be your next leading man," Mayer said. "I could just see the way Jimmy was looking at me," Eleanor recalled. "*That's* going to be my next leading woman?"[12]

During the making of the film, Mayer would ceremoniously gift Eleanor with her own private rehearsal bungalow, something no other MGM performer had ever received. Officially designated, with her name painted over the door, Eleanor's space included a roomy studio with a wood floor, mirrors, piano, barre, two changing rooms with showers, and a small office area. In the past, she had to wander from soundstage to soundstage in search of an empty spot to practice and choreograph; now, she was considered the studio's most important dancer.

By May 29, Porter had completed the score. All seven songs were confirmed, but there was still hesitancy about the finale, "Swingin' the Jinx Away." Del Ruth and dance director Seymour Felix had convinced Katz the song was not good enough. They were holding out for an idea they refused to let go of—a production number with motorboats filled with chorus boys and girls. Felix, who had recently staged the lauded "A Pretty Girl Is Like a Melody" number from MGM's *The Great Ziegfeld,* was then in high favor with Mayer. Now, he also had Katz on his side as they attempted to do away with Porter's version of the finale. Jack Cummings told Porter that Del Ruth was "very set against it and Eleanor says she can't dance to it." After continued discussion with an irate Porter, a meeting was set up for that afternoon. Porter, having confirmed that Eleanor was actually in support of the song, enlisted her in a last-ditch effort to save what he believed would make a stellar finale to the film. He asked Silvers to have Eleanor and Roger Edens quickly get a routine ready for the meeting. A few hours later, Porter and Katz joined Del Ruth, Felix, Silvers, Edens, Edward Powell (the film's orchestrator and no relation to Eleanor), Nat Finston (head of MGM's music department), Eleanor, and Blanche in a rehearsal hall. "When I came in, I realized there was battle in the air," Porter wrote in his diary. Del Ruth expressed his dislike for the song, which set off an argument among all the men. Finally, after hearing enough of the debate, Eleanor boldly stepped forward. "Nobody has asked my opinion, but the number suits me perfectly. In fact, I already have a routine which I would like to show you." Porter recalled, "[Eleanor] proceeded to do one of the most exciting dances I have ever seen in my life." Flabbergasted, Katz turned to Porter and said, "If the number suits our star . . . there should be no more discussion. . . . The number is definitely in."[13]

Still upset about losing his pet idea, Felix began to protest, but Katz refused to hear any more about girls on motorboats. He felt the number should focus solely on Eleanor. "The only way I will allow it is if you can shoot them out of cannons. . . . That would be a swell effect," he retorted facetiously. Soon afterward, Katz replaced Felix with dance director Dave Gould.

Mayer and head of production Irving Thalberg were the last to give input on the score and the production numbers. The final round of approvals was scheduled for June 3 in Mayer's office. Katz, Mayer, Cummings, Roger Edens, Silvers, Ida Koverman, Virginia Bruce, and Eleanor all waited with Porter for Thalberg. Finally, the producer arrived, "looking more dead than alive, and obviously angry at being disturbed to hear this score." Porter proceeded to play the entire score. Both executives were ecstatic about the music. After Porter finished, Thalberg congratulated him, calling it "one of the finest scores I have ever heard." Mayer, ever the businessman, immediately rushed over to convince Porter to finalize his contract for the following year.

Born to Dance began shooting on July 7. In the final version of the story, Ted Barker (James Stewart), a sailor on leave, falls in love with Nora Paige (Eleanor Powell), a dancer trying to get into a show. After Ted saves the dog of Broadway star Lucy James (Virginia Bruce), Lucy follows up with a play for Ted as a publicity stunt. Nora sees photos of them together and refuses to see him again. To win Nora back, Ted purposely leaks a fake story to the press, which causes Lucy to quit on opening night. Nora replaces her and becomes a star.

Eleanor's first number, "Rap Tap on Wood," takes place in the lobby of the Lonely Hearts Club after Jenny (Una Merkel) introduces Nora to the crowd. While Eleanor did record the vocal, the version used in the film was dubbed by Marjorie Lane. This number was the first that Eleanor shot after her return to the studio, and the soundstage became a regular stop for stars who ventured over from neighboring sets. Joan Crawford, Greta Garbo, and Clark Gable were among the regulars who came by to watch. Soon the studio had to build bleachers for the crowds of visiting stars. Because songs were prerecorded and the dances were shot silently, Eleanor's curious colleagues could be accommodated on the set without any danger of noise affecting the take. Clapping, cheering, and calling out encouragement as she danced, the lively crowd fueled her energy. Teenagers Mickey Rooney and Jackie Cooper visited while they were filming *The Devil Is a Sissy*. After Eleanor finished her dance, Rooney glanced around at the pretty chorines and commented to Cooper, "I told you we were in the wrong picture."[14]

The lighthearted "Hey Babe Hey" included the whole cast dancing in waltz clog rhythm, with vocals sung in rounds. Audiences were given a rare opportunity to see James Stewart tap dance. Stewart suffered through weeks of intense training in order to achieve some semblance of comfort in the role—early morning dance lessons with Eleanor and evening vocal lessons after shooting was finished for the day. Unsatisfied with Stewart's singing, the studio ended up dubbing him with the voice of singer Art Jarrett. While the dubbing for Eleanor's voice is very similar to her own, Jarrett's professional, timbred vocal did not at all match Stewart's slow, drawling voice. Preview audiences burst into laughter the moment the song began. The dubbed vocal was quickly replaced by Stewart's own.

Despite their unfortunate first meeting, shy Stewart became smitten with Eleanor over the course of the production but was convinced she was impossibly out of his league. Afraid to ask her out, he sought advice from Del Ruth. "She's very nice," Del Ruth told him. "I'm sure if you ask her . . ." But Stewart backed down. Eleanor recalled a convoluted series of events that finally led to a date. She had bought four tickets to an important annual event that MGM asked all their stars to support. Because she had no friends to invite, she decided to use just two tickets and attend with Blanche. Hearing from Del Ruth that Eleanor had tickets available, Stewart asked the director to act as a go-between so he could buy them. Eleanor found it amusing that even though they were filming a picture together, Stewart still felt the need to communicate through a third party. She offered to give him the tickets, despite his insistence on paying her. He made it clear that he wasn't taking his most recent girlfriend Ginger Rogers, then later told her he was taking his roommate (actor Henry Fonda). A few days before the event, Fonda decided to go sailing. Finally, Stewart said, "I don't know why I don't pick you up and just drive you down."[15]

When Blanche heard that Stewart was going to attend with Eleanor, she suddenly developed a bad headache so the two could have the evening alone together. Throughout the evening, the intensity of Stewart's crush was apparent. Eleanor had heard tales of Stewart's convertible Ford that was notoriously filthy. To protect her hair from the breeze, she tucked a shower cap in her coat pocket. When Stewart arrived, the top was up, and his car was immaculate. Eleanor was stunned. When she asked what happened, he replied, "Well, I thought I should have it cleaned up. We are going out." The adventure continued as they started down Sunset Boulevard. Stewart was so nervous that he was driving on the wrong side of the road but quickly corrected it when Eleanor gently brought it to his attention. After the event, they went to the Trocadero nightclub to dance, but his dancing efforts produced little more than a stilted sway.

On the drive home, Eleanor was again perplexed when Stewart began to drive slower and slower as they approached her house, in order to make the evening last as long as possible. At her door, a bashful and stammering Stewart faced her, eyes full of emotion. "'J-just-just stand there. Just let me look at you with the moonlight shining down on you like that. Just beautiful. Just beautiful. You know, there's something I've been wanting to tell you all evening with the music and dancing and I haven't had a chance to tell you but I, well, what I really wanted to say is . . . Didn't we have a wonderful time?'" Gazing back at him, Eleanor leaned in close. "I wanted him to kiss me so badly, and I'm leaning forward, and then he just tipped his hat and said, 'Well, see you tomorrow,' then got in his car and drove off." Stewart never again got up the courage to ask her out. The next time they saw each other on set, he told her, "'Gee, I guess I made a fool of myself the other night.'"[16]

On set, and behind a camera lens, however, Stewart was bolder. An amateur photographer, he spent his off-camera moments shooting his co-stars with his new Leica camera. "[Fonda] was always wandering around with his camera or setting himself up in his darkroom and then yelling for us to come and see something. First we knew, all the rest of us—Joshua Logan and John Swope and myself, who shared the house with Hank at the time—got Leicas, too, and began shooting." Stewart experimented with lighting, using bridge lamps and flashes, but found the studio lighting made his hobby significantly easier. "I got a good portrait of Eleanor Powell on the set of *Born to Dance*, but there I didn't have to worry about lights."[17]

One of Cole Porter's most memorable songs, "Easy to Love," finds Ted and Nora on a romantic stroll in Central Park, where Ted launches into an earnest version of the ballad. Still unable to express his feelings directly, Stewart took the opportunity of the moment in the film where Ted tries to tell Nora how he feels and prefaced the scene by telling her, "When I say these words, I'm putting my heart into them. . . . I'm no singer, but you listen to these words." Touched, Eleanor replied, "Yes, I'm hearing you loud and clear."[18] Despite their mutual attraction, the relationship between Eleanor and Stewart never progressed. "I wasn't going to push him," Eleanor recalled, "but we never seemed to get with it."[19]

The tender scene is followed by Eleanor's lyrical solo. Wearing a dress with a full, flowing skirt, she shows off her graceful high kicks and backbends. Her choreography, reminiscent of the style of British dancer Jessie Matthews, is charming in the park setting.

Eleanor's original vision for the number was quite different. She wanted to perform a dance on pointe, which producer Cummings adamantly vetoed. He felt that Eleanor's ballet work did not show her off in the best light and would also be out of place in the setting. Upset with Cummings, Eleanor went straight to Mayer, who ultimately sided with his nephew.

As the scene continues, Nora and Ted encounter a policeman, played by Reginald Gardiner. On Eleanor's recommendation, her co-star from *At Home Abroad* made his film debut as the policeman who shakes his hair out and directs an imaginary symphony in a humorous send-up of conductor Leopold Stokowski's vigorous style.

After Lucy storms off stage during a rehearsal, Nora is asked to step in. She improvises a dance to an instrumental piano version of "Love Me, Love

My Pekinese." Utilizing her signature skill of adding humorous gestures to accentuate intricate rhythmic riffs, she builds the dance up to a joyful crescendo when Lucy James angrily stops her. The song had originally been planned as a number with Eleanor and five-year-old Juanita Quigley (who played Una Merkel's daughter). As the youngest member of the MGM singing and dancing classes, Quigley was being touted in the press as a "baby Eleanor Powell." The studio instead decided to shift focus and the song was reworked for Virginia Bruce.

"Swingin' the Jinx Away" was the film's big-budget finale. In an excited reaction to the confirmation of the song, Mayer had directed Katz to "go to town and spend $250,000 on that number alone," the equivalent of over $4.5 million today.[20] Designed by art directors Cedric Gibbons and Merrill Pye, the stylized battleship, complete with six working cannons, weighed in at over 120 tons. The production crew worked around the clock for two months to construct the set. Because of the height of the towering crow's nest where Eleanor would make her entrance, the number had to be shot in the tallest soundstage on the lot, the massive Stage 15. With a forty-foot ceiling and over forty thousand square feet of space, Stage 15 was at that time the largest soundstage in the country.

Following a musical prologue led by Frances Langford, the camera pans up to reveal Eleanor at the top of the crow's nest. She makes her entrance, stepping down a spiral staircase and sliding down a pole to the deck, where the chorus and band await. In her initial attempts to make the descent look effortless and smooth, she did not wear any protection on her hand, and the metal friction rubbed the skin right off her palms. This mishap was quickly remedied. In subsequent takes, she wore a protective glove, hidden from view as she grips the pole during the slide.

Eleanor alternates between bandleader and tap percussionist in her choreographic interpretation of Porter's patriotic swing tune. A challenging number with a variety of rhythms, it had not been easy to arrange, nor was it easy to choreograph or stage. "It was Powell's finale, and we had the very devil of a time trying to work out a vehicle for it," Roger Edens recalled. Eleanor worked hand in hand with Porter to fine-tune her choreography to the orchestrations. MGM succeeded in their goal to top the opulence that had set the high standard—*The Great Ziegfeld*—also designed by Gibbons and Pye. "It was a smash-finale, to say the least," Edens said. "It was that really monstrous epitome of nonsense. . . . I don't know what to say except that it haunts me as an embarrassment of bad taste. But the audiences loved it."[21]

After working so hard on choreography, Eleanor insisted that she have some control over the finished presentation of her numbers. She had witnessed indiscriminate slicing, and she began the habit of sitting with the film editor (usually veteran editor Blanche Sewell) to assure that her dances retained continuity in the final cut. Eleanor had discovered that when faced with a precisely choreographed sequence of steps, the cutter, not understanding the number from a dancer's perspective, could inadvertently cut out the more intricate steps and leave the easy ones. Sewell, who had been with MGM since 1925, welcomed Eleanor's interest and involvement. Eleanor found her "a wonderful cutter," and the two became friends. Seeing Sewell at work fueled Eleanor's thirst for production knowledge.

Eleanor's involvement in other aspects of filming kept her busy. Her daily schedule took her to all parts of the studio. If she wasn't in the rehearsal hall, she was in wardrobe, shooting dialogue scenes, filming a dance number, or sitting with a cutter—until she started the process all over again. She never truly had a day off. Eleanor's interest in camera angles and lighting techniques began to influence how she crafted her choreography. As she gathered insight from the studio technicians, she made friends in all levels of production.

Mayer may have been pleased with her quest for perfection; however, he was not happy when Eleanor socialized off the set with members of the crew. She was naively unaware of the degree of control the studios wielded over stars. After she was spotted having lunch with film cutter Bob Stringer in the commissary, Mayer called her into his office. "My dear child, I would rather you weren't seen with any of the lower echelon of employees," he told her. Eleanor was livid and once again had no qualms about speaking her mind. "You can't tell me who I'm going to have lunch with. I'll do anything on the set. I'll work harder than anyone you've ever had in the studio. But as for not speaking to my friends—sorry."[22] Not used to anyone, especially a young female star, talking back to him or refusing his requests, Mayer threatened to fire her. "If you don't go along with me, you're out," he said. Unintimidated, Eleanor disregarded the warning and continued to socialize with whomever she pleased. The fact that she was not fired on the spot demonstrated just how much Mayer valued her.

Before production ended on *Born to Dance,* the tragic death of the "Boy Wonder" producer Irving Thalberg on September 14, 1936, at age thirty-seven sent a wave of sadness throughout the studio. Thalberg, who had a serious congenital heart condition, had been in fragile health for many years and finally succumbed to a bout of pneumonia. Publicly, Mayer appeared deeply grieved, and all studio departments were closed down for several days. "I have lost my associate of the past fourteen years and the finest friend a man could ever have. There is so very much to be said about Irving Thalberg, but there are so few words with which to say it and the shock is too great," he said.[23] But privately, the two had not been on good terms for a long time. Looking upon Thalberg's passing as a blessing, Mayer cruelly commented to Eddie Mannix in the limousine as they left Thalberg's services, "Isn't God good to me?"[24] Mayer swiftly removed major elements of Thalberg's legacy by completely shutting down his production unit, including disposing of all the Technicolor footage of the Jeanette MacDonald–Nelson Eddy musical *Maytime,* which would have been MGM's first full-Technicolor feature film. The film was entirely reshot in black and white. Thalberg had produced *The Broadway Melody* in 1929, but there is no evidence that he had any involvement in *Broadway Melody of 1936* or *Born to Dance,* other than his enthusiastic approval of Porter's score. Though none of Eleanor's upcoming projects had been tied to Thalberg, she joined the scores of MGM stars who sat in the pews of the B'nai B'rith Temple for his services.

As was standard practice for many musical releases, MGM staged a preview of all the production numbers of *Born to Dance,* with the leads performing the songs and dances live over the radio from Grauman's Chinese Theatre in Hollywood. This was featured on the *Hollywood Hotel* radio show on November 13.

A few days later, Eleanor answered an unexpected knock on her dressing room door during lunchtime. Outside stood Clark Gable holding a blindfold. "Ellie, I've got a present for you, but you've got to be blindfolded," he told her. After she covered her eyes, Gable led her down the stairs, turning her around multiple times to misdirect her. All she could hear along the way was muffled laughter as Gable guided her to their destination. Finally, Gable removed the blindfold, to reveal a brand-new 1936 convertible Packard roadster adorned with a pink ribbon. For the girl famous for pedaling around the lot on her bicycle, it was both a useful and unforgettable birthday present. Later, when telling the story, she would proudly quip, "And I only had to dance for it!"

Born to Dance opened in theaters on November 27, and critics unanimously praised both Eleanor and the film. "Miss Powell is without question the most expert feminine tap dancer."[25] "The closing number is one of those magnificent Hollywood things," a *New York Times* reviewer stated, describing the monstrous set as an "exaltation of the set designer in his unlimited field of vision. . . . The producers have crammed the film so full of pleasantry and gaetry [*sic*], as a setting for Eleanor Powell's exquisitely tapped-out rhythms, that it leaves one ga-ga for a time."[26] The critics concluded that any excess would be forgiven, however, as soon as one saw "the pertly stepping Eleanor Powell lead the band." No one seemed to mind Stewart's timid crooning; he was described as "lank and amiable."

The film received two Academy Award nominations—Cole Porter for Best Original Song for "I've Got You Under My Skin," and Dave Gould for Best Dance Direction. Both lost to other nominees.

Even before *Born to Dance* was released, production was already announced for Eleanor's next film, *Broadway Melody of 1937*. Taking advantage of about a month's break, she and Blanche headed back to New York. When Eleanor arrived there on November 18, she was greeted by an MGM publicity team who wheeled a red grand piano and a tap mat onto the platform at Grand Central Station. Eleanor tapped for onlookers and posed for photos with a smiling group of bell caps.

The following month, on December 13, she was invited to a special celebration at the Cotton Club in honor of Bill Robinson's fiftieth anniversary in show business. Rare silent footage of the Golden Jubilee event taken by the Nicholas Brothers shows Eleanor being helped up out of the audience and joining Robinson onstage, where they went into a brief impromptu dance before she stylishly strutted back into the audience.

With Eleanor's future now secure in Hollywood, it was finally time to close the East Coast chapter of her life. She and Blanche packed up the home in Crestwood and boarded the train west with Susie, Harold, and young Betty Meyer. Though Harold was healthy, sixty-four-year-old Susie had been diagnosed with diabetes and was experiencing some heart issues. They arrived in time to once again spend Christmas together as they looked forward to a brand-new year.

10

"Feelin' Like a Million"

In early January, Eleanor started work on *Broadway Melody of 1937*. She was thrilled to have the family together again, including her black cocker spaniel, Ruggles, and her canary, Tapper. Her grandmother's presence brought back comforting memories of life in Springfield and summers in Atlantic City. Though they had a cook, Susie often took to the kitchen to make comfort food for the family. She baked bread, and Eleanor loved to eat lots of it. Eleanor also had a fondness for her grandmother's apple dumplings. Her high level of activity often caused her to be underweight, so she was free to indulge herself.

Hoping to repeat the success of *Broadway Melody of 1936,* MGM had begun to publicize plans for the next edition of the series starring Eleanor Powell immediately after its release. Much like other projects that had been announced for her, plans for this film had been repeatedly scrapped and resurrected. MGM was determined to make this a blockbuster picture worthy of the *Broadway Melody* name. Roy Del Ruth was again assigned as director and Jack Cummings as producer; Nacio Herb Brown and Arthur Freed were to write original songs for the film. Dave Gould would again be responsible for the dance ensembles.

MGM booked Johnny Boyle, Eleanor's former teacher, to do a specialty number of his famous finger dances. He used finger movements to imitate the dance steps of Eleanor Powell, Buddy Ebsen, George Murphy, Fred Astaire, and Bill Robinson. Though this segment didn't make it into the film, Boyle apparently did, at some point, teach Eleanor his finger dances; and she used the technique to work out her choreography in the early stages, which cut down the wear and tear on her feet.

No leading man had been selected as yet, but plans for the supporting cast were taking shape. George Murphy, who had not had the opportunity to show off his strong dance skills in his previous movies, was given a major break when he was cast in a supporting role. Buddy Ebsen, featured in the last two Powell films, had another chance to showcase his comedic skills and eccentric dancing. Austrian baritone Charles Igor Gorin was engaged for a minor role that was pivotal to the plot. Lastly, the legendary Sophie Tucker was signed to play the role of mother to fourteen-year-old Judy Garland, who was finally making her first appearance in a big-budget feature film.

Ever since the aborted attempt to cast Garland in *Born to Dance,* the studio had been at a loss about how best to use her. She was loaned out to 20th Century-Fox, where her featured role in *Pigskin Parade* finally garnered her some attention. In the meantime, her *Every Sunday* co-star, Deanna Durbin, had become an overnight success in the Universal film *Three Smart Girls.* MGM, realizing their missed opportunity with Durbin, now turned their sights on Garland and earnestly groomed her for stardom. She began to make regular appearances on radio, gaining national exposure. The studio saw the new Powell extravaganza as the perfect vehicle to showcase Garland's unique talents in a feature film.

Though production wasn't to begin until February 10, Eleanor reported to the studio on January 6 to begin work on her dance numbers. The holidays had not given her sufficient time to rest before she resumed her daily work routine. She knew she had lost considerable weight while making her last film, but didn't realize just how much until she shopped at a local department store and discovered that her regular dress size was now three sizes too large. Mayer noticed, too, and, concerned that she would look too gaunt on film, continued to push the regular consumption of milkshakes from the studio commissary. Eleanor attempted to take better care of herself. She vowed to make it to bed by nine o'clock every evening, and she got a massage from a chiropodist every two weeks to keep her feet in the best condition possible.

News articles chattered about the interest she received from a wealthy Peruvian lawyer by the name of Manuel Yigorin. Introduced by her friend and physician, Dr. Lopez, Yigorin had squired her around New York during her recent visit. After his return to Peru, Yigorin continued to shower Eleanor with attention from afar, faithfully sending her flowers every Saturday. Throughout the entire production of the film, Yigorin sent cablegrams (to a special cable address he had purchased for her, "ELESWEET," directed to "Eleanor Powell, Bedford Drive, Beverly Hills, California"), along with orchids and even a llama wool rug. In April, the press amusingly announced that Eleanor had finally "taken up Spanish in order to give the right answers to her Peruvian beau."[1] It was a classic example of how romance was presented and embellished by the studio for the sole purpose of publicity.

On the day of Eleanor's return to the studio, MGM announced Robert Taylor as her leading man. After *Broadway Melody of 1936,* Taylor had risen from a lesser-known contract player to a popular leading man, playing opposite some of MGM's biggest female stars. His latest film, *Camille* with Greta Garbo, had opened at the Capitol Theatre in New York the week before. In reuniting the two onscreen, MGM hoped to repeat their successful first pairing.

Four dance numbers had been designated for Eleanor in the film. The plot once again featured the tried-and-true story of a small-town girl who comes to New York with aspirations of making it big on Broadway. This was the third such role for Eleanor, and she mastered it well—so well, that she later jokingly referred to herself as the Janet Gaynor of the musical, an allusion to Gaynor's role in the 1937 version of *A Star Is Born.* Stage door musicals were popular with Depression-era audiences, and MGM was not yet ready to tamper with this bankable formula.

The story opens with two out-of-work hoofers, Sonny Ledford (George Murphy) and Peter Trot (Buddy Ebsen), who get a job caring for Stargazer, a prize racehorse belonging to Caroline Whipple (Binnie Barnes). The horse is being transported to New York to recover after having pulled a tendon in a race. Sally Lee (Eleanor Powell), who raised him on her father's farm, stows away on the train so she can watch over him. She is discovered by Sonny and Peter and by Broadway producer Steve Raleigh (Robert Taylor), also on the train. Raleigh sees Sally dancing and wants to hire her for his new show, which is being backed by the Whipples. When Mrs. Whipple decides to sell Stargazer, Sally recklessly bids and wins the auction. Knowing that she does not have enough money, Steve borrows the remainder from Mr. Whipple and, wishing to remain anonymous, has Sonny give her the money. Mrs. Whipple learns that Sally is starring in the show and jealously threatens to withdraw her financial support unless Steve fires Sally. He refuses to do so, but Sally, overhearing his predicament, quits the show. She gets a job in a nightclub, and she and Sonny concentrate on getting Stargazer ready for the upcoming race at Saratoga. Stargazer wins the race, providing enough money to finance Steve's show.

A reflection of the high interest in horseracing in the late 1930s, three of MGM's 1937 summer releases featured a racetrack theme: *A Day at the Races,* *Saratoga,* and *Broadway Melody of 1938.* They all shared second-unit racetrack footage, and two of the three also shared a storyline about a crazed racehorse being propelled over the finish line by operatic singing blasted over the loudspeaker. MGM hoped to capitalize on the public's obsession with the champion horse, War Admiral, and his underdog rival, Seabiscuit.

Freed and Brown wrote seven new songs for the film, but only five of them were retained in the final cut. The opening number, "Follow in My Footsteps," featured Eleanor, Buddy Ebsen, and George Murphy. Reminiscent of "Sing Before Breakfast" in *Broadway Melody of 1936,* this time the trio playfully dances in a railroad car, complete with a horse. Murphy later recalled performing the entire number for a group of studio executives who, mindful of the length, kept their eyes on their watches more than on the dance itself. Irritated, Murphy spoke up in its defense: "If a number is lousy and it's on the screen for two seconds, that's too long. But if a number is good like this one is, it ought to be on the screen as long as the audience wants to look at it."[2]

One of the loveliest songs in the score was the ballad "Yours and Mine." Judy Garland briefly presents the song in the opening credits. An unusual practice at the time, it was reportedly awarded to her as a consolation prize by the director after two of her songs were cut from the picture.[3] Aboard the train, Steve and Sally "write" the song together, and he then prompts her to sing it. Marjorie Lane again dubbed Eleanor's voice, but Robert Taylor recorded a verse himself. Less successful than his rendition of "I've Got a Feelin' You're Foolin'" in *Broadway Melody of 1936,* his vocal part was removed after it provoked a burst of laughter from a San Diego preview audience. Though not allowed to sing, Eleanor became quite proficient at lip syncing, earning a reputation as one of the best on the lot.

The delightful "Feelin' Like a Million," performed by Powell and Murphy, marked the first time in her screen career that Eleanor was paired with a dance partner, which gave her the opportunity to step outside her solo tap choreography and explore a different type of dance. Set in Manhattan's Bryant Park, the number begins at a fountain. George Murphy introduces the song; Eleanor interjects a few spoken lines. When a thunderstorm breaks and it starts to rain, the two move to a gazebo for cover, then venture out to a grassy area, where they splash joyfully among the puddles in the falling rain. Grabbing an umbrella, they dance down the sidewalk, in a shot similar to that of Gene Kelly years later in the famous title number from *Singin' in the Rain* (1952). They continue spinning through the park until they end up falling into a disproportionately large puddle. All but their heads submerged in the deep hole, their laughing faces poke up from the surface.

While Eleanor and Murphy conceived of the idea and the setting together, Murphy actually directed the number. He had been working with film editor Blanche Sewell on a novel technique that would eventually revolutionize the way dance numbers were filmed. Instead of shooting the whole number in one continuous take as was the custom, they used the soundtrack as a guide to enable them to splice several segments together. Murphy then divided the dance into five sequences. Excitedly, he presented his idea to director Roy Del Ruth, complete with camera angles, even suggesting the lenses to be used. Impressed, Del Ruth allowed him to direct the dance number. Murphy's technique proved to be efficient; it cut the filming down from three days to one. Murphy and Sewell were never credited or compensated for this innovation, which would save the studio much time and money. Begrudgingly, Murphy later said: "The only thing I got out of working with Blanche Sewell . . . is the satisfaction of finding a new and better way of filming dance numbers, which doesn't always pay off at the supermarket."[4]

The number was filmed in mid-May, near the end of production. Even though Murphy's plan had cut the time needed to film the number, they still found themselves up against a deadline. The set where they were filming needed to be struck that evening so a large nightclub setting could be put in place for MGM's convention ball. Hard at work since early morning, Eleanor had developed two big blisters on her feet long before they were ready to finish. Dancing on so many surfaces in one number—wooden floors, macadam, composition floors, grass, and stone—had given their feet and shoes an extra workout.

Eleanor was assigned another number, "Got a Pair of New Shoes," which took place in the nightclub where her character was working after quitting the show. The music was recorded, and the dance was filmed, including the vocal by Marjorie Lane, but it was never included in the picture. Though the dance was cut, the song didn't go to waste. It was eventually sung by Judy Garland in another film made the same year, *Thoroughbreds Don't Cry*, and snippets of it turned up in soundtracks of other MGM films over the years.

Judy Garland all but stops the show in "Everybody Sing" when her character visits the theatrical agency, accompanied by her screen mother, Sophie Tucker. However, her most famous song from the film is "Dear Mr. Gable," adapted especially for her by Roger Edens. In early February, the young singer had captivated the studio executives when she sang the song to Clark Gable at his birthday party on the set of *Parnell*. She was given the opportunity to sing it on a few more occasions, each time making a hit, until the executives were persuaded that it would be an excellent song to include in the film. It was shot mostly in close-ups with soft lighting, which presented the young star to the public in a simple, but endearing, way.

Charles Igor Gorin was given a number, "Sun Showers," where he sang to Murphy, Ebsen, and Powell, all seated on the grass. Interestingly, this outdoor scene was filmed on a soundstage, complete with real grass, daylight-producing arc lights, and a wind machine gently blowing the blades of grass for an authentic effect. The number never made it into the final cut.

The film also featured comedians familiar to the audiences of the day. Robert Wildhack, the snorer from *Broadway Melody of 1936*, made another appearance, this time lecturing on the art of the sneeze. Willie Howard, a headliner on the bill from Eleanor's vaudeville days, had a minor but notable role as the waiter in the boardinghouse with a pack of dogs that scurried over furniture and the dinner table alike.

In keeping with the style of Eleanor's two preceding films, the finale of *Broadway Melody of 1938* was an elaborate and costly affair. She not only choreographed her own numbers but also contributed to their presentation. During each film, she consulted with Merrill Pye to explain her complete vision for the numbers. She would mention specific elements she wanted included in the set, such as a fountain or a staircase, and Pye and Gibbons would sketch the design accordingly, adding creative design in the best MGM tradition.

Naturally, the *MGM Studio News* boasted that the futuristic New York skyline in *Broadway Melody of 1938* surpassed the sets of both the "A Pretty Girl Is Like a Melody" number from *The Great Ziegfeld* and the battleship number from *Born to Dance* in size and opulence. The set—actually, seven sets in one—changed form for each of the specialty numbers that made up the finale. It featured a fifty-step, nine-ton glass stairway and twelve futuristic buildings that could be raised, story by story, by means of hydraulic pressure, to a height of eighty feet. Skyscraper curtains revealed the dazzling cityscape, while a series of cars, buses, and streetcars moved silently in the background, all controlled by an electrician in a booth.

The finale opens with Powell and Murphy in a ballroom-style number. For the first time on film, Eleanor is lifted and spun by a partner, proving her versatility and putting her ballet training to good use. George Murphy, undoubtedly her best partner in this style of dance, was the perfect match. Next, Judy Garland and Buddy Ebsen arrive onstage in a miniature town car to do a short dance, before climbing back in and driving off. Sophie Tucker essentially plays herself in the next segment, performing a nostalgic Broadway monologue and singing "Your Broadway and My Broadway," while all the neon signs in the background display her name. Igor Gorin is not given a solo, but his singing provides a transition between scenes. Eleanor reappears in her trademark top hat and tails, along with Murphy, Ebsen, and a line of chorus boys for a brief segue to her solo.

In the five-minute "Your Broadway and My Broadway," she incorporates different varieties of tap with each change of the music. Just as Sophie Tucker pays tribute to the stars of old Broadway in her monologue, Eleanor, opening with a fluid soft shoe, subtly samples styles of Broadway tap masters from Bill Robinson to George M. Cohan. As the chorus boys join her, the music shifts to a medley of Broadway-themed songs with diverse rhythms. Next, she interacts with the chorus boys, allowing them to lift and toss her, continuing into a series of acrobatic moves. In a unique duet, the orchestra drops out, and Eleanor dances to a drum solo, matching the beats with her taps. As the orchestra swells again, the lights dim and the neon words "Broadway Melody" rise slowly behind the spotlighted Eleanor in a dramatic finish. Robert Taylor and Stargazer join the rest of the cast onstage for a final bow. This was Eleanor's personal favorite of all her finales because of the many styles of dance she was able to perform.

Production had barely begun in late February, when Eleanor was sidelined for two weeks with a foot injury. As they waited for Robert Taylor to finish filming *This Is My Affair* with Barbara Stanwyck at 20th Century-Fox, the rest of the cast had begun to work on the dance numbers, the first of which was "Follow in My Footsteps." Originally, as Eleanor, George Murphy, and Buddy Ebsen clowned around in a boxcar, they were to wear big brushes on their feet for a short sequence in the number. To avoid hitting the camera crew during the filming of the dance, Eleanor attempted to kick the brushes backward off her feet. Her right foot caught on the brush, and she fell, spraining her ankle and one of her toes. After the studio nurse wrapped her foot, Eleanor attempted to finish the number, but found that she could barely stand on the swollen foot. On doctor's orders, the studio enforced a rest period of three weeks. Her strong work ethic made this difficult to endure.

Production worked around her but, conscious of the costly delays her condition would cause, Eleanor was relieved when she was finally given the go-ahead to get back to work a week early. Her many friends on the lot were also eager to see her return, and the press likened it to that of a New York reception for a popular hero. On the day she arrived on the lot, "everybody stuck their heads out of the windows, cheering and throwing showers of confetti. On the *Broadway Melody* set, 100 chorus girls greeted her with a banner of welcome."[5] Eleanor finished the number, but the brushes, deemed too dangerous for dancing, were only used in the form of mock musical instruments played by Ebsen and Murphy.

Because she spent so much extra time devising her own choreography, in April the studio modified Eleanor's contract to give her an annual twelve-week paid period to prepare numbers for her films. This was an exceptional clause that no other performer had at that time.

Later in April, Eleanor added Sophie Tucker to her list of dancing students. According to the press, Miss Tucker, to lose fifteen pounds, gave up dieting and turned instead to tap lessons from Eleanor and Buddy Ebsen.

For years, stars, contract players, and extras alike had been entirely at the mercy of the big studios. Stars had no say about which films they would appear in or how many hours they would work; their safety and meal requirements were often disregarded. The studio all but owned them and dictated every aspect of their lives. After many years of this abuse by the system, in May 1937, the Screen Actors Guild (SAG) attempted to negotiate a contract with the movie studios for the protection of actors. On May 2, picketers gathered outside the MGM gates. Movie stars from ten studios around town arrived at work with their stage makeup applied at home. Eleanor was among the stars to cross the picket line at MGM; she, Clark Gable, Greta Garbo, Jean Harlow, and Jeanette MacDonald managed to pass through without being stopped. A few days later, thousands of stars, contract players, and extras voted to strike if the guild was not recognized. On the morning of May 9, thirteen major movie producers signed the first SAG contract, which guaranteed a minimum pay of $25 per day for actors, $35 for stunts, and $5.50 per day for extras.

Also in early May, *Hats in the Air,* a musical by Dwight Taylor, was scheduled as Eleanor's next film. Shortly following the announcement, an interesting tidbit appeared in the press, describing her newest idea for a number—a dance on garbage can lids. In typical publicity exaggeration, she was said to have "visited a Los Angeles department store and tried over a hundred cans before she found one with the proper rhythm."[6] Eleanor gave up the idea but, years later in the 1955 film *It's Always Fair Weather,* the concept was successfully pulled off by Gene Kelly, Michael Kidd, and Dan Dailey.

Another novel idea for a number involved incorporating the help of the man who began designing both her shoes and her actual taps—Bill Morgan of the Hollywood Capezio store, a theatrical dance shoe supplier. As his nephew, Ralph Hadsell, later recalled, Eleanor wanted to create a tap number using skates. Instead of dancing in regular skates, however, she worked with Morgan to make a prototype of tap shoes that had tiny wheels embedded in the soles. "They tried for a long time to make that work," Hadsell recalled. "But she wasn't able to use it in a film."[7]

Two weeks before the end of production, it was decided that Robert Taylor would be given top billing in the picture. In order to get more mileage out of the film, the name was changed to *Broadway Melody of 1938*.

Production ended on May 25, 1937, but retakes were not completed until July 20. It was just as Eleanor was finishing up *Broadway Melody of 1938* that twenty-one-year-old Sid Luft, an old friend from New York, arrived in Hollywood and decided to look her up. Their acquaintance dated back to 1934, when both lived in Westchester County. Blanche frequented a dress shop owned by Luft's mother, Leonora, and the two ladies became friends. Back in Crestwood, their families had seen each other occasionally, and then Eleanor left for Hollywood and Luft for a European tour with his mother and sister.

Luft visited the set on the day the cast was celebrating the fifteenth birthday of Judy Garland (whom he would later marry). A newcomer in town, he became a regular visitor to the Powell home, where he was welcomed by the whole family. He claimed he got to know the three Powell women so well that Blanche even attempted to give him career advice.

On July 16, the entire *Broadway Melody* cast appeared on the *Hollywood Hotel* radio program to promote the picture. Two weeks later, on July 31, Eleanor received her first bonus—$25,000—for completing the film, a new provision that resulted from the renegotiation of her contract.

In mid-August, *Broadway Melody of 1938* previewed on a high note. *Motion Picture Daily* deemed it the best of the series yet, guaranteed to do well at the box office. *Variety* also praised Eleanor's performance: "Miss Powell is given wide latitude for her spirited and fascinating dancing and puts warmth and beauty into every rhythmic routine, both in the solos and in the duets with Murphy. She also stands forth as a splendid actress, skillful in her modulations and performing with appealing sincerity, a star by every right."[8]

Other reviewers were less enthusiastic. The summer had seen many horse racing–themed films, and one reviewer claimed that the picture resembled a cleaned-up version of *Saratoga*, with music. Others criticized Eleanor's acting, and one reviewer took offense at her perpetual nice girl demeanor. MGM took note and placed Eleanor in a film with a different type of role, with a budget to top all her previous films.

◉   ◉   ◉

MGM picked a ten-year-old Ziegfeld Broadway show to revamp as Eleanor's next project. Ziegfeld's original *Rosalie* had been inspired by the 1926 "royal tour" of Queen Marie, the Scottish aristocrat who had married the king of Romania. The queen, with her two children, had visited the United States in an effort to secure a loan and became the dazzling VIP of the season; she gave press conferences, visited places like West Point, and was a guest at fashionable parties. The royal visit set Ziegfeld's imagination in motion, and when Charles Lindbergh made international headlines that May with his *Spirit of St. Louis* voyage, his story was decided. He added a few years to Marie's princess daughter, renamed the character after his mother, Rosalie, then paired her off romantically with a West Point cadet who loved to fly. The show featured music by George and Ira Gershwin and starred Marilyn Miller and Eleanor's first tap teacher, Jack Donahue. MGM originally optioned Rosalie as a vehicle for Marion Davies in 1930, but the project was abandoned.

Preliminary work for the movie version of *Rosalie* began in early June 1937, less than a week after *Broadway Melody of 1938* wrapped. With an even higher budget slated for this film, MGM kept true to its goal of raising the production level for each subsequent musical. While the story was borrowed from the Ziegfeld show, Mayer decided to update it with an entirely new score by Cole Porter. Set to direct was Woody Van Dyke, as Roy Del Ruth had requested time off after *Broadway Melody of 1938*. William Anthony McGuire, one of the book's original writers, produced the film. Cast alongside Eleanor were operatic baritone Nelson Eddy (fresh from a national concert tour), Ray Bolger (in the role originated by Jack Donahue), Frank Morgan (reprising his role from the original stage production), Edna May Oliver, and Vienna Opera Company star Ilona Massey, in her film debut.

Eleanor plays Rosalie, a princess from Romanza, who is studying incognito at Vassar College. She meets West Point football hero Dick Thorpe (Nelson Eddy), and the two fall in love. When she is called back home by the king, she challenges Dick to prove his love by flying to her country and meeting her in the town square on festival day. Unaware she is a princess, he makes the trip, only to discover she is already betrothed to a prince. Heartbroken,

Dick returns home to West Point. When an uprising begins in Romanza, Rosalie and her family are forced to flee to the United States. Rosalie and Dick are reunited, marry, and live happily ever after.

Before the first week of prep was out, another tragic event cast a shadow over the studio with the sudden death of actress Jean Harlow on June 7, at age twenty-six. The actress had taken ill while filming *Saratoga* with Clark Gable and died just seven days later from uremic poisoning. Just as with Thalberg's death nine months earlier, the entire studio briefly shut down in reaction. The close-knit family of MGM stars was shaken by the loss. Because their studio dressing rooms were very close, Eleanor had seen Harlow often while on the lot, and the two had become friends. Eleanor fondly remembered Jean as a warm, down-to-earth girl who loved to cook—very different from the type of characters she played. As they got to know each other, Eleanor discovered Harlow shared her interest in collecting phonograph records. Harlow's passing left several members of her private staff out of work. The studio, in a bittersweet gesture, made efforts to keep them employed, and Harlow's personal hairdresser, Peggy McDonald, became Eleanor's hairdresser a short time later.

As production went back into full swing, preparatory work on *Rosalie* slowly resumed. Eleanor took advantage of delays to prepare choreography, but a frustrated Bolger, who had forsaken a road tour of *On Your Toes,* had been waiting at the studio with nothing to do since April. And then, in late July, Eleanor fell victim to what was becoming a chronic condition. Her intense practice schedule and tendency to overwork herself again took a toll, and severe exhaustion forced her to stay home with a nurse in attendance. Since completion of *Broadway Melody of 1938,* she had dropped seven pounds, and Louella Parsons noted that she "was sicker than anybody knows, and the studio is pretty worried about delays on *Rosalie*."[9]

In early August, with hopes she would be fully recovered within a few weeks, Cole Porter, Ray Bolger, and Nelson Eddy visited Eleanor at home and gave her a bedside preview of the score. With a tremendous budget at stake, each day she was out caused the studio increased concern. By late August, sufficiently recuperated, Eleanor resumed rehearsals for the film.

Prior to her illness, Eleanor had been working on a new concept for a dance. A performance by the Los Angeles Philharmonic Orchestra had given her a unique idea for the film's big production number. Inspired by the large timpani drums, she imagined a line of drums of various sizes as a setting for a dance, an intriguing idea that had not yet been done in films. Merrill Pye brought her concept to life; he designed a large set with sixteen round drums that descended like steps and ranged in height from sixteen feet to sixteen inches. More massive than the enormous battleship in *Born to Dance*, not even Stage 15 was big enough to accommodate the entire set. The festival scene, which took place in a large plaza in the tiny mythical kingdom of Romanza, was constructed outdoors on Lot 3. The set spanned a large swath of the sixty-acre backlot and was filled with over two thousand costumed extras. Into this setting, the star makes her entrance, carried through the crowd atop a large drum. *Rosalie* would prove to be MGM's most elaborate, as well as most expensive, musical to date.

Rosalie was faced with several unique production challenges. Extra care had to be taken in the on-screen portrayal of West Point and Army officials in the film. Uniforms had to be inspected for accuracy, and special attention was given to interactions between cadets and superior officers to ensure respectful representation. Certain scenes and dialogue required rewriting or deletion, pending the approval of the War Department and West Point. That the studio struggled with the extra burden is evidenced in the twenty-five pages of telegrams, letters of commentary, and script change requests found in the film's legal files.

It wasn't until September that the actors were put before the cameras. Eleanor's first number, "I've a Strange New Rhythm in My Heart," takes place in the girls' dormitory with her fellow students. Attired in satin pajamas, she dances through the room and out onto a moonlit balcony, ending the number in a romantic lyric style.

As in her prior films, MGM planned to have Marjorie Lane dub her voice. Lane, newly married to actor Brian Donlevy, requested permission to accompany her husband to England, where he was filming. She arranged to record the song before she left, but when it came time to work on the number, Van Dyke felt it lacked swing. Since Lane was no longer available to re-record it, he turned to Eleanor and said, "What's the matter with you doing it? You've been singing it around here at rehearsals, so why not sing it into the mic?"[10] Eleanor's version was used in the final cut—marking the first time her singing voice was heard on film. Throughout the rest of her career at MGM, she was never dubbed again.

Eleanor and dancer Ray Bolger choreographed a number together for *Rosalie*. Bolger recalled that, during the rehearsal, Eleanor expressed interest in some of his steps, so he taught them to her. The following day, Bolger had forgotten everything, and Eleanor had to teach it back to him. Unfortunately, the number, ironically titled, "I Know It's Not Meant for Me," was cut from the final release after the preview showing. It proved doubly frustrating to Bolger, cast in the same role as dancer Jack Donahue in the original, since this was his only dance number in the film.

Nelson Eddy introduced Cole Porter's romantic ballad "In the Still of the Night." Eleanor and Nelson had been friends since her first days on the lot. Though Eddy sometimes appeared stiff and stoic onscreen, his co-stars knew him as a jovial man with an endearing personality. Eleanor recalled his bringing a red rose every day to her dressing room as a gesture of appreciation.

An unforeseen conflict arose in early September. The press reported that Fred Astaire was planning to copyright a drum dance he was choreographing for his upcoming film, *A Damsel in Distress*. "If an appeal to Washington is successful, Fred Astaire will introduce a copyrighted dance routine in his new picture."[11] George Cohen, a member of MGM's legal team, was quickly in communication with RKO's attorney Ross Hastings: "There are a number of questions I would like to ask in connection with the 'Appeal to Washington' but professional courtesy prevents me from doing so."[12] Fortunately, Astaire's appeal was dropped, and Eleanor's drum dance was unaffected.

Indeed, the highlight of the film is the festival scene that features the drum dance to Cole Porter's title song, "Rosalie." Filmed over two weeks between October 11 and 22, 1937, the scenes were shot at night on MGM's Lot 3, about one mile from the main studio. With ample room for the sprawling set, Gibbons and Pye went wild on what was advertised as "the biggest set since *Ben Hur*."[13] A large portion of the castle, flanked with ornate columns and dancing fountains, was built, with hundreds of steps that descended onto an enormous open plaza. Here, Ilona Massey sang "Spring Love Is in the Air," and the Albertina Rasch Dancers performed to Alexander Borodin's "Polovtsian Dances."

The elaborate construction created much excitement in both the local Culver City neighborhood and the MGM star community. When the time came to film Eleanor's dance, security patrolled the surrounding wall on horseback to prevent children from climbing over into the lot. The hundreds of extras were allowed to invite family and friends to watch, and many stars that would normally have filled the soundstage bleachers made their way down to Lot 3. Bill Robinson was present as Eleanor's mentor and colleague, and *Life Magazine* sent over photojournalist Margaret Bourke-White to take photographs for an editorial spread on upcoming film productions. Several of her stunning photos, shot from a high vantage point, show a tiny Eleanor perched atop the winding row of massive drums. The number displays the excessive lengths to which MGM had gone to uphold their "bigger is better" credo; and, at the pinnacle of her skill, there was no one better than Eleanor to be placed on this literal high platform of tap, not even Fred Astaire.

Once the drums were in place and the covers were removed, a fearless Eleanor was hoisted up to the tallest one. There was no edge or railing on any of the drums, and her own feet were blocked from her view by her short, frilly skirt; this was the most dangerous dance Eleanor had ever attempted. Blanche was understandably worried as she watched from the crowd below. During production of Eleanor's first three films, Blanche had joined her at the studio every day, serving as her daughter's trusted companion. She mothered the cast and crew and often brought homemade cookies and snacks to set. By the time production began on *Rosalie,* Blanche only visited periodically, choosing to spend more time at home with her aging parents. This extravagant number, however, was one not to be missed, and that night her eyes were fixed anxiously on Eleanor.

With all in place, the production encountered an unanticipated problem. Fog from the nearby Pacific Ocean had rolled in, and the damp air made every surface slick and slippery. One of Albertina Rasch's dancers had already fallen on the stairs during the filming of their segment. As Eleanor stepped onto the drum, she nearly lost her footing. "I was like Sonja Henie up there," Eleanor recalled. "I took one step and I slid from here to there!"[14] The risk of falling from a sixteen-foot-high platform was not taken as seriously then as it would be today. Eddy and Bolger, "as a gag, had an ambulance out there and had Red Cross coats and bandages," Eleanor later recounted. "They said, 'Don't worry, Ellie. We're down here if you need us!'"[15] By this time, it was nearly midnight when she tried out a few steps. But, after cautiously jumping from drum to drum, the woman who never showed fear or hesitation suddenly announced to director Van Dyke, "I can't do it."[16]

Van Dyke called for a meal break until 1:00 a.m., and the whole crowd of extras was herded off to the food tent. As the cast ate, the crew applied a layer of cork to all the drum tops, hoping this would provide enough traction. Every minute was important. Due to the excessive amount of lighting needed for the night shoots, $30,000 worth of electricity would ultimately be consumed, and the production number was costing $300 a minute due to the number of crew and cast involved.

When Eleanor tried out the new surface, it was not perfect, but much better. "I had to learn to do a line of turns down those drums . . . but not break the flow of the turns. I could have done that number better," she recalled. "But I was just holding back a little bit because I was afraid of the dew."[17]

Another problem arose; at the bottom of the drums, as she turned, she was to break through a long row of hoops, each covered with a thin piece of plastic film. On the first take, she only made it through a third of the hoops before the camera ran out of film. Because they were shooting on a location far from the main prop department, the crew chose to use what was handy to recover the broken hoops. It proved to be a much thicker plastic than the original. When Eleanor hit the new plastic film, it held firm and bounced her right off the unbreakable surface, sending her "flying through the air," as she recalled. In the final cut, the taped plastic film used on some of the hoops during retakes is clearly visible.

Finally, after four nights of shooting with a total of nine cameras until about 2:00 a.m., the number was complete. All that remained was for Eleanor to dub the taps. In order to correctly time the distance of jumping from drum to drum, some of the drums had to be brought into the sound room. The entire dubbing process required two eight-hour days to complete.

Van Dyke chose to break up the intense week of shooting by holding one of his famous parties for the cast and crew. On October 16, he and his wife, Ruth (daughter of MGM's Eddie Mannix), hosted the event at their Brentwood home. Louis B. Mayer and Ida Koverman also joined, along with film editor Blanche Sewell, Albertina Rasch, Merrill Pye, and other personnel working on the production. Blanche, Nelson's mother, Isabel, and Van Dyke's mother, Laura, were there as well to celebrate their talented children.

Eleanor's final number in *Rosalie*, "Who Knows,"[18] finds her disguised as a cadet, scouring West Point in search of Dick Thorpe. To prove her identity, she is asked to lead the group in a marching drill. For authenticity, she was trained by actual West Point cadets (who also appeared in the number) in the use of command calls and marching technique.

Sid Luft, who was on set with Eleanor and Blanche, was used as one of the leaning cadets lined up behind Eleanor in her solo. He remembered, "Our shoes were nailed to the floor to facilitate a type of Raggedy Ann-doll movement as we bent in different directions."[19] Luft had befriended the Heasley twins, Jack and Robert, who were also in the chorus. The talented duo were skilled ice skaters who appeared in many films with Sonja Henie. Luft found the handsome pair great cohorts when making the rounds of Hollywood parties.

Luft didn't appear to be attracted by work as an actor, but to try to steer him into viable employment, Eleanor and Blanche urged him to look into camerawork as a career. "Eleanor thought this was the road up in the industry, as moviemaking was such an inside business," he recalled. But at twenty-one, Luft wasn't as interested in steady work as he was in having fun. He quickly grew bored with the long days on the set and started a floating crap game around the lot. When the game was discovered, he was thrown off the lot and barred from the studio.

This was the third picture in which Eleanor wore men's garb for a dance number. While a top hat and tails had begun to be known as her trademark, the cadet's uniform was somewhat of a departure. It inspired another "gag" from practical joker Nelson Eddy. During a break in filming the number, Nelson took a blindfolded Eleanor for a walk around the lot. When he let her go and she removed the blindfold, she found herself in the men's room. "Did I get out of there fast!" she recalled.[20]

Rosalie and Dick are married in a massive art deco wedding scene finale that features a giant stylized pipe organ, flanked by long rows of bridesmaids, guards, and soldiers. After the final scene was shot, Eleanor took advantage of her costume to shoot one of her humorous home movies. "I'd never had a wedding gown on before, and I had scenes with the director on bended knee, proposing, and Nelson Eddy making tragic love." Even the prop boy and other crew took part in the scene. Noticing Merrill Pye watching the antics nearby, she finally invited him over to do the honor of placing the ring on her finger. In an unusually serious mood, Pye complied. "He was so convincing, I told him he should have been an actor," Eleanor said.[21]

The studio held a private preview of *Rosalie* for military personnel in Pomona, California, on November 26, after which both Army and Navy officials gave their final approval. A sneak preview for the public was screened at the Westwood Village Theatre in Los Angeles on December 16, attended by Eleanor, Nelson Eddy, and other cast members. Child actor Tommy Bond, also appearing in the *Our Gang* comedies on the MGM lot, had a featured part in the film as Mickey the mascot. Tommy fondly remembered that when the two stars arrived and sat in the theater next to him and his mother, Eleanor pulled him up to sit on her and Nelson's laps. "I have only the highest admiration for that sweet, warm lady," he recalled. "She was a hard worker and a great dancer."[22]

The day before the film premiered, December 23, 1937, Eleanor was the fortieth honoree at one of Hollywood's most iconic locations; she placed her footprints and handprints in cement at the plaza in front of Grauman's Chinese Theatre on Hollywood Boulevard. She inscribed her section, "To Sid (Grauman), You're 'Taps' with me, Eleanor Powell." Hers was the most unusual footprint of all, complete with metal taps embedded in the cement. Fred Astaire was honored a few months later, on February 4, 1938.

The same day, the *Rosalie* cast appeared in a special edition of *Good News of 1938. Good News,* produced by MGM and sponsored by Maxwell House Coffee, was a popular radio program that ran from 1937 through 1940. The shows provided the audiences with a behind-the-scenes glimpse of Hollywood life while promoting the release of MGM's latest films. In this case, the listeners joined the "party" in progress on the MGM lot, held to celebrate the upcoming premiere of *Rosalie*. The show was broadcast live from Studio 30; Louis B. Mayer acted as host for the evening and Jimmy Stewart as emcee. Nelson Eddy, Eleanor Powell, Frank Morgan, Ray Bolger, and Ilona Massey each made an appearance alongside series regulars Fanny Brice (as Baby Snooks), Alan Reed (Lancelot "Daddy" Higgins), and Meredith Willson and his studio orchestra. Songs from *Rosalie* were featured—the most notable being the baritone–tap duet between Nelson and Eleanor.

MGM had ultimately put an incredible $2 million into the making of *Rosalie* ($200,000 was spent on the drum dance sequence alone), and the expense is clearly visible in the overly opulent sets, all-star cast, and new score from Cole Porter. Unfortunately, it did not prove to be a good investment. Reviews were dismal, signaling that enough was enough. Audiences no longer wanted to be transported so far from reality. "In one of the most pretentious demonstrations of sheer mass and weight since the last Navy games, Metro-Goldwyn-Mayer brings forth nothing more impressive than another musical," said the *New York Times*. "Eleanor Powell tap dances . . . among sets entirely divorced from reality."[23] "The story and its variously happy items seem profoundly lost in the gargantuan settings," said another.[24] Bringing the film out on Christmas Eve was a good strategic move, in keeping with the fairy tale quality of the sets. Despite poor reviews, *Rosalie* still ranked among the top twenty box office films of the year.

Eleanor was long overdue for a vacation, and since she was invited to perform at President Roosevelt's Birthday Ball in January, she decided to travel to New York by ship instead of train. On Christmas Day, Blanche and Sid Luft left with her for a two-week voyage on the SS *Santa Paula,* which would sail through the Panama Canal and make stops in Mexico, Guatemala, and Havana, Cuba, before docking in New York. Luft had been staying with Blanche and Eleanor at the Bedford Drive house. Though he later admitted to being infatuated with Eleanor, she still thought of him as a younger brother. Because he had been brought up by a stylish and fashionable mother who loved to dance, he was an excellent ballroom dancer. Having a handsome dance partner who knew how to do all the Latin dances came in very handy for Eleanor and Blanche on the cruise, and it helped Eleanor fend off any unwanted attention from male admirers.

In pre-Castro Havana, shore trips included visits to supper clubs with music and floor shows. Although Luft referred to the trip as "all perfume and stars over Havana" where they "drank and ate at the lavish casinos with Meyer Lansky and other celebrities,"[25] it was not all leisure. Eleanor was met at each stop by the MGM publicity department, who arranged interviews for her. During a stop in Cristobal in the Canal Zone, she signed autographs for hours and promoted *Rosalie* by singing a song from the film on deck. But even the grueling obligatory duties were a thrill to her, such as when she found hundreds of children waiting for the boat in Colombia, crying "We want Eleanor!" She posed for pictures all day and did dance steps for the crowd in between shots. Even people of the humblest professions recognized her. In Guatemala, a diver in a boat kept staring at Eleanor. After a moment of sudden recognition, he pointed excitedly and exclaimed, "You!" as he launched into a rhythmic shuffling of his feet. In Havana, she was asked by a Cuban man whether she drank, smoked, or gambled. When she denied all three, he then said, "Okay, I'll marry you."[26]

When the ship docked in New York on January 12, she was again met by a crowd of reporters, but they were shocked to discover a handsome young male had traveled with her party. While Eleanor quickly referred to Luft as her secretary, gossip columns were filled with photos of Luft accompanied by innuendo-filled captions: "Nice Work If You Can Get It" and "He-Men Secretaries Best, Says Eleanor Powell." Reporters went wild with both subtle and obvious speculations, stating, "At Havana, young Mr. Luft made the cheeks of the caballeros blanche with envy as he rumbaed with Eleanor."[27]

But as soon as news of the unapproved escort reached MGM, various conflicting explanations began to flood in. One paper reported that Luft was sent over to Eleanor in Los Angeles by an employment agency. Columnist Dan Walker suggested, "Eleanor Powell will crack down on MGM's cheap and fluky publicity stunts if she is wise. The latest being her arrival on a boat from California with a male 'secretary,' one Sidney Luft, who is being secretly groomed by MGM as a screen possibility."[28] By this time, it was clear that MGM had stepped in twice with alternate stories given to the press to divert from any perception of loose morals on Eleanor's part. Photos taken of Eleanor dancing a few days later at Manhattan's La Conga nightclub with a dapper, tuxedo-clad Luft were popping up in all the papers. But within a week, all discussion of male secretaries and publicity stunts had been suitably silenced.

On January 22, Eleanor made an appearance at a benefit for the Actors Fund. George M. Cohan was on the bill and reportedly stopped the show, but newspapers also praised the tap dance duet by Eleanor Powell and Bill Robinson as one of the high spots of the evening. Their "Tap Shim Sham Shimmy" number intrigued even those waiting in the wings, who edged their way onto the stage to better see what was going on. A burst of applause from the audience greeted Robinson as he announced that on May 25, he would be sixty years old.

A few days later, Luft stayed on in New York as Eleanor and Blanche continued to Washington, DC, where Eleanor was to participate in several events in connection with President Roosevelt's Birthday Ball. Her first scheduled event was a reception and luncheon on Thursday, January 27, where she and Ray Bolger were introduced to Lady Nancy Astor, the wealthy American who had gained her title by marrying into British aristocracy. She was the first woman to become a Member of Parliament in the House of Commons. The event was hosted by all-star football player Carter Barron, and other attendees included Fredric March, ballet dancer Vera Zorina, Joe E. Brown, Italian dancer Maria Gambarelli, and Janet Gaynor. Lady Astor and Eleanor then visited the Senate, where deliberations were paused for twenty minutes in order to welcome them.

The president's birthday balls took place on January 29, with the dual purpose of celebrating Franklin D. Roosevelt's fifty-sixth birthday and raising funds in the fight against infantile paralysis. There were seven charity birthday balls in all; Eleanor Roosevelt visited each and cut the big birthday cake at the last one.

The company attended a luncheon hosted by Mrs. Roosevelt at the White House on the afternoon of the twenty-ninth. Fearing the afternoon would be rather stiff and polite, Eleanor was relieved when she arrived and heard Jimmy Roosevelt's booming "El!" as he called out in greeting. She had known both Roosevelt sons, Franklin and James, for six years, dating back to her shows at Casino de Paree in New York. Of Franklin, Eleanor commented, "He's full of swing, and if he wasn't a Roosevelt, he'd be a saxophone player." Mrs. Roosevelt later recounted for *Photoplay*: "Pretty Eleanor Powell made two of my daughters-in-law extremely jealous . . . and I noticed that my boys were extremely anxious to act as guides through the White House. . . . Franklin Junior remark[ed], 'We had better check on our history, Mother. We are not really sure that the stories we have told about the rooms are entirely correct.'"[29]

Later, in the president's private sitting room, a nervous Eleanor sat with the entire Roosevelt family. The family's humorous bantering quickly put her at ease. At one point, the president turned to her and said, "I never saw anyone dance with the spirit you put into it. After seeing you in a picture I've always felt just like getting up and dancing myself." Eleanor felt it was "the greatest compliment . . . from the greatest man." During her visits to the White House, Eleanor enjoyed interacting with everyone in the household. Later, in a visit to the kitchens she delighted the staff with an impromptu tap dance after they had waited patiently to meet her.[30]

In a police-escorted motorcade, Eleanor was accompanied to Baltimore by Senator George L. Radcliffe, chairman of the general committee for the celebration. The ball at the Fifth Regiment Armory was the largest and most prestigious of the night, with many Washington elites in attendance. Eleanor and orchestra leader Vincent Lopez were the principal attractions of the evening. The local newspapers painted a vivid picture of her popularity: "After she finally reached her box, the crowd surged forward, almost tearing down the railing in an effort to touch the star, brandishing autograph books and focusing small cameras." Astounded, Eleanor remarked, "I never saw anything like this in my life. . . . I'm just one of the mob who got a lucky break."[31] The estimated crowd of twelve thousand people made such a commotion when she got onstage that she could not be introduced, nor even heard through the PA system. She simply blew a kiss and went into her dance.

Publicizing her original "Chuck-a-Boom" dance step, she invited six young people who had been dancing the Big Apple to get up onstage with her, and she taught them her dance. While the crowds were still clamoring for more, studio representatives joined with the police to lead Eleanor and her mother out to the waiting car. Another mob converged as she left. The night finished up with the Golden Plate Breakfast at 3:00 a.m., and she recalled: "When it was over, the orchestra played a waltz, and I danced down a line of 200 officers. It was a beautiful end of a beautiful time."[32]

Back in New York, Eleanor made a "barnstorming" tour of the Manhattan area, with personal appearances in six theaters. At around 7:30 p.m., she began at the Pitkin Theater and then jumped to others on the Loew's circuit: the Kings, Metropolitan, Commodore, Orpheum, and State theaters, all in one night. At the Pitkin, there was a group of high school students who carried a banner with her name on it. "People at those houses were old friends," she remembered. "Because I played there as a kid, they felt they had put me in pictures."[33] In truth, Eleanor was as appreciative of her audiences as they were of her.

11

Fulfilling Dreams

Despite the poor reception of *Rosalie,* MGM had not yet abandoned their penchant for a yearly big-budget musical. In her February 24, 1938, column, Louella Parsons announced MGM's plans for a new film for Eleanor, based on the *Broadway Melody* series. *Hollywood Melody* would feature co-stars George Murphy, Judy Garland, Billie Burke, and Frank Morgan. Parsons lamented to her readers: "Eleanor Powell, one of the nicest girls in Hollywood, has had a really bad break on the screen. *Rosalie* was not up to expectations, and it is important now for the studio to get her a good picture if she is to continue at the top."[1]

No sooner had Parsons given her scoop than *Hollywood Melody* reverted to the Great White Way, and *Broadway Melody of 1939* (with essentially the same all-star cast) was announced as the next big extravaganza. *Honolulu* was also included in a list of big-scale productions MGM planned for the year.

In the month of March, Eleanor would experience a deep, personal loss. On the morning of the seventeenth, her grandmother died at home of a heart attack. She was only sixty-four. Though she hadn't been in the best of health, it nevertheless was a shock to the family. While Blanche was Eleanor's best friend and confidante, it was always her frank and outspoken grandmother who kept her grounded. "I would have grown up to be a very overbearing, conceited thing without [her]," she said. The loss had a deep impact, but her grandmother's guidance resonated as she slowly returned to her normal routine.

MGM had renewed her contract and she prepared to return to work. Her next film would now be *Lucky Star*. Even though production had not yet started, she was already at work on her new dance routines. It was always challenging to come up with something new and fresh, and Eleanor looked for inspiration from every aspect of her life. At night she would often wake up and jot down ideas for new dances as they came to her in dreams, something she had in common with Fred Astaire.

Preparation began on production #1048, alternately called *Honolulu* and *Lucky Star*. The project had already undergone several iterations and was now set in the Hawaiian Islands. A destination only the wealthy could afford in the late 1930s, it held a special fascination for mainland audiences. Magazine spreads showed photos of Shirley Temple vacationing on Hawaiian beaches with her family. Jeanette MacDonald and Gene Raymond chose the romantic location for their honeymoon in 1937. George Burns and Gracie Allen had also recently returned from a trip to the islands. By 1938, Hawaii had become a popular setting for movies. At the same time *Honolulu* was in production at MGM, 20th Century-Fox was making *Charlie Chan in Honolulu*.

In July 1937, trade papers carried the news that Arthur Freed had been promoted to producer, and *Honolulu* would be his first assignment. It would star the seventeen-year-old singer from the Chicago opera, Betty Jaynes, who had been under contract to Metro-Goldwyn-Mayer for the last six months. Jaynes would play opposite Robert Taylor, with Una Merkel and Buddy Ebsen in the supporting cast. The film would undergo many changes over the following months. Jack Cummings took the place of Arthur Freed, who would ultimately debut his career as producer with the film *Babes in Arms*. Betty Jaynes ended up with a small role in another film, playing Jeanette MacDonald's understudy in *Sweethearts*, as did Douglas McPhail, who played the role of understudy to Nelson Eddy. The two were later set to perform an imitation of MacDonald and Eddy at the costume ball in *Honolulu*, but this segment was cut. In the final version, Jaynes, the originally intended star, can be spotted as a background player with McPhail, wearing their costumes from *Sweethearts*.

Eleanor began her twelve-week allotted time to devise new dances for the film, one of which was an impersonation of Bill Robinson. MGM sent a letter to 20th Century-Fox on April 11, requesting permission to use his name in *Lucky Star*. Robinson's studio responded favorably, with one condition. As they were currently working on a film entitled *My Lucky Star* with Sonja Henie, they expressed concern over the similar title. MGM complied, and the film became definitively known as *Honolulu*.

Weeks dragged on with no real progress in casting. Finally, by May 20, Allan Jones was set as the leading man. Una Merkel and Helen Troy were listed as the supporting cast. No director had been named for the film yet.

On June 18, Eleanor began filming her musical numbers, starting with "Got a Pair of New Shoes." Since the number had been cut from *Broadway Melody of 1938,* she decided to update it for *Honolulu.* Taking place in a nightclub, the first part of the number is set to a song written for her by Sigmund Romberg and Gus Kahn, "Where's the Girl?" Wearing a short, beaded costume, Eleanor begins with a soft shoe dance, picking up the pace as the music segues into the upbeat "Got a Pair of New Shoes." Unfortunately, the number was again cut. In the 1940s, the dance was partially salvaged and appeared in the film *The Great Morgan,* initially released only in the United Kingdom. Years later, when the full soundtrack was discovered, a reconstructed version with a portion of the dubbed taps appeared on YouTube.

Ever eager to affirm its industry status, in 1938, MGM set the very lofty goal of producing fifty-two films within one year. This ambitious overload of productions ended up creating a backlog, which in turn caused multiple delays in the production schedule. *Honolulu,* which was to have begun production mid-July, was delayed until mid-August, held up by what the studio simply termed a "production situation" that would continue for months. In the meantime, MGM continued to announce new vehicles for its stars. The latest to appear in the trades was *Ziegfeld Girl,* with Joan Crawford, Virginia Bruce, Eleanor Powell, and Margaret Sullavan.

Even though she was still working six hours a day on her routines and taking voice lessons, *Honolulu*'s slow production pace allowed Eleanor to indulge herself in a little fantasy. She had some time on her hands before filming began, so she took a break from her rehearsals to visit Luise Rainer and Fernand Gravet on the neighboring set of *The Great Waltz.* Enthralled by the elaborate waltz scene staged by Albertina Rasch, she arranged to switch places with one of the chorus girls. Her partner, dancer Louis Hightower, didn't quite realize what had occurred until the next take, when he was shocked to notice that his partner was Eleanor Powell. Hightower was an experienced chorus dancer (he had even been used as the movement model for Prince Charming in Disney's animated *Snow White*), so he took it all in stride. They continued the charade for about an hour, giving Marsha Kent, the chorus girl who had lent her the costume, a welcome chance to rest.

In mid-September, production was pushed back again to late October. In the interim, Eleanor threw a party for the *Honolulu* crew at her house. From her earliest days at the studio, she greatly valued her production team and considered them friends. She wanted to acknowledge the work that they had already done on her dance sequences. The afternoon featured a picnic lunch,

Hawaiian melodies, and ice cream in the form of MGM mascot Leo the Lion. Of course, the party would not be complete without a huge cake. This one was adorned with the inscription "For Powell's MGM Gang."

While the cast was still being finalized, the MGM publicity department got to work. To lend a touch of authenticity to the film, Kealoha Holt, a native Hawaiian girl (known in Hawaii as Alice Kealohapau'ole Holt), was hired. As Miss Kauai, Kealoha had also earned the title of Queen of the Hula in an inter-island hula contest; she won a trip to Hollywood and a chance to dance in the film. With no Hollywood aspirations, she wisely intended to use the money she earned on the film to put herself through business school. On October 12, Holt arrived in San Francisco by ocean liner. Dressed in full native costume for publicity shots, she was greeted by MGM's PR department.

Promotions continued the following day when Eleanor appeared on the *Good News of 1939* radio program along with Lionel Barrymore, Frank Morgan, Fanny Brice, Robert Young, and Allan Jones. She was introduced by Robert Young, and she gave an exciting demonstration of her skill. After she performed a waltz tap and a lightning-fast tap number to "Limehouse Blues," she then sang and danced in a fun number with Frank Morgan. During the broadcast, neither Allan Jones nor Robert Young was mentioned in the context of *Honolulu,* but Young was announced as the leading man the following day. Young, best known today for the iconic television show *Father Knows Best,* as well as his seven seasons as the kindly doctor in *Marcus Welby, M.D.,* started his career at MGM in 1931. A prolific and reliable actor with many films under his belt, he had a reputation for being pleasant to work with. Young later joked that he got most of his parts only after other A-list actors turned them down.

Rarely has a film seen such an array of would-be leading men. Robert Taylor, Allan Jones, Robert Montgomery, George Murphy, and Robert Young were all considered for the part before the final selection was made. Later, Eleanor alluded to some of the development issues the film faced while pre-production dragged on for over six months. "The picture was intended to be a straight drama starring Robert Taylor. Then somebody changed his mind and decided to make it a musical. . . . Finally, the script was ready, and they put me in it, with Allan Jones. They took some publicity stills of us, and we were about ready to go to work, when they told me that Allan was out. I never did understand why."[2]

Jones had repeatedly been disappointed in his casting assignments and had lost out to Nelson Eddy on several roles he wanted. Growing more and more dissatisfied with his experience at MGM, he felt he would be happier at another studio. His contract was terminated soon after, and he moved on to Paramount.

Comedians George Burns and Gracie Allen had now been added to the cast. Edward Buzzell was selected as director, and production was finally slated to start. Written by Herbert Fields and Frank Partos, the zany plot features look-alikes, music, and dance, set against the exotic backdrop of the Hawaiian Islands. Pineapple plantation owner George Smith from Honolulu (Robert Young) is mistaken for movie star Brooks Mason (also played by Robert Young) at the premiere of his latest film. Mobbed by fans, Smith ends up in the hospital. When Mason discovers the mix-up, he offers to switch places with his look-alike, hoping to take a long-awaited vacation in Hawaii. George Smith agrees, looking forward to the excitement of taking Mason's place in New York on a personal appearance tour arranged by his agent, Duffy (George Burns).

On the boat to Hawaii, Brooks Mason (disguised as George Smith) makes the acquaintance of Dorothy March (Eleanor Powell), a dancer traveling with her companion Millie De Grasse (Gracie Allen). He falls in love with Dorothy but is dismayed to learn that George Smith has a fiancée and, to make matters worse, is also wanted for embezzlement.

Meanwhile back in New York, George Smith's encounters with Mason's adoring fans land him repeatedly in the hospital. When George hears an announcement on a Hawaiian radio broadcast that Mason is about to marry his fiancée, Cecilia (Rita Johnson), he panics. George finally manages to convince Duffy that he is not Brooks Mason, and he arrives in Honolulu just in time to clear his name of the embezzlement charges and take Mason's place at the wedding. Dorothy forgives Mason, and they all happily celebrate at a luau.

Eleanor's first number takes place on board the deck of the ocean liner, re-created (with swimming pool) on Stage 19. Gracie Allen picks up her ukulele to sing the title song, "Honolulu," and Eleanor launches into an energetic number with a jump rope, flying down the deck as she jumps, taps, and spins. Her athleticism in the number prompted newspapers to liken her to a prize-fighter training for a championship fight. "Her rehearsal hall could be mistaken for a fighter's training camp. Rubbing lotions line the walls, the dance floor is roped off so that Miss Powell knows her stage space. It resembles a boxing ring. When she finishes her dance, she retires to a corner, sits on a chair and relaxes, while her legs and arms are rubbed. An attendant hands her a bottle of water, and another drapes a towel around her shoulders."[3] But the rigorous training was not without effect. Her close-ups for the number were shot before the dancing was filmed and in the time between the dance rehearsal and the actual filming of the numbers, she had lost fifteen pounds. The weight loss made it difficult to match up the close-ups.

Dancing with a jump rope presented its own challenges. On one occasion, Eleanor got her skirt so tangled up in the rope that director Eddie Buzzell had to stop the cameras and retake the number from the beginning. Good-natured Gracie Allen quipped, "I guess I'll have to do it over again. We've got to be patient with these beginners."[4]

On board ship, the passengers attend the "come as your favorite movie star" evening. The costume ball gave Eleanor the opportunity to do an interpretation of her mentor. Introduced as "the great Bill Robinson, the King of Harlem," she appears in blackface. The demeaning origins of the practice—cruel stereotypes popular in minstrel shows of the 1800s—make the number far from politically correct today. The dark makeup reflects the attitude still prevalent in the 1930s, but the dance is a flawless recreation of Robinson's steps and style. It is unknown whether Eleanor had any say in the decision to wear blackface, but it is clear she meant it only as an honor to her friend. Robinson sanctioned the tribute and personally taught Eleanor the choreography of his famous stair dance. The set was innovative, with a surprising set of stairs that popped up from the floor as she danced.

Robert Young enjoyed his dual role in the film, and when he wasn't on camera, he was on the sidelines watching Eleanor dance. "I didn't miss a tap step through the whole picture," he told an interviewer. "When she taps, I can't keep my feet quiet. You can't listen to Eleanor Powell tap and keep your feet planted, not if you're human."[5]

Like *Rosalie, Honolulu* did not have a finale. Instead, the largest production number was incorporated earlier in the story, set in a Hawaiian nightclub. Eleanor dances a traditional Hawaiian hula, followed by her own jazzy tap version.

MGM engaged Andy Iona and His Islanders, a Hawaiian musical troupe popular on the mainland who incorporated elements of the traditional island sound, such as steel guitar, with swing. While the dancers wore grass skirts, Eleanor's hula outfit had to be specially tailored to complement her dancing. Hers was made of a silver-beaded fringe, designed to flow with her movements.

Despite certain disparaging comments over the years that Eleanor Powell had little sex appeal, she managed to spark a minor uproar in her revealing hula costume. The Hays Office censored a good number of her publicity photos, deeming them too steamy for public consumption. Her original hula skirt was modified. To avoid showing too much midriff, extra fabric was added to raise the waistline. Whether it was the suggestiveness of the photos or that she was simply showing too much leg, she never did grasp what the objections were about.

Eleanor learned the hula from native Hawaiians, and she was quick to admit that it was one of the toughest dances she had ever attempted to master. She brought in three professionals to teach her. To learn their movements, she observed them from all angles. "I thought it would be easy. . . . I wanted to do it right, so I got some native dancers . . . and they nearly killed me. You've got to stand absolutely straight. Then you've got to bend your knees and keep them bent while you dance."[6] After a few hours of practicing these unfamiliar movements, she joked that she was ready for the wheelchair. True to her perfectionist nature, she had all her dances photographed in slow motion. Then, each night, using a projector installed in her home, she would study her technique and begin practicing her steps all over again.

The nationwide release of *Honolulu* was scheduled for February 3, 1939. Hawaiian locals were very proud to learn that the world premiere would be held at the Waikiki Theater the day before, and a special print was rushed to them for the occasion. Before the film, Kealoha Holt and Rita Lum Ho (Miss Maui) joined the festivities on a special radio broadcast heard throughout the territory. This was the first time that Honolulu would host a world premiere. In an era when Hawaii saw only a fraction of the tourism it does today, the local papers excitedly claimed that Honolulu would reap great benefit from the awareness created from the promotion of the picture.

After viewing the picture, however, the enthusiasm quickly soured when the locals took offense at Eleanor's interpretation of the hula. Eleanor herself had predicted this when she told a reporter, "I get over to the *Honolulu* set and do the hula with a lot of new taps that no Hawaiian ever heard of and will probably die of chagrin when he does. I look for the islands to start a mutiny after I get through with a grass skirt."[7] She was not entirely wrong. Outraged, the Hawaiian Society called her tap version of the hula "sacrilegious," and they planned to meet to "adopt resolutions against Miss Powell's dance, which they declared was no more a hula than the Black Bottom or the Big Apple."[8] They found her movements too rapid; true hula body movements should be slow, symbolizing trees moving in the wind. "We wouldn't mind it so much," said Mr. Allen of the Hawaiian Society, "if the whole thing had been a burlesque. But to have the Hawaiian scenes correct, to have the music the best of the Hawaiian type and to have the whole picture correct except for this one misinterpretation of one of the most highly revered ceremonials of the islands—it's bad." Others simply did not understand what the fuss was about, as this was clearly a specialty tap version and not meant to be the real hula. Nevertheless, Eleanor was hurt by the negative reaction.

In August, Eleanor took a day off from filming to spend the day posing for miniature silver statues of herself. These would be presented to the students of the Dancing Troupes of America, who had named her their honorary president. Her interest in dance students had begun as a child when she led the baby classes, then continued years later when she was on the road doing vaudeville. She was asked to give dancing lessons to a group of children one morning before a performance in Baltimore. Enjoying the contact with young dancers, she did the same in Washington, Cincinnati, Kansas City, and all over the Midwest. "Clubs were formed, and today there are seventy-five Eleanor Powell clubs. I've sent photographs and written greetings to all of them. It makes me feel like the president of a huge class, and it also makes me very happy."[9] Now, as Grand Trouper, she began writing a monthly letter that appeared in the Young Dancer section of *Dance Magazine.*

Well into the filming of *Honolulu,* the production team realized that the comedy duo of George Burns and Gracie Allen didn't have a single scene together. Burns and Jack Cummings conferred, and Burns agreed to write a scene for the film. The next day, when Cummings asked to see what he had written, Burns had nothing to show. Lifting his hands with a shrug, he told him that they had worked something out, but it was impossible to put on paper. "'That doesn't make sense,' said Cummings. 'Well, neither does the scene,' replied Burns, who tried to explain that the lines and business were so hopelessly intermingled that it couldn't be explained. 'It's . . . well, it's just Gracie,' George concluded."[10]

A special connection developed between Eleanor and Andy Iona, which would continue after the film was released. She came to deeply respect the rich history of Hawaiian music and culture, and the experience of learning the hula was pivotal in her appreciation. As production came to a close, Iona gathered a company of 150 Hawaiians to perform a special show for the cast. Eleanor sat in a chair while each of the Hawaiians came to her, knelt, and presented her with a gift. Among the presents she received were ukuleles and fifteen leis of gardenias.

◉   ◉   ◉

The Bedford house had grown to be a true home to the Powell household, providing a sense of stability and becoming a joyous place for celebrations, gatherings, and parties. The door was always open to Eleanor's friends, old and new.

November was always a festive month, as both Eleanor and Blanche had birthdays near Thanksgiving. For Eleanor's twenty-sixth birthday, Blanche welcomed a small group to the house, where they dug into platters of fried chicken and all the trimmings of a sumptuous dinner. Blanche's elaborate cake design was a masterpiece. With the theme of Eleanor's journey up the ladder of success, the three-tiered cake had just that—a molasses candy ladder with a tiny figure in a full dress perched near the top rung. Various other candy scenes depicted Eleanor's climb: one for her work on the stage, a microphone for her radio days, and palm trees, cameras, and lights for her success in film. At the top, a theater marquee read: "Now appearing, London—?" referencing her dream of someday performing in Europe. The countless gifts, cards, wires, and letters, as well as forty-two baskets of flowers, were a far cry from her frugal childhood in Springfield or birthdays on the road during her vaudeville years.

On the twenty-fourth, they celebrated both Blanche's birthday and Thanksgiving Day by attending the UCLA–USC football game with friends. To end the "birthday season," they had an elaborate dinner at the Powell home for the birthday of Eleanor's secretary, Helene Stebbins, nicknamed Stebby. She, too, had a special cake, topped with a girl seated at a typewriter, surrounded by hundreds of letters made of peppermint.

While production on *Honolulu* was wrapping up in December, Eleanor regularly found time to attend the roller derby in Los Angeles. In the past year she had become friendly with skating stars Wes Aronson, Ivy "Poison Ivy" King, Buddy Atkinson, and Peggy O'Neal, who all visited her on the set of *Honolulu*. In her honor, Aronson's team renamed themselves "Eleanor Powell's Hollywood All-Stars," and rumors began to circulate of a romance brewing between Eleanor and Aronson.

Eleanor was joined at the events by such Hollywood celebrities as W. C. Fields, Eddie Cantor, George Burns, Gracie Allen, Jack Benny, Milton Berle, and Cary Grant, as they flocked to see the popular sport nearly every night. She was seen several times with Mickey Rooney. Eight years her junior, he was a studio buddy she frequently spent time with. One reporter acidly remarked that seeing tall Eleanor and the boyish five-foot-two actor together made her look like his maiden aunt.

Over the Christmas holidays, the Powell household welcomed a visit from Capt. Theodore Thomas ("Ted") Teague, an Army officer whom Blanche and Eleanor had befriended on board the SS *Santa Paula* during their trip to New York in January. While in town on leave, he enjoyed a pleasant dinner with them at their home. During the evening, upon learning that he was known as Tiger to his Army friends, Blanche and Eleanor ribbed him mercilessly. The press reported a strange story. Not willing to let them have the last laugh, on the final morning he was in town, the captain disappeared for a few hours. Sometime later, Eleanor opened the door to find a mysterious package. Discerning movement and hearing odd sounds emanating from inside, she opened it gingerly. She was surprised to find a baby tiger with an accompanying note that read, "Never tease a tiger."

In late January, Eleanor again headed east to attend the president's annual birthday ball. The only guest to receive a repeat invitation, Eleanor had been unable to confirm her attendance because *Honolulu* was still in retakes. A special request via phone from Eleanor Roosevelt to Mayer quickly secured her release from her MGM duties. She boarded the Super Chief, where, during an hour-and-a-half stopover in Chicago, she hosted a press conference at the Blackstone Hotel and cut a huge birthday cake dedicated to the president.

Shortly after her arrival in Washington on a rainy January 29, Eleanor attended a cocktail party at the Mayflower Hotel given by Representative Caroline O'Day to welcome the visiting stars. Among this year's guests were Mitzi Green, Ralph Bellamy, George Brent, Bruce Cabot, Erroll Flynn, Lili Damita, Jean Hersholt, and Paul Whiteman. Eleanor, in an eye-catching fuchsia purple ensemble with a wimple hat, stood out as a bright spot on the rainy day.

Although the birthday balls had been going on since 1934, the annual list of visitors had grown bigger and the festivities increasingly elaborate. With more Hollywood stars coming each year, the press joked that Hollywood was as empty as a ghost town during the season. Washington locals excitedly waited to get a glimpse of the movie stars. This year, twelve-year-old Nancy Server made the news when she went missing for twelve hours. Armed with her new autograph book, the spunky girl set off in search of famous folk. As Eleanor stepped off the train at Union Station early in the morning, Nancy was there to greet her with her little book. In search of other stars, in particular Errol Flynn, the child visited several hotels until she landed at the Mayflower, where she found most of the celebrities gathered for the congresswoman's reception. Still in search of the absent Flynn, she managed to find Eleanor's suite. "She watched photographers make pictures of Miss Powell, then the star kissed her and gave her another autograph. 'That was for my mother,' the little girl explained." In the meantime, the frantic mother had been searching high and low and, when the girl finally returned home at 7:15 p.m., was much too relieved to scold her. Nancy recounted her adventure: "Eleanor Powell was awful nice. She kissed me. I liked her best of all, and her hair is so pretty and curly."[11]

The presidential program was much the same as that of the previous year. The next day the group of stars attended the luncheon at the White House, where Mrs. Roosevelt asked Eleanor to lead the tour afterward. By now she was so familiar with the landmark home that the First Lady considered her almost one of the family. Then Eleanor was again whisked off to Baltimore to attend a tea at the Belvedere Hotel, followed by a small dinner given by Senator Radcliffe, again chairman of the committee. As the stars made their rounds before arriving at the final destination of the evening, it was noted that Eleanor Powell and Mitzi Green had danced and sung fifteen times within three hours, never in the same spot twice. Eleanor also carved some spare time from her full schedule to make a stop at the Children's Hospital. All in all, she had given a total of forty-three speeches during her three-day stay in Washington.

Joining in the benefit to raise funds to fight infantile paralysis, Eleanor was again the guest of honor at the Armory Ball, assisted by Ben Blue and Helen Morgan. Despite bad weather, over fifteen thousand packed the venue from 8:00 p.m. until midnight—a diverse crowd dressed in evening garb, military uniforms, and even everyday clothes. "Young people of several nationalities, members of youth groups of Baltimore's foreign colonies, came in the costume of their ancestral lands and gave folk dances during the intermission."[12] Those who did not come to dance enjoyed watching the festivities from their boxes. Eleanor performed one of her numbers from *Honolulu* and sang an encore.

Honolulu premiered on February 3, 1939, over a year since the release of her last film. The gap had given the public sufficient time to recover from the overblown ambitions of *Rosalie,* and they turned out in large numbers to see her again.

While *Variety* considered *Honolulu* a fairly amusing comedy with attractive stars, they found the story unsteady and slow. The film received a positive response from film exhibitors across the country, however, and did well at the box office. One exhibitor declared that, after Eleanor's all-too-long absence from the screen, her dancing was better than ever. Another, from the small town of Lebanon, Kansas, praised her performance as Bill Robinson as one of her best, echoing the sentiment of most reviewers, who thought it the finest number in the film. Another declared that, after *The Great Waltz* and *Idiots' Delight,* it was a relief to show a film like *Honolulu*. Indeed, by comparison, *Honolulu* was an unpretentious and enjoyable comedy romp, showcasing three of Eleanor's most unusual dance numbers.

Back in Los Angeles, on February 9, Eleanor joined the cast members from *Honolulu* for *Good News of 1939*. Starring Eleanor and Robert Young, the broadcast opened with a medley of music from the film, followed by a rhyming dialogue among composer Meredith Willson, Young, and Eleanor. Guest Tony Martin sang "This Night Will Be My Souvenir" from the film, followed by Fanny Brice's Baby Snooks sketch, a regular feature of all the *Good News* series. Other guests included the film's composer Harry Warren and Andy Iona and his band. Eleanor and Robert Young joined series regular Frank Morgan for a comedy sketch set forth in rhyme, and Eleanor performed her tap hula.

Eleanor gave a final Hawaiian-themed party for her friends, including Andy Iona and his group, George E. Stoll from the MGM music department, and pianist Walter Ruick. Eleanor described the party in detail in her Young Dancer column for *Dance Magazine*. Once again, a specialty cake was a popular feature. "Each guest received a lei as he entered, just to put us all in proper Hawaiian spirit. We had our dinner served on . . . table(s) decorated in Hawaiian style, and for dessert, we had the most wonderful cake. . . . On top were little dolls, dressed to represent the boys in the band. In the center was a girl with red hair in a fringed hula skirt, and at one corner, a tiny cameraman was taking a picture of the scene with his licorice camera. The entire cake was surrounded with candy leis."[13]

After dinner, Eleanor pulled out her tap mat and everybody in the party took a turn at trying to hula. It was a memorable and celebratory end to the production for Eleanor and the cast and crew.

For the first time during her tenure at the studio, MGM decided to send Eleanor on a five-city personal appearance tour. To promote the film, Eleanor and Andy Iona and His Islanders would perform multiple shows a day with a sampling of numbers from *Honolulu*. Her contract was modified to guarantee her the same weekly salary she earned working at the studio. Her pianist, Chris Schonberg, would accompany her as music director. In June, two films awaited her upon her return—*Broadway Melody of 1940* and *The Dancing Co-Ed*.

The pairing of Eleanor and Fred Astaire in a film had been anticipated by eager audiences ever since her rise to fame in *Broadway Melody of 1936*. MGM was finally able to secure Astaire in a deal for *Broadway Melody of 1940*. He officially signed for the film in early April. Eleanor would be his first dance partner since Ginger Rogers. But while Astaire's on-screen partnership with Ginger Rogers was a match of chemistry, the impending pairing with Eleanor was always about technique—like scheduling a friendly match between two championship prize fighters or a paint-off between Da Vinci and Rembrandt. Everyone wanted to see the result of the pairing of this masterful twosome.

Before Eleanor left for New York, the studio arranged an important meeting to introduce the two stars. The first order of business was to assure their physical compatibility. Mayer arranged for a morning meeting in Mervyn LeRoy's office. Eleanor was understandably nervous, as she idolized Astaire. She knew the main concern would be whether she was too tall for him. Eleanor arrived about forty-five minutes early and spent some time talking with LeRoy, in an attempt to calm her nerves. As she later told author John Kobal, "I said to Mervyn, 'I'm so nervous. I took a bath in Lux last night, hoping I'd shrink.'" Finally, Astaire and his agent, Leland Hayward, arrived and were waiting in the outer office. LeRoy quickly told Eleanor to hide. Instead of questioning the wisdom of the move, she rushed over and hid behind the door just before Astaire and Hayward entered the room. After a few minutes of small talk, Astaire mentioned how nervous he was to meet her. At that point, LeRoy called her out. "I slunk out and sat in that chair, red as a beet," she later remembered. "I was so embarrassed."

As they were politely making small talk, Mayer, Mannix, and several other executives walked in. Finally, the moment arrived. Eleanor and Astaire rose and stood back-to-back. At five foot eight, Fred was a mere two inches taller than Eleanor, but it was enough. The project was on.

On April 22, as Astaire and his wife headed to England, Eleanor took the train to New York City, where with Blanche, Stebby, and family friend Cookie, she checked into the Waldorf Astoria for the week. This tour would mark Eleanor's return to the vaudeville stage after a five-year absence. Visitors from around the country had come to the city to attend the World's Fair in nearby Flushing Meadows, Queens; its opening coincided with hers at the Loew's State Theater on the twenty-seventh. The exhibitors, anticipating a successful week, packed in the audiences for five shows a day. Eleanor occupied the final spot on the program. She had lost none of her skill onstage and captivated the audience with, as *Variety* put it, her "fine hoofing proficiency, a winning manner, rare showmanship, attractive looks, and becoming duds."[14] She opened with a long introduction, plugging her upcoming picture with Fred Astaire. After she charmed the audience with imitations of Katharine Hepburn and Jimmy Stewart, she followed with two dance numbers. She took advantage of the tour to use "Got a Pair of New Shoes," which had been cut from *Honolulu.*

Andy Iona and His Islanders played two songs during a quick costume change into her hula outfit for her final two dances from *Honolulu.* She added tacet sections to her tap hula, much like she had done in the Mademoiselle Arlette number in *Broadway Melody of 1936. Variety* noted that she held a packed house enthralled for a full twenty-eight minutes (nearly half of the show's entire running time and one of the longest acts of its kind). The audience was left clamoring for more as she took her bows and exited the stage. One evening during the New York run, audiences were in for a special treat when Bill Robinson, in town performing in *The Hot Mikado,* came to see the show. Spotting him in the audience, she called him onstage where he joined her for an impromptu dance.

At five (and sometimes six) shows a day, by midweek the schedule was already taking its toll on everybody. They were cramped in the small dressing room backstage, and the activity never stopped. In between shows Eleanor was asked to greet groups from local schools, and she rarely turned down a fan who showed up at the dressing room door. Unable to leave the theater for twelve hours at a stretch, she lived on sandwiches brought in from the outside. With the constant flurry of telephone calls and visitors, there was little time for rest. Her costume changes required almost as much energy as she expended onstage. After they peeled off a dress soaked in perspiration, Blanche and the ladies doused her with rubbing alcohol before they helped her slip into a dance belt and the tight-fitting hula skirt. She repeated this marathon several times a day. At the end of each show, she could hardly wait to plunge her aching and swollen feet into a bucket of ice water.

The following week the company moved on to Washington, DC, where they checked into the Mayflower Hotel. Eleanor's next appearance was at the Capitol Theatre. She was already a favorite in Washington before she went into films, and her popularity had only increased after her visits for the president's birthday balls. Crowds flocked to see her. On her second day in town, she was deluged with requests for radio and benefit appearances, and she even received an invitation to tea from Eleanor Roosevelt. But Eleanor was near exhaustion from her time in New York and, to guard her health, she declined all of them. The unfortunate and unfair result was that she earned, for the first time in her career, a reputation for being difficult.

On tour Blanche's greatest concern was for Eleanor's health. "I don't mean that Eleanor's health isn't good," Blanche explained. "I simply mean that I intend to keep it so, and that's a job when she's working. There will be no more of those collapses like the one she had during *At Home Abroad*. I am the one who got tough about this Washington date—all the extra shenanigans they want to put the child through." Blanche put her foot down and flat out declared that she would cancel the rest of Eleanor's tour unless her daughter was guaranteed some quiet and rest between shows.

The next stops on the tour were at the State Theatre in Cleveland, Ohio, followed by the Stanley in Pittsburgh, Pennsylvania, where "the mob couldn't get enough of her. She could have stayed on all day." The critics described her as "so gracious, spontaneous, personable, and eager to please. That combo of talent and personality . . . almost overshadows her spectacular hoofing. . . . She makes an earnest effort to ingratiate herself with the crowd, talking to the kids down front, tossing souvenirs at them." The reviewer remembered Eleanor from the last time she had played vaudeville at that same theater as a timid young lady who "balked at doing a couple lines in a skit when the principal fell ill. Talking scared her to death." He added, "That phase of her career has gone with the wind, however."[15]

Eleanor excitedly told the audience that MGM was hoping to get Artie Shaw's band for her next picture, *Broadway Melody of 1940*. Although negotiations were in place, the deal ultimately fell through, and the studio musicians were used instead.

The final stop on the tour was at the RKO Palace in Chicago on May 30. This engagement was not originally planned as part of the tour and, as the Palace was not on the Loew's circuit, her financial arrangements had to be modified. She no longer collected her studio fee, but instead, split the proceeds fifty–fifty with the theater. Considered one of the top billings at the theater, she was the only act besides Eddie Cantor and Mae West to have obtained those terms.

Before she made the trip back to Los Angeles, Eleanor had one additional piece of business in Chicago. Sid Luft was no longer welcome on the MGM lot, and his stint as her secretary had ended. Though his reckless actions had thwarted Eleanor's efforts to get him studio employment, she and Blanche had not given up on helping their problematic old friend—until, finally, they closed the book on their association. Luft had the idea to capitalize on the popular practice of car customization. He had spotted a large empty storefront on Rodeo Drive in Beverly Hills, not far from where his mother had moved her dress shop, and he had asked for Eleanor's help in opening the business. Eleanor had previously had some custom car work done herself—a pair of tiny tap shoes painted on her car with her initials—so she was well aware of the trendiness and interest in custom car work in the Hollywood community. She felt it was a viable venture that could provide Luft with a promising career. After putting up $5,000, she now had a vested interest in making sure her loan was repaid. So, while in Chicago, she made an appointment to meet with twenty-five-year-old automotive designer and customizer Alex Tremulis, who had done special work on another car she had seen.

"I met her at her hotel, and she explained her custom auto company operation," Tremulis recalled. "If I was interested, her public relations and partner in the company, Sid Luft, would be by the next day to fill in the details. She hired me to go to California and put Sid's business on a business basis."

Soon, with Eleanor's funds as seed money, Tremulis and Luft were catering to wealthy Beverly Hills residents who brought their Cadillacs and La Salles in for glamorizing. But it was a short-lived venture. Tremulis recalls that Luft, after finding a buyer for one of Eleanor's cars, ruined the deal. "He had taken the car, no insurance, and eight miles out of San Francisco he went off the road at 100 miles an hour. He totaled the car which ended his automotive business."[16] Tremulis, already noted in the field, would go on to design the stunning but ill-fated Tucker car for automotive visionary Preston Tucker in 1949, and would later be inducted into the Automotive Hall of Fame. But Luft seemed ultimately more concerned with fast living than hard work. Once the initial investment had been recouped, Eleanor and Blanche abandoned any further efforts to lend a hand in Luft's career. As he admitted, "I didn't see myself working for a weekly salary."[17] After his repeated abuse of her generosity, this would be the last time Eleanor would help Luft in any way.

Baby Eleanor in an early portrait sitting in 1913. Metro-Goldwyn-Mayer production and biography photographs, Margaret Herrick Library, Academy of Motion Picture Arts and Sciences. (hereafter AMPAS)

Eleanor's father, Clarence "Sonny" Powell, in Springfield. Scott Arno Collection

Seventeen-year-old
Blanche Torrey Powell
holds baby Eleanor.
Lisa Royère Collection

Eleanor as a young child. Lisa Royère Collection

Eleanor, c. 1920. Lisa Royère Collection

Eleanor as a snowflake for the H.P. Lane Studio recital in Springfield, 1922. Lisa Royère Collection

Right: Eleanor with Dorothy Warfield in 1925. *Top left*: The "Dot and El Sisters" on the Ambassador Hotel float in Atlantic City. *Bottom left*: Eleanor poses in the burnt orange costume sewn by her grandmother. AMPAS

Eleanor with the cerise fan after the glamorous makeover for her debut at Cafe
Martin in Atlantic City, 1926. AMPAS

Fourteen-year-old Eleanor strikes a dance pose. AMPAS

Portrait of Eleanor at fourteen. AMPAS

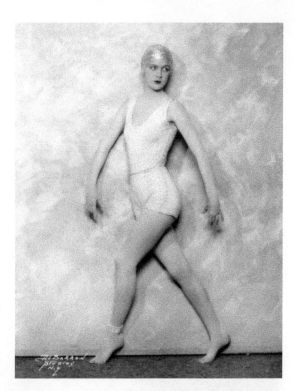

Newly arrived in New York, Eleanor loathed tap and clung to her lyrical acrobatic style in 1927. Lisa Royère Collection

Eleanor's risqué "showgirl" portraits from the De Mirjian Studio, 1928. Paula Broussard Collection

Photo session from the late 1920s. Paula Broussard Collection

A portrait from Eleanor's early Broadway years. Paula Broussard Collection

Left, Eleanor dancing in *George White's 1935 Scandals*. *Right*, Bill Robinson coaching Alice Faye and James Dunn on the film set. AMPAS

Eleanor in the gown she wore to the Mayfair Ball with L. B. Mayer, 1935. David Joiner Collection

"Sing before Breakfast" with Eleanor and Buddy and Vilma Ebsen in *Broadway Melody of 1936* (1935). D. Scott Calhoun Collection

Eleanor in the "You Are My Lucky Star" dream ballet, *Broadway Melody of 1936*. AMPAS

Robert Taylor serenades Eleanor, in her disguise as Mademoiselle La Belle Arlette, on the set of *Broadway Melody of 1936*. Lisa Royère Collection

Eleanor in her "Broadway Rhythm" costume with songwriters Arthur Freed and Nacio Herb Brown on the set of *Broadway Melody of 1936*. Lisa Royère Collection

Margaret Herrick Library, Metro-Goldwyn-Mayer Collection

Eleanor in "The Lady with the Tap" from *At Home Abroad*, 1935. *Upper row,* John Payne stands to the right of Eleanor. The Shubert Archive

Carrying her tap shoes and scripts, Eleanor waves to friends on the MGM lot. AMPAS

Eleanor performs "Rap Tap on Wood" in *Born to Dance* (1936). Lisa Royère Collection

Joan Crawford visits Eleanor on the set of *Born to Dance*. Lisa Royère Collection

The cast of *Born to Dance* in "Hey Babe Hey." *From left*: Frances Langford, Buddy Ebsen, Eleanor, James Stewart, Una Merkel, Sid Silvers. Lisa Royère Collection

Eleanor confers with director Roy Del Ruth on the set of *Born to Dance.* Paula Broussard Collection

James Stewart takes a photo of Eleanor during *Born to Dance*. Lisa Royère Collection

Filming a close-up in the big-budget finale "Swingin' the Jinx Away" from *Born to Dance*. Paula Broussard Collection

Virginia Bruce, Eleanor, and James Stewart at the *Hollywood Hotel* radio broadcast, November 13, 1936. Lisa Royère Collection

Eleanor and Blanche pose with a Packard roadster at MGM, 1936. D. Scott Calhoun Collection

Eleanor poses with the chorus boys of *Born to Dance*. AMPAS

Getting ready to rehearse in her studio bungalow. David Joiner Collection

From left: Blanche, Eleanor's Aunt Hattie Dougherty, grandmother Susie Torrey, Eleanor, and grandfather Harold Torrey. AMPAS

Eleanor, George Murphy, and Buddy Ebsen in "Follow in My Footsteps" from *Broadway Melody of 1938* (1937). After Eleanor's accident, the brush shoes were abandoned. Margie Schultz Collection

Shooting "Feelin' Like a Million" from *Broadway Melody of 1938*. Lisa Royère Collection

Jack Dawn touches up Eleanor's makeup. Lisa Royère Collection

The cast of *Broadway Melody of 1938* in the film's finale. Lisa Royère Collection

The cast of *Broadway Melody of 1938* at the *Hollywood Hotel* radio broadcast. Museum of the City of New York

Celebrating Eleanor's twenty-sixth birthday with the "ladder of success" cake. Sid Luft, Leonora Luft, Eddie Mannix, and Lee Bailey (Eleanor's stand-in) are among the guests. Collection of Lee Bailey

Eleanor poses with Eleanor Roosevelt and dances at the President's Birthday Ball in 1938. AMPAS/Paula Broussard Collection

Ray Bolger and Eleanor rehearse a number for *Rosalie* (1937). Lisa Royère Collection

Director Woody Van Dyke places Nelson Eddy and Eleanor for a scene in *Rosalie*. Lisa Royère Collection

Eleanor poses with West Point cadets and costumed extras on the set of *Rosalie*. Sid Luft stands on the far right. Paula Broussard Collection

Eleanor and Blanche share a laugh with Ray Bolger and Ilona Massey on the outdoor set of *Rosalie*. Lisa Royère Collection

Eleanor is carried in on a drum for the massive production number in *Rosalie*.
Paula Broussard Collection

Eleanor breaks through plastic hoops in the title number from *Rosalie.* Lisa Royère Collection

Eleanor places her hands and feet in the wet cement at Grauman's Chinese Theatre, December 23, 1937. Lisa Royère Collection

Eleanor dances on shipboard in the title number from *Honolulu* (1939). Paula Broussard Collection

Robert Young embraces Eleanor as Gracie Allen and George Burns look on in *Honolulu.* Margie Schultz Collection

Eleanor performs onstage with Andy Iona and His Islanders during the *Honolulu* promo tour in 1939. Paula Harmon Collection

Eleanor and Fred Astaire rehearse for *Broadway Melody of 1940* in her bungalow at MGM. Margie Schultz Collection

Eleanor with George Murphy in "Between You and Me" from *Broadway Melody of 1940.* Lisa Royère Collection

Eleanor and Fred Astaire in "Begin the Beguine" from *Broadway Melody of 1940*.
AMPAS

Eleanor shows off a record from her collection. AMPAS

Eleanor and fiancé Merrill Pye at their engagement party at the Beverly Wilshire Hotel in 1940. D. Scott Calhoun Collection

Blanche and Eleanor pose in her newly decorated dressing room during the filming of *Lady Be Good* (1941). David Joiner Collection

"Fascinating Rhythm" from *Lady Be Good.* Paula Broussard Collection

Dancing with the chorus in "Hawaiian War Chant" from *Ship Ahoy* (1942). Lisa Royère Collection

Eleanor in the matador costume from *Ship Ahoy*. David Joiner Collection

Drummer Buddy Rich trades beats with Eleanor in "I'll Take Tallulah" from *Ship Ahoy*. Lisa Royère Collection

Eleanor wields a lasso in her "So Long, Sarah Jane" costume from *I Dood It* (1943). Lisa Royère Collection

Eleanor dining with Glenn Ford at the Brown Derby. Paula Broussard Collection

Blanche and Hannah Ford flank the newly married Eleanor and Glenn, October 23, 1943. AMPAS

Eleanor holds baby Peter in 1945. Lisa Royère Collection

Taking bows at the London Palladium, 1949. Paula Broussard Collection

Husband Glenn Ford and son Peter visit Eleanor on the set of *The Duchess of Idaho* (1950). Lisa Royère Collection

A mid-1950s portrait of Eleanor. Margie Schultz Collection

Eleanor writes on the blackboard during a taping of *Faith of Our Children.* Hearst Corporation *Los Angeles Examiner,* USC Libraries Special Collections

Eleanor with one of five Emmy Awards she won for *Faith of Our Children*. Margie Schultz Collection

Opening night at the Dunes Hotel, Las Vegas, April 19, 1962. The bandage on her leg is visible from her March injury. Paula Broussard Collection

In trademark top hat and tails for her comeback, 1961. Hearst Corporation *Los Angeles Examiner,* USC Libraries Special Collections

Hollywood Palace television show, 1964. Paula Broussard Collection

Dancing with Gene Kelly at a premiere event for *That's Entertainment, Part 2* (1976). Lisa Royère Collection

With protégé Jeff Parker and friend Eleanor Debus. D. Scott Calhoun Collection

Eleanor makes a stylish exit after her panel presentation at the Academy of Motion Picture Arts & Sciences in 1979. With co-author Lisa Royère and Marvin Paige. Lisa Royère Collection

Dedication of Eleanor's star on the Hollywood Walk of Fame, February 15, 1984.
Lisa Royère Collection

Eleanor checks her top hat before the next take. *Broadway Melody of 1938*. Lisa Royère Collection

12

King and Queen

Both Eleanor and Astaire arrived back in Los Angeles the first week of June 1939. Though shooting would not begin for several months, Eleanor started working on ideas for numbers for the film. Six weeks of choreography and rehearsals were planned with Astaire; the prospect filled her with a mixture of excitement and trepidation. Seeking inspiration for the ballet sequence planned for *Broadway Melody of 1940,* Eleanor had attended all ten performances of Leonide Massine's Ballet Russe a few months earlier in Los Angeles. Excited about the film—this time to be in color—and full of innovative ideas, she envisioned a "Flame Ballet." She would be costumed as the sun, in gold with red accents, and the background dancers would be a corps of girls dressed as clouds and boys as flames, ignited by the appearance of the sun. In a dramatic climax, rain would douse the flames. "It would be grand in Technicolor," she told a reporter.[1] She continued to toy with more ideas for the number as she worked on her solo.

By now, the remainder of the film's production personnel had been confirmed. Norman Taurog was set to direct and Jack Cummings to produce, with a story by Jack McGowan and Dore Schary. Once again, Cole Porter would write the score. During the filming of *Rosalie,* a tragic horseback riding accident had seriously injured both his legs. Porter now wore double leg braces and was able to walk with the help of canes but would never regain full mobility.

Ever the consummate professional, Porter completed five new songs for the score by fall: "I Happen to Be in Love" (ultimately discarded), "Please Don't Monkey with Broadway," "Between You and Me," "I've Got My Eyes on You," and "I Concentrate on You." An instrumental piece by Walter Ruick, "Italian Café Routine," was penned for a duo with Astaire and Eleanor. The final song would be one previously written by Porter for the show *Jubilee,* "Begin the Beguine." In January 1939, Artie Shaw's swing version of the song had catapulted it to the top of the music charts and prompted the choice for the film's most elaborate production number. Also added was a song with a nautical theme, arranged by Roger Edens: "All Ashore (I Am the Captain of This Boat)."

"Please Don't Monkey with Broadway" introduces Johnny Brett (Astaire) and King Shaw (George Murphy), a down-on-their-luck dance team aspiring to make it on Broadway. When producer Bob Casey (Frank Morgan) sees them perform, a mix-up causes him to hire King as a new partner for star Clare Bennett (Eleanor Powell) instead of Johnny. King ultimately finds out about the mistake and feigns being drunk on opening night so that Johnny can step into the starring role.

The nautical number, "All Ashore," introduces Eleanor as Clare Bennett. It appears early in the picture but was filmed last because the producers were concerned about the potential for injury from her rigorous acrobatic moves. Reminiscent of "Swingin' the Jinx Away," Eleanor makes her entrance atop the mast of a yacht—this one a dizzying five feet higher than the mast in the *Born to Dance* battleship. To avoid the mishap of the previous film, she was lowered with one hand holding a rope while her foot rested on a small platform. At the bottom she joins a group of chorus boys dressed as sailors and launches into her song. This number marks the second time Eleanor's own singing voice was used. As Johnny watches from the theater audience, he marvels at Clare's lively solo, punctuated by her trademark high kicks and acrobatics.

Eleanor always sought to add exciting elements to the choreography. Her hairdresser, charged with devising ways to keep her coiffure neat during strenuous numbers, remarked that Eleanor "works twice as hard as any other dancer I've seen. She always schemes around for someone else to try a stunt first, and if anyone else can do it, Eleanor won't. She figures out a harder way."[2] Incredibly, MGM did not take out insurance on their stars at that time.

In the ballroom dance, "Between You and Me," George Murphy proved once again an excellent partner for Eleanor. Her ballet training gave her an ease and fluid grace; she never appeared out of her element. Most impressive were the standing slides she performed alongside Murphy down sloping ramps, a difficult move even for experienced dancers. Set designer Merrill Pye became frustrated when it seemed to him that Eleanor and Murphy were not sliding down quickly enough. The bemused dancers then dared him to try it for himself. After Pye fell flat on his face, Eleanor and Murphy continued at their own pace.

Eleanor's favorite number from the film was the "Italian Café Routine" (also known as the Jukebox Dance). Johnny and Clare try out a difficult step from Clare's show, and it evolves into a spontaneous duet when a waiter inserts a coin into the jukebox. The premise of finding common ground with a starting step proved to be an icebreaker in the scene just as it did in the real-life rehearsal sessions between the two.

The ballet, "I Concentrate on You," was another departure from the many tap numbers in the film, but the finale number, "Begin the Beguine" proved to be the showstopper that would achieve iconic stature in Hollywood film history.

On July 7, Eleanor and Astaire began their long-anticipated dance sessions together; the big finale production number would be the first to shoot at the end of August. This would be Astaire's first film after his longtime RKO film partnership with Ginger Rogers. Audience expectations were high, not only because Eleanor would be Astaire's partner but also because he had not been seen on screen for a full year. Astaire had been looking forward to his first film in Technicolor; he and Eleanor were disappointed to learn that the studio had changed its mind due to the economic situation in Europe. With Technicolor no longer planned for the film, Eleanor's ambitious "Flame Ballet" had been set aside.

Eleanor found it difficult to enter into a comfortable working relationship with Astaire. To make Fred feel more at ease, she tried to arrange for them to work with his personal pianist, but union regulations prohibited him from working at a studio where he was not under contract. Once settled in the studio rehearsal bungalow, still intimidated by each other, they initially remained very formal, calling each other "Mr. Astaire" and "Miss Powell." Neither one was willing to make the first move when it came to choreography. Astaire said, "Well, now, just how are we going to work this thing out?" They put on a few Benny Goodman records for inspiration, but neither dared make a move. "We just sat there and fidgeted," Eleanor recounted. Neither wanted to be the first to dance. Finally, Eleanor said, "'Look, here's something Jack Donahue taught me.' And I did the steps. Fred yelled, 'Say, that's great—teach me.' So, he got up and did the steps. Then he went into a bit of his own routine. And I asked him to teach me the steps. This interchange of dance steps broke the ice."[3]

Eleanor's greatest concern about working with Astaire was that their choreography and performance styles were so different. "Fred is very aerial and covers a lot of space, while I dance close to the ground," she explained.[4]

Both were well aware that much was riding on this partnership and were willing to compromise for the sake of the finished product. Fortunately, they were alike in one important way—both were excessively hard workers and perfectionists. Astaire admired Eleanor's skilled precision taps, while she admired his clean balletic lines and attention to detail. Like Eleanor, he rehearsed a step again and again, never satisfied until the result was as close to perfection as possible.

They also shared a musician's approach to tap. Like many tap dancers, Astaire was an amateur drummer, and he loved jazz. Choreographing the rhythms of their steps was approached with a serious musical ear. Their conversations during rehearsal were often music related. "That should have been a half-beat," Eleanor recalled. "That should have been a whole beat." She admitted that average viewers wouldn't know the difference. "We were really knocking out the musicians who were sitting out front . . . if we could get a musician to say, 'Wow, look at that!' it was a challenge."[5]

Eleanor's daily schedule reflected her rigorous discipline and dedication to her work. She arrived at the studio at 9:00 a.m. A one-hour singing lesson was followed by a dramatic lesson and then rehearsal in the bungalow with Fred for six hours. Calling the sessions "exhaustive, and exhausting," Eleanor was pleased they "had really achieved some breathtaking combinations." Later, after production started, she and Astaire would "hang around until all hours" working with the music after the rest of the cast and crew had gone home.[6]

In his previous partnership, Ginger Rogers was the one working hard to match his skill. Now, it was Astaire who was pushed to his capacity in order to keep pace with Eleanor, working well outside of his comfort zone. His previous habit had been to work in close collaboration with choreographer Hermes Pan. The two liked to bounce ideas off each other, with Pan acting as the female counterpart in ballroom dances as they worked out routines. Pan would then teach and fully rehearse Astaire's partner so she would be prepared when she joined him.

Due to the high interest in the Powell–Astaire partnership, special studio security was placed outside the rehearsal hall to allow complete privacy. No one was allowed to view their rehearsals or visit the set. The studio was confident in the successful future of the pairing and announced at least two potential upcoming projects for the two even before production had completed—*Broadway Melody of 1941* and a retooling of the Gershwin show *Girl Crazy*.

The collaboration Eleanor and Astaire had spent weeks perfecting would culminate in a spectacular ten-minute finale, "Begin the Beguine." It was divided into two sections, each presented in a different rhythmic style. A lyrical version with a languid Latin pulse is introduced by sultry mezzo-soprano Lois Hodnott, who provided the vocals for actress Carmen D'Antonio, costumed in a strapless, tropical print dress. Suzanne Garland, sister of Judy and part of the original Gumm Sisters singing act, was one of the supporting singers and can be seen behind D'Antonio in this scene. The camera pulls back, rising from the orchestra pit to the stage, to reveal two lines of swaying Albertina Rasch girls in flowing skirts. The dancers make their way across a sloped riser and over a vast mirrored floor. Overhead, a deep sky twinkles with artificial stars. Eleanor appears atop the slope in a sequined midriff top and full skirt. As she dances, Astaire's reflection appears in the tall, mirrored backdrop, before he joins her for their duet. Eleanor and Astaire continue with a smooth bossa nova–styled dance with elements of Spanish flamenco.

The pair exit and the music shifts into the swing version of the song, introduced by The Music Maids. The lively interlude gives a fun nod to MGM's recent release by interjecting "in the merry land of Oz" into the lyrics. The vocals end, and the stars return. Eleanor now wears a street-length, full-skirted white dress, and Astaire, a tailored white suit. Their duet starts off with nonchalant, playful ease as they make their way out onto the vast mirrored floor, then soon it moves into an intricate interplay of beats and syncopated rhythms. Finally, the music drops out and a tacet challenge ensues between the two, giving the audience a rare display of the ultimate tap prowess. Astaire would go on to dance with many other partners in his career, but none would prove to be as formidable a match as Eleanor.

The visual magnificence of the set designed by Merrill Pye featured a unique use of mirrored surfaces. The soundstage was covered in sixty-five hundred square feet of mirrored floor tiles, so many that MGM had to resort to manufacturing their own. Both the floor and tall mirrored panels were constructed on tracks so they could be easily positioned to reflect the dancers. The huge movable panels towered sixty feet in height and weighed four tons each. These were placed in front of a midnight blue cyclorama embedded with thousands of twinkling lights to represent the night sky. MGM proudly touted in advance publicity that the floor was the largest mirror ever fabricated. But while the mirrors provided a stunning visual, they were a challenge to work with. They required constant cool air and regular cleaning with dry mops to clear away the condensation caused by the hot lights. Made of shatter-resistant glass, they still could crack under the pressure of tap dancing, even without tap shoes, so Eleanor and Astaire were not allowed to rehearse on them. During production, the two stars cracked a total of thirty tiles, but none are evident in the film. The final effect was stunning. The number, coupled with the spectacular elegance of Pye's set, would prove to be a perfect closure to MGM's magnificent black and white musical era.

Rapidly becoming one of the most respected art directors at MGM, Pye was so admired by department head Cedric Gibbons that he commissioned him to design interior sections of his own home. It was during the filming of *Broadway Melody of 1940* that Pye's professional relationship with Eleanor began to blossom into a personal one. This was their fifth production together, and though they had butted heads many times in the past over budgets and artistic decisions, their shared passion for the presentation of dance on film had eventually fostered a strong bond. Pye, as devoted to his work as Eleanor was to hers, spent long hours at the studio, sometimes more than sixty hours per week. Though the studio and his work held high priorities in his life, he also enjoyed socializing with stars and film personnel at MGM.

Pye's marriage to Mary Halsey, a dancer who had appeared in the *Rosalie* chorus, as well as a host of other musicals, was over. They were already living apart, and their divorce would become final in the fall of 1940. Eleanor and Merrill's relationship grew, and soon they were spending nearly every day together, both on and off the set. Merrill appreciated Eleanor's independence and understood her love of her craft. They enjoyed each other's company and had an easy rapport. Until now, she had refused any relationship that would divert her attention from her work, but Merrill made her reconsider her position.

After "Begin the Beguine" was completed, production shifted back to dialogue scenes on September 12. Though Eleanor had not seen any rushes from the first number, she was pleased with reports. She felt confident that things were going well enough that production would be finished by Christmas.

By October 19, all the dramatic scenes had been filmed. Cummings and Taurog began to clash on how Taurog had been handling the script and story elements. Unable to resolve the conflict, Cummings complained to Mayer—if Taurog stayed, he would leave. "Jack was unhappy with a lot of the things I had done," Taurog remembered. Mayer asked for a screening of the work done so far, about two reels of film. After the viewing, a pleased Mayer sided with Taurog and told his nephew, "Jack, if you want off the picture, you can get off the picture. This man has done a fabulous job with Ellie Powell, who never proved she could act before. He's done a terrific job with George Murphy. If you don't think your script is strong enough, that's your job as the producer. Now why don't you fellows get together and any discrepancies that you see—I'm sure can be worked out—and go back and continue. You're making a fine picture."[7]

Contradicting the common criticism that Eleanor's acting abilities were weak, Taurog shifted the blame to her previous directors. "They used to say it was hard to get a performance out of [her] . . . because she didn't have the warmth. The hell, she didn't have the warmth. She had it but they didn't know how to get it out of her before," he recalled. "My God, Eleanor certainly gave a performance for me in *Broadway Melody*. She was magnificent, delightful, charming."[8]

They returned to shooting musical numbers on October 22, and by December 2, Eleanor had two remaining numbers to film—the Pierrot and Pierrette ballet with Astaire ("I Concentrate on You") and, finally, Eleanor's nautical number, "All Ashore."

The ballet number presented a unique set of problems. As the plot called for the performers to be disguised, both dancers wore a mask, and in addition, Eleanor wore a platinum wig. Made visually dramatic by a total of fifty-three different lighting changes, Eleanor and Astaire strike a series of poses framed by columns as they travel up a sweeping staircase to a high platform. The narrow field of vision caused by the mask's eye openings made the series of turns up the staircase, which had no railings, treacherous. "[Eleanor] has to be exactly the right distance from Astaire, and she must depend on memory as she goes, looping and leaping up a set of unevenly spaced stairs into the shelter of some towering black columns," one reporter described. Eleanor commented, "When I [got] up there I [said], 'Thank God, home at last!' Any second I expected to fall flat on my nose."[9]

Astaire was also troubled about the appearance of his hairpiece. He had worn a toupee for his entire film career and was very self-conscious about it. After he made a photo test in his costume, Astaire was so uncomfortable that he left a note for Cummings begging him to destroy the test. He despaired of his Harlequin costume, calling it "god awful and ill-fitting." He lamented that Eleanor appeared slightly taller than him in the number and felt ill that his hair looked so different from George Murphy's. As a result, the costume was altered. A tight cap now covered his hair, and Eleanor's toe shoes were replaced by flat ballet slippers for their sequence together. Privately, Astaire was as self-deprecating as he was talented, and he was rarely fully satisfied with any number, scrutinizing his appearance as much as he did every move in a relentless push for perfection. Now, faced with a partner of Eleanor's caliber, the challenge was proving a difficult one, and he could not fall short.

Eleanor celebrated another birthday on a film set with her fellow cast members. Blanche gifted her with a three-month-old schnauzer puppy that she named Tanzer (German for "dancer"), affectionately nicknamed Tanz.

About two weeks later, on the day they were filming the first section of the Albertina Rasch ballet, famed conductor Arturo Toscanini was taking a tour of the studio. All the stages were notified to prepare for short visits by the maestro. Eleanor idolized Toscanini and was thrilled to be able to perform for such an important guest. She was especially pleased that the conductor would be able to view a classical number, as she felt it would be more to his liking than a jazzy tap dance. When the seventy-two-year-old maestro and his wife finally arrived, accompanied by Mayer and a full entourage, Eleanor and the Rasch dancers performed the opening ballet section of "I Concentrate on You." As Eleanor made her final curtsy, the maestro seemed disappointed. He conferred in Italian with his wife, then approached Eleanor and, in his heavily accented English, asked, "Where is . . . the dance with the noise?" When she realized he wanted to see tap dancing, Eleanor looked around for a prop man to pull up the sound-deadening tiles that covered the set. "Nobody came, so I yanked up some of the boards myself and tossed them aside until I had a space to dance," she later told a columnist. After hurriedly changing out of her ballet costume and retrieving her tap shoes, Eleanor tried to bring over her pianist Chris Schonberg. "He was so scared, with Toscanini on the set, that he couldn't move." As all the dancers sat in a wide circle around her, she launched into a long improvised rhythmic sequence for the now-grinning Toscanini. "I danced without music, and all the time I could see Toscanini beating his chair with his fist." She continued for two hours. Every time she would pause, he would motion excitedly to her, "More! More!" Later, with tears streaming down his face, the elderly maestro kissed Eleanor on both cheeks. She, too, was crying. "My child, never have I cried before, except at music. Your feet are a symphony! And that you are a lady and can dance like this . . ."[10] He turned to Mayer and said, "'I go now. I see nothing else!'" Eleanor recalled.[11] About a week later, she received a very special letter from the maestro that said, "I want you to know that the three things I will carry with me in my memory when I pass on to the world beyond will be the sunset, the Grand Canyon, and your dancing."

Her final number, "All Ashore," completed shooting on December 30, thankfully without any injury; this left only tap dubbing and retakes to be completed in early January. The year had seen several seemingly impossible dreams come true for Eleanor—she made a film with Fred Astaire, danced for Toscanini, and was developing a relationship with a special man.

But the new year of 1940 started with the dampening of one of those dreams. Though MGM was initially anxious to continue the Astaire–Powell partnership, Astaire was not so enthusiastic. He felt the differences between himself and Eleanor were impossible to overlook, and he admitted that it was challenging to dance with her, clearly a more skilled tapper than he. He felt she was too tall for him and, perfectionist that he was, knew he simply had to work too hard to make it successful. Even before the film was released, plans for subsequent films were scrapped as he chose not to extend the contract. "I had twenty-nine partners, but I met my match with Ellie," he later stated. In 1952, he told columnist Hedda Hopper that Eleanor was "one of our greatest talents," but lamented that she was "a bit too powerful for me. She has a mannish style but is very easy to work with."[12] He went on to Columbia to make *You'll Never Get Rich* with Rita Hayworth and did not return to MGM until 1945 for *Yolanda and the Thief* with Lucille Bremer.

Critics called *Broadway Melody of 1940* "easily one of the most enjoyable pieces of entertainment that the screen has offered in some time. . . . There are no dull moments, no backing and filling from plot to music. The picture moves. . . . Eleanor Powell has never been seen to such advantage . . . and Astaire is the same safe Astaire without a peer."[13] Another noted, "The picture isn't great . . . but it is gay and amusing and a lot of fun and you feel the lift of the audience as it responds to the dancing and the Cole Porter music."[14] While fans of Ginger Rogers were loyal in their belief that no other partner could take her place alongside Astaire, it was clear that pairing tap masters Eleanor and Fred was a historic opportunity MGM could not ignore.

13

Love and Disappointment

By January, Eleanor and Merrill Pye's names were regularly linked in the gossip columns. The *Hollywood Reporter, Variety,* Louella Parsons, Hedda Hopper, and Sheilah Graham all commented on their frequent outings. "Miss Powell, sotto voce, is seeing a lot of Merrill Pye," one noticed in February. The pair made the rounds of Hollywood nightspots, and Pye felt right at home when they dined in the art deco splendor of Earl Carroll's. "At Victor Hugo's . . . Eleanor Powell and Merrill Pye, dissecting a rumba," remarked another. They attended opening nights at the opera and ballet and planned cozy dinner parties at home with Blanche. An avid golfer, Pye took Eleanor to a golf course for the first time and set about teaching her to play. "The Eleanor Powell–Merrill Pye flame is still burning," affirmed another mention in the press.

For several months, Eleanor had been looking forward to the Hawaiian vacation she and Blanche had planned for mid-March. "*Broadway Melody* meant seven months of hard work, and I'm just about as tired as anyone could possibly be," Eleanor wrote actor and filmmaker Robert "Bob" Board on February 20, 1940. "I'm going to take a trip and have a nice long rest." But as the date for the trip approached, Blanche made an astute observation. "Eleanor and Merrill looked so woebegone at the idea of being separated that I turned in the tickets," she told a reporter.[1] Instead of sailing to Hawaii, the three went to La Quinta, a local desert resort, where they rented bungalows and enjoyed a few days of swimming and relaxing.

By April 5, newspapers and Hollywood columns were full of the exciting news they thought they would never hear from the workaholic dancer— Eleanor and Merrill announced their engagement. "Merrill and I found ourselves very much in love," she told reporters. Since it would be several months until Pye's divorce was final, they had not yet set a date for the wedding. "We won't make any definite plans until we can tell when we will be able to get away from our jobs," she told the press and friends at their engagement party at the Beverly Wilshire Hotel.[2]

MGM again teased notices that Eleanor was cast in *Ziegfeld Girl,* this time with Lana Turner, Frank Morgan, and George Murphy. While she waited for a definitive start date, she focused on her fiancé. In addition to evenings at nightclubs, opera, and the ballet, they went to boxing and wrestling matches and rodeos. They took Blanche to the famed Brown Derby for lunch and to the fashionable Florentine Gardens ballroom to watch the chorine basketball games, in which chorus girls played against studio execs. Other times they stayed in, and Eleanor cooked a meal.

On hearing that her father was ill, Blanche decided to take a trip to Springfield to make sure he was being well taken care of. While it was not to be a long trip, it would be the first time she and Eleanor had ever been separated. In her mother's absence, Eleanor cooked dinner nightly for Merrill, enjoying a preview of their domestic future.

Suddenly, the columns reported that Eleanor and Merrill were on the outs. Informants from the MGM lot reported they simply nodded when passing each other. Shortly afterward, on May 24, Eleanor attended the gala opening party at the celebrity-owned nightclub, The Pirate's Den, on the arm of bandleader Vic Irwin. Merrill was nowhere in sight. Whether her appearance with Irwin was just a friendly outing or was intended to show that she was moving on, within a few weeks it would no longer matter.

While at a concert by Jeanette MacDonald at the Philharmonic Auditorium on April 25, Eleanor suddenly began to experience abdominal pains; she felt so weak and uncomfortable during the event that she wanted to go home. The pains were fleeting, but over the next few weeks, they became more frequent and severe. Her doctor quickly brought her into Cedars of Lebanon Hospital for tests; she was found to have gallstones and was scheduled for surgery on June 6.

Initial reports were that she was "recovering comfortably," but the following day her condition suddenly worsened. Her body temperature soared to 106 degrees, and hyperpyrexia set in. She was unconscious for several days, suffering the effects of a severe infection. "I felt like I was going to die," she recalled. Finally, her fever subsided. Their differences forgotten, Merrill was again at her side. He brought her home on July 3, after she had spent nearly a month in the hospital.

MGM was finalizing details for *Ziegfeld Girl,* now scheduled for production later in July, but Eleanor's doctor insisted on a full month's rest. Already lean, she had lost a full ten pounds as a result of her illness. MGM continued to ignore the severity of her situation and went so far as to suggest that she and George Murphy make a personal appearance tour to Argentina. The idea was scrapped, and, on July 10, the studio officially pushed production on *Ziegfeld Girl* to September, "if Powell is better."[3] The other stars were placed into other projects: James Stewart in *The Philadelphia Story*; George Murphy in *Little Nellie Kelly* with Judy Garland; and Hedy Lamarr in *Come Live with Me*.

By early August, Eleanor appeared improved enough that MGM bumped up the start date for *Ziegfeld Girl*. She was to report to the studio on August 19 to begin rehearsals. But it was clear she was not yet physically ready for the rigors of another film.

Eleanor and Merrill, joined by Blanche, spent Labor Day relaxing on a yachting trip to Catalina, a small island just off the coast of Southern California. Realizing how much a sea voyage would do to help her regain her strength, Eleanor made arrangements to take a cruise to New York via Panama. Three days before she left, she went to MGM for a photo portrait session with Clarence Bull. This was her first visit to MGM since her operation; while there, she visited Merrill and Jeanette MacDonald on the set of *Bitter Sweet*.

As Eleanor continued to recuperate, rumors began circulating that she would be replaced in *Ziegfeld Girl* because she needed further time to recover. Trade papers sometimes added Judy Garland to the list of cast members, with no mention of Eleanor Powell. Others had Eleanor Powell, but no Judy Garland. Nevertheless, the studio repeatedly assured Eleanor that she was still a part of the film. Behind the scenes, it was a different story. Scripts dating from as early as June 1940 already show the role as one clearly meant for a singer, ultimately played by Judy Garland; and no versions of the script show any role for a dancer in the ensemble. It appears that even if Eleanor had fully recovered for the original start date, she was never intended to have much more than a supporting role, if any. Positive reaction to Judy's rushes from *Little Nellie Kelly* sealed MGM's decision early on to put her in the film.

At noon on September 19, Eleanor and Blanche boarded the SS *Washington* in dock at Terminal Island in Long Beach. Merrill had planned a stateroom surprise with a small group of friends and a picnic as a festive sendoff, but ship's regulations unfortunately foiled the effort. Non-passengers were no longer allowed on board before departure, so the group was forced to eat their basket of food on the dock below as Eleanor and Blanche watched from the railing. Eleanor and Blanche were never far from MGM connections—

also on board for the voyage were screenwriter Sylvia Thalberg (sister of Irving) and Fredric March's wife, Florence, with their two children, Penelope and Anthony.

They settled in for two days of sailing until they reached the first port, Acapulco, Mexico, on September 21, where they made a five-hour stop. Writer Tennessee Williams, who lived there at the time, happened to describe the town on that very day in a letter to his family. The bay was "as blue as the Mediterranean" and the area was full of palms and mango trees. It was a far cry from the modern resort city of today, filled with tall hotels. Williams remarked that "the poverty there is depressing" and "the natives live under almost animal conditions."[4] Nevertheless, the balmy climate and beautiful vistas must have proved exotic and fascinating for Eleanor and Blanche, especially as the town was holding a fiesta in the gaily decorated streets on the day the ship came into port. The cruise continued down to Balboa, the capital of the Canal Zone. The zone was now under control of the United States, and security had been heightened due to war having been declared the previous year. They docked the evening of September 25 and stayed overnight; in the morning, military personnel boarded and remained on the ship as it traveled through the canal to Cristobal. All cameras and binoculars had to be checked with the purser before the ship made the twelve-hour crossing. No one was allowed to board or leave the ship. There were numerous requests for celebrity autographs from the crew handling the locks, and the ship's chef devised a method to wrap the autographs around lemons. They were tossed to the men, who unwrapped the lemons and threw them back. The next stop was Havana.

Every day Eleanor sent a radiogram to Merrill, and the two spoke regularly through ship-to-shore phone calls. It was an expensive habit, but it bolstered Eleanor's spirits to share details of the trip with Merrill and allowed him to keep her up to date on the studio happenings, specifically with regard to *Ziegfeld Girl*. It was a film Eleanor very much wanted to do.

The plan had been to spend a few days in New York before returning by train to Los Angeles. It was not smooth sailing out of Havana, however, and the ship ran into a storm near Cape Hatteras so severe that they had to dock and wait out the heavy weather. Finally, after a twenty-four-hour delay, the SS *Washington* sailed into New York on October 2.

The trip's stormy finale did not dampen Eleanor's spirits. She felt renewed. "The cruise was delightful," she wrote in her Young Dancer column. "I have gained eight pounds, caught up on all my rest, and feel like my old self again."[5]

Eleanor was looking forward to going back to work on October 9. Two days later she received the news that she was no longer in the cast of *Ziegfeld Girl*. Strung along for months when the studio clearly had other plans for the film, Eleanor now felt betrayed and used. She vehemently expressed her feelings to the studio executives. As a result, she was placed on hiatus on October 14.

Though there were discussions about *Broadway Melody of 1941* as her next film, in early December the studio confirmed her for *Lady Be Good*. MGM bought the rights to the book in October and completely revamped the 1924 Gershwin show. Production was not due to start for several months.

During her hiatus, Eleanor visited Merrill on the set of *Ziegfeld Girl* often, as interested to see him as she was curious to see how the film was progressing. And though she did not appear in the film, one of the gowns Lana Turner's character pulls from her closet is Eleanor's own gold lamé costume from her "Between You and Me" number with George Murphy.

Eleanor managed to keep herself occupied with another interesting hobby during her layoff. In early 1941, the sport of midget auto racing was all the rage in Hollywood, and Eleanor became a big fan. She was seen posing with her own miniature race car, and she was said to have built her own private track at her home.

As the holidays approached, Eleanor and Blanche enjoyed the time at home. For their first Christmas together after the finalization of his divorce, Merrill gifted her with "a sparkler 'this big'" according to newspaper reports. But with shooting scheduled to start in less than six weeks, Eleanor took stock of this turning point in her career and decided to slow things down.

It was a shock to all when, on January 6, May Mann reported in her column that Eleanor Powell and Merrill Pye, who had been waiting all year for his final divorce decree, had finally decided that a marriage date was now off the calendar. To stir the pot further, she added another piece of drama for her readers. According to Mann, Eleanor, who had cooked dinners for Merrill, gifted him with an automobile, and practiced signing her name "Pye," was now being seen about town with Dan Dailey.

◉　◉　◉

Eleanor finally emerged from her eighteen-week layoff from the studio when *Lady Be Good* began production in early February. It had been a year since *Broadway Melody of 1940* had wrapped. In the time away, she realized her place in the MGM family was changing, and she no longer felt confident in the direction her career was taking. Her contract was up for renewal, and it was a mutual decision to limit it to three years. She would now be earning $2,250 per week with a guarantee of $90,000 per year. But while her salary was increasing, her status was not. Studio priorities and politics were evolving as the studio added more projects to producer Arthur Freed's roster. The latest was the stage hit *Panama Hattie,* purchased for $150,000, beating out the competing bidder, RKO. In an interesting casting choice, it was announced for Eleanor, Ann Sothern, and Shirley Temple.

On a personal level, she was also at a crossroads. She sensed that serious life choices were impending. Despite the rumor mill, her friendship with Dan Dailey had played no part in the wedding postponement. It was simply that her relationship with Merrill had deepened to the point where she knew she had to make a choice—marriage or career. She didn't see a place for compromise. The outside world saw only the romance, and May Mann's comments sparked other press mentions that belied the cooling of the relationship: "It will surprise *Ziegfeld Girl* crew members who've watched their on-set cooings."[6] But Eleanor's conflicted feelings went deeper. She would be not only relinquishing her career but also entering into marriage with a man who had been married twice before and had a young son. For now, she was at an impasse.

Pushing past feelings of doubt, Eleanor stepped back onto the lot ready to work and genuinely enthusiastic about the new project. Though her role was secondary to the two leads, she still received top billing. *Lady Be Good* was also to give her three dance numbers: a unique dance with a little dog to "Lady Be Good," the production number "Fascinating Rhythm," and a third number, "I'd Rather Dance."

In the cast were Robert Young, Ann Sothern, Red Skelton, John Carroll (in the part previously assigned to Tony Martin), Virginia O'Brien, and Dan Dailey in a small dramatic role. The Berry Brothers, a flashy acrobatic dance trio, were to perform two specialty numbers. Arthur Freed would produce the film.

Since November 1940, Busby Berkeley had been set to direct. According to Sothern's biographer, Sothern and Eleanor were both unhappy about this and complained to Mayer. Although Eleanor had never worked with Berkeley, Sothern had recently, in *Fast and Furious* (1939), as well as in a bit part in his "Shanghai Lil" number in *Footlight Parade* (1933). As a result, Berkeley's assignment was changed to dance director, and Norman Z. McLeod was brought on as director.

The project started well for Eleanor. With top billing and three numbers, she was confident about her status in the film and viewed her secondary role as one that would give her a certain amount of freedom to play a new type of character. At Freed's request, on January 9, she resumed training with acting coach Lillian Burns. Freed arranged for a car to pick her up at her bungalow for her hour-long sessions at noon each day.

The storyline focuses on the relationship between a songwriter and lyricist, Eddie Crane and Dixie Donegan (Young and Sothern), told in flash-backs from divorce court. Eleanor plays Dixie's best friend, dancer Marilyn Marsh.

Eleanor recorded her vocals for her first number in the film, "I'd Rather Dance," on February 25, 1941, and the dance was filmed three days later. The number takes place at Eddie's penthouse party, where Marilyn removes the skirt portion of her gown and performs a dance for the guests in her sequined peplum top.

The previous year, producer Arthur Freed had brought out Vincente Minnelli from New York to be a part of his new unit. "You won't have a title, but you'll be learning the business," Freed told Minnelli. "You can read scripts and make suggestions . . . direct musical numbers." It was the start of one of MGM's most famous production units. "Other producers had put together similar units before, but this was the first to be composed of newcomers to the industry," Minnelli recalled.[7] One of Minnelli's earliest assignments after coming on the lot was the direction of "I'd Rather Dance." It inspired him to try some innovative camerawork, and the number was shot with three cameras positioned in a half circle around Eleanor, as well as one overhead and one shooting up from a pit. Unfortunately, the number was cut from the film, and the footage has never resurfaced.

Over the course of the coming months, Sothern's growing esteem in the studio's eyes spurred a change. "The bosses decided she needed a fourth song," Eleanor recalled. Prompted by the devastating situation in Europe, Jerome Kern's "The Last Time I Saw Paris" was added. Sothern sings the song in a close-up over a montage of scenes of Paris. The addition of the song was another worrisome indication that Eleanor was no longer a priority in the film. "Louis Mayer was ecstatic about her singing. . . . I didn't realize they would cut one of my already filmed dance numbers to insert it," she said.[8] Although Eleanor was notified while shooting was already under way, the reality is that Sothern's "newly added" song had actually been on the shooting schedule the entire time, even before her number was shot.

With the removal of "I'd Rather Dance," Eleanor does not dance until midway into the film. It was easy to feel that the ambitious Sothern had somehow sabotaged her. Though she remained professional and civil to Sothern for the remainder of the film, their previous warm interactions now turned cool and impersonal.

The two remaining numbers were memorable. Eleanor, once again in search of something unique for the film, wanted to try doing a number with a dog. Her agent, Billy Grady, had arranged for a dancing dog named Wing to appear with Eleanor in the number, and the two started rehearsing on December 2. Wing's owner, Billy Black, signed a contract for the dog's services at $150 a week. Despite his theatrical experience, however, Wing was let go after two weeks. Other dogs were sent Eleanor's way. "I auditioned dogs. I had dogs of every size and shape," Eleanor recalled. "But they didn't have the personality that I wanted." Finally, prop boy Jack Ackerman told her of his daughter Arlene's clever dog, Buttons, who had already shown an aptitude for learning tricks at home. The match proved ideal, and Eleanor began working with the little fox terrier on December 23, taking him home to spend the next six weeks with her. She trained the dog to walk through her legs as she danced, jump through hoops formed by her arms, and leap over her extended leg. "He had to get used to my taps going, and that threw his little ears down there," Eleanor said. By the time they returned to the studio, Buttons was a pro. "And what a ham! When we went through rehearsals, his little body would quiver. He'd want to do his part."[9] The number was shot without a hitch, ending with Buttons bounding across the room and into Eleanor's arms. The successful number launched Buttons' film career. He would go on to appear with Bing Crosby in *The Emperor Waltz* (1948).

"Fascinating Rhythm" was an elaborate piece of staging that allowed Berkeley to stretch his creative wings. His initial list of elements included the swing singing group "Six Hits and a Miss," thirty-four male and female dancers (later changed to eighty male dancers), with a forty-piece band and numerous other sideline musicians. Wary of Berkeley's reputation for elaborate and expensive concepts that often went over budget and racked up overtime, Freed set limits. "You've got three days to rehearse and one to shoot," Freed told him, but Berkeley would end up disregarding both directives.[10] Freed allowed a budget of $81,000 for the number. As was typical in her production routines, the number involved Eleanor being swung head over heels down a long row of chorus boys at the conclusion. Even though it had been nine months since her operation, her entire abdomen was bound tightly with medical tape for support and protection.

The distinctive number was creatively staged by Berkeley. "I start my number with seven choruses of 'boogie-woogie' on six pianos, each playing a different strain," Eleanor said. She performed to a piano version of the song, traveling backward for the majority of the number as tall curtains swirl open behind her to reveal pianists as they played. A marvel to watch, Eleanor's crisp and clean choreography is matched only by the smooth "choreography" of the crew who swiftly moved, wheeled, and positioned the pianos and stages behind her in a seamless manner. Getting this exactly right, according to Eleanor, was an exhausting experience that was performed under extreme discomfort. Equally elegant was Merrill Pye's set, with swirling curtains and precisely designed lighting that produced distinct shadows across them during the number.

On Friday, April 11, Pye and his unit laid in the set elements on Stage 27, rigged the curtains, and brought in the platforms and piano. After Pye and Berkeley reviewed the full setup and rehearsed the movement of the dolly, they were ready for filming.

Several days were occupied with the Berry Brothers' opening segment. On April 14, Berkeley finally shifted his attention to Eleanor's portion of the number, which would take two laborious sixteen-hour days to complete. After several rehearsals with Eleanor and Berkeley, Freed visited the set to check on the progress. By 6:00 p.m., Berkeley had still not started on Eleanor's section, the largest part of the number. The evening ahead would be grueling.

Between 9:30 p.m. and 10:55 p.m., Eleanor performed twenty partial takes of the dance and then took a brief break. Another six takes were done by 11:30 p.m., when a rip in her shirt required repair. The next hour resulted in eight more takes. A thirty-minute lunch was finally called at 12:35 a.m. After another eight takes, Berkeley was dissatisfied because the curtains created too much of a bulge as they flowed around the pianos during the dance. The curtains were then cut shorter, and shooting resumed at 2:00 a.m. After three more takes, the first section of Eleanor's dance was finally on film, and she was released from set at 2:30 a.m.

Shooting resumed two weeks later at 9:00 a.m. on Thursday, May 1, with Berkeley filming the second half of the number with Eleanor. By 10:00 p.m., the remaining segments had still not been completed to Berkeley's satisfaction. The cinematographers were switched out, and Oliver T. Marsh was replaced by George Folsey (union rules required a twelve-hour break between wrap and the next day's call time). The dance segment was run again for another eighteen takes. After thirteen hours on set, Eleanor was running a fever, but Berkeley was anxious to wrap up the shoot by 3:00 a.m. The grumbling crew continued on. At 2:40 a.m., Eleanor was flipped head over heels down the line one last time, finishing with a bright smile as a semicircle of canes framed her face. This final take was the version used.

The hard work put in by Eleanor and the crew paid off. The stylish number ranks as one of the most memorable of her films. Later, Berkeley stated that though Astaire was best for him to work with, his favorite dancer was Eleanor. "Eleanor was by far the finest female dancer we ever had in films and a very hard-working perfectionist," he said. "I've known very few women that talented and that gracious."[11]

Lady Be Good received mixed reviews. Most criticized the film for being too long, underusing talent, and lacking any wit. Much of the advertising featured stills that showed Eleanor in her leggy "I'd Rather Dance" costume, which never appears in the film. Audiences who expected the usual number of Powell dances were sorely disappointed. Today, the film's only memorable standouts are Eleanor's numbers. "Modestly sentimental and friendly as a tail-wagging dog, *Lady Be Good* never seems to be able to pull itself together to become a more than fair to middling musical comedy," said the *New York Times*. The reviewer praised Berkeley's inventiveness with "Fascinating Rhythm," saying, "Miss Powell is caught by an agile camera whirling through an endless series of gauze curtains." But ultimately, little could save the film as a whole. "Despite the performers, despite the imaginative handling of the production numbers, *Lady Be Good* deserves little better than a passing mark."[12]

Though "The Last Time I Saw Paris" won an Academy Award for Best Song, there were considerable complaints since it was not original to the film. It beat out such classics as "Chattanooga Choo Choo" from *Sun Valley Serenade* and "Boogie Woogie Bugle Boy of Company B" from *Buck Privates*. Eleanor was frustrated; she lamented her time with the Freed Unit and the loss of her number "I'd Rather Dance." Still, she forged on, hoping that the next project would be a better experience.

14

Hollywood at War

*L*ady Be Good had been a frustrating departure from the norm for Eleanor. Her new film (with the working title *I'll Take Manila*) seemed like a return to familiar territory when, in spring of 1941, her *Honolulu* director Eddie Buzzell was named for the picture and Robert Young set as her co-star. Arthur Freed was again named producer. Freed had been a fan of Eleanor during the *Broadway Melody* series; but, after he produced the successful *Babes in Arms* in 1939, he felt musicals were taking a new direction—one that required different stars. Nevertheless, his regard for her star appeal never wavered. "Talent, that's what she had. Eleanor represented a showstopper to me, which she was," Freed told interviewer John Kobal in 1974. "She was ideal for the kind of film they were doing then, but she didn't last the period. She was not a good actress like Judy was."[1] Eleanor could sense that Freed perceived that her appeal was slipping; however, unlike *Lady Be Good,* this project had a true starring role for her. She would play the part of a dancing star on an ocean liner who was deceptively recruited by Nazis to transport a mine on a trip to Manila, Philippines. Perhaps still inspired by Paul Haakon's toreador ballet in *At Home Abroad,* "Death in the Afternoon," she was already working out ideas for her own bullfight-themed tap dance as the main production number, but it would be months before shooting would actually begin.

While she waited, Eleanor kept busy. On June 29, she appeared on the *Million Dollar Broadcast,* a radio show to benefit the USO. A few days later, she traveled up the coast to the Santa Barbara Biltmore with Blanche and Merrill for the Fourth of July weekend. Even when on vacation, she found reasons to train and learn new skills. She took high-diving lessons from the Olympic trainer Fred Cady and, after working with him, could "already do a slick jack knife off a twenty-four-foot board."[2] It was not a new pastime; Eleanor had in fact been taking diving lessons for the last few years. She loved the feeling of launching herself through the air and remarked that the skill required engaging an entirely different set of muscles than tap dancing.

Back in December 1940, MGM had announced plans to do a vaudeville story, *The Big Time,* with Eleanor Powell, Judy Garland, and Walter Pidgeon. It was originally to feature two female leads, one a dancer and the other a singer. By July 1941, as *I'll Take Manila* worked through production delays, the studio finally began to put the plans in motion. *The Big Time* was retitled *Me and My Gal,* and Dan Dailey was cast as the lead opposite Eleanor.

Eleanor was Dailey's longtime friend and champion and had been instrumental in bringing him to MGM. Although Dailey had performed as a dancer for years in vaudeville and on Broadway, his initial roles in Hollywood were all nonmusical. Dailey was tall and good-looking and would play well alongside Eleanor as a leading man and dance partner. MGM made numerous screen tests of the two dancing together and moved on to recording songs for the film. On July 8, they began with the title song, "For Me and My Gal." Existing recordings show that Eleanor's singing lessons had borne fruit; her voice was rounder and much improved, and she carried the bulk of the song. However, MGM reworked the casting when Dailey was drafted and decided instead to feature only one female lead. After the project was shelved for eight months, it went into production as *For Me and My Gal,* starring Judy Garland with Gene Kelly in his film debut.

On July 11, Eleanor began dance tests on *I'll Take Manila.* In the interim, Jack Cummings had taken over as producer from Arthur Freed. The studio was now actively pursuing Cuban entertainer Desi Arnaz for one of the male lead roles; Arnaz had recently made a hit on Broadway and on the screen in RKO's *Too Many Girls.* RKO was focused on their own project that teamed Arnaz and his new bride, Lucille Ball. As it turned out, Arnaz was busy until October with his work in *Four Jacks and a Jill,* and he was ultimately not cast.

As casting decisions on *I'll Take Manila* were being discussed, on August 19, Eleanor recorded two Gershwin songs, "Do, Do, Do" and "Do It Again" (with piano accompaniment by Roger Edens) for a project that was never realized. The purpose for these recordings remains a mystery.

As a diversion from the heaviness of the escalating events on the world stage, audiences were now craving comic relief. The press noted a distinct rise in popularity among comic actors such as Abbott and Costello and Bob Hope; they singled out the young red-headed comedian, Red Skelton, who had played in *Lady Be Good* and in two editions of the *Dr. Kildare* series. After Skelton's successful first starring role in *Whistling in the Dark,* followed by equal success in *Panama Hattie,* MGM was keen to establish him as a comedy star. They placed him in the lead role previously assigned to Robert Young. "Give a newcomer a chance," the studio asked of Eleanor. By mid-September, singer Tony Martin was also added to the cast.

Late October found Eleanor learning Morse code for the picture. In a scene in which she sends out an SOS on board a ship, her challenge was to tap out a message in authentic Morse code while still making the dance interesting to the viewer. She worked with a special "automatic wireless machine to pace the speed and timing of the dots and dashes to [her] taps."[3] Though Eleanor's choreography was pleasant, the tapped message section was less successful and came across as overly obvious.

Months before America officially entered World War II, young men from all over the country were being readied for an eventual conflict. Private Eddie Brach, Eleanor's dancer friend from her Broadway and vaudeville days, was stationed in boot camp at Camp Haan Army Base, not far from Los Angeles. Eleanor and Blanche invited him to dinner along with two other Army buddies, Ted Foster and Elmer Fuller. In his prolific letters sent home to family, Foster provided a detailed account of the memorable evening spent with Eleanor, Blanche, Merrill, Lee Bailey (Eleanor's stand-in), and another unnamed family friend.

The festive dinner party featured a patriotic red, white, and blue floral centerpiece in honor of the servicemen, and an all-American dinner of fried chicken, homemade rolls, and what Foster called "a fine salad." The guests were treated royally with champagne and an after-dinner liqueur, along with an ice cream dessert served creatively in "frosted tumblers" of red ice. Merrill was deemed "a hell of a swell fellow," and Foster was thrilled to find Eleanor and Blanche "not at all 'Hollywood.'" He wrote that "they make you feel right at home and are the kind that it seems you've known them for years." The soldiers were treated to a screening of Eleanor's home movies and given full access to her record collection of three thousand tunes. "I had a big time playing all my old favorites," Foster wrote. "I even had to be the yokel boy and dance with her once so that now I can say I danced with Eleanor Powell—some fun."[4] After Merrill snapped a few photos for the group, Foster, Brach, and Fuller were driven back to their hotel at midnight by Eleanor and Blanche. Later, their tale of dinner with Eleanor Powell was the hit of the barracks.

I'll Take Manila started production on November 11. Three days later, Tommy Dorsey and his Orchestra were signed along with their young vocalist, Frank Sinatra. Tony Martin was more appealing on screen than the skinny singer from Hoboken, but Sinatra came as part of the band. Martin was reluctantly let go. After the preview, Eddie Mannix found scrawny Sinatra so unattractive on screen that he stated, "You can't photograph him," and asked for his songs to be cut. Cummings convinced him that the numbers should stay.

Filming was barely under way when Eleanor celebrated her twenty-ninth birthday on the set. The crew presented her with a special cake with "Happy Birthday, Eleanor" cleverly spelled out in Morse code, in a nod to the recently filmed number. The same day, the *New York Times* reported that Eleanor Powell and Merrill Pye would be wed in February; Louella Parsons quickly reacted, wondering the following day if that meant Eleanor was about to retire. Blanche stepped in to clarify the issue. "I am devoted to Merrill," she said, "and he and Eleanor are in love and will get married—but I don't think it will be in February."[5]

The bombing of Pearl Harbor by the Japanese on December 7, 1941, profoundly shocked the country. First Lady Eleanor Roosevelt spoke to all Americans via a national radio broadcast with an admonition that Eleanor took to heart. She urged them to "go about our daily business more determined than ever to do the ordinary things as well as we can and when we find a way to do anything more in our communities to help others, to build morale, to give a feeling of security, we must do it. Whatever is asked of us I am sure we can accomplish it. We are the free and unconquerable people of the United States of America."

America was now at war, and Hollywood quickly rose to the occasion. Films in production were quickly reevaluated in light of the times. In the case of *I'll Take Manila,* when the Philippines were invaded by the Japanese the day after Pearl Harbor, the film's title suddenly became inappropriate. The FBI, who had been consulting on the picture, ordered MGM to change the title, or they would withdraw their approval of the film.

I'll Take Manila now became *Ship Ahoy* and underwent a series of other modifications. The setting was moved from the Philippines to Puerto Rico, but the title song, "I'll Take Manila," had already been recorded. A rewrite was problematic since the phrase was used extensively in the lyrics. To avoid affecting the tempo and rhyme, Eleanor's character—originally Kay Winters—became Tallulah Winters, and the song was re-recorded as "I'll Take Tallulah," with some very creative (and silly) new lyrics. The studio tried to salvage as much footage as they could, and overdubs are still apparent in the final version. Ultimately, it cost MGM $75,000 to make the necessary changes to the film.

The plot, blending espionage and comedy, was a departure from earlier Powell vehicles. Tallulah Winters (Eleanor Powell), star of a dancing troupe, is sailing from New York to Puerto Rico with her friend Fran Evans (Virginia O'Brien) and Tommy Dorsey and his Orchestra to appear in a floating night club. As she is about to set off, Tallulah is approached by a man posing as a government agent who asks her to smuggle a magnetic mine on board and deliver it to fellow agents. Unaware that he is really an enemy agent, Tallulah accepts the mission. Also sailing is Merton K. Kibble (Red Skelton), a hypochondriac pulp fiction writer, and his friend, Skip Owens (Bert Lahr). Tallulah and Merton meet on the ship and fall in love. When Tallulah overhears Merton describing the plot of one of his stories to Skip, she thinks he is planning to jilt her after the voyage and breaks off the relationship. The ship docks, and Tallulah unknowingly turns the mine over to enemy agents. Realizing the truth, she devises a plan to alert the US agents on board by tapping out an SOS message in Morse code during her performance. The plan succeeds, and the enemy agents are captured.

Critics agreed that Powell and Skelton had a pleasant chemistry, and Eleanor appeared more relaxed and warmer in her acting. As in *Lady Be Good*, she exhibits a certain flair for comedy, possibly as a result of the fun rapport she had with her co-star. Each day on the set, they tried to top each other in a silly game they called "Prop Puns." "For instance, Red comes into the dancer's dressing room with a length of rope—'You've roped me in,' he cracks. Miss Powell counters with: 'Get along. I'll brush you off.' A broom illustrates."[6]

In the first of the three numbers Eleanor shot for the film, the bullfight number "La Torria," she deftly shows her prowess with a matador's cape. Always game to learn a new skill, she worked for weeks with a professional matador, Dr. Alfonso Gaona, who was engaged as technical advisor and teacher. Pianist Walter Ruick composed the music for both "La Torria" and "Tampico," the dance immediately following. But more than just showing off a new skill, Eleanor loved the idea of using a dance to tell a story, just as in ballet.

Eleanor's insatiable desire to learn all she could about behind-the-scenes aspects of filmmaking resulted in a significant evolution of her skill sets during her years at MGM. Her extensive production knowledge had become so well-known that columnist Paul Harrison predicted, "When rheumatism sets in, Eleanor Powell can earn her keep as a production designer."[7] Eleanor was an anomaly in that era; at the time, female dancers were not given much production input, and female choreographers in musical features were extremely rare. A few years later, Gene Kelly would successfully battle to be active in the decision-making process in the staging of his elaborate numbers, such as the ballets in *An American in Paris* and *Singin' in the Rain*. It would be years, however, before a female choreographer would be allowed the same freedom. Eleanor's input was limited to the conception of the number. She presented her vision at the outset, but the final iteration of the number was entirely dictated by studio executives with little creative bent—a reality that increasingly frustrated her.

The evolution of the matador number in *Ship Ahoy* was a classic example of how studio decisions sometimes worked against her and made her unable to present her best work. She approached the dance not just as choreography, but with a director's eye, staging a full story; she visualized shots and specific lighting and even the creative involvement of other cast members. The café set had originally been described as a pirate-themed floating nightclub in an old Spanish galleon docked at the pier, which would have allowed a large area for the number. Eleanor envisioned a walled-in bullring with tables on platforms. As the matador, she would arrive through a tunnel and toss her hat to Red Skelton. From another tunnel, a spotlight would appear in the shape of a bull's head. Eleanor would dance, incorporating authentic bullfighting movements while wielding a large red cape. At the conclusion of the bullfighting ritual when she kills the bull, the spotlight would go red and pulse until it faded away. Then, in an adjacent area, the celebration would begin with a challenge dance between two matadors. "I wanted José Greco," she told John Kobal years later, "who so badly wanted to work with me, to be the other leading matador who gets up and does his flamenco work to 'Jealousy.' José and I [would] have a real challenge . . . with the heel work."

Unfortunately, Eleanor's plans were drastically curtailed when the script was changed to add a comedy scene between Skelton and Lahr, which cut the time allotted for her number. When she arrived to rehearse, she also found the space was much smaller than she expected. If given the opportunity, she would have developed an alternate idea, but there was no time to change. "I'd have done a pirate's number, come flying down as a pirate on a rope. So, it was a throwaway, no story to it—just a girl coming out and doing a tap dance in costume."[8] While she was satisfied with her dancing and cape work, which she would later incorporate into her nightclub act in the sixties, the end result in *Ship Ahoy* was a huge disappointment to her.

167

The same day the company finished shooting the bullfight routine, they went directly into filming the cabaret number on the ship. Accompanied by Tommy Dorsey and his Orchestra, featuring the Pied Pipers and Frank Sinatra, Tallulah tries to signal to US agents that enemy agents are also on board and that everyone is in danger. Wearing a satin version of her signature top hat and tails, Eleanor does a soft-shoe routine (to "Moonlight Bay"), backed by four chorus boys. As she dances, she cleverly integrates an SOS message in Morse code, spelled out in taps.

While the cape dance in its original concept was certainly intended to be the principal number of the film, "I'll Take Tallulah" was the blockbuster that stole the show. As a rhythm dancer and percussionist, Eleanor relished the chance to work with the Dorsey Orchestra's star drummer Buddy Rich. One of the most influential drummers of all time, Rich was also an excellent tap dancer. The two masters had a great respect for one another.

Unlike the massive production numbers of the thirties, the success of this number stems solely from Eleanor's matchless energy. She flies through the set, her rhythmic use of props and furniture propelling her onward in an effortless flow of movement. She fearlessly dances on tables and chairs and swings across the pool on a ring, ending the number in an intricately synchronized interchange with Rich. The number exudes pure contagious joy.

But the number was not without risk. Eleanor took inspiration from her diving lessons and incorporated a swan dive into the arms of a man on a platform in the middle of the pool. Timing was critical. They rehearsed the number perfectly several times, but on the first take all did not go quite as planned, and she ended up in the pool. "To save my hair and face for makeup, I grabbed the edge of the pool and kept my head up out of the water. Now this poor guy . . . sees I'm hanging, and . . . he dives in, grabs me by the waist and pulls me down to the bottom. But in so doing, he pulled all the ligaments in my arm. We couldn't do any more shooting that day because my arm was just torn."[9]

Ship Ahoy marked Frank Sinatra's second and final film appearance with the band. Since he had begun singing with Dorsey in 1939, Sinatra's popularity had increased dramatically, and a successful series of solo recordings had convinced him it was time to go out on his own. Eleanor remembered him as rather aloof during the making of the picture; he kept to himself or played poker with the boys in the band. Sinatra recorded three songs from the film with Dorsey in February: "I'll Take Tallulah," "Poor You," and "Last Call for Love." By August, Dorsey released him from his contract.

In December, the war felt a little closer to home when Eleanor received an unusual package while on the set of *Ship Ahoy*. Richard Norton, a long-time fan in London, had been writing to her every month since he had seen her in *Follow Thru* during a visit to New York in 1929. This time, instead of a letter, she received a charred scrapbook. Norton's home had been bombed by the Nazis, and the scrapbook was the one item they were able to salvage. He wanted Eleanor to have it.

The situation in Europe was becoming increasingly dire, and the first Christmas following Pearl Harbor was a somber one for many Americans. To spread a little holiday cheer to the servicemen based locally, Eleanor performed at a camp on Christmas Day. Later in the afternoon, Blanche, Eleanor, and Merrill held an open house.

With long hours at the studio and little rest over the Christmas holidays, Eleanor began to feel run down. Trying to push through, on December 27, she reported for work with a bad cold. She was immediately sent home, and the company was dismissed for the rest of the day. This went on throughout the first week of January, holding up production. Eleanor had again lost twelve pounds during the making of *Ship Ahoy*, which caused the wardrobe department grief as they were forced to alter sixteen of her costumes.

Increasingly involved in the war effort, Eleanor made personal appearances at camps whenever she could. The boys of the 143rd Field Artillery made her a "major" at an impressive ceremony, and she was chosen Sweetheart of the Regiment. Later she was honored to receive a special pin with an inscription engraved in gold: "Every star is a bomber to us—but you are our B-19."[10]

Toward the end of production, a final number was added—"Hawaiian War Chant," used as the film's opener. Tommy Dorsey's signature song introduces the band, highlighting Buddy Rich with a trick photo effect that makes him appear to float over the orchestra until he lands in his usual spot. During the last few bars, Eleanor makes her entrance with the chorus girls. Dressed in hula skirts, they do a very short dance that Eleanor dubbed the "Hawonga" (a conga that incorporates some Hawaiian movements).

In February 1942, the production of *Ship Ahoy* came to an end. It also marked the end of the two-and-a-half-year Powell–Pye relationship. This time would be a final break for Eleanor and Merrill. She told the press it wasn't right to enter into marriage when her career was her priority and took every ounce of energy. "I simply had to decide which one was more important to me," she said. "I found out my career came first." She never spoke publicly of the relationship again. Merrill, on the other hand, displayed hope that things would eventually work out between them. On February 14, he registered for the draft. Under the section that asked for the contact information of "someone who will always know your whereabouts," he carefully printed Eleanor's name and home address.

Audience response to the sneak previews in March was positive, but Virginia O'Brien's number, "I Fell in Love with the Leader of the Band," was cut from the film. Shooting of an additional scene was delayed while Eleanor recovered from another bad cold. The film finally premiered on June 30, 1942.

With only perfunctory nods to the lightweight story, critics were unanimous in their praise of Eleanor and they complimented the comedy skills of both Skelton and Lahr. "It sags and labors rather heavily in spots . . . but it skips along right merrily when Miss Powell is doing her turns," said the *New York Times* critic, Bosley Crowther.[11] The *Hollywood Reporter* claimed that "Powell was at her best with Dorsey rhythms" and that she "has never stepped more delightfully than in her dazzling routine around the ship's swimming pool." Singling out Eleanor's much improved acting, they added, "All deliver for Buzzell, and he gets from Miss Powell her warmest screen performance." Neither Sinatra nor Rich was mentioned by name, just that "the drummer and vocalist with Dorsey's orchestra have their moments."[12] Critics acknowledged Red Skelton as an up-and-coming comedy star and claimed that Bert Lahr's work in the film was some of his funniest since *The Wizard of Oz*.

Eager to take full advantage of Skelton's radio success, Howard Dietz gave the publicity department a new direction: "Believe it might be advisable to switch billing on *Ship Ahoy* wherever possible and feature Skelton ahead of Powell. Skelton's radio build-up makes this logical." While she retained top billing in the film, newspaper ads showed a mix of split-billing, with many giving Skelton top billing and visual prominence. MGM decided that repeating the Powell–Skelton combination was smart business. But first, Eleanor would join her Hollywood colleagues in a massive war effort on the road.

◉　◉　◉

By early 1942, America's involvement in the war was being felt at home. From the sale of war bonds to the planting of Victory gardens, every citizen was encouraged to pitch in. Hollywood was also called upon to do its part in the war effort, and it put together the biggest touring show ever produced. The sponsoring Hollywood Victory Committee of Stage, Screen and Radio—chaired by Clark Gable, George Murphy, and Sam Levene—organized over seven thousand events between 1942 and 1945.

The largest and most successful of these was the Hollywood Victory Caravan; twenty-two top stars and seven "starlets" (who served as chorus girls) traveled cross-country by train and played one-night shows in twelve cities. All proceeds benefited the Army and Navy Relief Society. The long list of stellar names for the three-hour show included Cary Grant, Bob Hope, Groucho Marx, Risë Stevens, Bert Lahr, Charlotte Greenwood, Bing Crosby, Merle Oberon, Desi Arnaz, James Cagney, Laurel and Hardy, Claudette Colbert, and Olivia de Havilland, among others.

Eleanor was added to the list on April 14 and was featured in several numbers. Costumed as Uncle Sam, she was the sole dancer in a massive patriotic production number, "Keep the Light Burning Bright," a finale that rivaled "Swingin' the Jinx Away" in a celebratory overload of Americana. One reporter noted that "Eleanor Powell brought the house down with her tap dancing, and when she was brought back for more, made the audience participate in her act" by joining in song. "I can't shoulder a rifle," Eleanor told the press. "But if these machine gun taps of mine can help this magnificent cause in even a small way, I am thrilled to be able to do my share."[13] Her finale alternated in some cities with a number by James Cagney, who danced to "Yankee Doodle Dandy."

In a departure from their usually glamorous accommodations, during the two-week tour the stars lived on a custom-outfitted train made up of seven Pullman cars provided free of charge by Southern Pacific Railroad; these were furnished with pianos and dance floors for on-the-road rehearsals. All the stars carried their own costumes. Eleanor brought along several from her recent films.

Mark Sandrich was hired as director/producer, and Alfred Newman, music director at 20th Century-Fox, served in the same capacity for the show. Fourteen of his studio musicians traveled with the tour, and local musicians were added to supplement the orchestra along the way. New songs with a patriotic theme were penned by Johnny Mercer, Jerome Kern, Arthur Schwartz, and Frank Loesser. By the final week of April, rehearsals were in full swing in Hollywood, lasting till the early hours of the morning. With much fanfare, the stars boarded the train at Union Station on Sunday, April 26, bound for Washington, DC. There, they had tea with First Lady Eleanor Roosevelt and then prepared for the first evening show.

Crowds turned out in such numbers that the police were brought in to manage the horde. "A cheering, whistling, applause-crazy audience of 16,000 persons, nearly every one a movie addict, jammed Convention Hall . . . right up to the eaves," said one reporter of the Philadelphia show. He dubbed the spectacle "an unforgettable extravaganza" that was surely "the stage show of all stage shows." Every stop along the way was met with crowds of boisterous fans, and the stars would often put on a short preview of the entertainment upon arrival at the depot. In Chicago, Charles Boyer clowned as part of a barbershop quartet with Cary Grant. At the city's Navy Pier, Eleanor greeted her half brother, Cliff Powell, with a kiss on the cheek. The twenty-five-year-old was then a seaman first class in the Navy. Naturally impressed with a celebrity sister, Cliff was one of the three siblings who established contact with Eleanor after discovering their connection. Later, she would be instrumental in helping him get work as a cameraman at MGM.

Blanche had joined Eleanor partway through the tour and rode alongside her daughter in a motorcade through the streets of Boston. Over five hundred thousand people packed the route, shouting greetings to the stars as they passed. Incredulous, Ellie waved happily to the cheering fans. A reporter noted that, "pointing to the sea of happy faces, Eleanor Powell's mother whispered in Eleanor's ear, 'This is better than money, for you can't buy that.'"[14]

Life on the train with the stars quickly turned the trip into a license for free-spirited debauchery, with lots of drinking and nightly bed hopping. Some stars, like friendly actress Charlotte Greenwood, steered clear, and focused on practicalities such as how to keep one's wardrobe wrinkle free. She helped Eleanor rig up a clothesline with sheets to hang up their costumes. When they returned to the train after each show, many would gather around the piano and take turns singing popular songs and clowning late into the early hours. Bert Lahr recalled that, because it was so hard to sleep on the train, a studio doctor freely dispensed sleeping pills to the stars at night, then gave them Benzedrine pills in the morning to keep them energetic—an unfortunate practice MGM had started several years earlier with some of their stars.

Many evenings, while traveling from one city to the next, Eleanor relaxed by chatting and playing cards with new friend Pat O'Brien. He was one of the few in the cast who was a devoted family man, married to the same woman, Eloise Taylor, since 1931. They had four children and would remain together for life. One of their conversations turned to recent films and young actor Glenn Ford. O'Brien had just finished shooting *First Lieutenant* with the twenty-six-year-old actor. Eleanor was intrigued by Ford's style, likening him to a young Paul Muni. She had casually dated several men since the breakup with Merrill, but none had piqued any serious interest. Sensing the spark in Eleanor's questioning, O'Brien had the idea to introduce them. Though Ford had been seeing Universal actress Evelyn Ankers steadily enough to have introduced her to his mother, Hannah, O'Brien knew Ford was not serious about her. He promised Eleanor to set up a dinner when they were finally back in Los Angeles.

After an exhilarating but exhausting two weeks, with shows in Washington, DC, Boston, Philadelphia, Cleveland, Detroit, Chicago, St. Louis, St. Paul, Minneapolis, Des Moines, and Dallas, the train rolled into Houston for the last big show, where eleven thousand patriotic fans applauded the close of the run.

Just one smaller show remained a few days later in San Francisco, as many stars had to leave the tour for other commitments when the train stopped briefly in Los Angeles. Spearheaded by Walter Winchell, the remaining stars set off on May 18 from Glendale for the final show at San Francisco's Civic Auditorium the following night. Additional cast members Al Jolson, Milton Berle, Eddie Cantor, the Andrews Sisters, and Dinah Shore joined them. The shows raised a total of over $750,000 for the war effort, making the campaign the most successful for any cause to date by the entertainment community.

MGM had little for Eleanor to do until July, when dance rehearsals would start on her next film, *I Dood It*. An avid swimmer, she started to frequent the pool at the nearby Beverly Hills Hotel. After connecting with Al Jolson during the San Francisco show, Blanche and Eleanor had dinner with him when he was in town briefly on his way to more camp performances. Because Jolson had recently broken up with Ruby Keeler, columnists speculated a romance was brewing between the older star and Eleanor. While Jolson may have harbored other intentions, Eleanor quickly clarified that it was just a friendship. With no one to take the place that Merrill had filled in her life for so long, she was spotted out with a variety of dinner and dancing partners, among them her music director, Walter Ruick, and actor Philip Reed. Both were only friends. After coming so close to marriage and with her career becoming more and more a disappointment, she was cautiously on the lookout for a change.

With matchmaking in mind, Pat O'Brien followed through on his promise to introduce Eleanor to Glenn Ford. Along with several other guests, O'Brien invited the two to his house in late May for a post–Victory Caravan celebration. O'Brien's spacious family home was just a block north of famed Sunset Boulevard in the star-studded neighborhood of Brentwood. Ford described his first view of Eleanor from across the room, stunning in a lavender suit that showed off her beautiful legs. "I had only seen her in black-and-white movies. . . . I was struck by her coloring, her chestnut hair, worn in soft waves to her shoulders, this glowing complexion, and her beautiful cornflower blue eyes. And when she smiled, I was just captivated."[15]

But while Ford was taken by Eleanor, he was still dating others. Singer Dinah Shore was his latest steady, and he was also linked to recent flame Ankers, Joan Crawford, Janet Blair, and starlet Alma Carroll. On Thursday, June 11, Ford attended the ball for the Navy Relief Society at the Ambassador Hotel's Cocoanut Grove nightclub, where Red Skelton was the emcee. Both Eleanor (who later joined her date John Carroll at a table) and Shore were on the bill with the Berry Brothers, Risë Stevens, Dick Powell, Abbott and Costello, and Freddie Martin and his Orchestra.

Once the show was over, Ford cut in on a dance as Eleanor and Carroll were out on the floor. The two finally had an opportunity to talk after the brief meeting at O'Brien's crowded party. They made a date for dinner the following week at the famed Musso & Frank Grill, Hollywood's oldest restaurant. It was clear that they were strongly attracted to each other.

The relationship began to blossom, and Eleanor and Glenn were seen about town on a regular basis. They attended the gala premiere of *Mrs. Miniver* on July 22, 1942, then dined afterward at the Trocadero. Glenn was in no rush to give up his bachelorhood. At the same time he was dating Eleanor, he was also pursuing actress Hedy Lamarr. "Glenn Ford, the lad who finally hit the social success ladder by his romance with Joan Crawford, has gone onto more beautiful conquests," columnists reported. "Now he's calling Hedy Lamarr, but she's too busy to bother with the youngster."[16]

Eleanor's *Born to Dance* co-star, James Stewart, now a lieutenant of the US Army Air Corps, invited her to come entertain the troops at Mather Field near Sacramento, California, where he was stationed. Joining her for two days of shows in July were Nelson Eddy, Virginia O'Brien, and Milton Berle. "This we were too happy to do," Eleanor recounted, "and we were amply repaid by the appreciation of the boys, and the courtesy and hospitality of their officers, who all but gave us the Field."[17] By the end of July, she was back in the rehearsal hall at MGM working on dance numbers for *I Dood It*.

Glenn returned from Utah in late August, where he had been working on the film *The Desperadoes* with Randolph Scott. Soon he resumed dates with

Eleanor. Surprisingly, he told columnist Harry Mines that he and Eleanor were engaged. "The question of a wedding date remains unsettled in the couple's mind because of the Army draft. They'll have an announcement probably during the next two weeks."[18] Eleanor, though confident about the romance, was hesitant to talk of marriage. "We are quite serious," she told a reporter. "However, I don't know about marriage. I'd rather consider carefully than make a mistake and be faced with a divorce."[19]

Eleanor was deep into preparation for *I Dood It* when their relationship took a significant turn. There were no more mentions of Glenn with other starlets. Back on the lot and occupied with choreography, Eleanor continued to see Glenn when she was able, but she soon fell into her routine of spending long hours in her bungalow and heading to bed early. Difficult days on the set would soon occupy her thoughts.

15

Disillusion and Hope

Eleanor was about to embark on her last starring film at MGM, and from the outset, *I Dood It* (known as *By Hook or By Crook* in the UK) would be different from all previous projects. Wartime now impacted all aspects of the economy, and previously generous budgets were slashed dramatically. "Save film! Help win the war!" was admonished on every script. Originally planned for Technicolor, the film was eventually shot in black and white. MGM recycled a plot from one of their old productions, using the silent Buster Keaton film *Spite Marriage* (1929) as inspiration. The title—taken directly from a radio catchphrase of Red Skelton's Mean Widdle Kid character ("If I do, I get a whipping . . . I dood it!")—made it clear the primary star of the picture was Red Skelton. MGM was now positioning Skelton to compete with Paramount's big comedy star who had also been successful in radio, Bob Hope. The studio used the services of an uncredited Buster Keaton, who had been on the MGM payroll for several years as a "gag" consultant, for comic input on the scenes taken from *Spite Marriage,* as well as new ones.

The plot centers around humble pants presser Joseph Rivington Renolds (Red Skelton), who carries a torch for Broadway star Constance "Connie" Shaw (Eleanor Powell). Joseph has a bad habit of borrowing the customers' suits from the valet service to go out on the town. Nightly, he goes to see *Dixie Lou,* the show in which Connie and her fiancé, Larry West (Richard Ainley), are appearing. When socialite Suretta Brenton (Patricia Dane) makes a play for Larry, Connie, to spite her fiancé, marries Joseph, believing that he is the owner of a gold mine. She soon regrets her hasty decision and discovers Joseph is an imposter. However, he wins the day and the girl when he foils a Nazi plot.

Though dance rehearsals began in July, filming did not begin until November 19, 1942, which meant that Eleanor's choreography was planned out well before decisions on story elements were set.

"So Long, Sarah Jane" (with Bob Eberle on the vocals) was the only number shot for the film. Eleanor's idea for a western-themed dance number was not a new one. Back in April 1939, she had begun taking lessons in fancy roping, twirling, and riding from film star and rodeo champion Hoot Gibson, and Sam Cope of the California State Police had shown her how to use a six-shooter. Press reports indicated that this was for a number she was working on for *Broadway Melody of 1940,* but it is possible that it was intended for *Girl Crazy,* announced as another vehicle for Eleanor, Astaire, and Eddie Cantor. Though *Girl Crazy* eventually went to Judy Garland and Mickey Rooney, the rodeo theme was revisited for *I Dood It.*

This time, cowboy Sam Garrett was hired to (literally) teach her the ropes. Instructed by Will Rogers, Garrett was a champion trick roper from Oklahoma who had been roping from the age of fourteen. He had earned the title of World's Champion Trick Roper an unprecedented seven times. During the 1930s and 1940s, Garrett frequently was employed as a riding and roping teacher in Hollywood and also worked as a double in films.

With her customary dedication, Eleanor set out to conquer the difficult art of roping. It took her an intense six weeks to learn. She underestimated how difficult it would be. "That hondo [a metal part at the base of the loop] is very heavy," Eleanor said later. "When you get the rope going, it's about fifty miles an hour and you have to have a very strong arm."[1] Maintaining a spinning rope at high speed was tiring work. If her arm dropped, the hondo would hit her head. After being knocked out more than once, she finally resorted to rehearsing in a football helmet and shoulder pads. As an unforeseen result of the rigorous training, Eleanor developed such a muscular arm that costume designer Adrian had to replace the right sleeve on every one of her dialogue dresses. In the end, Sam Garrett was so impressed with her skills that he suggested she give up films and go on the rodeo circuit.

When it came time to stage the number, in lieu of chorus boys, Garrett hired actual cowboys to rope along with Eleanor and himself. Dance director Bobby Connolly added some pretty chorus girls into the mix to soften the effect. Eleanor dazzled the audience by throwing eight successive lassos. "For six weeks we worked on that number, and that whole [part] was shot in one take. The crew had cigar boxes and they were taking really big bets—like $50, $100—that I wouldn't make it in one take." Eleanor succeeded after just three tries. "I got so good that I could lasso anybody who came on that sound-stage!"[2] As an appreciative gesture for her hard work, MGM executive Sam Katz gifted a proud Eleanor with a 16mm film copy of the number.

The number was filmed under director Roy Del Ruth, but by the time the entire script had been sorted out by writers Fred Saidy and Sig Herzig in late December, Del Ruth had been replaced by Vincente Minnelli. With so much time and budget invested, Eleanor had planned it for a prominent place in the film. Unfortunately, the number fell victim to the dictates of the script, the details of which came much later. Eleanor later described the entire process in a letter to a disappointed fan from the Navy, Douglas Ebersole. Story ideas were told to her verbally along with options for how many numbers could be included. The usual pattern was a simple dance number, then a novelty number, and finally a large production number. She explained:

> I work out my numbers alone in the rehearsal hall for about four months, all the while the script is being written. Sometimes I don't even see the completed script until I'm on the set; you see, I must therefore have implicit trust in my producer.
>
> The roping number, which is absolutely authentic and took me over three months to perfect, was to be the highlight of the picture. But in the writing of the script, the charity bazaar had to come at the opening of the picture, and I felt therefore the entire number was lost, as it came too soon.[3]

Eleanor's frustrations were warranted. MGM continually refused her creative input about the placement of the numbers or revisions to the script. Despite her valiant efforts to educate herself on the production process, they chose to keep her as a dancing workhorse. Just how many of the decisions on the remainder of the film were actually made by Minnelli or simply mandated by MGM is unclear. Even though he had worked with Eleanor in *At Home Abroad* and directed an unused number for *Lady Be Good,* his biographer attested that he "never liked her dancing much, which was too athletic for his taste."[4] In any case, Minnelli took the assignment, not out of any particular interest in the film, but out of obligation. He had just finished directing his first film, *Cabin in the Sky,* three weeks before starting on *I Dood It.* The studio was unhappy with the first results from Roy Del Ruth. Though Jack Cummings was producer, Arthur Freed's enthusiasm after seeing early *Cabin in the Sky* previews led him to recommend Minnelli as Del Ruth's replacement. Freed's influential stature was evident. Given their confidence, Minnelli felt it imprudent to refuse.

Stuck with "So Long, Sarah Jane," Minnelli had no issue with "burying" it early in the picture. As further evidence of wartime budget cutting, MGM used two recycled numbers in the film and misleadingly promoted them as unused numbers from previous films. However, the dance numbers ultimately used in *I Dood It* were not outtakes from earlier films.

Eleanor had simply been told *I Dood It* would not need a finale number. She was then left with one ill-placed number and a recycled number disguised as a "dream" sequence. Already unhappy with the entire experience, she was shocked to discover at the preview screening that the studio had borrowed "Swingin' the Jinx Away" from *Born to Dance* and placed it as a finale. "The hula number was acceptable, since it was highly logical Red would be dreaming of something he'd seen me do before. But I never knew about the finale from *Born to Dance* until the night of the preview. . . . I came home and cried myself to sleep. . . . I had been told there would be no finale . . . and it would be that much money saved."[5]

Eleanor was devastated by this treatment, which sadly clarified how little her input was valued in the production process. It would become one of the tipping factors in her decision to leave the studio. She felt that the studio had not only mistreated her but also, by presenting a shoddy film patched together with mismatched numbers, had cheated the audience. As she explained in her closing thoughts to Ebersole, "I feel it's more important to give the public something for its money beyond just collecting it at the box office and letting it go at that."[6]

The finished film did allow her to display her comedic gifts, but, overall, her dance talents were underused, which made her seem a mere foil to Skelton. As the *New York Times* observed, it was essentially a "one-man comedy . . . with an assist from Eleanor Powell."[7]

Although a disappointment for Eleanor, the film was a triumph for Skelton. The *Hollywood Reporter* called it "the funniest musical in which Skelton has ever appeared on the screen,"[8] mentioning the pantomime scenes where "no one could have heard a cannon drop in the screaming audience." Though taken move by move from *Spite Marriage,* the scene in which Skelton tries to maneuver a drugged Eleanor into bed has been considered by film historians as "one of the funniest sequences in American comedy." One astutely observed: "Eleanor Powell's flair for comedy suggests acting ability completely overlooked during most of her dancing career."[9]

Variety found the film much hindered by a weak screenplay and not one of MGM's best. The critics applauded Eleanor's contributions, ignoring the reused numbers: "Eleanor Powell is the co-star, dancing and twirling ropes in a dazzling novelty number, tapping out a hula in a dream insert, and stepping expertly and leading the stunningly staged battleship finale. Her performance ranks with her best on the screen."[10]

⊙ ⊙ ⊙

Eleanor's personal life took an important turn during the production of *I Dood It*. Her relationship with Glenn was growing stronger, and they were seeing each other as often as they could. In December, Glenn enlisted in the Marine Corps. He was working on *Destroyer* (1943) and was expected to go to boot camp in a few months. With his impending departure, he felt an urgency to seal his relationship with Eleanor. While they were out Christmas shopping one day, they stopped for chocolate sodas. Glenn began to propose, but Eleanor stopped him and suggested they find a more meaningful setting for the occasion. They deferred it until Christmas day. Glenn proposed again, this time kneeling in a pew at St. Augustine Episcopal Church in Santa Monica. Eleanor accepted, but they kept the news to themselves and their families for the next few weeks.

Eleanor danced for the first time in Technicolor in *Thousands Cheer*. The big-budget film in support of America's war effort starred Kathryn Grayson and Gene Kelly. A highlight of the picture was a camp show, now a common type of entertainment to boost the morale of servicemen across the nation, with numbers performed by the MGM Star Parade. Eleanor's sequence evolved greatly from the original concept. Early scripts from October 1942 show her in an elaborate sketch teamed with Mickey Rooney. Eleanor was to be a mind reader in a harem costume, Princess Fatima Powell, trading clever dialogue with Rooney. Abandoning the character, she and Rooney would end with impersonations—she of Jimmy Stewart and he of Katharine Hepburn. Finally, Eleanor would perform a dance. The sketch was continually shortened over the next month and ultimately eliminated from the final film. Simply introduced by Rooney as "America's Greatest Dancer, Eleanor Powell," she dances a boogie-woogie tap number to music written by Walter Ruick.

On January 20, 1943, the *Los Angeles Times* carried the "scoop" that Eleanor Powell's engagement to Glenn Ford was confirmed. According to their publicity-spun version, she had visited him on the set at Columbia, where he presented her with a diamond solitaire ring. Speculation immediately began on when they would tie the knot; some reports suggested that they might wait until after the war to marry. Ten days later, Eleanor officially announced their engagement in the press.

A sign of the times, in early February, columnist Sheilah Graham noted the sudden increase in Hollywood marriages. Ginger Rogers had recently married a marine after only ten dates, and "Hollywood's old maid, Eleanor Powell, [was] finally altar bound." Graham attributed this to the wartime urgency to grab a man "while he was still around."[11] The wartime climate could account for Eleanor's jumping into an engagement with both feet a mere six months after she and Glenn met. They were all too conscious that time was limited and precious.

Nothing could have demonstrated this more than the sad news that her friend, Colonel Ted Teague of the United States Army Signal Corps, was now a prisoner of war, held by the Japanese at the Taiwan prison camp in Formosa. Having no family, the colonel listed Eleanor as his next of kin. While on the set, in mid-February, Eleanor received a record with a message from him, made several months earlier. He wished her a happy birthday, recalled the fun times spent at her home, and sent his fondest greetings to her "guardian angel," Blanche.

About this time, Glenn and his mother, Hannah, moved into a two-bedroom apartment on Camden Drive in Beverly Hills. This would help save some money during his time in the service since he was no longer earning a studio paycheck.

On March 22, 1943, Glenn arrived at the Marine Corps base in San Diego to begin boot camp. Promoted to sergeant by the end of the seven weeks, he moved on to Camp Pendleton in nearby Oceanside, where he became part of the motion picture unit.

The day following Glenn's departure, the trade papers announced that Bobby Connolly had begun screen tests with Eleanor and Gene Kelly for a new project to be filmed in Technicolor, *Broadway Melody of 1943*. A Freed favorite since *For Me and My Gal*, Kelly was next cast in another musical, *Du Barry Was a Lady*, and the war drama *Pilot #5*. Even though Kelly would not work under Freed again until 1946, Mayer recognized his potential to play a strong part in the next decade of the studio's musicals. But pairing Kelly with Eleanor would have proved an odd match. Though they were the same age, their dance styles were vastly different. Eleanor was also partnered best with taller men. A muscular five foot seven, Kelly was a mere half-inch taller than Eleanor. *Broadway Melody of 1943* cycled through Hollywood columns that listed various other possible participants such as Victor Borge, impersonator Dean Murphy, and Rita Hayworth, before the *Broadway Melody* series was abandoned. A few days after the initial announcement, Eleanor was purportedly set for the leading role in *You Can't Fool a Marine*, which later became *Anchors Aweigh*, starring Kathryn Grayson, Gene Kelly, and Frank Sinatra.

In the meantime, Eleanor was still being considered for other projects. On April 28, it was announced that she and George Murphy would co-star in *Up and Down Broadway*, eventually retitled *Broadway Rhythm*. The film was to be a major Technicolor production directed by Roy Del Ruth and would start filming on June 1.

Despite all the potential projects, Eleanor was becoming increasingly dissatisfied with her life at MGM, and she felt it was time to take a new direction. Producer Arthur Freed, whose unit would handle the majority of MGM musicals through the next decade, had already categorized her as belonging to an old style of musicals and preferred to develop his unit primarily around rising stars Garland and Kelly.

As music evolved, dance styles had also begun to change. The success of the musical *Oklahoma* on Broadway in March 1943 played a significant part in dethroning tap from its prominent place in musicals, giving way to jazz dance. MGM no longer saw bankability in vehicles built around a strong solo female tapper, especially one in her thirties. Eleanor was the last of her class. Her successor, Ann Miller, would only ever be awarded supporting roles. However, iconic male dancers such as Astaire and Kelly retained their star status and were permitted to age on screen with grace.

Eleanor had no intention of slowly being edged out of lead roles. Instead, she preferred to make any decision to leave on her own terms—and she wanted to quit while she was still on top. Less than two weeks before she was to begin production on *Broadway Rhythm*, Eleanor told Louella Parsons: "I have worked for seventeen years, and I have promised myself and my mother when I marry, I will retire. I want to be a wife and have children and you cannot do strenuous dance routines and keep a home going at the same time. If Glenn doesn't go overseas, we will probably wed this summer. If he does—I don't know, because I don't want to be one of those hurry-up war weddings."[12]

Her decision finally made, in May she requested an early release from her contract, which still had nine months to go. After negotiations, Eleanor and MGM parted ways on June 5, 1943. She received $39,000 in pay that was due her and walked away from the studio that had been home to her for the past eight years. It was the end of an era. As she explained in her letter to Ebersole: "So, I retired from the screen and MGM. I felt that after all the years of hard work, I wouldn't have my career ruined and have to quit at the bottom because of poor stories and circumstances beyond my control."[13]

After Eleanor's departure, Ginny Simms took over Eleanor's part in *Broadway Rhythm,* and the trades speculated that MGM would consider Ann Miller to fill future dancing roles. Eleanor had plans of her own. As a free-lancer, she was now at liberty to pick and choose her projects as they suited her. But first, she had important personal projects to attend to.

With marriage on the horizon, she decided that now was a good time to look for a house for Blanche. The first week of August, she purchased a small English Tudor two-story house at 484 Hillgreen Drive in Beverly Hills for $20,000 (about $310,000 today). Blanche would remain in this house for the rest of her life.

Since her release from MGM, Eleanor had been putting together her own revue. While MGM was still doing trade and fan magazine screenings of *I Dood It,* in mid-August the press announced that Eleanor would be heading to New York to appear at the Roxy Theatre in September. She would be earning $7,500 a week, which would have made her one of the highest paid artists to play the venue. Rumor also had it that she would shortly be signed for a Broadway contract, to appear in *Dancing in the Streets* for producer Vinton Freedley. The show, previously starring Mary Martin, had never made it to Broadway after it required numerous rewrites following its Boston tryout. Though Eleanor would have enjoyed returning to Broadway, with the war intensifying and Glenn's deployment looming in the future, she canceled all plans to go to New York and flatly refused to leave California. Meanwhile, *I Dood It* premiered on September 1, 1943.

Shortly after, Eleanor found an engagement closer to home. She opened at the Golden Gate Theatre in San Francisco on September 22. Fellow William Morris Agency clients appeared on the bill: songwriter Pinky Tomlin and the "suave deceiver" Cardini, with whom she had appeared on the vaudeville circuit years earlier.

On Eleanor's return to Los Angeles, continued uncertainty about Glenn's deployment finally convinced the couple to be married as soon as possible. Glenn submitted a request for a brief leave, and the two began the wait for approval.

Act Three

(1943–1959)

16

Mizpah

Glenn's request for leave had been approved, and he and Eleanor set Saturday, October 23, as the date for their wedding. On October 17, photographers captured the couple getting their marriage license at the Santa Monica Courthouse. Eleanor was stylish in a white fur coat as she beamed at the camera, glowing with the promise of her new life. A boyish Glenn grinned sheepishly next to his bride-to-be.

Anxious for a simple ceremony without celebrity fanfare, Eleanor planned a small, quiet wedding at home. The only concession they would make was to allow the necessary presence of studio photographers. The next few days passed quickly. Glenn's minister, Reverend Ray Moore, was secured as officiant; Stebby was Eleanor's matron of honor, and Glenn's old friend Ned Crawford would be his best man.

With the wedding date decided, Eleanor, Blanche, Hannah, and Stebby went shopping to buy items for Eleanor's trousseau. After making the rounds of the shops, the four ladies ended the excursion with a girls' night out at the Florentine Gardens, the famed Hollywood nightspot known for great live orchestras and a large dance floor. A group of visiting English soldiers begged Eleanor for a dance. By the end of the evening, each soldier had taken a turn with her on the dance floor.

Still in search of a wedding gown, Eleanor, Blanche, and Stebby headed to I. Magnin. The salesgirls in the women's department knew and liked Eleanor, who never failed to remember their names and ask about their spouses and children. Eleanor soon found a dress she loved—a cap-sleeved gown designed with a soft draped twist that crossed the front of the bodice. It was stunning but only available in black. The store promised to have their team of seamstresses create a cream satin version for her on a rush basis, to which she added a matching cap and veil. Glenn would wear his dress blues for the occasion.

Eleanor chose a pair of shoes she had never worn for her "something old." Her "something new" would be her wedding dress. Stebby loaned her a beautiful handkerchief that she had worn at her own wedding for "something borrowed," and the seamstresses provided the "something blue" with a tiny, embroidered clover and rosebud in the neckline of her dress. For the double ring ceremony, Eleanor had a special message inscribed inside Glenn's ring—"Mizpah"—the Hebrew word for watchtower, a remembrance signifying, "May God watch over thee and me." She would discover at the ceremony that Glenn had the same message inscribed in her own ring.

The wedding day finally arrived. Blanche surprised Eleanor with a lovely spray of white orchids for her wedding bouquet and decorated the mantelpiece with fragrant flowers. Eleanor's new pianist Dave Gussin played "Sweet Leilani" for the short ceremony—one of Eleanor's favorites. Afterward, the new Mr. and Mrs. Ford cut the wedding cake, and their small group of friends and family enjoyed food catered by the Brown Derby.

Eleanor's recent performances in San Francisco prompted her to suggest that they revisit the city for their honeymoon. After a leisurely train ride up the coast, the couple checked into the St. Francis Hotel, where she had stayed the month before. As usual, Eleanor had made friends with the staff, and when she returned as a new bride, they welcomed the couple with romantic amenities and special treatment.

The couple enjoyed dining out, leisurely strolls in the bustling Bay city, and time alone in the quiet luxury of the hotel. Famed Chinese American physician Dr. Margaret Chung, who had developed connections with many celebrities and politicians, threw a party in their honor. They sent a short wire to columnist Louella Parsons saying they were "very, very happy."

Eleanor's star status made it impossible for her and Glenn to roam incognito. The handsome couple turned heads wherever they went, especially out on the dance floor, much to Glenn's dismay. "People recognized us and stared," Glenn recalled. "I felt like they were expecting me to be as good a dancer as Eleanor, and of course I never was."[1]

The intimate time together passed quickly, and nearly a week later they were already on their way home. Glenn was due to report back to Camp Pendleton on November 1. *I Dood It* was playing in theaters all over the city. Eleanor felt a pang of loneliness when her new husband left for San Diego, as she was both alone and without an upcoming project.

Eleanor soon received an offer from director Andrew Stone to appear in his film *Sensations of 1945*, to be released through United Artists. "I felt this was no time to sit back and twiddle my thumbs when the world was so badly in need of all kinds of entertainment," she wrote Doug Ebersole.[2] And so, she accepted the picture offer from Stone, who felt Eleanor "had not been done right by" at MGM. She liked Stone and recognized that "he has some grand ideas which jibe with mine about shooting dance numbers."

She was already at the studio rehearsing when surprised columnist Harold Heffernan visited. "The other day we dropped into the General Service Studios and found Eleanor making the walls shake going through her routines," he commented. "She was hop-step-and-skipping all over the place, working out new routines and thrill stunts. In short, there was evidence that Eleanor Powell was not through with movies after all."[3]

Stone's film was a far cry from Eleanor's high-budget MGM productions, but it allowed her the opportunity to display her acting and comedic ability. Stone also booked Russian ballet choreographer and dancer David Lichine for the film. Eleanor began training with Lichine and was soon back to her former routine of six-hour daily rehearsals.

In *Sensations,* Eleanor plays a dancer turned press agent who falls in love with a rival publicist (Dennis O'Keefe). As they try to outdo each other in creating extravagant publicity stunts, various novelty acts are showcased throughout the picture. Also co-starring are Eugene Pallette, C. Aubrey Smith, Sophie Tucker, and W. C. Fields (in his final film appearance), and there are special appearances by the bands of Woody Herman, Cab Calloway, Dorothy Donegan, and the Les Paul Trio.

Sensations gave Eleanor a chance to be an actress first and a dancer second. By this time in her career, she more than adequately held her own throughout the movie even though the thin plot did not give her much to grasp.

The film opens with Eleanor's "jitterbug ballet" duet with David Lichine. Dancing to boogie-woogie music, and dressed in a tight-fitting skirt and top, Eleanor shows a different dance persona from all her previous films. Lichine is her swaggering, gum-chewing partner, and the two mix tap with elements of jitterbug style. Eleanor has two other numbers in addition to the opening dance—one as a twirling, tapping live pinball in a set designed as an actual machine, accompanied by Woody Herman and his orchestra; the second, a short number alongside a prancing horse, "Starless Night." Unfortunately, unlike Buttons the dog, Starless Night proved to be extremely difficult on set; the horse repeatedly balked as she walked it around the ring in an attempt to do a rumba. Other issues beset the number. One take was ruined simply because the seams on Eleanor's stockings were crooked and another because Eleanor's sparkly costume was too shiny. After about eighty takes, finally the circuit was completed satisfactorily on film. A fourth number, the song "One Love," was cut from the film due to length.

Though Stone had plans to make two more successive films with Eleanor as the lead, critics did not rate *Sensations* highly. "The show is made up of so many good acts," said one reviewer, "but they are interrupted by the dull story." They complained about having to wait so long to see Eleanor dance, discounting the opening duet, and added, "then she goes into a straight role she is unsuited for."[4] Another critic called the film "a far-fetched formula affair."[5] While the musical features with Calloway, Herman, Donegan, and others added interest, they were so detached from the story that there was not much left to stand on.

After retakes on *Sensations* were finished in April, Eleanor was anxious to join Glenn. He still had several weeks before receiving his assignment location, and they had no idea where he would be stationed. She wanted to stay as close as possible because he might be sent overseas. She searched for an affordable rental near Camp Pendleton and found a small two-room garage apartment on the grounds of an estate in the town of La Jolla for $60 per month. The little apartment was just two blocks from the beach. Formerly used as servants' quarters, it came furnished with quaint wicker furniture, a kitchenette in the living area, and an iron bed that nearly filled the tiny bedroom. Only a thirty-minute drive to the base, it would allow Glenn to easily join her when on leave. It was there she and Glenn would spend what she later described as the happiest time of her married life.

For the first time, Eleanor was on her own without Blanche. She threw herself into her new domestic routine of shopping, cooking, and cleaning. Far from Hollywood, she and Glenn went unrecognized and enjoyed normal life, free of photographers, gossip columnists, and studio dictates. Word reached Los Angeles that Eleanor was "keeping house for her Marine hubby . . . and she loves it." Noting that Glenn had gained fifteen pounds as a result of her home cooking, reporters admiringly pointed out: "Eleanor does all the housework herself—everything from cooking to laundry. She's a real Marine's wife."[6]

On Saturday, June 17, just eleven days after D-Day, Glenn was granted a three-day leave and was able to spend the weekend with Eleanor in Los Angeles. The *Los Angeles Times* headlines screamed "England Battles Nazi Robot Planes" and "Americans Cut Germans' Cherbourg Escape Road." The world was in disarray, but a glowing Eleanor had happier news to share with Glenn that morning. She had just found out that she was pregnant.

The papers were abuzz with the news of the stork's impending visit to the Ford household. The pregnancy was the best of news to Eleanor, but Glenn was less than enthusiastic. Eleanor had looked forward to starting a family since the day they were married; Glenn saw the arrival of a baby as an interruption of their brief married life together. It was all too soon for his liking. Glenn was focused on his career in the Marine Corps, preparing for Officer Training School and a possible deployment overseas. He had been assigned to duty in a radio production unit, then to the Army Motion Picture Unit in Culver City to work on military training films, where his film background was put to use.

Just a few weeks later, Eleanor's joyful mood turned to concern as Glenn was hospitalized with serious stomach problems. Doctors feared the condition may have been caused during training when Glenn swallowed mustard gas after not putting his mask on fast enough. He remained at the Naval Hospital in San Diego for six weeks and was ultimately diagnosed with duodenal ulcers.

Relieved that Glenn's condition seemed to be stabilizing, Eleanor blissfully began preparing for the baby. In October, the couple celebrated their first wedding anniversary together in La Jolla. However, Glenn continued to struggle with health issues over the next few months, and finally received an honorable discharge from the Marines on December 7, 1944.

With the baby's due date projected for January 28, the couple relinquished the apartment in La Jolla and moved back to Beverly Hills. Due to the wartime housing shortage, finding a place of their own was a challenge. Each moved in temporarily with their respective mothers. Though an odd decision for a newly married couple, given Glenn's physical condition and Eleanor's impending delivery, both felt that their mothers could best take care of them at that time. Nevertheless, after so much time spent apart while he was on base, the lack of intimacy in their new living arrangements did nothing to strengthen their marriage.

The medical discharge was a great disappointment to Glenn. Like many who had voluntarily enlisted, he had looked forward to both officer's training and active duty. After his extended absence from the studio, he was now unsure if work would be available to him. He immediately let Columbia studio head Harry Cohn know of his return to civilian life. Cohn had nothing for him, but Glenn's situation took a fortuitous turn when Bette Davis noticed him on a visit to the Warner Bros. commissary. She expressed interest in testing him for a role opposite her in the picture she was also producing, *A Stolen Life*. Davis hesitated at first, thinking that Glenn might appear too young to play her husband, but she scheduled the test anyway.

On the afternoon of Saturday, February 3, a few days after her projected due date, Eleanor checked into the Cedars of Lebanon Hospital in Hollywood in the early stages of labor. Glenn stayed beside her throughout the night, but labor was not progressing. A caesarian section was advised, which Eleanor flatly refused. The next morning when Glenn was to report to the studio for his screen test, his state of exhaustion worked in his favor. The sleepless night added just enough maturity to his look that he now suited the part.

After thirty-two hours of labor, on February 5, 1945, at shortly past midnight, Eleanor gave birth to a strapping boy, weighing in at close to nine pounds. During the pregnancy, based on the baby's heartbeat, doctors had told Eleanor and Glenn to expect a girl. When the child turned out to be a boy, it took them a day to regroup and decide on a name. The press ran a sentimental story claiming the baby would be named after their friend, actress Susan Peters (Susan for a girl or Peter for a boy), who had recently suffered a crippling accident that landed her in a wheelchair and nearly ended her career. Though the veracity of the story seems questionable, the child was indeed named Peter, with the middle name of Newton after Glenn's father.

Eleanor's difficult labor extended her stay at the hospital a full week, but how much rest it gave her is unsure. Warners wanted Glenn for the Bette Davis film and would be paying Columbia handsomely for the loan, so he seized the opportunity to renegotiate his salary. Relying heavily on Eleanor's seasoned advice, he consulted her regularly over the next few days. Finally, after extensive discussion, a satisfactory new contract was agreed upon. She later joked that she "gave birth twice—once to her son, and again to her husband's contract."[7]

Eleanor went home to the house on Hillgreen with Blanche and baby Peter, while Glenn returned to the apartment with Hannah. The living arrangements were hardly ideal for a new family. Glenn placed an ad in the newspaper seeking a home in Beverly Hills, close to their mothers, but housing was still scarce. They still had found nothing when Glenn reported to Laguna Beach for location shooting on *A Stolen Life*.

The April 1945 issue of *Good Housekeeping* displayed the Fords' simple birth announcement that read:

> Now we are three
> Peter, Ellie and Glenn
> February 5, 1945
> 8 pounds, 14 1/2 ounces.

The Fords had planned to wait for Peter's christening until they were settled in a home of their own, but the date was suddenly hastened when Glenn's Marine buddy, Captain Eddie Lyon, was about to be transferred. On April 22, the ceremony took place at the Little Chapel of the First Methodist Church in Santa Monica with Glenn's minister, Reverend Ray Moore, officiating. Photos depict a solemn event with Peter surrounded by his parents and godparents, Eddie and his wife, Russene. Peter's two grandmothers were also present. Sadly, the Lyons would divorce less than six months later, and it is unknown if Peter had much contact with them afterward. Later, Eleanor's friends Bill Robinson and Pearl Bailey would be considered his honorary godparents.

Eleanor and Glenn's odd living arrangements did not go unnoticed by the press, but they were quick to qualify that it was only due to the housing shortage. In answer to frequent speculation about whether Eleanor would resume her career, Glenn assured reporters that she had lost all interest in returning to film. "I had the glamour, now I wanted the other side of the coin," she later said.[8] She also felt it was necessary to allow Glenn to take responsibility as the breadwinner in the marriage.

For Glenn, things were going well on the set of *A Stolen Life*. Bette Davis had taken a special liking to him and was pleased with his hard work. Production on the film came to a close in mid-July 1945. In late August, *Variety* announced that production would soon begin on Rita Hayworth's new picture, *Gilda,* with Charles Vidor directing and Glenn Ford in the male lead.

After months of living with their mothers, Glenn and Eleanor finally found a home to call their own—at least for the time being. High on a hilltop in Beverly Hills, the new house afforded the family ample space, with a library large enough to house their seven thousand records and its own projection room. A new addition to the household was Mary Pickford's excellent cook, Agnes Clarke, whom the Fords managed to woo away from Pickfair. The house would do until they could buy a home of their own, but Eleanor was already concerned that, because there was no backyard and the house was located on a cliff, it would be too dangerous for Peter to play outside when he got older.

On September 2, 1945, victory was declared over Japan and the turmoil of World War II was finally over. Two days later, back at Columbia, production began on *Gilda*. Glenn and Rita had previously co-starred in *The Lady in Question* (1940), when they were both still relatively unknown. Now Rita was married to Orson Welles and the mother of a baby girl Peter's age. By this time, marriage to the complex and unpredictable Welles had made Rita miserable. Finding a familiar friend, she reached out to Glenn for comfort. While Glenn was sufficiently in love with Eleanor to resist the advances of Bette Davis during the making of his previous film, whatever resolve he had mustered utterly crumbled at the hands of Rita Hayworth. Despite his wife and new baby at home, a romance soon developed with his glamorous co-star. "You couldn't help but fall in love with Rita," Glenn later told Peter.[9]

As the spark ignited between them off as well as on the set, it was hard for Hollywood not to take notice. Rumors of their affair certainly reached Eleanor's ears as well. She realized the temptations actors experienced while being thrown together in intimate situations on movie sets, but she was devastated to think her beloved Glenn might be cheating on her. The news of the affair also infuriated Harry Cohn, who was personally obsessed with Rita himself. Cohn "ran Columbia like a private police state."[10] It was a common habit of Cohn's to place listening devices on his soundstages so he could interject reactions over a loudspeaker and surprise the actors when any conversations angered him. To satisfy his curiosity, he did not hesitate to place listening devices in Rita's dressing room.

Though Eleanor had consistently stated over the years that she did not believe a career and marriage were compatible, now she appeared to reconsider her feelings. Glenn repeatedly claimed he would not dictate to Eleanor whether or not she should resume her career. Eleanor, all too aware of his insecurities, was hesitant. So, for the time being, she devoted herself to raising her child with the same single-mindedness and determination she had exhibited throughout her dancing career. She resolved to be the best mother she could be, but this, too, caused conflict. With all her efforts focused on Peter, Glenn felt he was no longer the center of attention in his home.

As Glenn was working on *Gilda*, Eleanor, unsettled in her marriage and struggling to find balance in her life, began to earnestly feel the call to return to work. She told columnist Sheilah Graham that she would be ready to make another movie once she and her family were settled in their new house.

The press patriotically reported that Glenn and Eleanor celebrated their second wedding anniversary on October 23 by giving each other Victory bonds. Two days later, Hedda Hopper reported that Rita had taken to sleeping in her dressing room at the Columbia studio. There was little doubt that she was not alone. "Dressing rooms are so comfortable," Hedda slyly remarked. "I've wondered why stars didn't do that more often." On December 10, production ended on *Gilda*. Glenn's affair with Rita also came to a close, but it would be only the first of dozens of infidelities to come.

17

Back on the Boards

The new year brought a continued resolve on Eleanor's part to resume her career. By February 1946, the press was full of the news of her upcoming seven-week engagement at the Copacabana nightclub in Rio de Janeiro. Glenn was to go with her, and they were busy trying to find a reliable nurse to take care of Peter during their absence. Then, Glenn was cast in *Gallant Journey* and was no longer available to accompany her. Reluctant to leave them both, Eleanor canceled her engagement.

While Glenn was busy on the set, Eleanor trained at a Hollywood dance studio. She continued to receive new offers to appear on Broadway. One interesting press notice mentioned director Carlos De Angelo's plans to star Eleanor, French actor Jean Sablon, and Reginald Gardiner in a new musical inspired by Booth Tarkington's *Monsieur Beaucaire* shortly after the Bob Hope film of the same name had completed shooting.

Perhaps as a result of all the talk of Eleanor going back to work, gossip soon followed that the Fords were in trouble. The premiere of *Gilda* on April 25, 1946, which propelled Glenn's career to new heights, added fuel to the fire and rekindled rumors of the affair between Glenn and Rita Hayworth.

In one of the first of a number of damage control articles that would appear over the years to dampen the rumors, Glenn gave an interview for the September 1946 issue of *Screenland,* with the somewhat telling title "How Are the Glenn Fords Doing?" Supposedly answering this question "frankly and honestly for the first time," the article painted a picture of an ordinary household, with the joys and challenges that faced any young family. Although the article was filled with embellishments common to fan magazines of the time, some grains of truth showed through the Hollywood veneer even while the author attempted to reassure fans that all was well in the Ford household.

Several weeks later, Eleanor paid a visit to MGM for the first time in months and showed off her fifteen-month-old son to old friends on the lot.

Back in the environment where she had seen such great success, she felt strengthened and encouraged to continue honing her act for a potential engagement at the swanky Chicago nightspot Chez Paree. Always eager for a scoop, the press prematurely announced that she would appear in June and, after that, she would begin rehearsals for the lead in a West Coast stage production of Ziegfeld's original *Rosalie*. Duties at home once again delayed her plans.

In August, the Fords found the house of their dreams. With Glenn's career finally established, they chose a twenty-two-room mansion located in the heights of Beverly Hills at 1012 Cove Way. The furnished house had previously belonged to Max Steiner and featured a unique Chinese-themed room where he had composed many of his notable film scores. While the Fords eventually remodeled the other rooms in the house, they left that one unchanged. Not unusual for wealthier couples of the time, Glenn and Eleanor had individual bedrooms at opposite ends of the hall. Less usual was that Glenn's mother, Hannah, occupied a room right in the middle.

Glenn did not waver in his decision to have his mother move into the Cove Way house with them. The two shared such a devoted relationship that Hannah could not stand the thought of them ever being separated. This may have stemmed from her own abandonment issues: she had been left behind with friends in Canada at the age of four when her parents returned alone to England. It may also have been related to the trauma of nearly losing Glenn in a home fire on the night before his birth. In any case, Hannah clung fiercely to her son, and after Glenn's father died in 1940, her attachment increased. Glenn promised he would never leave her, and Hannah was installed in the household as the reigning matriarch. She was a prime witness, as well as one of the catalysts, to the slow erosion of Glenn and Eleanor's relationship.

Reminders of Glenn's infidelity plagued Eleanor. Nearly a year after production was completed on *Gilda*, a drunken Orson Welles stumbled angrily down the driveway at the Ford home. Brandishing a gun, he called out to Glenn with Shakespearean theatricality, demanding he come out and reveal where his wife, Rita, was hiding. A shaken Eleanor telephoned the police, but Welles was gone by the time they arrived. Eleanor's trust in Glenn was further damaged and would never be quite the same. Rita and Welles would divorce the following year.

Though Eleanor tried hard to surmount the difficulties that arose in her marriage, it was becoming more difficult to ignore that she and Glenn were very different people. Eleanor was friendly and outgoing while Glenn was increasingly aloof and withdrawn. An interviewer remarked: "He has a certain shell of reserve about him and is a little cautious about picking friends. You get the feeling that perhaps at some time in his life someone who he trusted betrayed that trust and left him on his guard forever afterwards. Eleanor is peppy, gay, and vivacious."[1]

Glenn's insecurity proved to be a constant challenge to the relationship. "He had such an inferiority complex—it was sheer hell," Eleanor recalled. "When we went out together, everyone flocked around me. I couldn't see they were ignoring him, but he thought they were."[2] Glenn was not a good dancer and was terribly self-conscious about it. This was especially hard for Eleanor. When they frequented clubs and she wanted to get up and dance, just as during their honeymoon, Glenn continued to insist that they sit it out. "People think we're going to put on an exhibition," he explained to a reporter. "They have an idea that being Eleanor's husband, I must be a terrific dancer. Instead, I look like a young Abe Lincoln type, stumbling awkwardly around."[3] He would only participate if the lighting was dim enough to hide their identities.

Another issue was that, until *Gilda* was released in April 1946, Glenn was rarely recognized in public, while Eleanor had been an established star for years. When Glenn approached a maître d' about a table, he would often be told nothing was available or that a long wait would be necessary. As soon as Eleanor came into sight, suddenly there would be a change of attitude, and a table would quickly be found. After the meal, his manly pride sorely bruised, Glenn would tell Eleanor he did not want to return there. "We were running out of places to eat," she recalled. To avoid the conflict, they mostly stayed home, where they enjoyed reading or listening to their record collection.

After *Gilda*, Glenn's star status and salary greatly increased, but at $215,000 (well over $3 million today), the house proved to be a stretch for their budget. Eleanor had been working on her act for some time; now was the opportune moment to use it to earn needed funds. Out of pride, Glenn preferred to be the breadwinner for the household, but this time he made an exception.

In need of new costuming, Eleanor contacted old friend Charles LeMaire, now under contract to 20th Century-Fox Studios. LeMaire's exclusive agreement forbade him to design for anyone outside the studio, but, out of love for Eleanor, he slyly suggested that if he happened to sketch something out and she happened to pick it up and take it to a production house to construct it, no one would be any the wiser.

On Peter's second birthday, on February 5, 1947, Eleanor headed out on the road for a three-month tour, taking Blanche with her just like old times.

Also traveling with her was her pianist, Dave Gussin. Peter stayed behind with Glenn, supervised by his nurse, Gussie, Agnes the cook, and his grandmother Hannah. With an average salary of $5,000 per week, Eleanor would make a substantial contribution to the house payment, even after subtracting the expenses of the show.

Eleanor opened in Buffalo, New York. With fourteen hundred seats, the Town Casino was the city's most elegant supper club and the perfect venue to break in her act before they headed on to larger cities on the tour. She had not been forgotten. Crowds stood in line for two hours in the snow, and the act broke the box office records of such notables as Sophie Tucker, Joe E. Lewis, and Harry Richman.

After her long absence from the stage, life on the road and doing multiple shows a night was grueling work, but Eleanor rose to the occasion. While she experienced great joy in returning to her first love, she missed her family and regretted leaving her little son behind. She knew Peter missed her, too, and that he struggled to grasp that his mother had gone on a "long, long ride," as his daddy had explained to him. Without the daily pressures at home, absence did indeed appear to make the heart grow fonder. Glenn called nearly every night, and letters flowed freely between the two of them. On one occasion, he listened to her entire act over the telephone, a sizable expense in the 1940s. The time away made it easy for Eleanor to forget the bad times and to forgive Glenn's indiscretions. She hoped that her return would mark a fresh start; this time she was sure they could make it work.

Before her next engagement in Chicago, Eleanor was invited to perform at the prestigious White House Correspondents' Dinner in Washington, DC. Despite a snowstorm on the evening of March 1, all Washington's elite came out to the Statler Hotel, including President Harry Truman and General Dwight D. Eisenhower. Other guests included cabinet members, Supreme Court justices, high-ranking Army and Navy officers, and government officials and their guests; it was the largest attendance in the dinner's twenty-four-year history. Performers on the bill were Metropolitan Opera tenor Ferruccio Tagliavini, singer Dinah Shore and her husband, actor George Montgomery, comedian Sid Caesar, veteran pantomimist Gene Sheldon, and popular pianist, Frankie Carle. Closing out the evening was Eleanor Powell.

Columnist Earl Wilson, acting as emcee, later recounted that the thought of President Truman in the audience caused him the most severe stage fright he ever experienced. He was not alone. "Dinah Shore was trembling. Frankie Carle couldn't eat. He took a pill to quiet himself. Sid Caesar was shaky.

Appearing before the President is a big thing. Only Gene Sheldon, Eleanor Powell, and Ferruccio Tagliavini were calm."[4] Indeed, this was not the first time Eleanor had performed before a sitting president, and she was quite familiar with the Washington scene. At the end of the evening, the president graciously thanked the performers for a "magnificent show," signed autographs, and presented each with a signed scroll.

Eleanor and her company moved on to Chicago, where she opened at Chez Paree on March 7. Well aware of the evolution of her craft since she had begun in the movies and especially over the last four years, she developed her "Concerto in Tap" to reflect that. Her act varied in musical styles from Debussy to the rumba and showcased her skills as a tap percussionist, which significantly elevated her art from that of a mere hoofer. The supper club was so packed that one reviewer complained of not being able to see. She engaged in a warm patter with the audience and did requests all through the show. Critics found she had lost none of her skill during her time away but had instead come back better than ever.

Eleanor had a worrisome issue to contend with during her stay in Chicago. Blanche had caught a cold on opening night that later developed into pneumonia. Glenn, stuck on location filming *The Man from Colorado*, reportedly called every night to check on his mother-in-law's condition and to console Eleanor. Fortunately, the stay in Chicago was long enough for Blanche to sufficiently recover before they moved on to Cincinnati.

The last stop on the tour was the Beverly Hills Country Club in Newport, Kentucky. Just across the Ohio River from downtown Cincinnati, the venue was a popular nightclub and gambling establishment. It was host to some of the most popular entertainers of the day.

Eleanor's tour was successful, but all the adulation of the public could not provide what she really longed for—to be foremost in her husband's regard. Fully aware of his straying eye, she feared she could not compete with the glamorous co-stars in his life. In a letter to Glenn while on the road, Eleanor revealed her personal struggle:

I did fourteen numbers during the evening and still had to beg off. Isn't that wonderful, darling? I thought I was all washed up. I'm so proud, Glenn, not for myself but for you. I want you to be so proud of me. Do you know when you play opposite Rita Hayworth and people like that—Bette Davis, etc., I feel in my heart, Oh! Golly, he admires them so, and I want that same feeling from you. Not just as your wife, but as a top performer. I want those people you play opposite to look at me and say, "She really is tops." Not for me but for you. I want to shine in your eyes, not only as a wife and mother but in your profession also. I want to be the sun, the moon, everything to you.[5]

Eleanor returned home at the end of April approximately $150,000 richer than when she had left but with a relationship still deeply in need of repair. Not long after her return, Eleanor received a phone call from Harry Cohn; he complained about Glenn's misbehavior at the studio and asked her to keep an eye on him. Furious and hurt, she confronted her husband. Glenn in turn took his anger out on Cohn; he stormed into his office and threatened him with a small baseball bat Cohn kept on his desk.

Eleanor slipped back into her role as a mother for the next several months. By mid-July, the press was sharing the news that she would start a six-week run in Las Vegas at the end of the month, followed by a stint in Miami. Glenn had plans to join her there with Peter, followed by a family vacation in Havana. About this time, the press also announced that for their fourth anniversary, Glenn and Eleanor would renew their vows before their "big families" in Quebec, who were not able to attend their small wartime wedding. It was yet another effort to put to rest the rumors of the Fords' troubles of the past year. Neither the vacation in Havana nor the second wedding in Quebec came to pass. Eleanor's Las Vegas plans were modified, and Miami scrapped altogether.

Glenn was regularly working, but despite his contract renegotiation, his salary was still not comparable to what other actors of his stature were earning. The expensive Cove Way house continued to rapidly drain Eleanor's savings until Glenn's contract was up for renegotiation. When a generous offer came for a national tour, it was too tempting to turn down. She had high hopes that in about two years, Glenn's higher salary would end their financial worries and allow them to consider having more children. She longed for a baby sister or brother for Peter. She deeply regretted that the tour would keep her apart from Peter for so long and turned down additional bookings that would have kept her away through Christmas. She held out some hope that a potential movie offer from Fox might come through instead. "If I like the script, I may stop my tour any day now and go back where I can see my son and husband every night," she said.[6] But the offer did not pan out.

She readied herself for performance and kicked off a two-month tour at the Last Frontier in Las Vegas. Because she had some excess weight,

Eleanor began intense rehearsals along with a diet regimen. When she also contracted the flu, the combination pushed her to collapse. Her doctor advised her to postpone the opening, but she felt compelled to continue.

On September 28, Eleanor opened at the Latin Quarter in Boston, where she would dance nightly until October 10. During the run, she also made appearances at two benefits. The first, on October 5, was a show alongside Frank Sinatra and Jack Haley to benefit the building fund of the Christopher Columbus Catholic Center. More than twelve thousand fans packed the Boston Garden, many of them bobbysoxers there to see teen favorite "Frankie" Sinatra. On October 7 she appeared at a large rally for United Jewish Appeal, a drive to raise funds to aid needy Jewish survivors of the Holocaust in Europe. Throughout the tour, when not on the nightclub stage, she visited children's hospitals and veterans wards, where she danced for free. She especially enjoyed the pleasure it brought ailing youngsters. She missed Glenn and Peter and looked forward to the daily letters with news from home or wherever Glenn was shooting.

The tour continued on to Club Cairo in Washington, DC, where columnist Harry MacArthur called Eleanor, "with all due respects to the town's drummers, the finest percussion artist who will ever set a tempo . . . and elaborate rhythmically on a melody."[7] MacArthur observed that though Eleanor was "no longer an enthusiastically girlish" dancer, "this in no way diminishes the pleasure of watching her"; he added that "she's fast, she's nimble, she's subtle and she is equally at home in a variety of rhythms."[8] She was visited at the club by policeman Joe Osterman, one of the officers who had regularly assisted her during her Roosevelt Birthday Ball appearances. Eleanor recognized him and received him warmly.

A week at the Bowery in Detroit was followed by another stint at the Beverly Hills Country Club in Kentucky in late November. Over the weeks, feeling at ease with her act, she incorporated some comedy into the performance. She resurrected her impression of Jimmy Stewart and played off comic and mimic Arthur Blake, who was on the bill with her. In a spontaneous moment, they ad-libbed together, with Blake impersonating Katharine Hepburn.

Back at home, Glenn was about to begin a new film, *The Loves of Carmen*—his third film with Rita Hayworth. The memory of Glenn's affair during *Gilda* made Eleanor uneasy. "I don't trust that hussy," she wrote Glenn. "You know I'm jealous of her."[9] Glenn asked Eleanor to cut her tour short and meet him in

California, but though she was concerned about Glenn's inability to resist Rita's charms, she also felt obligated to finish out her final date. He left for Lone Pine, California (about four hours from Los Angeles), on November 14.

Four weeks later, Eleanor headed home on December 17 to spend Christmas with Peter after eleven weeks on the road. Producer Milton Sperling sent her a proposal for a role alongside Doris Day, Sophie Tucker, Dinah Shore, and Gloria De Haven in a film based on Fannie Hurst's story *Sister Act*. As was the case with so many others, this project was never realized. Fred Astaire had also reached out to Eleanor with a business venture. He was starting a chain of Fred Astaire Dance Studios and was looking for someone to partner with him. He offered a salary of $50,000 to be a supervising consultant for the West Coast chain. Though the project was solid, she ultimately decided it was not for her and that she already had too much on her plate to manage the responsibility.

Happy to be back at Cove Way, Eleanor was unaware her worst fears were playing out between Glenn and Rita on location. Rita had filed for divorce from Orson Welles on October 1, just six weeks before production started, and in her vulnerable state she turned to Glenn for consolation. Their intense affair rekindled during the two-month shoot, and Rita discovered that she was pregnant not long after the production ended in late January. During her affair with Glenn, Rita had also been romantically involved with Howard Hughes. When Hughes found out about the pregnancy, he was livid. He had no interest in marrying Rita or having children and pressured her to get an abortion. There are differing versions of what followed. One of Rita's biographers, Barbara Leaming, states she had the abortion in the United States shortly before she left for a scheduled trip to Paris in early June. There, serious complications developed, and she was taken to the American Hospital in Neuilly, just outside of Paris. The press was told she "grew ill" while dining with Otto Preminger and "had to be carried back to her hotel." Later reports stated she was suffering from severe anemia, but curiously, a gynecologist and close friend of Howard Hughes was the doctor who gave information on her condition.

According to Peter Ford, many years after the fact, Rita intimated to Glenn that the baby was his. Rita said she traveled with a close girlfriend to Paris, where she had the pregnancy terminated at the American Hospital. However, an abortion in early June would have placed her pregnancy at nearly four months after the very last day of shooting on *The Loves of Carmen*. Though Eleanor was aware of the affair, she did not know of Rita's pregnancy.

When the production returned to town for interior shoots at the studio, Eleanor made her presence actively known. Not about to lose her husband to his "hussy" co-star, she made visible efforts to stake her claim. She and Glenn were spotted holding hands, a fact that Hollywood columnist Ruth Brigham found remarkable, "and after five years of marriage, too!"[10] Columnists kept quiet about the affair, well-known in industry circles.

Shortly before Peter's third birthday, Eleanor was presented with the offer she had been waiting for since the earliest days of her career—an opportunity to perform in Europe, specifically a four-week stint at the acclaimed London Palladium. With increasing frequency, American performers were being invited over to entertain postwar British audiences, and Eleanor was the most recent addition to the list. As negotiations for her London dates continued over the coming months, domestic bookings were lined up for the remainder of the year.

In September 1948, she opened her third tour in Las Vegas at the Flamingo Hotel for two weeks; from there, she continued on to Cleveland, the Latin Quarter in Boston, the Town Casino in Buffalo, and the Beverly Hills Country Club in Newport, Kentucky. "Eleanor has a style that makes it possible for her to go through some of the most intricate tap steps with seemingly little or no exertion," said one reporter. "At the opener last night, she performed virtually everything in the book—fox trots, waltzes, rumbas and boogie-woogies, and after three or four encores finally had to demur."[11]

At the close of another impressive tour, Eleanor headed home to spend Christmas with Peter and Glenn. She received word that the Palladium had confirmed her dates for the following spring. The American entertainment imports, dubbed a modern "invasion" by the press, were now being assembled for Palladium audiences by British producer Val Parnell. Eleanor had never been readier.

Eleanor, Blanche, and musical director Dave Gussin left New York February 27 on the *Queen Mary* and arrived on March 4 in Southampton. Eleanor was scheduled to perform one week at the Empire Theater in Glasgow, Scotland, starting March 14, followed by three weeks at the Palladium to open the 1949 London variety season on March 21.

Eleanor met with the British press and shared her joy at being able to fulfill her goal of performing in Britain. As a guest on John Ellison's radio show, *In Town Tonight,* she also told of her plans to finally meet longtime fan Richard Norton, the young man who had sent her the charred scrapbook during the war. Now married, Norton was employed as a tea taster in London.

In Glasgow, the Scots were thrilled to discover that Eleanor was no stranger to their particular accent because Agnes, her cook/housekeeper, was from the Scottish town of Perth, and Andrew Aitchison, her gardener, hailed from the town of Coldstream. The habit of daily tea had even been instigated at the Ford household, and Eleanor enjoyed the practice. While in Glasgow, Scottish music hall legend Sir Harry Lauder visited her backstage. A piano was rolled into her dressing room and the seventy-nine-year-old, then in his last year of life, delighted her with songs for over an hour.

Structured much like vaudeville bills of the past, the London Palladium shows included a diverse variety of novelty acts that ended with the headliner performance. Appearing with Eleanor was a mix of British and American acts, not all of which successfully appealed to British audiences. By the time Eleanor closed out the evening with her "Concerto in Tap," they had seen everything, from a dog and pony act to Señor Wences and his tiny hand puppet to a cross-dressing acrobat.

Eleanor's casual and conversational style of presentation at first seemed a bit unusual to the British but, according to the press, audiences quickly warmed to her personality. "Although Miss Powell confessed to nervousness, there was little sign of it at the first house," said one critic. "Her quiet, confidential style of talking to the audience soon gained their good will." The British press commented that she spoke about "the ideals and ordeals of her art with the unaffected simplicity and good nature of a true craftsman," and they remarked that her dancing "had the touch of a virtuoso. Miss Powell taps her feet as great Spanish dancers use their castanets—poetically."[12] Keeping to her established program of a variety of rhythmic styles peppered with light conversation, Eleanor charmed the British audiences. "She . . . for half an hour kept a capacity crowd enthralled with intricate steps in a rumba, 'Clair de Lune,' boogie-woogie, 'The Blue Danube,' and other numbers."[13] Other reviewers were frankly astounded at the physical demands of the program. She tapped for nearly forty minutes without any real break. "As a feat of sheer endurance, it is almost terrifying, but her charming unaffected personality seemed unruffled at the end of it."[14]

Eleanor reluctantly bid farewell to London. Her successful appearance was celebrated with a party at the elegant Saville Row Albany Club the night before she was due to set sail for home on the *Queen Mary*. Having seen little of the sights, she called upon Henry, the cabby who had regularly taken her to the theater, to serve as tour guide for her, Blanche, and pianist Dave Gussin on their last day. "I loved every moment I was here."[15] It had been a long and hard road from the birthday cake with the London topper that Blanche had so hopefully designed over ten years earlier. It was the only time Eleanor would ever perform in London.

⊙   ⊙   ⊙

Back in September 1948, producer Joe Pasternak had presented Eleanor with the idea of making a comeback appearance in one of his upcoming MGM films. For his project, *The Duchess of Idaho,* Pasternak proposed a specialty for Eleanor as part of a larger number featuring Fred Astaire and Judy Garland. Delayed by the pregnancy of Esther Williams, the project finally came to fruition in late 1949. Instead of Astaire and Garland, cameos were made by Eleanor, Red Skelton, and Lena Horne. The press jumped to cover Eleanor's return to film after a seven-year absence. "Happy sounds of tapping feet are again coming from the Eleanor Powell bungalow, long a landmark at MGM Studios," wrote columnist Bob Thomas. "Miss Powell has returned to the studio where she once reigned as a musical queen."[16]

The film's headliners were Esther Williams and audience favorite Van Johnson. Williams had made several films with Pasternak and respected his strong work ethic. "Pasternak believed in happily-ever-after entertainment," she recalled. "It was Pasternak who gave me the longevity I enjoyed in the movies from then on, because he showed that there was a market for me as me, not just as some circus performer diving through hoops and doing stunts."[17] Pasternak felt the same about Eleanor's trajectory.

Since her retirement from film, Eleanor had done live appearances, but she was curious to know whether movie audiences still wanted to see her on screen. During her years at MGM, she had given audiences numbers that had grown consistently more daring as her career progressed. As Eleanor jokingly recalled, "I would start out with a fast number, follow that with a faster number and keep punching harder until at the end of a picture they shot me out of a cannon." She recalled that training for various novelty production routines at MGM had built up her muscular strength; one day, after Mayer greeted her on the street, he commented, "Ellie, you've got a handshake like a wrestler!" Now, she had put the showy numbers behind her. Her focus was on her footwork, without the extraneous distractions of being thrown around by chorus boys or sliding down a pole. Eleanor's new "feminine" style (as the studio dubbed it) was tested out at a sneak preview. "The audience's reaction to that will determine whether or not I do any more pictures."[18] It was a gentle way of telling the audience not to expect the elaborate productions of the previous decade.

The film was already well into production by the time Eleanor shot her cameo sequence in November 1949. In the film, Van Johnson's character spots her seated in a nightclub, introduces her as herself, and invites her up to dance. After a lyrical ballroom opening, she removes her long skirt and launches into a boogie-woogie tap segment. She utilized many elements from her nightclub act, including a mix of rhythms and her signature tap turns. She looked stunning in color; her lightened hair softened her features and her vivid blue costume complemented the shade of her eyes and accentuated her trim figure.

Williams recalled that Eleanor, in her dedication to perfection, rehearsed her number to the point that her feet bled. Shocked that Eleanor would put in so much effort for just a cameo, she commented, "Eleanor, it's only a guest shot. Is it really worth it?" Eleanor replied, "If they're filming it, it has to be better than good, it must be perfect. My feet will be alright."[19] Critics responded well to Eleanor's number. "There are brief guest appearances by Miss Lena Horne and Miss Eleanor Powell, who in three or four short minutes prove that there's still no substitute for talent."[20]

MGM thought enough of Eleanor's turn in *The Duchess of Idaho* to offer her another long-term contract with one picture per year. She was still adamant that two ongoing film careers would not make a successful marriage. Bob Hope also offered her a spot on his Easter television special, which Eleanor declined for a different reason. She was not thrilled about how tap was being presented on television. "It's not right for tap dancers yet," she told reporters. "They either cut off your head or your feet. And who wants to watch a pair of feet on the screen?"[21]

Glenn's next project was *Follow the Sun*, a film about champion golfer Ben Hogan, who had suffered serious injuries the year before in a car accident and had spent months recuperating. When the time came to cast an actress to play Hogan's wife in the film, Hedda Hopper printed a valiant proposal in support of Eleanor for the role, but Fox did not take up the suggestion. Anne Baxter was cast. Glenn spent many weeks rehearsing his golf moves with Hogan in preparation for the shoot. Later, a dinner was held at Chasen's restaurant in Hogan's honor, attended by Glenn and Eleanor. As Hogan was praised and cheered, Eleanor felt his wife, Valerie, was being ignored. She addressed the crowd with a noble toast, saying, "How about a little cheer for his wife? She's a champion, too. I'll bet she's spent as many hours in the clubhouse praying for his success as he has on the golf course. Let's give the wives who stay behind the lines some of the credit they deserve."[22]

The allusion to devoted wives praying for their husbands echoed the depth of Eleanor's spiritual beliefs. Over the trying years, she had increasingly come to rely on God as the only constant in her life. She did not press her faith on others but taught by example. She had also recently begun teaching five-year-old Peter's Sunday School classes at the Beverly Hills Presbyterian Church.

No stranger to dedication, Eleanor never missed a Sunday teaching class. As she threw herself enthusiastically into raising her son, she attended lectures on child psychology, became active in the Parent Teachers Association, and would become the very first female Cub Scout leader (due to rules, she was listed in registers as "Elmer" instead of Eleanor).

Eleanor wholeheartedly believed in her marriage and family and yearned to work with Glenn to create a nurturing environment for Peter. But as Glenn's career grew, his public and private personas were at distinct odds. He had slowly changed from the caring young man she had married, and Eleanor became concerned about his marked lack of interest in parenting his son. Publicly, however, Eleanor, Glenn, and young Peter were seen as an idyllic family, presented as many celebrity families were in the 1950s press—wholesome, patriotic, and without scandal. Even so, rumors concerning the couple's problems and impending separation became so frequent that in mid-1950 Glenn issued a blanket statement to the press, "They're not true, so we don't bother to deny them."[23] Privately, not only was Glenn uninterested in Peter but he also began to criticize Eleanor for her efforts to compensate for that very lack of interest.

Glenn's primary focus was on his career. He was now making between $100,000 and $200,000 per film and had plenty of offers to choose from. Eleanor was still receiving film offers but consistently turned them down—the most recent was a co-starring role with Jane Powell in the film *Athena*. She occasionally took time out from her family duties to appear at benefits or special events. She joined the cast of Bob Hope, Jack Benny, Dan Dailey, Danny Thomas, Donald O'Connor, and others for a performance at the annual show at the Shrine Auditorium with a week's run to benefit the families of sick or deceased policemen.

Glenn's next film, *The Green Glove* with Geraldine Brooks, was to be shot in Europe. There were plans for Eleanor and Peter to join him on location, but ultimately Eleanor decided that March was not a good time to take six-year-old Peter out of school. Eleanor herself was not eager to travel and admitted that "travel, to me, is always associated with work. I can't remember ever visiting a city without feeling I had to put on a performance."[24] Constant travel during the years of vaudeville made her appreciate her home all the more. "I practically lived out of a trunk until I was married." She summed up their natures in a prophetic statement—"Glenn's a goer . . . I'm a stayer."[25]

The press and public assumed there was a deeper reason for her staying behind when Glenn announced that he was instead taking his mother on the trip. Louella Parsons came to his defense. "Unkind rumors will probably start popping when Glenn Ford leaves for Europe March 24 with his mother. . . . Any gossip will be silly. Eleanor does not want to take the boy out of school in the middle of his term and that's the only reason she's not going."[26] Parsons went on to say that Hannah Ford would be visiting a sister she had never met, Mrs. Dorothy Harris, in London.

Before he left, Glenn went to a premiere screening of the Ben Hogan biopic in Fort Worth, Texas, on March 23, a gala affair that attracted six thousand people. At the reception afterward, Ben and Valerie Hogan joined celebrities who mingled and greeted the crowd, but Glenn kept to himself. "Shy Glenn Ford, who portrays Hogan in the film . . . quietly retired to a corner and was cordial but somewhat embarrassed when spoken to."[27]

Glenn and his mother set sail on the *Queen Mary* on March 30, bound for Southampton, England. At home, Eleanor continued her routine. On Mondays, she would go to her bungalow at MGM and put in about four hours of practice. She made efforts to run through all her previous dance numbers. "The dance routines are like children to me," she told Louella Parsons. "I don't want to forget them." According to Parsons, Eleanor had hopes for her own television show in the future, and it was a way to keep in good shape. She received calls from Glenn with updates on how the film was progressing, and newspapers stated he sent her a French bikini as a gift from the Riviera. Most of all, as on many of his long location shoots, she missed the closeness of her husband. They had spoken frankly in the weeks before he left and had rekindled something they had not experienced since the days alone in La Jolla. While Glenn was still in England, visiting relatives with Hannah, Eleanor's earnest, heartbreaking letter reached him at the Savoy Hotel: "We grew so close together in the weeks before you left that I don't even want to leave the house. . . . I smell your clothes, look at your pipes and think of you and wonder what you are doing. . . . Remember darling, how happy I was in La Jolla? I am so afraid you will change. Don't let anything happen to this."[28]

But on the set of *The Green Glove,* another drama was unfolding all summer. Glenn and co-star Geraldine Brooks had begun a torrid affair that had grown serious. Ironically, he reported from France to columnist Parsons that he was "homesick for his wife and son," and that he was "happy that his next film will keep him in Hollywood."[29] Eleanor's intimate urging to hold on to their love was in stark contrast to the hard reality of Glenn's pursuit of Geraldine Brooks. The affair progressed, and the two even spent a romantic weekend together at a hotel in Vienna. But after serious discussions, Brooks began to retreat. She realized the effects their actions would have on Glenn's marriage, family, and, of course, both of their livelihoods. The 1950s public was not forgiving about extramarital affairs, and scandals could easily mean the death of a career. Glenn took Brooks' rebuffs hard and chose to drown his sorrows at the local bars. At one point, fueled by a night of drinking in a bar with co-star George Macready, he decided the solution to his problems was to enlist in the French Foreign Legion. In 1978, Glenn told an interviewer it was due to "a bad love affair," but failed to mention that he was married at the time. Both were in an inebriated state, and Macready accompanied Glenn to a recruiting location, where Glenn filled out paperwork and proceeded to sleep off the remainder of the night on a cot.

The next morning, realizing what he had done, Glenn went to the recruiting sergeant to explain but was unsuccessful in obtaining his release. "Next thing I knew, they had issued me a uniform and were cutting orders to send us to . . . Algeria," he explained.[30] When Macready informed director Rudy Maté what had happened, Maté worked for five days to obtain Glenn's release from the commitment. Though Brooks refused to speak to Glenn off the set for several days, they finished the film without further incident. Glenn returned to England to join his mother, and the two sailed back to New York on the *Queen Elizabeth,* arriving on July 26.

Reports of the serious affair between Glenn and Geraldine Brooks had reached Eleanor, and the Foreign Legion debacle was also eventually revealed. She met Glenn and Hannah on arrival in New York, and the three returned together on the train. Hurt and humiliated, particularly considering how close she had felt to Glenn before his departure, Eleanor had lost what remaining trust she had in him. The repeated disregard for their marriage both saddened and angered her, but she was determined not to shatter Peter's upbringing with a painful divorce. No number of explanations or temporary reconciliations would ever bring back the sheer happiness they had both experienced in the tiny apartment in La Jolla.

18

Walking through Fire

Daily life at Cove Way soon slipped back into its regular routine, a life now more than ever at odds with what was shown to the public. The family was presented as loving and close-knit, and the public never suspected that happy moments shared by that family could turn stressful and angry in an instant. Eleanor later recalled an incident one morning around the breakfast table. She had made pancakes—Peter's favorite as a child. Eager and all thumbs, the three-year-old grabbed the syrup bottle and knocked it over, spilling the contents into his plate. Glenn, in a stern disciplinary move, told Peter that it was unacceptable to waste the syrup. A shocked Eleanor watched as Glenn forced Peter to drink the entire plate of syrup.

In the fall of 1951, Glenn started filming a romantic comedy at MGM with Ruth Roman, *The Young Man with Ideas*; he was brought in to replace Russell Nype in the role of a family man with three children. Glenn's next film was just the opposite. *Affair in Trinidad* with Rita Hayworth was a comeback picture for the actress after her four-year break from the screen. Because *Gilda* had proved such a success, the studio was keen to rekindle the on-screen chemistry between the two with a similar story and international setting. That Glenn was working closely again with Rita worried Eleanor, but by now she realized there was little she could do to control his straying behavior.

The remainder of 1951 was relatively uneventful for the Fords. Their eighth wedding anniversary passed without much fanfare in October. Eleanor performed for a church dinner in late November and the two attended premieres of two of the year's biggest film releases—*An American in Paris* and *A Streetcar Named Desire*.

Glenn rarely had more than a month's downtime between films, and the household routine revolved closely around his schedule. Eleanor remarked that she liked to read his scripts in advance of each film so that she would know who she would be living with for the next month or so. Not only did each role heavily influence his personality but he also demanded extreme quiet and attention to protocol as he worked to hone his character. Most nights he would simply eat dinner and immediately retreat into his room to prepare lines for the next day's shoot, spending no time at all with Eleanor, Hannah, or Peter. He installed a red light outside his bedroom door, just as on a film soundstage, along with an intercom system that enabled him to communicate with Eleanor. The family was forbidden to make noise or disturb him when he was at work in his bedroom. After studying his lines for hours, he would then go directly to bed.

Glenn and Rita had been in rehearsals for *Affair in Trinidad* for nearly a month when production was unexpectedly halted due to Rita's sudden dissatisfaction with the script. As a result, she was put on suspension December 13 for failure to report to work. By January 2, a frustrated Glenn threatened to pull out of the film, as the delay would affect his participation in subsequent projects. After an additional week of debates, Rita finally agreed to start work on the film, and rehearsals resumed January 23. Eleanor read Sheilah Graham's column with a certain trepidation that week. Graham wrote, "Rita Hayworth will have to use all her charm to thaw her leading man and director. Both Glenn Ford and Vincent Sherman are extremely miffed with the Princess."[1] Since her last picture, Rita had married and divorced Prince Aly Khan, which gave rise to her regal nickname.

What actually happened during the filming of *Affair in Trinidad* remains in question. Decades later, Glenn told a story of this time period to actor Burt Reynolds in the wake of a scandal that Reynolds was involved in. Supposedly, certain actions by Harry Cohn had upset Rita, and when filming ended, she asked Glenn to have a drink with her. Later, in his dressing room, Rita went into the bathroom. After a long time passed, Glenn went in and found her lying unconscious on the floor, nude, with sleeping pills scattered around. He called the switchboard and asked them to discreetly call an ambulance. Cohn's listening devices evidently picked up the conversation, as minutes later, he burst into the dressing room with four cameramen who began taking photos of Glenn and Rita. "'Then, in a moment of stupidity, I dove on top of her so they couldn't photograph her nude body,' [Glenn] said. 'As soon as they got that shot, next day, headlines everywhere. My career and my marriage were over. I was married to Eleanor Powell at the time, and we were Mr. and Mrs. America. It was over.'"[2] However, no part of this version can be verified, and neither Glenn's career nor his marriage to Eleanor ended in 1952.

While no proof had yet reached her that an affair between Glenn and his co-star had recommenced, Eleanor was nonetheless on edge. She did not trust Hayworth around her husband, and, like many wives after several years of marriage, she feared her initial allure had faded, that she was "just plain old Ellie."

Eleanor also missed the joy and satisfaction that dance never failed to give her. Though she was wary about television and had refused the many offers that had come her way, Eleanor changed her mind in early 1952 and agreed to appear on *The Danny Thomas All-Star Revue* in May. It would mark her television debut. Eleanor diligently rehearsed in her old bungalow at MGM. Shortly before the appearance, she received a wire from Bill Robinson's widow wishing her well: "He will be with you once again, only this time from the shadows of the wings. I join my late husband in repeating his words: 'You're the tops.'"[3] Robinson's words were a joyful reminder of the old days, a much-needed boost during this difficult patch in her personal life.

Eleanor chose a number she had choreographed for her London Palladium appearance and performed on a simple set. She was careful to request that the camera cover her entire body, not just her feet or torso. She missed the days at MGM when she could sit alongside Blanche Sewell as her numbers were carefully cut for the screen; television was an entirely different medium. Gone were the expensive and elaborate sets that took weeks to construct. Gone also were the numerous retakes. The bleachers of cheering MGM stars were now replaced by a live studio audience. Early television was low budget and lacked any frills, but Eleanor saw to it that the sound of her clean and intricate taps was properly recorded.

She appeared as vibrant as ever in her four-minute tap medley, dubbed the "Powell Goulash." She also held her own in a humorous skit alongside June Havoc, Bob Hopkins, and Danny Thomas; the skit envisioned a futuristic all-female White House with comic speculation about what female presidency might entail. Ever the professional, she appeared happy and at ease with her co-stars. Critics praised her debut and predicted more engagements to come: "Eleanor Powell was such a hit on Danny Thomas' TV show that she's a cinch for his shows in the fall."[4] Unfortunately, Glenn was not able to see her television debut. On April 2, he sailed for London on the *Liberté* from New York to work on the film *Terror on a Train*.

Shortly after Glenn's return from London the last week of May, tales of serious issues in the Ford household began to make their way into Louella Parsons' column. On June 20, when Parsons made one of her regular calls to

Eleanor to check in for news, she was shocked. Eleanor answered the phone in a hysterical state; unable to speak coherently, she pleaded, "Please give me a little time to get myself together. I've never been so unhappy." Questioned about Glenn, Eleanor stated she did not know where he was or where he had been staying. For the first time in years, Blanche intervened. She called Parsons back and told her, "I cannot deny to you that they have had serious trouble," but she clarified that Glenn had been found and was in the house. Parsons told her readers: "[Blanche] had put Eleanor to bed in hysterics, and Eleanor had taken a sedative."[5] The strange narrative indicated a problem, but specific details were not released.

It was clear that Eleanor and Glenn had had a serious dispute. They separated for a week, and Glenn sought refuge in a bungalow at the Beverly Hills Hotel. Numerous other columnists jumped on the story, and finally on June 23 a brief article appeared: "Film star Glenn Ford and his wife Eleanor Powell announced today that they have ended their week-long separation and are back together again."[6] Peter Ford later recalled, "While Mother wanted things to work out, I think she knew that she and my father could never put all the pieces back together. These were stressful years for her . . . trying to keep her sometimes humiliating private life separate from her beaming public persona."[7]

Whatever may have caused Eleanor to be in such an agitated state on June 20, another issue arose that caused her great anxiety and humiliation. Glenn had been brought home late one night, drunk, by the Beverly Hills police. On the first occurrence, the officers discreetly explained that Glenn had been found in compromising circumstances in the company of young sailors. In the small, close-knit community of Beverly Hills of those days, the officers were always respectful and apologetic toward Eleanor, and each time they kept the matter private and made no official reports.

It's unknown exactly when Eleanor first became aware of his activities, but she was faced with hard truths about her husband. She had to deal with his hurtful dalliances not only with other women but also with men, and she was overwhelmed.[8] In those days, even a hint of any homosexual activity, no matter how isolated, would have destroyed Glenn's career. Such goings-on were not uncommon in the movie colony, where wealth and privilege (and sometimes studio intervention) allowed a blind eye to be turned and any incidents discreetly forgotten. While his publicist at Columbia worked hard to cover up his indiscretions, Glenn made little effort to curtail his infidelities and late-night carousing. "Some nights my father did not come home at all, or he came home very late, well after my bedtime," Peter recalled. "Later, I would hear about the 'homes away from home,' the bachelor pads and party houses."

Indiscretions of all types had been going on for years. As far back as 1939, Harry Cohn had set up discreet accommodations in penthouse suite 54 at the Chateau Marmont in Hollywood for Glenn and William Holden, with these instructions: "If you must get into trouble, do it at the Marmont." Glenn recalled that, "We were constantly . . . going places where we shouldn't have gone and mixing with the wrong people."[9] The suite soon became a bachelor pad where he could have his fun away from Hannah's prying eyes. Other Hollywood actors such as Humphrey Bogart, Errol Flynn, and John Barrymore regularly stopped by, either alone or with extramarital partners. The Marmont was just one of many such apartments and rooms maintained in the Hollywood circle for men carousing away from their spouses.

Eleanor knew she could end this unhappy cycle at any point. Each time she consulted divorce lawyer Jerry Geisler, she instead chose to continue with the marriage. As hurt as she was, she still loved Glenn enough to keep his indiscretions from seriously damaging his career and causing embarrassment for their young son. Many nights, she cried herself to sleep and prayed for courage and guidance.

Inevitably, in an attempt to alleviate the negative press from the reports of the Fords' short separation, studio requests were sent to the publicity machine. "Fan magazines and photo offices are being asked to shoot home layouts on Glenn Ford and Eleanor Powell to offset the news stories about their brief separation. Glenn and Eleanor are as anxious as their press agents about the whole thing."[10] Eleanor, criticized throughout her career for her weak acting skills, was now giving the most convincing performance of her life.

The family was pictured in various domestic activities—Glenn helping Peter with his homework, the family relaxing together in their den or camping and fishing together, or father and son building a treehouse. However, these moments were nearly always staged for the cameras and were far from a true reflection of their life. Eleanor perfected the habit of dutifully posing as a graceful and supportive wife and loving mother. In her heart, she longed for this to be true, but harsh reality intruded as soon as the magazine crews left the house. Glenn was no longer the attentive family man. "Most of the time my father was just not around, and when he was, he was either distracted or exhausted," Peter Ford recalled. "When making a movie he was so preoccupied when he got home at night that he hardly seemed to recognize any of us."

Eleanor and Glenn also made public amends by announcing they would be going on a fishing trip with Peter to Mammoth Lakes. They left on July 15 for a ten-day vacation at the Barker's Family Manahu Lodge and enjoyed the rustic outdoor life far from Beverly Hills. Despite the brief respite, life would soon return to normal.

Immediately after completion of *The Man from the Alamo* for Universal, Glenn went to Mexico to shoot *Plunder in the Sun,* and Eleanor planned to join him there. Sheilah Graham, alluding to the affairs on previous location shoots, remarked, "Eleanor Powell now plays it smarter—she'll go with Glenn Ford and son Peter to Mexico when he does *Plunder in the Sun.*"[11] But Eleanor did not go to Mexico. The film was set in four different regions, areas where conditions would be too rough for her and a seven-year-old; and again, it would have required taking him out of classes for part of the school year.

Eleanor and Glenn had not been photographed together publicly for months when they stepped off the 20th Century Limited in New York on January 21, 1953. Glenn was doing the radio drama show *Cavalcade of America.* Whether urged by press agents or out of personal resolve, Eleanor also decided to join Glenn on his next trip—the shooting of the film *The Americano* on location in Brazil. This time Peter could come along without missing school, and the three left Los Angeles by train for New Orleans on June 22, 1953. From there, they would take the SS *Delmar* for a fifteen-day voyage to Santos, Brazil. Curiously, on the visa immigration card, Eleanor listed Blanche's Hillgreen house address as her and Peter's residence, while Glenn listed his as Cove Way.

Glenn had made it a contractual requirement that Eleanor and Peter accompany him, or he would not participate. Perhaps the couple hoped that the trip might serve as a bonding experience and help bridge the chasms in their relationship. "For the first time in a long while I think they really did discover the happiness in each other's company that they once had known," Peter recalled. "I can remember seeing them strolling on the decks holding hands and embracing. I felt happy for them, for all of us."[12] But the closeness was short-lived once they landed in Brazil. The profuse adulation Eleanor received the moment they arrived in Rio de Janeiro and a few days later in São Paolo created the first crack in their fragile connection. The people of Brazil held Eleanor in the same esteem as they had during the height of her career. The large welcoming banners—"Brazil Greets Eleanor Powell"—gave Glenn flashbacks to their early dating days. The couple, constantly mobbed by crowds while sightseeing, was unable to spend any moments in public alone. Once they moved to the film location in the jungle, other mishaps arose to mar whatever progress they had made during the journey. Peter remembered finding a worm in his food. A parasite sickened all three soon after, and they were sidelined by stomach issues. Peter emerged from a river with leeches clinging to him. Ticks and red ants infested the ranch where they stayed. On top of this, problems with the crew and money issues with the production's bank turned the trip into an ongoing nightmare. For Eleanor, who had made a sacrifice to join her husband despite her dislike of extended travel, the trip was disastrous on all levels. Glenn was embarrassed to have Eleanor witness such a fiasco. Not close enough to draw support from each other, they simply retreated. By the end of the shoot, they were barely speaking.

Delays held up the production so long that they reached the end of Glenn's contracted date, September 9, without completing the film. The lack of funding forced Glenn to cover return tickets for himself and several others in the company. On September 11, they sailed back home. The film would ultimately be finished later, using Southern California locations. Exhausted and frustrated, Eleanor and Glenn returned to Cove Way with Peter.

The ill-fated trip to Brazil depleted Eleanor's physical and mental reserves, and after their return, Glenn simply went back to his previous ways. He would have affairs with the co-stars of his next two films, Gloria Grahame and Barbara Stanwyck. His other activities also continued. Nothing in Eleanor's life had prepared her for the events in her marriage, and she turned increasingly to the two things she had learned to rely on the most—her faith and her dancing.

She resumed teaching her Sunday School classes, resolving to keep a positive purpose in her life and not sink into depression. Little to her was more rewarding than sharing her faith with the children in her class, who gave her hope as well as humor each Sunday morning. She recalled a class the day after one of her films had played on television. Several of her young students had seen it for the first time and remarked with amazement, "You didn't tell us you were an old, old movie star!"

Eleanor was in her fifth year of teaching classes at the Beverly Hills Presbyterian Church when she was approached by Reverend Clifton Moore, minister in charge of radio and television for the Southern California region of the United Presbyterian Church. Searching for new programming ideas, he was impressed with Eleanor's dedication and rapport with her students. He asked if she would consider turning her class into a television broadcast. The program, titled *Faith of Our Children,* would be groundbreaking as the first religious program created for children. Eleanor was initially hesitant, thinking audiences would feel she was only doing it to be on television. But when she considered the benefits to children, she warmed to the idea. "I think it will do a lot of good in getting children to go to church," she told a reporter.[13] She refused any salary, but was obliged to take minimum scale due to union regulations—about twenty-seven dollars per show. What she made, she immediately put back into the program by buying supplies, props, costumes, and other materials. To provide whatever the show lacked, she canvassed other church members and celebrity friends. Any sponsorship money received was donated to charity.

Eleanor wrote the scripts, interviewed celebrity guests, led a question-and-answer session with the students, staged a costumed Bible story skit, and personally selected the weekly cast of children. She occasionally enlisted Glenn to help as narrator and to wrangle the large group there for each shoot, and Peter continued to be a member of the class. The studio audience was also composed of children. During production of the first show, Glenn, who had to corral eighty-four youngsters, was amazed at Eleanor's calm demeanor. "I was a wreck at the end of the day," he told Sheilah Graham. "It's a good thing Ellie kept her head."[14] Filming took place at NBC Studio D, located in Hollywood on Vine Street. Also filmed at the same studio was Groucho Marx's popular game show, *You Bet Your Life,* a bonus that was gleefully discovered by some of the children. "I wasn't too interested in who the adults involved in the production were, I just knew that it was fun being in the Groucho Marx Studio for the pre-show rehearsing," recalled musician John Case Schaeffer, one of the children who successfully auditioned for the show's choir. "I found the place where the pulley controlling Groucho's 'duck' was . . . and we would play with that until we saw the adults coming." Like most of the other youngsters on the show, he and his friends had fun until the responsibility of the actual shooting started. "I remember successfully fighting off the temptation to pluck the single feather on that goofy looking duck's tail." But while Eleanor thrived in the studio full of lively and curious children, Glenn was out of his element.

The most distinctive aspect of *Faith of Our Children* was Eleanor's emphasis on diversity. She insisted on including children of all races, a bold move that provoked many irate letters and calls. She received an especially concerned call from a prominent minister who complained about the number of Black children in the class. Eleanor replied politely and assured him that she would "address that issue in the upcoming episodes." The following week, not only did she make sure she had Black children in the class but she also invited an entire Black audience as well as a Black celebrity guest, gospel singer Mahalia Jackson. The show made its debut on October 3, 1954, and was broadcast locally every Sunday afternoon, first on KNBH-TV and then on KRCA-TV, Los Angeles.

Just as she had once brimmed with production ideas for her MGM numbers, Eleanor now dove headfirst into *Faith of Our Children*. She felt an increased calling to share Christian principles with children, and it was exciting to give them the opportunity to hear celebrity guests talk about their spiritual experiences. "I don't know of anything that has given me more satisfaction," she told Louella Parsons.[15] Soon singled out as a star who loved to speak about her faith, Eleanor was included in an NBC documentary, *Religion in American Life,* which was broadcast from October 30 to November 6 over television and radio. It was hosted by Art Linkletter, and guests Eddie Cantor, Gene Lockhart, Ruby Goodwin, and Eleanor spoke about the influence of religion in their lives.

Faith of Our Children consistently sustained strong ratings and won a total of five local Emmys for its first and second year. Eleanor took home the award for Most Outstanding Female Personality, beating out, among others, campy horror actress Vampira.

To the public, Eleanor and Glenn continued to epitomize the ultimate wholesome couple. Eleanor was much respected for her dedicated church and charity work. Glenn, due to his recent success with *Blackboard Jungle,* was instrumental in drawing attention to the battle against juvenile delinquency. Despite appearances, 1956 would prove to be the turning point in their fragile marriage. Hannah's reigning position in the household, literally midway between their bedrooms, mirrored her divisive role in their relationship. Eleanor had finally had enough. After years of putting up with Glenn's numerous infidelities, drunken adventures, and antisocial behavior, she decided to take a stand—starting with Hannah. Around June 1955, she informed Glenn that Hannah would need to move into her own home. Surprisingly, Glenn put up little protest. Instead, he saw a solution in the unused garage apartment of next-door neighbor, Charlie Chaplin. Then living primarily in Europe, Chaplin agreed to sell that portion of the adjacent lot on Summit Drive to Glenn. Glenn then refurbished the former chauffeur's residence for his mother and turned the large area of the former garage into a "rumpus room" for himself.

Nevertheless, tension continued to grow between the couple. Eleanor would regularly tap dance around the house, something that Glenn now detested. During the filming of *The Fastest Gun Alive* early that year, he checked in on a rehearsal with choreographer Alex Romero and dancer Russ Tamblyn, who were working on a routine for the hoedown scene in the film. When they began to work out some tap steps, Glenn interjected, "Listen, if you're going to do tap, I'm leaving. That's all I hear at home. [Eleanor] taps in the bathroom and kitchen. . . . I absolutely hate it!"[16]

Even as the rift widened between Eleanor and Glenn, the accolades continued. At the gala Photoplay Achievement Awards in February 1956, the Fords were honored with a Special Bronze Achievement Plaque for their "untiring devotion to religious and civic life and their contribution to the youth of our nation." Eleanor was radiant in a white crepe beaded gown with a diamond necklace, her hair now styled short and blonde. She publicly soldiered on, but there was little hope for a turnaround in their relationship. Soon, she would release the only sliver of hope that remained. A gathering at home with too much alcohol was the catalyst.

Parties at the house on Cove Way were a far cry from the happy holiday open houses and cozy dinner parties Eleanor had once hosted with Blanche on Bedford Drive. Most of the guests were Glenn's film buddies. Blanche rarely came to the house. Though Eleanor and her mother's closeness never diminished, Blanche felt unwelcome in Glenn's domain. "Glenn didn't care for my friends," Eleanor recalled. "So, I would not invite them over."[17] Many of Glenn's friends were heavy drinkers and, as the alcohol flowed, tempers often flared. On this particular night, several guests had brought their children, who gathered in the den to watch television with Peter. As the night wore on, it became clear that some guests had overindulged, including the host. As Peter recalls, writer Jack Holland had wandered into the den and, in his inebriated state, stood right in front of the television as the children were trying to watch a show. Peter attempted to talk to Glenn. "I quietly explained to him about Holland blocking the TV. . . . My father responded angrily . . . and seemed to act as if I was the troublemaker about to ruin his evening."

Glenn told Peter to go to his room. Eleanor intervened, and an argument started. "My father marched me upstairs, and my mother followed after him," Peter said.[18]

When they reached his room, Peter tried to explain the situation. He recalled, "My father grabbed me, shook me, and threw me down. My mother came forward to stop him, and he backhanded Mother, and she flew across my bed. I threw myself on her to protect her, but by then my father had rushed out of the room."[19] Despite Glenn's state, his violent actions took them both by surprise. Eleanor quickly told Peter to pack some clothes. They left the house and headed to Blanche's.

The small house on Hillgreen already hosted a young boarder that Blanche had taken in a few years earlier. Harlan James "Jim" Juris, then twenty-six, had become a handy helper for Blanche around the house. Both he and Blanche now rallied around Eleanor and Peter.

Eleanor once again contacted divorce lawyer Jerry Geisler. Ironically, at that same time Geisler was also handling another matter with a tie to Eleanor. Judy Garland had just filed for divorce from husband, Sid Luft. In 1959, Geisler would state that Eleanor had consulted him three times over the course of the marriage with serious intention to divorce but had ultimately backed down on each occasion.

Looking back at the marriage, her hesitation seems incomprehensible. Eleanor had blinded herself to many serious issues until it became impossible to continue. She spent the next two weeks at Blanche's, and each time she spoke to Glenn of divorce he countered with vicious threats. Eleanor had not been a breadwinner for many years and had no idea how she would support herself. "He promised to get the best lawyers in town, leave her broke, and take full custody of me," Peter recalled.[20] It was that prospect that frightened her the most; it was a sure way to keep her from taking action. Glenn knew Eleanor had the ability to ruin his career if she made the domestic violence public, disclosed his numerous affairs, or worst of all, revealed his bisexuality. He wasn't sure how far she would go but did not want to find out. His strategy worked. Defeated, Eleanor and Peter returned to Cove Way.

Until Peter turned fourteen, when he would no longer be under the direction of the court in a custody decision, Eleanor felt she had little choice but to stay in the marriage. "My father . . . had a powerful position in the company town where we lived," Peter said. "She stopped thinking about divorce for the time being. But from her perspective, from that point on, the marriage was over."[21]

Around this time, Glenn took unusual action to monitor private phone conversations. Just as Harry Cohn had installed listening devices throughout Columbia Studios to exert control, Glenn, in a fit of paranoia, decided to do the same in his own home. He enlisted the skills of a young electronics whiz—a student at Santa Monica High School—to install a secret bug on all the telephones in the house. Sixteen-year-old Ken Wales Smith was the 1956 recipient of an annual award set up in Glenn's name at his high school alma mater. After he won the award, Smith became a close family friend, and Glenn had him install stereo equipment and other devices. But the phone bug was not discovered until years later. "With a flick of a switch, my father could activate his secret audio-taping system and record any and all conversations to and from the house," Peter recalled.[22] From that point on, no conversations Eleanor or Peter had over the phone were private from Glenn.

The rest of the world saw little difference in their relationship. Glenn was soon voted scoutmaster of Peter's Troop 17, with Eleanor as secretary. The movie magazine articles continued to cover their activities as a family, with spreads full of cozy photos with bright smiles and feigned closeness, staged for the camera to boost Glenn's career. According to Louella Parsons, one of Eleanor and Glenn's friends attested that "they have worked out their marriage better than any other Hollywood couple who had once been threatened with marital troubles. They are so happy now."[23] Only the closest of friends knew of the problems, and even they did not know the full extent of Eleanor's concerns.

Eleanor continued with *Faith of Our Children,* now going into its third year. Sheilah Graham praised the show as "a solid hit . . . looking for an open spot to go network."[24] With network placement a possibility, the format of *Faith of Our Children* was still in question. Eleanor insisted that it remain as it was. But signing with the national networks would necessarily bring big changes to the format—the show would be limited to only one denomination, there would be no mixing of races, and the networks would have full control—none of which she was willing to agree to. "Eleanor Powell has confided to close friends that unless *Faith of Our Children* . . . is shown nationally with its present format, she will give it up."[25]

On November 27, she rode on the show's float in Hollywood's famous Santa Claus Lane Parade. Finally, in December 1956, Eleanor officially left the show, which had been on a break since June. After a short hiatus, the show resumed under several rotating hosts, but it markedly lacked the diversity she had fostered. The end of her position as hostess of the show also marked her break with the Beverly Hills Presbyterian Church, where she had been an active member for well over a decade. She had been frustrated because some members of the congregation had had reactions to the show that surprised and greatly saddened her. Each time she had asked for small loans of props and costuming for the show, she had been rejected; it had become obvious that the other ladies were jealous and unwilling to help out of spite. The rejection hurt her deeply. She no longer felt wanted. It was not the supportive environment she desired in a place of worship.

Even though she was no longer hosting the show in 1957, she was awarded an Emmy for Most Outstanding Personality, and the show also received another for Best Children's Program in the local Los Angeles Emmy Awards covering 1956.

Soon after her departure from *Faith of Our Children,* plans were under way with producer John Guedel to package a brand-new show, *Sunday with Eleanor Powell,* and present it as a national option to networks. Two networks expressed interest, pending securement of sponsors. Eleanor's lofty goal was to convince them that her idea was bankable, but in the conservative, pre–civil rights era, it proved to be an impossible challenge. "Sponsors run away from religion," she said. "They feel it's too touchy a subject for comfort." Moreover, no sponsor was willing to back a show that had children of different races mixing together. "I received a number of crank letters asking how I dared to have colored and white children in the same Sunday School classroom. Some even accused me of being a Communist and threatened to report me to the authorities. It was very disillusioning."[26] Sadly, *Sunday with Eleanor Powell* was never to be.

Eleanor realized her battle was fruitless and abandoned the idea for a religious show. She returned to her work with scouting and charities and became active in a variety of causes dedicated to aiding disadvantaged children, combatting discrimination, and raising money for children's health issues.

CBS may not have been willing to produce her religious show, but they were enthusiastic about reuniting her with Fred Astaire in a television special. Plans were to have the two trace the history of dance styles over the course of a ninety-minute production. But Eleanor did not feel ready for a dance comeback of this scope. Astaire would film the first of his *An Evening with Fred Astaire* specials beginning the following year with young dancer Barrie Chase.

Throughout 1957 and 1958, Eleanor kept busy with constant charity events, and Glenn carried on his regular schedule of filming, both locally and abroad. Tensions and jealousy continued between the two. On location in Colorado during the filming of *The Sheepman,* a young Shirley MacLaine told Glenn that Eleanor was her father's favorite dancer. "Glenn was not amused," she recalled. "He was competitive with Eleanor."[27]

In 1958, Eleanor began to pursue a longtime dream of opening a chain of Eleanor Powell Dance Studios. Like Astaire, she had desired to lend her name to further dance education. She had enjoyed her involvement with the Dance Troupers and loved helping children fuel their passion for dance. But by 1959, her life with Glenn had finally reached an impasse, and the business venture was not pursued.

Eleanor now discovered that Glenn had diverted large portions of their joint funds in purchases and cash for his mother. All her life she had been a pillar of optimism, to the point where Blanche said of her, "I know that it's good from time to time to have a release for one's own hostility. But not Eleanor. If a car passed a red light and knocked her down, she would get up and apologize to the driver for having caused him any worry."[28] Now, despite Eleanor's optimistic disposition, she could no longer look the other way. The extreme stress she had internalized over the course of the marriage caused her to seek a doctor's care for nervousness. It was time to act. "I found that a woman could only run so fast and so far. . . . I decided to stop running and face the truth," she said.[29] She told Hedda Hopper, "I'll be so glad when it's over. I'm no longer in love."[30]

When Peter turned fourteen on February 5, 1959, Glenn's threat to take full custody of their son no longer held weight. At the frazzled end of her rope, Eleanor announced to Glenn that she was seeking a legal separation and then divorce, just as he was packing to leave for Europe to film *It Started with a Kiss* with Debbie Reynolds. Glenn saw that Eleanor was finally serious and said they would discuss it when he returned. Unlike her three previous meetings with attorney Geisler, this time she would actually follow through with her plans.

Jerry Geisler was Hollywood's number one divorce and criminal defense attorney. He and Robert Neeb Jr. had teamed up on high-profile cases like the incest case against sinister Black Dahlia murder suspect Dr. George Hodel and Marilyn Monroe's divorce from Joe DiMaggio. No one was better suited to face off against Glenn. But Geisler was undergoing serious health issues; by August he handed the case over to his equally strong partner, Neeb. Glenn's attorney, Alfred I. Rothman, another experienced Hollywood divorce lawyer, had represented actress Lili Damita against Glenn's old friend Errol Flynn. By late April, Glenn had returned from Europe. The fight was about to begin.

On Glenn's birthday, May 1, Eleanor served him with divorce papers on the set of *The Gazebo,* his current film with Debbie Reynolds. When Glenn questioned the ironic timing, Eleanor said, "I've given you the best birthday present you could possibly have—your freedom."[31] Glenn had tried to share his side of the story with Reynolds while on set in Spain, but she had little sympathy. Not only had she recently gone through a very public divorce from Eddie Fisher but she had also observed firsthand how Glenn was with women. At the same time he was telling Reynolds about his marriage woes, she was astonished to see him try to flirt with actress Eva Gabor. "He had this fabulous wife and son, and he was upset, but he couldn't resist looking and patting," she later told Peter. "He was hot to trot. . . . I think Glenn flirted with every woman he ever worked with. He liked to play, and he always wanted to have his cake and eat it, too."[32]

Eleanor named Hannah Ford as codefendant in the suit, claiming that Hannah had "received certain funds and properties" that belonged to the couple. The lot purchased from Chaplin where Hannah was living was part of the community property. Shockwaves echoed across the headlines and gossip columns churned out speculative commentary. Curiously, though it was common knowledge in Hollywood circles, no one mentioned Glenn's extramarital affairs. These contributed greatly to their troubles, but, as Eleanor later confided to a close friend, the most serious problems with Glenn, ultimately, were due "not to the girls, but the boys."[33] She was tired of being forced to repeatedly forgive and forget and could no longer overlook his serial philandering.

Eleanor took responsibility for her own slowness to act. "Some people are stupid. I guess I'm one," she told Hedda Hopper. "I was like an ostrich with my head in the sand, refusing to believe things I knew were true. Finally, I got smart. I had to, for my son's sake."[34] She gave no details; she cited "extreme mental cruelty" as the reason for her action and told reporters "and that's exactly what I mean."

Glenn expressed complete shock to reporters and refused to comment. He tried to convince Eleanor to reconsider, but she would not change her mind. Finally, after he attempted to continue living together in the same house for several months, Glenn packed up his things and carried them down to Summit Drive, where he moved in with Hannah.

Over the summer, numerous court continuances delayed the proceedings. As the divorce negotiations continued between Eleanor and Glenn, the tense atmosphere had an adverse effect on adolescent Peter, who had just started at Beverly Hills High School. Unable to cope with a home in the process of splitting in two, he fell in with a bad crowd. "I managed to find the worst element for friends," Peter recalled. "I was angry. I got into fights. I still have scars on my hands from being knifed."[35] His attitude and his behavior continued to deteriorate over the coming months. "I refused to go to school. I would slip out at night to meet and travel with my hoodlum friends. I'm sure strings were pulled to keep me out of reform school and that if my parents hadn't been who they were I'd have been sent away."[36]

By late October, there had been eleven continuances, many times with both Eleanor and Glenn appearing before the judge. Finally, at 1:00 a.m. on October 23, exactly sixteen years to the day after Eleanor and Glenn's small home wedding on Bedford Drive, a tentative agreement was reached between both parties. The two attorneys had been conferring continuously from noon the previous day.

Four weeks later, on November 23, testimony in the case continued. Bess Randall, a friend of the couple, testified that Glenn and Eleanor often came to their home for holiday dinners. "As soon as he finished with his Thanksgiving dinner, he'd pick himself up and leave. My husband or one of the other guests would take her (Eleanor) home."[37] Randall also added that Glenn's conduct necessitated Eleanor seeking medical treatment for a nervous condition. Eleanor complained that Glenn was moody and antisocial and shared little to nothing about finances with her. "He was very secretive in his financial affairs. I have been considerably left in the dark so far as they are concerned."[38] Judge Allen T. Lynch granted the interlocutory decree that ended the marriage.

In a departure from the years of vehemently denying rumors, Eleanor finally gave herself permission to be honest with reporters. "I have been unhappy for a long time, and this is no sudden thing. My marriage wouldn't have lasted this long except for my religion and my feeling that I should keep my marriage together," she said. "I am sure Glenn will be much happier alone. He isn't happy now."[39]

Although her hard-nosed divorce attorney had wrangled over alimony and settlement issues, Eleanor's agreement was a far cry from typical Hollywood divorces. After thirteen hours of debate, Glenn would budge only so far, and Eleanor, mentally depleted, had no energy left to push for more. She had originally expressed a need for $3,700 per month for expenses. According to the details in a twenty-two-page property settlement document, she ultimately received an "iron-clad agreement," as she called it, that awarded her the home on Cove Way, $40,000 a year ($3,333/month) for the first six years, and then $30,000 a year ($2,500/month) for life, unless she remarried. If she went back to work, the amount earned would be deducted from the allowance. She had also agreed to assume responsibility for paying off $50,000 in community debt. In addition, she would receive $250 monthly support for Peter until he turned twenty-one. At that time, Glenn was earning over $250,000 a year. Eleanor had no other income.

An unnamed lawyer, when shown the agreement by reporter Lloyd Shearer, was shocked. "Frankly, the terms of the Powell-Ford agreement . . . amazed me. It's dirt cheap. Take a poor guy like Eddie Fisher . . . married to Debbie Reynolds for three years. You know what he had to pay in child support? From $2,000 to $4,000 a month."[40]

Despite the unfair settlement, an exhausted Eleanor felt victorious. Her sixteen-year ordeal was over.

Finale

(1959–1982)

Part X

(1861–1861)

19

The Phoenix

"'Ellie, you've got to work,'" Blanche told her.[1] It was the only solution, but it wasn't going to be an easy road. She was easily thirty pounds over her former dancing weight. Motherhood had softened her body. While she could still "tap dance in her sleep," her body had lost the needed tone and stamina. Except for the single television appearance in 1952, she had been away from the daily demands of rehearsal and performing since 1949. Entertainment itself had changed in recent years. If she returned to the stage, what kind of show could she put together? Would audiences remember her? Accept her? All these questions swirled in her head in the days following the finalization of the divorce. The morning after Thanksgiving, she felt drained and defeated. She found Peter and told him they were taking a trip. They were heading to Las Vegas.

Six people motored across the long stretch of desert toward the Nevada border, filling the spacious interior of Jim Juris' black 1959 Cadillac sedan— Eleanor, Blanche, Peter, Jim, Peter's young friend and next-door neighbor Scotty McComas, and the family cook, Agnes. It was the dawn of the "Rat Pack" era, and the long Cadillac with the distinctive fins was a fitting vehicle for their arrival about six hours later at a sprawling, sand-colored hotel with a neon-topped ranch-style sign that read "Wilbur Clark's Desert Inn." Frank Sinatra had made his Las Vegas debut there just eight years earlier. They had left town with so little notice that Eleanor hadn't even had time to return a phone call that morning from Hedda Hopper about her column. Hopper had written: "I'm happy Eleanor Powell's and Glenn Ford's divorce didn't erupt in fireworks. It could have if Eleanor hadn't been the fine girl she is."[2] On arrival, Eleanor sent a quick telegram to the columnist: "Leaving for a much-needed rest with Peter. . . . I was grateful for your kind mention in today's *Times*."[3]

The casino showrooms were full of star headliners, and each night they went to a different show. Marlene Dietrich was at the Sahara, Dean Martin at the Copa Room, Louis Prima and Keely Smith at the Desert Inn, singer Billy

Eckstine at the Frontier, and comic Joe E. Lewis with Lili St. Cyr at the El Rancho. Donn Arden's scantily clothed showgirl revue Lido de Paris was at the Stardust, and the Folies Bergère girls pranced the stage at the Tropicana. The heyday of Las Vegas was just about in full swing.

Eleanor and her entourage saw act after act, but it was the final night of their stay that moved her the most. Pearl Bailey had just opened at the Sahara, and Eleanor and Blanche couldn't leave without seeing her show. "She started delivering a eulogy to a celebrity in the house," Eleanor recalled. "And then she introduced me." Shocked, Eleanor got to her feet and bowed to the applauding audience, but Pearl protested. "You can't get by with a low bow here, honey. Get up on the stage with me." Eleanor quickly joined Pearl. "I was up doing the shim sham with Pearl's troupe. The audience cheered and applauded—and I thought they'd forgotten all about me."[4] Backstage, during a heartfelt hug, Pearl assured her they hadn't and encouraged her to take it a step further and consider making a comeback. This, combined with the adrenalin from the applause, touched her deeply. "I was as giddy as if I had been drinking champagne," she recalled.[5]

By the time she returned home, Eleanor was resolute. "Suddenly it was as if a voice said, 'Here are your shoes, your boy is grown.' It was a wild idea, and I didn't accept it easily. I was fat, my muscles were flabby, the mirrored reflection of a forty-seven-year-old face and figure was anything but encouraging."[6] She had never shied away from hard work; however, this might be the toughest uphill battle she had ever begun.

In May of the previous year, Eleanor had mused about the only way she would ever consider a comeback. "I can't afford to come back unless I am as good as I once was," she told reporters. "I'll start all over at the beginning. That's the best way to get your muscles toned up in the proper manner."[7] This is exactly the road she chose. She contacted her old friend, Russian ballet dancer David Lichine, who had partnered with her in *Sensations of 1945*. They set up daily sessions of ballet barre work, which she followed by an intense tap workout, dancing a total of six hours each day. Her doctor prescribed a draconian high-protein diet, just nine hundred calories a day, along with diuretics and appetite-suppression pills. For the next nine months, as Eleanor devoted herself to this rigid routine, she dropped weight while she slowly increased her strength and stamina. To bolster her spirits as the weeks passed, she wore the same slacks so she could noticeably view the progress of the diet. Only those in her closest circle knew of her efforts.

Each passing month brought a new infusion of confidence. "I danced like I never danced before . . . six and seven hours at a stretch. My muscles ached and hurt so much that tears ran down my cheeks," she recalled. "It was the most challenging thing I've ever done. . . . I did a powerful lot of praying."[8] She added daily singing lessons from vocal coach Harriet Lee to round out her training.

As she honed her figure and refined her technique, she put out feelers to potential interested bookers and producers, focusing on Las Vegas as a starting point. At the Sahara, Pearl Bailey's manager Stan Irwin was lining up future acts for the hotel's state-of-the-art space, which he described as "the best lounge ever." After Eleanor successfully auditioned with Sahara owner Milton Prell, Irwin booked her for a one-week trial beginning on February 28, 1961, with an option for extension. She would open at the Congo Room, the very spot where she had been pulled up onstage with Bailey just months earlier.

Next, she gathered a team of professionals to help stage and shape the act for modern audiences—some were from her MGM days, others were new. She hired Lichine as dance director and brought in Vegas veteran Donn Arden as show director. She added four strong singer/dancers, dubbed her Four Gentlemen (Tom Allison, Howard Krieger, Gordon Cornish, and Jerry Madison), to move the show forward during her costume changes and provide some song breaks. Musical director Richard Priborsky handled arrangements and wrote some additional new material for her. Percussionist Steve Dweck would serve as a strong match for trading rhythmic beats. Lastly, Eleanor decided to engage old family friend Jim Juris as her personal manager. A formal contract was drawn up that put him on a monthly salary with a percentage of earnings.

In the early 1960s, tap dancing was, as Eleanor aptly described it, "dead as a doornail." She was one of the few dancers from the golden era of Hollywood still performing tap. In recent years, it had almost become a lost art, and she felt the time was ripe to champion a revival. Her challenge now was to appeal to 1961 audiences.

The opening date was just five months away, but Eleanor's efforts to procure the financial investment needed to mount the act on her own were unsuccessful. She was finally forced to take out a second mortgage on the Cove Way home. The private loan would provide her with $100,000 to staff and costume the show, but it was a loan she would need to repay, whether or not the show was successful. In addition, in October she was hit with a tax lien of $10,481 from the IRS for funds owed from 1959.

As the pressure to succeed on both financial and creative levels fueled Eleanor's quest, Peter was still reeling from the effects of the divorce. The more he watched his mother struggle to keep her head above water, the deeper he sank into his own juvenile rebellion. During this crisis, he admitted to being "angry and very hostile" toward her.[9] After much consideration, she decided to take Peter out of Beverly Hills High and enroll him in the Chadwick School in the nearby beach community of Palos Verdes. Long known as a top educational facility for children of wealthy families, Chadwick was a boarding school where Peter could live on campus during the week. The school would be an added burden of $250 per month for tuition, an expense Glenn did not cover. It was just one more reason her comeback needed to be successful.

By the end of 1960, word was out about Eleanor's comeback. She staged a formal press conference on January 24, 1961, where she gave reporters a preview of her stunning, newly toned figure and also a taste of the crisp and intricate tap rhythms that had always been her signature. Journalists and photographers packed a Beverly Hills synagogue, where a nervous Eleanor dispelled all rumors that she was anything near a "has-been."

The following week, columnist Whitney Bolton described with unabashed admiration Eleanor's demeanor and proud admission of her age. "I am forty-eight years old and that's that." The image of Eleanor at the press conference was one Bolton "wished every eighteen-year-old in America could look at. The legs are poems. The head is up in honest pride and the eyes look at you straight and deep in," he wrote. "You have to love a woman like that. . . . Not many of the kind around these days."[10] In terms of technique, she was back at the top of her game. Both the press and the public were rooting for her. Bolton closed his column with a rousing, "Eleanor, get out there and kill the people."[11]

A little over a month remained until the show opened. In early 1961, *Life* magazine sent noted photographer Ralph Crane to the Sahara, where final rehearsals were in full swing. His documentation shows Eleanor in the full spectrum of emotions during the days just before the opening. Though Crane took over six hundred photos over the course of several days and also on opening night and backstage, only a few would end up in the resulting one-page article, which appeared in the March 24, 1961, issue.

Arden worked to put the numbers into place; each required special staging, props, wigs, and costuming. Eleanor's production notebook detailing the show inventory included designer costumes, special microphones to clearly capture the sound of the taps, trunks of tap shoes, and, of course, her personal tap mat. Eleanor would only perform with a specially constructed mat made of maple, the wood she felt produced the best sound for tap. Though she owned several, including a small one in a rehearsal room at home, the one that she would install on the floor of the Sahara measured sixteen by twenty-four feet, weighed a thousand pounds, and could be rolled up for transport. She considered it one of the most important tools of her trade. "In essence, my feet are my voice, and it is as necessary for me to have my dance mat as a singer who must have a microphone," Eleanor explained. "I can't take the chance of having a floor that is waxed or made of the wrong type of wood and therefore not be heard."[12] She also wore specially constructed shoes that had a layer of fiberboard attached to the soles and were very slippery.

So far, Arden had been overseeing the direction of the show with Eleanor's input. His original concept for the opening involved a bedroom setting. Eleanor would lounge sensuously on a bed as she talked to the audience, and, after some brief dialogue, would go behind a screen and change, emerging in a beautiful gown to begin the first number. While this was a signature style for Arden, Eleanor felt the concept was at complete odds with her persona.

Arden also began to criticize Eleanor's dance technique. She had long had a habit of performing her turns and pirouettes with her hands bent at the wrist and hanging in front of her, instead of the traditional form of holding them taut and close to the body. Arden nagged her about it, and Eleanor balked. She felt this method anchored her balance and had served her well for decades. She wasn't about to change now.

More importantly, Arden disapproved of Eleanor's matador number. He considered the eight-minute extravaganza (reminiscent of her dance from *Ship Ahoy*) unauthentic. But Eleanor had a clear vision and trusted her own instinct for showmanship. She loved coupling tap rhythms with Spanish beats and had longed to do more with the idea ever since MGM had squelched her original concept for the number. She stuck to her convictions, and Arden was let go in early February. He was replaced by Nick Castle barely three weeks before the show was scheduled to open.

Castle had a long history at 20th Century-Fox Studios. He had worked extensively with the Nicholas Brothers and other dancers in the 1940s and 1950s, and his input would be invaluable. The matador number, with its showy $7,000 French-cut, black and silver beaded costume, matching bolero-style jacket, and the accompanying bullfighter's cape lined with crimson and white baby ostrich feathers, was kept in. With such a huge investment in time, costuming, and personnel, Eleanor prayed her instincts were on target and her fans would return.

Her prayer was answered. The Congo Room on opening night was packed with reporters from fifty of the nation's top newspapers and the six-hundred-seat room was sold out. Peter and Blanche were in the front row, cheering her on.

An audio tape and film footage of the show reveal a confident, chatty Eleanor at the top of her game in a smoothly crafted presentation. In a show that featured new songs as well as material from her Broadway and MGM days (some with clever new updated lyrics), her tap rhythms ran the gamut from soft shoe to waltz to Latin beats to lyrical to an impressive percussive exchange with drummer Steve Dweck. She amused the audience with an introduction to her close-to-the-ground tap technique contrasted with a humorous demo of various versions of the time step. She also demonstrated the mechanics of her famed "top-spin" move, still an impressive technical feat. But by far, the most ambitious and one of the most crowd-pleasing moments was the matador number.

Eleanor had developed a creed, which she often shared with others: "What we are is God's gift to us, but what we become is our gift to God." She was deeply thankful for what she had been able to accomplish and as an expression of this attitude, before each show she gathered her team for a short meditation and reading from the Bible. Forming a circle, they ended in prayer. "You'd be surprised what this does for us," she told the press, "bringing harmony to a bad situation."[13]

Reviews exploded with praise. "Eleanor Powell, for precious moments on the Congo Room stage of the Hotel Sahara," said one review, "stops time in its flight." "Her dancing is still fast, precise, and exciting, but there is a subtle new character in her movements."[14] "Dance-wise, she's a knockout," wrote esteemed New York dance critic Walter Terry. "The nostalgia comes not because we are seeing Eleanor Powell, but because we are seeing live on stage, first-class hoofing and we realize that we have not seen it for a long time. . . . She is giving us a star act in the old variety tradition."[15]

The audience gave her three standing ovations, and a tearful Eleanor humbly acknowledged their love. At a crowded reception backstage after the show, dancer Ann Miller gave Eleanor a congratulatory hug. Peter smiled and kissed his mother's cheek as press photographers flashed photos. Eleanor had done the near impossible. She was back.

◉   ◉   ◉

Though Eleanor's act was initially booked for just one week, the response was so overwhelming that the Sahara extended her booking for an additional three weeks until March 26. Back home in Beverly Hills the first week of April, she took a short break as she mulled over other offers. According to Harrison Carroll, those included "two pictures, a TV spectacular, many guest spots, and night club bids that could keep her busy for months."[16] Among these were venues in Paris and New York. During this time, she decided to take up an offer of full management from the Music Corporation of America (MCA), who convinced her she no longer would need the services of her personal manager, Jim Juris. She broke the news to Juris. Though he was not pleased with the situation, he temporarily let the matter rest.

Buoyed by her successful Las Vegas debut, Eleanor took her act on tour. First, she played the Latin Quarter in New York, where crowds were so enthusiastic that "a ringsider threw a diamond bracelet onstage. Eleanor handed it back with thanks."[17] Next was the Cork Club in Houston. The show was then revamped before it returned to Las Vegas at the end of summer.

Back on the road, she played the Town Casino in Buffalo in September. Touted as the "biggest nightclub between Chicago and New York City," the casino had a dinner show at 7:30 p.m., followed by shows at 10:30 p.m. and 1:30 a.m. By the final show, the audience would often be more focused on their cocktails than Eleanor's elegant footwork. At one performance, recalled dancer Roy Fitzell, a table of drunken partiers were particularly loud and boisterous during Eleanor's act. Unable to ignore it any longer, she took her cane and motioned for the orchestra to stop. As the room quieted, she stared pointedly at the revelers. After they stopped their loud talking and laughing, she thanked them and then continued the show.

That same month, her grandfather Harold, who had returned to live in Springfield after his wife's death, came to see her act at Blinstrub's in Boston. At eighty-nine, Harold was still active and in good health.

In October, she performed at the New Latin Casino in Merchantville, New Jersey, then crossed the country for a November engagement at Harrah's in Lake Tahoe. Feeling strong and confident that she would continue working for many years, she extended publicist Milton Weiss' contract through 1972.

In recent months, ever since they had appeared together on the bill at the Dunes in Las Vegas, Eleanor had been seeing comedian Allan Drake. Though she was much too occupied with her career for a serious relationship, Drake pursued her relentlessly. The press began to comment on their keeping steady company and went so far as to predict marriage. "Eleanor Powell may follow Lucille Ball's path to the altar," wrote Dorothy Kilgallen. "She's more than a bit interested in a comedian named Allan Drake."[18]

After a week at the Vapors Club in Hot Springs, Arkansas, in early December, Eleanor headed back home to Beverly Hills for a few weeks. She wanted to be with Peter, who was scheduled to undergo a tonsillectomy. "That's another opening for me," she jokingly told reporters. "I have to be at that one."[19] She spent Christmas Day through New Year's Eve at the Chi Chi Club in Palm Springs, then settled into a well-earned two-month break. It was during this break that the disagreement with Jim Juris finally escalated into a lawsuit. On February 22, 1962, Juris, still angry over being fired the preceding April, sued Eleanor. He cited breach of contract and faulted Eleanor for favoring MCA over his existing written agreement. The outcome of the suit was never made public, and it is assumed they resolved the situation with a private settlement.

In March, Eleanor traveled to Florida, where she was booked at the Diplomat Hotel. Her first visit to the state would be a memorable one. There are few better examples of Eleanor's stubborn dedication to her craft than the incident on March 8, 1962. While she performed the Bill Robinson stair dance tribute on opening night at the hotel's Café Cristal—the second number in the show—a loose brace on the prop steps caused her to lose her footing. Immediately assuming it was her own error, she held fast to her vaudeville training, reattached the brace, and started the number again. Once more the stairs shifted and she fell, this time severely gashing her leg in the process. Despite the three-inch wound, Eleanor was not about to let the audience down. A sympathetic patron tossed a dinner napkin onto the stage. Eleanor used it to daub the cut, then glanced up to heaven and said, "I'll get it this time, Bill." Cries from the audience erupted as she went to start the number once more. Again, the stairs wobbled as the brace again detached, but she held her footing and replaced it for the third time. Finally, Richard Priborsky, who was conducting the orchestra, stepped over, convinced her to stop, and moved the faulty prop away.

Ending the show was unthinkable, but Eleanor stepped over to the offending stairs, gave them a quick spank, and exited. "Leaving the stage still smiling and apologizing, the wonderful dancer returned to finish the remaining three-quarters of her show," wrote one critic. "She did it with color, style and an injured leg and showmanship that ended with a near standing ovation."[20] The audience's applause acknowledged not only the dedication Eleanor showed her audience by completing the show that night but also her return to her fans at this point in her life. The talents of the young Eleanor Powell had met the needs of Depression-era audiences, and now the mature

Eleanor Powell had returned in full force to bolster the same audience, now middle-aged, who had weathered the years alongside her.

Backstage later that night, the hotel doctor put eighteen stitches in her leg and gave her a sedative. In addition to the gash, her right knee was also injured. But the accident did not sideline her for long. She resumed performing the following night and successfully finished out the run with a bandage on her leg. Critics lauded both her professionalism and her undiminished talent. "When Eleanor Powell floats on the stage . . . rhythm drips from her toes and heels," said the *Miami News*. "She's slender, unpadded, and a wholesome lady to watch work."[21]

With the stairs securely rebuilt, this time at a much lower height, the number was reintroduced in the act. A film clip of the number shows Eleanor performing the dance with more swagger and verve than in her earlier effort in *Honolulu*; she incorporated her mentor's sass as she exited with a strut. During the week-long engagement in Florida, she met Miami hotelier Manfredo Sepia. They spent a pleasant time chatting and, during Eleanor's appearance at the Caribe Hilton in San Juan the following week, she received a letter from him. He asked if he could meet her at the Miami airport on her return and take her to dinner. Though she was still occasionally seeing Drake, she found Manfredo's company interesting. His previous marriage of four years had ended in divorce in 1961. As the two shared many of the same views on life issues, conversations were comfortable. "I never thought I'd find a man with exactly my philosophy of life, but Manfredo has it," Eleanor told reporters.[22] Manfredo was easygoing in social settings and pleasant to be around.

Eleanor returned home to Los Angeles to revise the show for her upcoming engagement at the Dunes in Las Vegas. She booked a rehearsal hall at the Goldwyn Studios for two weeks, where the full company rehearsed new additions and changes. The new version of the show was produced and staged by Tony Charmoli, Emmy Award winner for television's *Your Hit Parade,* and was choreographed by Ron Lewis. Sharing the bill were comic Gary Morton in his Las Vegas debut, featured dancer Maybin Hewes, Arturo Romero and his Magic Violins, and singer Bob Newkirk. Richard Priborsky continued as music director.

An old friend of Priborsky's, forty-year-old Charmoli had long idolized Eleanor. He had novel ideas about how to refresh her act, suggesting an opening soft-shoe number: "In the darkened theater you hear taps, the spotlight hits the curtain and slowly moves . . . and tap shoes come into the spotlight . . . now the spotlight widens to full head to toe as Eleanor turns, taps her cane, taps her top hat, strikes a pose and the announcer says, 'Ladies and Gentlemen, Miss Eleanor Powell.'"[23] Hesitant about the opening, Eleanor told Charmoli, "You can't open the show with a soft shoe." He replied, "No, you can't—but Eleanor Powell can!"

Eleanor previously had a habit of giving out her pancake recipe while chatting with the audience during her act, which annoyed Charmoli. "I kept reminding her she was a movie star, not Betty Crocker."[24] Recipes aside, famed Spanish dancer José Greco later assured Peter backstage that his pancake-making mama was now "cooking with gas."

Eleanor's new show opened at the Arabian Room at the Dunes Hotel on April 19, and critics once again applauded her return. "Eleanor Powell put an even stronger claim to the title 'America's Queen of Rhythm Dancing' when she tapped her way into the hearts of everyone who packed the Dunes Hotel . . . for the opening."[25] The personality that had charmed movie audiences in 1935 had not diminished. "She can charm and dazzle an audience by merely stepping on a stage and striking a dancing pose," another reviewer wrote. "Maybe it's her bright, little bursts of happy laughter as she dances . . . or the bewildering assortment of complex terpsichore she throws at you . . . but whatever it is, the sensuously writhing Eleanor has it just like Astaire, Robinson, DiMaggio, Dempsey, and Babe Ruth."[26] Dancer Maybin Hewes recalled Eleanor's tremendous generosity and encouragement and the "glorious" audience appreciation and reception of the show. "She was magic," Hewes said. "Her footwork was unbelievable."

During her Broadway years, Eleanor's innocent and wholesome demeanor had often kept men away, but now, potential suitors were intrigued and attracted by her glamorous, confident image and newly single status. Manfredo continued to send her flowers regularly, and Drake maintained his pursuit. Hewes, who had become a close friend of Eleanor's during the run of the show, grew concerned about Drake's persistent interest. "He was not a good guy," Hewes later recalled.[27] Familiar with the Las Vegas scene, she knew all too well of Drake's mafia connections. Drake's wife had been killed in a 1959 hit while in the company of his friend and sponsor, mobster Anthony "Little Augie" Carfano. Hewes also knew that Drake had a serious gambling problem and was just an all-around "low class guy." Drake persisted in his attempts to woo Eleanor, but the romance cooled as Eleanor grew closer to Manfredo.

Smitten with Eleanor, Manfredo offered his services to help her career, and in coming months would become part of her traveling entourage. Eventually, he became a personal support and joined her on the road when able.

With the success of the nightclub tour, television offers poured in, but Eleanor turned down most, holding out for her own special. Chrysler expressed interest in sponsoring the show. Dancer Roy Fitzell recalled Eleanor's disappointment when, during her ongoing negotiations for the program, Chrysler requested that Astaire introduce her. Fitzell had stopped into her dressing room before the show in Reno while she was on the phone with Astaire. "He said no," she told Fitzell after she hung up. "And then he said, 'Eleanor, you were always better than I.'"[28]

While Eleanor toured, Peter completed his senior year at Chadwick School. She arranged to be in town for his graduation on June 15 and canceled the remainder of her summer tour until her return to the Dunes on July 26. Glenn, held up in France while shooting *Love Is a Ball* with new girlfriend Hope Lange, was unable to attend. Peter planned to enter Lake Forest College, a private liberal arts institution in Illinois. At that time, he expressed interest in being a lawyer.

Eleanor returned to the Dunes for another five weeks in late July with comedian Rip Taylor, who was making his Las Vegas debut. By now fully acclimated to her new performing life as she neared fifty, she told a reporter, "I've never been more happy and relaxed in my life. . . . Tired? I should say not! Right now, I could easily take a five-mile walk. Wanna come along?"[29]

Acknowledgment of her achievement came on July 26 with an award from the Dance Educators of America in "recognition of her lifelong dedication to the dance." Since she would be onstage at the Dunes when the award was presented in New York, dancer Gwen Verdon agreed to accept it in her place. A unique arrangement was made to have a long-distance phone call between Verdon and Eleanor during her show played over a loudspeaker for the audience to hear.

In the fall, Peter started his term at Lake Forest and once again fell into his former ways. "The weather was cold, I was homesick and frankly, I had been medicating myself liberally with pills to get through the Illinois winter."[30] He joined with several other students and also began dealing the pills. When the school administration found out, Peter was expelled; after just one semester, he was back at home in Beverly Hills. He enrolled in Santa Monica Community College and turned his sights to acting options.

Eleanor, devastated, blamed herself and questioned her own decisions. "Only a parent can instill the character you want a child to have," she said. "I was president of the PTA. I organized baseball teams. I worked with the Boy Scouts. . . . I taught Sunday School for twelve years without missing a Sunday."[31]

Though she made efforts to be home and attentive to Peter when she could, at nineteen he was an adult. She now had the sole responsibility to earn the money needed to maintain the house. She had finally had the opportunity to pursue her talents again. She knew the time was not far off when performing would be over for her and wanted to enjoy dancing while she still was able.

In December, Eleanor was back in New York and appeared on *Perry Como's Kraft Music Hall* on the 26th. She performed a medley from her act as well as a song and tap dance with Caterina Valente, "Follow in My Footsteps." The press erroneously stated it was her television debut—evidently forgetting her appearance on *The Danny Thomas Show* in 1952. At fifty, Eleanor was still surprised at the second life of her career. "I thought they would have forgotten by now. But they haven't," she said. "When I finish my act and go around to tables shaking hands, many of them are crying. . . . They seem to be glad I made it back."[32]

Nineteen sixty-three started off with a return appearance on *The Perry Como Show* on February 20. In the fall, she returned to the Dunes for a month, and on December 10, she was back in New York, where she made her only appearance on *The Tonight Show* with Johnny Carson. Her old tap jam buddy, John Bubbles, was in the audience that night and was called up onstage. The two danced together for the first time in nearly three decades. The following week, she was a guest on *The Bell Telephone Hour* for the December 17 show. She finished out 1963 at the Chi Chi Club in Palm Springs.

Throughout her packed performance schedule during the early 1960s, Eleanor tried to maintain regular contact with close friends and to keep her mailing list of over two thousand updated with her touring schedule. Though she was working constantly, finances were still a struggle. The secretary she engaged not only had to handle the heavy correspondence but also had to help with household duties while Eleanor toured.

On January 25, 1964, she made a return appearance on *The Hollywood Palace* show. She danced to a medley of numbers from her films, backed by chorus boys dressed as sailors, and participated in comedy sketches with the other guest stars Ernest Borgnine, Carl Ballantine, and Joe Flynn.

Manfredo had been working to help set up connections overseas, and Eleanor had received some tempting offers from producers for international appearances. Though she found her career rewarding, Eleanor realized that touring with her act was not something she could sustain indefinitely. Updating her show each year with new costumes, music, and ideas was expensive and difficult to maintain.

While Eleanor was intensely worried about Peter's future and the turn his life was taking, she found some respite in her relationship with Manfredo, which had deepened over the months. She announced their engagement with a projected wedding date for the spring of 1964.

Over the next six months Eleanor appeared in the final bookings of her nightclub act. She performed at Harrah's Lake Tahoe in Stateline, Nevada, then the Cave Supper Club in Vancouver. Next up were the Vapor's Club in Hot Springs, Arkansas, and the Latin Quarter in New York. As a fitting close to the tour, she ended in her hometown of Springfield, Massachusetts, with three weeks at the Storrowton Music Fair, June 7 through 21. Her time in Springfield was filled with reunions, including one with childhood best friend Gabriella Bonfitto (whose Italian family had embraced her decades earlier), now Mrs. Gabriella Howard. It was an emotional moment. "I didn't care if I was on camera. We just bawled our heads off."[33] The theater owners gifted Gabriella and her husband with a new wardrobe, appliances, and dining room set; they also provided childcare so that they could both accompany Eleanor around town during her visit. The reunion was a timely one. Gabriella passed away from a heart attack the following year.

City officials designated a special welcome committee to coordinate all her activities, including the proclamation of an "Eleanor Powell Day" on June 11, 1964. In an unprecedented move, the city essentially closed down to celebrate Eleanor—schools, markets, and stores took a holiday in honor of the triumphant return of their hometown girl. She rode in a festive motorcade down Main Street where, along the way, shop owners ran out to hand her flowers. She was deeply touched by the outpouring of love and reciprocated by making the performance one that neither she nor the audience would ever forget.

Eleanor was grateful for the opportunity to spend time with her grandfather. Harold Torrey was now ninety-two years old and was excited to be able to be with his "Ding" in their hometown once more. Though her visit was packed with a heavy schedule, she made the effort to see him daily, and when the show opened, he proudly sat in the front row at each performance.

Though Clarence Powell had passed away in California the year before, her Powell relatives still in Springfield came to greet her. For the first time, she met her half sister Judy, twenty-three years her junior. Eleanor welcomed her sister warmly and would continue to correspond with her for years to come.

It was the first time Eleanor had played a theater-in-the-round, and special attention was paid to the presentation of the show at the Storrowton

Music Fair. A translucent screen was arranged so that audiences could see the film clips from multiple sides. The performance was a moving experience that both Eleanor and the audience cherished. The Springfield crowd gave her multiple standing ovations and a warm send-off. She promised to return.

While the Springfield performances were emotionally fulfilling and moving, a special invitation to travel abroad for a command performance in Monaco in August 1964 was an offer Eleanor could not refuse. She would perform as part of the prestigious annual Red Cross Ball. Comic Rip Taylor would also share the bill. Overseen since 1958 by Princess Grace, the gala performance and ball were star-studded events that featured luminaries each year, such as Maria Callas and Sammy Davis Jr. This year, all eyes were on the princess, as just four days earlier she had announced she was expecting her third child with Prince Rainier.

Eleanor was thrilled to visit Monaco, a first for her. As she had for her tour in Britain in 1949, she would transport her large maple tap mat across the ocean. She arrived a week early for preparations and rehearsals. Her mat was installed on the outdoor stage and readied for the evening show on August 7. As Eleanor was introduced and began her set, something happened that had never occurred in the seven-year history of the show—instead of the usually warm and balmy summer weather of the Riviera, a freak storm of "torrential rain, thunder, and lightning" erupted. At the royal table, Princess Grace covered her head with a napkin as the rain came down. "Next to her, David Niven sat drenched, but bravely grinning," a London paper reported. The guests who did not brave out the storm in their seats ran for cover nearby.[34]

Soaked and heartbroken, Eleanor never stopped dancing as the rain destroyed both the opportunity she had greatly looked forward to, along with her $3,000 tap mat. The press reported, "Hollywood star Eleanor Powell struggled through her performance with tears and rain streaming down her face." The remainder of the show was canceled by the performers set to follow Eleanor, "Miss Bluebell" and her troupe of young British dancers. "It was the first time in my life I danced between raindrops," she later wrote her friend, the New England artist Stanley Woodward, as she recounted the fiasco.[35]

Later that month, Eleanor announced to the press that her engagement with Manfredo Sepia was over. The relationship the two had struggled to maintain was just not working. "What can you do with a long-distance romance like this?" she told the press. "I haven't seen him since I was at Lake Tahoe." As a result, they split amicably as a couple, but remained friends for years.

Offers to perform continued to be plentiful. Particularly tempting was a six-month tour around Sydney and Melbourne, Australia, as well as an appearance in Russia organized by impresario Sol Hurok. But Eleanor could not bring herself to accept them. It was increasingly apparent that Peter was in need of strong parental guidance at this stage of his life. "I couldn't think of leaving Peter that long," she wrote to Woodward. "He has many decisions to make . . . and needs someone to turn to . . . someone interested in his grades, etc." In her eyes, Glenn had essentially rejected Peter, and she could not rely on him to provide the fatherly attention and support Peter needed. After much reflection, she declined the offers and resigned herself to "playing the role of 'Mom' which is after all the most rewarding role of all."[36] Feeling the performing chapter of her life would need to close, her attention now shifted back to the home front.

20

Winding Down

Eleanor slipped back into her role as a full-time mother with dedication, attempting to fill the void dancing had left. Though enticing offers were still coming in, she was firmly resolved to be there for Peter. She busied herself with home life and enjoyed the tranquility of tending her garden, where she cultivated roses, carnations, gladiolas, and old-fashioned hollyhocks sent to her by a friend in the East. She loved the huge white magnolia blossoms on her trees and the heady fragrance of night-blooming jasmine in the summer evening. "My love of nature and all of God's wonder is all I need to make me happy," she declared.[1] She tapped into her domestic side and did much of her own cleaning and laundry. It was an effort to be frugal, but one that also brought her joy. "I adore the days I wash. I like to hang things on the clothesline in the sun. Can't get away from that New England background," she wrote to a friend.[2] Still active in charity work, she supported no fewer than sixty-five organizations and frequently received awards for her work.

With just Peter and herself and no income other than her alimony, it was increasingly clear that she needed to focus on selling the house. She had first put it on the market in 1963, but it was hard to find a buyer for a large estate in a tough market. It would be years before she could finally unload what Peter later termed "the white elephant."

In the years since her departure from the Beverly Hills Presbyterian Church, Eleanor had explored a wide range of spiritual avenues, still hoping to find one that resonated with her inclusive attitude. She was a voracious reader and had ventured into the array of metaphysical books that filled bookstores in the 1960s, a time of spiritual expansion and exploration for many. During this quest she happened upon a group that advertised itself as the Spiritual Science Unity Church, an offshoot of the Unity Church that emphasized a doctrine of metaphysics. Spearheaded by John T. Ratekin, this new group, which he called "The Symposium," held their weekly services at the Beverly Theatre, not far from Eleanor's Beverly Hills home. Ratekin's upbringing was in the Foursquare Church, where as a teen he often appeared in theatrical pageants. In the mid-1930s, he became associated with Aimee Semple McPherson and her Angelus Temple and wrote and directed her elaborate stage presentations. When Semple McPherson died in 1944, Ratekin occasionally spoke at events as an evangelist before he segued into a full-time career as a landscape architect. By the time his church activity resurfaced in the 1950s, his beliefs had dramatically shifted and he no longer subscribed to any particular dogma.

After her experience with parishioners and the hierarchy at the Beverly Hills Presbyterian Church, Eleanor found the Symposium's services welcoming. She was glad to oblige when after several visits, she was asked to speak at the Sunday gatherings.

Before long, Eleanor had gone through an "ordination" and her status was elevated to "associate minister." The group's organizational meetings were moved to her home on Cove Way. Eleanor was giving sermons nearly every Sunday and became heavily involved with planning the future of the group, as well as supporting their grandiose plans for the design and building of a massive church structure. She wrote Stanley Woodward: "We intend to build an edifice that will be thirty-five stories tall and will be a large glass dome holding 4,000 seats at the top with twelve pillars . . . below will be the Gardens of Civilization which will hold 10,000 people . . . and twelve ministers of all faiths preaching seven days a week." In 1965, the building would have been the tallest structure in Los Angeles, topping even the thirty-two-story city hall. Though Ratekin's team included only Eleanor, Dr. Peter Riggs, and former actress Ellenora Rose, the group had extremely lofty ambitions. It also had the alarming trappings of a potential cult, given the charismatic Ratekin, the efforts to attract celebrity names, a goal of raising large donations from the public, and an ever-evolving, all-inclusive philosophy without any actual doctrine. In a desperate effort to appeal to young searchers, and inspired by the popular nightclub on the Sunset Strip, Ratekin placed a sign reading "Faith A-Go-Go" in front of the theater on service days. He wanted to present it as a hip church that accepted all beliefs because it itself had "no dogma or creed"; but his teachings, which he called "spiritual science," were an odd mélange of motivational thinking and metaphysics. Church meetings and sermons increasingly consumed Eleanor's time, coming to monopolize a large portion of her day. She was also tiring of her role as a celebrity ambassador for the group and the continual effort it took to be "Eleanor Powell."

As she began to feel less at home with the church and its teachings, personal issues also began to demand more of her time. Peter fractured his heel in a gym accident and was on crutches as it healed, and dental problems sidelined her temporarily as well. By late fall 1965, she decided to take a leave of absence, which turned into a permanent break from Ratekin and the Symposium. Within a few months the church ads featured only Ratekin's name and then completely disappeared. By 1966, Ratekin had abandoned his landscaping career, separated from his wife and his young children, and moved to Mykonos, Greece, where he lived for seventeen years and became an artist. At this time, the island began to attract a growing gay community. Ratekin gained prominence in Mykonos for his art and also penned the island's first tourist guidebook. His unfulfilled metaphysical aspirations may have been a precursor to even more elaborate manipulations that caused him to suddenly break from his family and escape overseas, or he may just have been an unhappy man on a quest for peace. In any case, Eleanor realized that the Symposium was not the spiritual base she needed. When later questioned about her time with Unity, she succinctly stated, "I don't do that anymore" and did not elaborate further—her usual method for dealing with experiences she preferred to leave safely in the past. She never joined a specific denomination or church again, but over time she found comfort in her simple, but personal, faith in God.

The Symposium services had introduced Eleanor to a variety of people, among them attendee Lou Slater and his friend, theater director and screenwriter Barry Baumgarten. Slater, described by Baumgarten as "a maverick Jew," had happened upon the services as a "positive living kind of church." After he heard Eleanor speak multiple times, the two became friends and he introduced her to Baumgarten, who had dreams of forming a repertory theater group. In August 1965, the three met at Eleanor's home to discuss his vision. "After listening to my plan to form a repertory theater . . . she decided to let me use her name to get started," Baumgarten recalled. "And so, Eleanor Powell's Repertory Theater began."[3]

Baumgarten set about auditioning actors as well as gathering an illustrious group to join Eleanor on the board of directors. Though none contributed financially to the venture, celebrities including Edward G. Robinson, John Raitt, Roger Wagner, Arthur Kennedy, and Ruth Warrick agreed to lend their support through the inclusion of their names on the board. "It seems that Miss Powell and Mr. Baumgarten are approaching the entire 'business' with more forethought, know-how, and cash outlay than any of the others [local repertory companies] and could very possibly accomplish what everyone else has failed at," the local press reported.[4] Seed money was provided by a sponsor, and the first production, *Long Day's Journey into Night,* was set to open on November 30. A flexible season was planned that would include one musical revue that Eleanor would choreograph.

Similar to the start of her involvement with the Symposium, Eleanor was enthusiastic about her part in a creative theatrical vision and told the press that she would "even sharpen pencils if it will help out in any way."[5] All appeared full speed ahead until Eleanor paused and took stock of all she had committed herself to. Though she was no longer overworking herself physically, the level of responsibility she had accepted from multiple directions was gradually overwhelming her. Citing a case of the flu, she bowed out of a meeting at the Brown Derby with Baumgarten and *Los Angeles Times* theater critic Cecil Smith. She discussed the theater project with Glenn—given his own roots in local theater, his insight was valuable. In late October, Baumgarten received a surprising letter from Eleanor. "She had been advised by her former husband, Glenn Ford, to not have her name associated with the company," he said. Her decision to step aside from involvement with the theater company coincided with her separation from the Symposium.

Glenn had been pursuing Kathryn Hays, a young actress in her early thirties. Though his relationship with his son had been strained in the early years after the divorce, by this time it had improved significantly. Peter was best man at their wedding in March 1966. When the marriage ended after only two years, the press began to carry stories of a possible reconciliation between Eleanor and Glenn. Though the two were now on friendly terms, nothing came of it. Eleanor was happy on her own.

During the next few summers, Peter occasionally worked with Glenn in his films as an actor or dialogue director, but then he began to concentrate on his first love—music. He and three friends formed a band, Peter Ford and the Creations, and in October 1964, he accepted a contract with Capitol Records. *Variety* noted that he was joining the ranks of other children of famous show business personalities who were trying to make their way as recording artists. Dino Martin (son of Dean Martin), Desi Arnaz Jr. (son of Lucille Ball and Desi Arnaz), Jack Jones (son of Allan Jones and Irene Hervey), Rick Nelson (son of Ozzie and Harriet Nelson), and Gary Crosby (son of Bing Crosby) were among the up-and-coming recording artists. Liza Minnelli (daughter of Judy Garland and Vincente Minnelli) had already gained a solid reputation as a vocalist and stage performer. The Sinatra children, Nancy and Frank Jr., were also making a name for themselves.

In December 1964, Eleanor accompanied nineteen-year-old Peter (still legally a minor) to court for judicial approval of his contract, and his career was officially launched. The band had some success, cutting a few records and playing clubs in Los Angeles, San Francisco, and Las Vegas. Peter moved over to Phillips Records and recorded a few singles. But the success and life on the road had a detrimental effect. "I pursued the sex, drugs, and rock-and-roll lifestyle with a vengeance. But I finally reached a point where I literally all but self-destructed."[6]

In the summer of 1966, as Peter was preparing for an important gig with his band, he was suddenly stricken with excruciating pain in his bones and joints. He was diagnosed with severe arthritis. Peter could barely walk, and his doctors expected him to be confined to a wheelchair for the rest of his life. All sorts of remedies were tried, but none were successful. Despairing for her son, Eleanor began to pray. "She prayed over me for a week or so. . . . One day, I woke up . . . completely free of arthritis. It's really a miracle. I don't know how else to explain it."[7]

On July 24, 1968, Eleanor was saddened to learn of the passing of her favorite aunt (her grandfather's sister, Helen). Just two days later, her grandfather, Harold Torrey, passed quietly at age ninety-six. Eleanor had lost a mainstay of her childhood and the only father she ever knew. After a local funeral in Springfield, her grandfather's ashes were brought to California to be placed in the niche at Hollywood Memorial Park (now Hollywood Forever Cemetery), next to those of his wife.

By 1969, the financial situation at the Cove Way house had become critical. Glenn's alimony payments barely kept the lights on. Eleanor and Peter cut corners where they could. They let the household help go and did the cleaning themselves, and they existed on simple, inexpensive meals. Despite previous efforts to sell the house, there had been no viable offers. Now, at a financial impasse, Eleanor had little choice but to take any reasonable offer, even one below the full asking price.

On days when the house was to be shown, Eleanor and Peter scrambled to prepare everything. Peter recalled that Eleanor purposefully scheduled appointments in the afternoon; that gave them time to make sure the house was sparkling clean. By the time the agent appeared, she would be lounging by the pool, playing the part of the glamorous retired movie star to perfection. "Just minutes before she had been furiously scrubbing toilets, with me following behind with the vacuum and dust cloth," Peter recalled.[8]

In preparation for the move, Eleanor donated the bulk of her vast record collection to the University of Southern California. She kept only twelve albums (78s) of the Fats Waller records that had been a staple in her life since the age of sixteen—she could not bear to part with them. She kept two tap mats and relegated many other items to storage. Anxious to downsize her life, she also made the decision to destroy much of her personal memorabilia.

The Cove Way house was finally sold in December 1969, and collections of "antiquities and fine art" from the estate were sold at auction in March 1970. Eleanor eventually moved into the upper apartment of a duplex situated in a quiet neighborhood on Roxbury Drive in Beverly Hills, across from a park. The apartment, very small in comparison to her former home, was comfortable; it had two bedrooms and a cozy den with a built-in bookcase that filled an entire wall. This was where she spent most of her time. Her favorite pastime was reading, and she had a particular fondness for mystery and crime novels. Conveniently, Eleanor's new apartment was located less than a mile from her mother's house on Hillgreen. She went daily to look in on Blanche, now in her seventies and happy to have her daughter nearby.

For the past three years, Peter had been dating Lynda Gundersen. He met her at the University of Southern California, where he had enrolled after graduating from Santa Monica College (he received a BA in English in 1968). Eleanor had taken to Lynda immediately and was pleased at the prospect of having a daughter-in-law. On December 6, 1970, Peter and Lynda were married in a small ceremony at Glenn's house on Oxford Way, with Eleanor, Glenn's mother, Hannah, and friends of Peter and Lynda in attendance. Following the ceremony, Eleanor hosted a reception for the wedding party at Don the Beachcomber, a Polynesian-style restaurant in Hollywood that she and Glenn used to frequent in their early dating days.

With Peter and Lynda settled, Eleanor continued her quiet life on Roxbury Drive. She enjoyed going to see plays and musicals at the Los Angeles Music Center with friends and family. Her closest friend was a longtime fan, Eleanor Debus. From Buffalo, New York, Debus had been in the audience for Eleanor's first performance of her initial road tour in 1947. They had kept in touch over the years, and when Debus moved to Los Angeles in the 1960s, Eleanor took her friend on as her private secretary. Having a good friend was a new experience for Eleanor, who had found it difficult to sustain close friendships while working. Debus proved to be a reliable aide and soon was also acting as Eleanor's business manager.

Eleanor's tranquil existence came to a halt with the Los Angeles opening of MGM's blockbuster film *That's Entertainment* in May 1974. Celebrating MGM's fiftieth anniversary with an astonishing array of clips that displayed the highlights of its Golden Age, *That's Entertainment* was the catalyst for a revival of interest in classic musicals. It was also the vehicle by which many discovered Eleanor's talent for the first time.

The film featured clips of Eleanor in the drum dance from *Rosalie* and the showstopper "Begin the Beguine" with Fred Astaire from *Broadway Melody of 1940*. Astaire was struck anew by Eleanor's talent. "There was a number in the film that amazed me. A slapdown tap dance with Eleanor Powell, a helluva hoofer who dances like a couple of guys. . . . I didn't remember it at all."[9]

MGM gathered as many of its former stars as it could for the preview of the film. Instead of attending the star-studded event, she and Eleanor Debus chose to see it in a nearby movie theater a few weeks later. As they waited for the film to begin, a man sitting in the row behind them suddenly said to his wife, "I'm here for just one reason—to see Eleanor Powell!" Eleanor sunk lower in her seat. A fan since his Navy days, he cheered and whistled each time she appeared on screen. Finally, at the end of the movie he exclaimed, "I'm still in love with her. I wonder what the hell she's doing today!" Eleanor waited quietly and left the theater after they had gone, saying to Debus, "Let him have his illusions!"

Though Eleanor had maintained a regular correspondence with fans and old friends throughout the years, suddenly the amount of mail she received increased dramatically. A gracious correspondent, she sent warm and detailed responses to each letter and card she received. At the request of her friend Loretta Young, Eleanor granted her first interview in years, to London-based film historian John Kobal. She spent two days with him and felt that the interview, which appeared in *Films in Review,* was the best she had ever given.

When Eleanor was working at MGM, she rarely had the opportunity to see her own films. So, in November 1974, when the Gary Theatre, a tiny revival movie house on Santa Monica Boulevard, was showing a retrospective of her films, she thought it would be fun to go. Watching herself on screen nearly forty years later was a bittersweet experience. As she was about to leave the theater, the owner, Ray Sandlow, caught sight of her. "You're Eleanor

Powell!" She assured him she was not, but he would not back down. "I'd know that smile anywhere. Won't you come back tomorrow night and let me introduce you?"[10]

By the next night he had hired a small spotlight and a microphone. When he introduced her, the delighted audience gave her a standing ovation as she went to the front to share a few anecdotes from her films. The young audience was made up largely of college students and film buffs, and Eleanor was deeply touched by their enthusiastic response.

Sandlow invited her back the following week to see two more films. Unbeknownst to Eleanor, Sandlow had arranged a birthday celebration for her, spanning two nights. She was surprised by guests Virginia O'Brien, Sybil Jason, Cass Daley, and Jane Withers, who presented her with flowers and a cake. To the delight of the audience, Eleanor donned the jacket she wore in *Rosalie* (the film being shown that night), brought by a collector of memorabilia.

With the success of the event, the following year Sandlow planned another retrospective and celebration for her birthday. Many of the guests from the prior year returned. This year, Una Merkel came along at Eleanor's invitation. They hadn't seen each other since 1936, but when Eleanor learned Una was still living in town, she surprised her with a phone call. The two shared fond memories of working together in *Broadway Melody of 1936* and *Born to Dance*. Eleanor offered to pick her up for the November 15 screening. "She doesn't know I get up and talk," said Eleanor to an interviewer beforehand. "I'm going to get her to come up and say a few words." Although Eleanor succeeded in getting her to the theater, nothing could get the shy and somewhat reclusive Una, who was nothing like the brash and self-assured characters she often played, to speak.

The new interest college students showed in her career also prompted invitations. University of Santa Barbara film student James Scott Bell began to correspond with Eleanor after one of the Gary Theatre screenings. "I invited her to come speak to a film class, and she readily agreed," Bell recalled. "So, I drove my Ford Pinto into Beverly Hills, picked up her and her secretary, and drove us up to Santa Barbara. She gave a lecture and then, to demonstrate a point, she stepped out from behind the podium and started to tap . . . she was still poetry in motion."[11]

In 1974, she took on a gifted dancer as her protégé. Forty-year-old Jack "Jeff" Parker had met Eleanor eight years earlier when she was appearing at Harrah's in Lake Tahoe and, over the years, their friendship had grown. He was then performing as one of Ginger Rogers' backup dancers. Though he had dance training, Jeff had never had any formal tap lessons and Eleanor noticed the lack of technique. "Jeff, would you mind if I showed you?" was her surprising offer—something that she had never done before. On Saturdays, she would arrive at Jeff's house for a session. Installed in his garage, along with her tap mat, her Victrola, and her Fats Waller 78s, the two of them would go to work. "We dance up a storm. We don't even sense the time passing. I'm teaching him all of my steps and he's thrilled, but not any more than I am because, as always, this is how I'm happiest—dancing."[12]

She taught him numbers from her films and from her nightclub act. Indefatigable even at sixty-two, she would say, "Jeff, you rest while I noodle a little." Jeff recalled, "Her 'noodling' was improvisation of the highest caliber . . . artistry and rhythm. And it had been years since she had donned a leotard and stepped into her tap shoes."[13]

After the huge success of *That's Entertainment*, MGM began almost immediately to plan its sequel. *That's Entertainment, Part II* was released in 1976. The film featured clips of "Fascinating Rhythm" from *Lady Be Good* and "Swinging the Jinx Away," the finale of *Born to Dance*. Thanks to *That's Entertainment*, Eleanor's popularity was experiencing a resurgence in Europe as well. In June 1976, she received a special tribute at the 26th Berlin International Film Festival.

While Eleanor was enjoying the renewed interest in her career, she was busy with her family. She lived close to Blanche and did her weekly shopping and cleaning, something she truly enjoyed. "I love to clean. . . . I could get somebody; but it isn't the same," Eleanor explained. "We are together and it's exercise for me. First of all, she makes me breakfast and gives me too much to eat."

Blanche's health was failing, and she could no longer be left alone. She suffered from pulmonary edema and began having dizzy spells; once she fell and hit her head against the stove. The lawsuit long forgotten, Jim Juris still lived in the house and acted as a caretaker, but Blanche now needed more specialized attention. Eleanor spent as much time as possible with her mother during the day, and she hired a nurse to come in late afternoon and stay with her at night. Peter, who had gotten his contractor's license and had started a construction and renovation business with Lynda, often called upon Eleanor for help. When they moved into the house for their newest renovation project in December 1976, she cheerfully lent a hand as Lynda was heavily pregnant with their first baby.

To Eleanor's great joy, her first grandson, Aubrey Newton Ford, was born on January 20, 1977, and she proudly shared the happy news in her letters to friends and fans. But this joyful time was soon shadowed with sadness.

Only one month later, on February 25, Blanche died at home on Hillgreen Drive at the age of eighty-one. The loss of her "angel mother"—her mainstay who had faithfully championed her through each season of her life—left an unfathomable void. Eleanor grieved deeply for months. Every week she visited the cemetery where Blanche's ashes rested next to those of Eleanor's grandparents. She cried and gently kissed the glass of the crypt as she placed flowers in the vase. She could no longer watch her own films; Blanche had been on the movie set with her so often that the memories were too much to bear. During this dark time, she found sweet comfort in her little grandson. As she expressed to a friend, "God took one life away and gave me another to fill the void."[14]

Eleanor took care of Aubrey often and wholeheartedly embraced her new role as a grandmother. Letters to friends were filled with details of weekly babysitting dates. In September 1977, she stayed with Aubrey while Peter and Lynda attended Glenn's wedding to his third wife, Cynthia Hayward. While she loved being with her grandson, Eleanor admitted that taking care of an active toddler was hard work. "I thought my twilight years would be easier, but then I became a grandmother and wow! Days on Stage 15 were easier than what I'm doing now."[15]

As time went by, Eleanor began to go out in public again. She was a frequent guest of honor at the Jeanette MacDonald International Fan Club banquets, where she delighted fans with her warmth and graciousness. Wherever she appeared, she tirelessly signed autographs and was often the last to leave.

Over the next few years, she also was the recipient of several awards and honors. On February 10, 1979, she was honored at a Dance in Action luncheon on the *Queen Mary*, which was now permanently docked at the Long Beach Harbor. The venue brought back memories of her 1949 crossing to play the Palladium. She still was incredulous when people wrote to tell her of film tributes to her all over the country. She could not have dreamed when she was making her first film for MGM in 1935 that she would enjoy so much recognition decades later.

In August 1980, Eleanor acted as hostess at the Cinecon Film Convention, which had given her an award in 1975. She lectured at a presentation of her film clips and gave out twelve awards during the evening. It was with emotion that she presented one of the awards to cameraman George Folsey, who had worked with her in *Lady Be Good* and whom she hadn't seen for nearly forty years.

In April 1981, Eleanor was invited to speak at the American Film Institute's televised *AFI Life Achievement Award: A Tribute to Fred Astaire*. She was nervous to be in front of the camera for the first time in seventeen years, but she needn't have worried. As she stepped onto the stage, the audience of her peers rose to their feet to give her a long and heartfelt ovation. A radiant Eleanor shared her memories of working with Astaire in *Broadway Melody of 1940* and told of their common drive for perfection in their dancing, how they practiced over and over until each step was perfect. "You'd have thought we were two scientists in a laboratory—we were so serious. . . . Of course, the reason you work so hard is to make it look easy," Eleanor explained. "We would still be there now if somebody hadn't said, 'Print it. It's just fine.'. . . But Mr. Astaire, I still wish we could do it just one more time!"

Unbeknownst to the audience, Eleanor was already suffering the first signs of illness, but she put off seeking medical help until her condition could no longer be ignored. On May 31, she checked into Midway Hospital for surgery the following morning. The news was grim. The surgeons discovered a large tumor on her left ovary. She was diagnosed with advanced stage cancer, but Eleanor was not told the full extent of her illness. The doctors had been able to remove only 90 percent of the mass, and she soon began long and grueling chemotherapy treatments in the hopes of eradicating the rest. Chemotherapy at that time had severe effects; she was admitted to the hospital for two nights each month for a twenty-three-hour session that was followed by a week-long regimen of pills. She suffered nausea and a complete loss of appetite, and lost seven pounds the first week. By the time she would start to feel better, it was time for another treatment. She lost her hair, but never her sense of humor, joking that it was a good thing she looked great in turbans. Her strength waned, but her spirit remained strong.

Eleanor declined invitations for the next few months, but on October 24, 1981, she made a special effort to attend the National Film Society Convention at the Sheraton Universal Hotel. At the event, she was the first recipient of an award named for her—the "Ellie Award." The award, given to honor the accomplishments of dancers in film, was presented to her by Gene Nelson.

Wearing a white wig that she jokingly referred to as her "Martha Washington" wig, she spoke with her usual vivacity and graciously took time to speak with fans and sign autographs until she was coaxed away to rest. The event was poignant. Many fans sadly realized just how ill she was.

Against her wishes, word that she was battling cancer had become public, thanks to an article that appeared in the tabloid *National Enquirer,* morbidly titled "Eleanor Powell's Dance with Death." As a result, Eleanor received many letters from well-wishers from all over the country. One that particularly thrilled her was from Katharine Hepburn. After years of admiring Hepburn, in early 1980, Eleanor finally had the pleasure of meeting her backstage at the Ahmanson Theatre in Los Angeles, during the pre-Broadway tour of her play *The West Side Waltz.* Eleanor's response to "Dear Kate Hep" was one of the last letters she would write. Unable to contain her enthusiasm, in the middle of an effusive thank-you from the heart, Eleanor exclaimed, "Is this a fan letter, you ask? You're darn tootin' it is!"

In November, Eleanor was able to spend Thanksgiving Day with her family, and she even attended a performance of Sandy Duncan's *Peter Pan* at the Pantages Theatre in the evening. Two days later, she developed an excruciating intestinal blockage that landed her back in the hospital for another surgery. Learning to live with a colostomy bag was a trial for her, and she now required the services of a nurse twice a week.

In the last weeks of her life, Eleanor was in good spirits and appeared to be doing well. Up to the end, she remained hopeful. "I have such complete faith in the Lord. I know he is holding my hand and my trust in him is everlasting."[16]

Though Eleanor's expression of faith had taken several forms during her life, her love for God never wavered. Whenever asked who her favorite dancing partner was, she would reply without hesitation "God." She viewed her art as an act of worship and thanksgiving for all she had been given.

At 9:40 a.m. on February 11, 1982, her favorite dancing partner called her home.

Epilogue

Two years after her passing, Eleanor was honored with a much-deserved star on Hollywood's iconic Walk of Fame. As a final gift to her friend, Eleanor Debus worked tirelessly to raise money and awareness to make this happen, gathering donations from Eleanor's fans from far and wide. On February 15, 1984, in the presence of a large crowd made up of her family, friends, and colleagues from the world of film and dance, Eleanor's star was unveiled.

Similar to *That's Entertainment,* the catalyst that allowed new fans to discover her in the 1970s, today social media has given Eleanor Powell an ever-growing new audience. Both young and old marvel at her timeless dance numbers and continue to seek out her films. As Frank Sinatra said, "You can wait around and hope, but you'll never see the likes of that again."

Eleanor's heartfelt dedication to her art continues to resonate today.

◉　◉　◉

"Wherever you hear the sound of my feet, it's the beat of
my heart saying thank you."

—Eleanor Powell

Acknowledgments

This project originally began in 1975 with a concept for a modest book on the films of Eleanor Powell. Nearly four decades later, it matured into an in-depth biography. Along the way, many people helped us craft the telling of Eleanor's life. Without them, this book would not have been possible.

We would like to extend our thanks to Ashley Runyon and Patrick McGilligan of the University Press of Kentucky, who recognized the importance of Eleanor's legacy and believed in our ability to tell her story. Additional thanks go out to the entire staff of the University Press of Kentucky for their aid in the publishing process. We would especially like to thank Janet Yoe for her insightful editing of the manuscript.

Those who shared letters, interviews, insight, and recollections: Fayard Nicholas, Ralph Hadsell, Jack Cummings, Jennifer Lane, Anthony Slide, Kevin Thomas, Michael "Miguel" Bernal, Meghan Kirk, Stephanie Brody, Lori, Dori and Jim Pye, the family of Alice Kealohapau'ole Holt, Lille Foster, Conrad Doerr, Darryl Busby, James Scott Bell, Paul Brogan, Tom Young, Veronica Corrales, Heather Castillo, and Maybin Hewes Sherman.

We are grateful to those who graciously shared their photo collections with us—Margie Schultz, D. Scott Calhoun, David Joiner, Paula Harmon, Scott Arno, and Tim Smith.

Heartfelt thanks go to all of those who helped us in the writing process by providing thoughtful critiques and insight: Paula Harmon, Sharon Calkin, Carl Rollyson, Mary Jean Valente, and the Biographers International Organization (BIO). We deeply appreciate the encouragement and aid provided by Margie Schultz and Miles Eady, who both shared extensive research on Eleanor in support of our project.

We value the helpful diligence of staff at the many archival sources, libraries, and collections that we consulted: Karla Davidson and her secretary Donna of the MGM Legal Department for opening their doors to us in 1984,

ACKNOWLEDGMENTS

Sylvia Wang at the Shubert Archive, Maggie Humberston, Curator of Library & Archives at the Wood Museum of Springfield History, Genevieve Maxwell, Lynn Kriste, and Taylor Morales at the Margaret Herrick Library and the Academy Film Archive, the Institute of Jazz Studies at Rutgers University, Dorinda Hartman and Josie Walters-Johnson of the Moving Image Research Center at the Library of Congress, and the staff at the Billy Rose Performing Arts Collection at the New York Public Library, the Smithsonian Institution, University of Wyoming, American Film Institute, and the University of Southern California.

A special thanks to Melody Holzman for her generous aid with research at the Library of Congress.

We acknowledge our departed friends, Eleanor Debus, Jeff Parker, and Jim Taylor, for various parts they played along the way, and also the late John Graham, who believed in the project from its inception over forty years ago and encouraged us to research relentlessly.

Lastly, we are grateful for the patience and loving support of both our families: Claude, David, Marc, Paul, and Jonathan Royère, Harry and Theresa Broussard, Alma Murphy Harshman, and Gene and Jo Ann Shanklin.

Notes

1. First Steps

1. Phillip Torrey, will dated April 16, 1621, proved June 27, 1621, England, http://homepages.rpi.edu/~holmes/Hobbies/Genealogy2/ps28/ps28_480.htm.

2. James Savage, *A Genealogical Dictionary of the First Settlers of New England: Showing Three Generations of Those Who Came before May 1692, on the Basis of Farmer's Register* (Boston: Little, Brown, 1860).

3. "Divorces Granted," *Springfield Union,* November 19, 1913.

4. Until the 1930s, the term "motocycle" was often used instead of "motorcycle." "Indian Motorcycles through the Years," Condon Skelly website, January 15, 2014, https://condonskelly.com/Blog/indian-motorcycles-through-the-years/.

5. "Johnston-Powell Marriage Last Night," *Springfield Daily Republican,* June 2, 1917, 4.

6. Grace Wilcox, "The World's Greatest Feminine Hoofer," *Oakland Tribune,* September 15, 1935, 70.

7. John Kobal, *People Will Talk* (New York: Alfred A. Knopf, 1985).

8. "Thank You and You and You for Making It Possible," *Reno Evening Gazette,* November 22, 1961, 32.

9. "Benefit Performance for Wolcott Tent," *Springfield Daily Republican,* March 1, 1922, 8.

10. "Novel Features for Lane's May Festival," *Springfield Daily Republican,* May 17, 1922, 8.

11. "With Eleanor Playing on Home Stage, Everyone Wants to Get Into the Act," *Springfield Union,* June 16, 1964, 26.

12. Kobal, *People Will Talk.*

2. Atlantic City

1. Betty Penrose, "Just about People and Parties," *Atlantic City Daily Press,* August 28, 1925, 6.

2. Marie Leeds, "Recreation Club to Hold Affair in Ambassador," *Atlantic City Daily Press,* June 29, 1926, 3.

3. *Atlantic City Daily Press,* June 25, 1926, 16.

4. "Special Night at the Ambassador This Evening," *Atlantic City Daily Press,* July 2, 1926, 22.

5. "Talented Young Dancer," *Atlantic City Daily Press,* August 25, 1926, 4.

6. *Press of Atlantic City,* February 20, 1925, 12.

7. William Cavanaugh, "'Sweleanor' Powell, Hollywood Nicknames Springfield-Born Star Tap Dancer," *Springfield Sunday Union and Republican,* September 5, 1937, 3E.

3. Broadway and the Joyful Noise

1. *Broadway: The Golden Age,* directed by Rick McKay (New York: Masterworks Broadway, 2004), DVD.

2. "Film House Reviews," *Variety,* December 7, 1927.

3. "The Optimists," *Variety,* February 8, 1928, 48.

4. "The Century Roof Goes Informal," *Daily News* (New York), February 7, 1928, 25.

5. *Delaware Evening Journal,* December 12, 1928.

6. Kobal, *People Will Talk.*

7. Kobal, *People Will Talk.*

8. Cavanaugh, "'Sweleanor' Powell."

9. "Follies Girl, Now in Films, Shocked by Own Pictures," *Daily Mirror,* November 30, 1925.

10. *Theatre Magazine,* March 1929.

11. "'Follow Thru' an Easy Winner," *Daily News* (New York), January 10, 1929, 193.

12. "Follow Thru," *Variety,* January 16, 1929, 54.

13. Gerald M. Bordman, *American Musical Theatre: A Chronicle,* 3rd ed. (Oxford: Oxford University Press, 1978), 498.

14. "They Like Her: Producers 'Found' Her and Will Keep Her," *Daily News* (New York), August 25, 1929, 59.

15. Louis Stockman, "Craze for Tap Dance Sweeps Whole Nation," *Indianapolis Times,* August 20, 1930, 14.

16. Gilbert Swan, "If You Can't Tap-Dance You'd Better Learn," *Daily Mail* (Hagerstown, MD), September 16, 1930, 8.

17. James Haskins and N. R. Mitgang, *Mr. Bojangles: The Biography of Bill Robinson* (New York: William Morrow, 1988), 228.

18. Haskins and Mitgang, *Mr. Bojangles.*

19. Nicholas F. Weber, *Patron Saints: Five Rebels Who Opened America to a New Art, 1928–1943* (New Haven: Yale University Press, 1995).

20. Edwin C. Stein, "Fine and Dandy," *Standard Union* (Brooklyn, NY), September 24, 1930, 11.

21. *Chicago Sunday Tribune,* June 7, 1931, 64.

22. *Sunday Star* (Washington, DC), October 11, 1931, pt. 4.

23. James M. O'Neill, "Joe Cook Furnishes Laugh Every Second in Erlanger Comedy," *Courier-Post* (Camden, NJ), September 28, 1931, 18.

24. E. de S. Melcher, "From the Front Row," *Evening Star* (Washington, DC), October 19, 1931, A5.

25. *Ithaca Journal,* December 4, 1931, 5.

26. Louise Mace, "News of the Theater: Joe Cook in Good Dancing Show," *Springfield Republican,* November 24, 1931.

27. Marshall W. Stearns and Jean Stearns, *Jazz Dance: The Story of American Vernacular Dance* (New York: Schirmer, 1979).

28. Anthony Slide, *The Encyclopedia of Vaudeville* (Jackson: University Press of Mississippi, 2012).

4. Gaining Traction

1. Noralee Frankel, *Stripping Gypsy: The Life of Gypsy Rose Lee* (New York: Oxford University Press, 2009).

2. "Ziegfeld's Last Great Gesture was in Defiance of Depression," *Asbury Park (NJ) Press,* August 3, 1932.

3. E. de S. Melcher, "'Hot-Cha!' Scores a Knock-out," *Evening Star* (Washington, DC), February 16, 1932, A3.

4. Frederick Nolan, *Lorenz Hart: A Poet on Broadway* (New York: Oxford University Press, 1995).

5. Stanley Green, *Ring Bells! Sing Songs!: Broadway Musicals of the 1930's* (New York: Galahad, 1971).

6. "Ziegfeld's 'Hot-Cha' is to End its Run," *New York Times,* May 25, 1932, 23.

7. Irene Thirer, "Flicker at Capitol Surpassed by Revue," *Daily News* (New York), June 24, 1932, 46.

8. "Reviews of Acts for Picture Theatres," *Motion Picture Herald,* July 9, 1932, 66.

9. *Variety,* July 22, 1932, 29.

10. *Variety,* September 6, 1932, 27.

11. *Variety,* September 20, 1932, 35.

12. "Mr. White Experiments," *New York Times,* November 23, 1932, 15.

13. *Brooklyn Daily Eagle,* November 25, 1932, 21.

14. "First Radio City Show Is Announced in Part," *New York Times,* November 22, 1932.

15. Mordaunt Hall, "Will Rogers and Janet Gaynor in a Film Conception of Phil Strong's Novel, State Fair," *New York Times,* January 27, 1933, 13.

16. Cecelia Ager, "Music Hall's Swift Pageant," *Variety,* January 31, 1933, 11.

17. "Size of Music Hall Amazes Miss Keller," *New York Times,* February 2, 1933.

18. Joe Collura, "Easy to Love: Eleanor Powell," *Classic Images,* no. 82, n.d.

5. Traipsing the Boards

1. Elsa Brenner, "Old World in a Big City," *New York Times,* October 28, 2011.

2. Kobal, *People Will Talk.*

3. *Minneapolis Star-Tribune,* October 22, 1933, 20.

4. Edward Gloss, "Scandals Is Reason for Road Failures," *Akron Beacon Journal,* March 4, 1933, 7.

5. "George White's 'Scandals' Pleases Crowds at Indiana," *Indianapolis News,* March 20, 1933, 13.

6. "White's Scandals Is the Biggest Theater Buy Yet," *Indianapolis Times,* March 20, 1933, 12.

7. "Zippy Revue at Bargain Prices," *Dayton Daily News,* March 25, 1933, M27.

8. "'Scandals' at Keith Offers Great Entertainment Value," *Dayton Herald,* March 25, 1933, 12.

9. *Minneapolis Star-Tribune,* April 24, 1933, 10.

10. *Variety,* September 12, 1933, 24.

11. John Alden, "Speaking for Myself about the Movies," *Minneapolis Tribune,* October 22, 1933, 8.

12. John Alden, "Seeing the Movies," *Minneapolis Star-Tribune,* October 21, 1933, 16.

13. Alden, "Speaking for Myself about the Movies."

14. Allan R. Ellenberger and Robert M. Paton, *Anita Page: A Career Chronicle and Biography* (Jefferson, NC: McFarland, 2021).

15. *Evening Star* (Washington, DC), November 20, 1933, B16.

16. *Henderson Daily Dispatch* (Henderson, NV), January 18, 1934, 4.

17. *Lexington Leader,* March 4, 1934, 5.

18. "Billy Rose Quits Casino," *New York Times,* September 8, 1934.

19. Lloyd Scherer, "Eleanor Powell: World's Greatest Woman Tap Dancer Comes Back," *Independent Star News* (Pasadena, CA), January 22, 1961, 88.

20. "Bill 'Bojangles' Robinson Inducted as Mayor of Harlem," *New York Age,* March 3, 1934, 2.

21. *Daily News* (New York), June 9, 1934, 24.

22. "Stage and Screen," *Baltimore Sun,* August 29, 1934, 8.

23. *Pittsburgh Press,* October 6, 1934, 8.

24. Gary Marmorstein, *A Ship without a Sail: The Life of Lorenz Hart* (New York: Simon & Schuster, 2013).

6. Westward Bound

1. "Tap Dancers Getting a Play at Hollywood," *Chicago Tribune,* December 6, 1934, 18.

7. Taming the Lion

1. In an unprecedented move, the press announced that eighteen-year-old Black dancer Jeni LeGon had been placed under a five-year contract at MGM (surprisingly at $1,250, the same exorbitant weekly salary as Eleanor's), to begin with a featured spot in *Broadway Melody of 1936.* She is listed in production reports for the film in early April and appeared at a benefit alongside Eleanor in May. LeGon later reported that her contract was bought out that summer, and she was never used by the studio.

Craig Delahunt, "Jeni Le Gon," YouTube, May 19, 2014, https://www.youtube.com/watch?v=t-geMH6LbCA.

2. Kobal, *People Will Talk.*

3. Kobal, *People Will Talk.*

4. Kobal, *People Will Talk.*

5. Kobal, *People Will Talk.*

6. "Interview with Roger Edens," *Sight & Sound* (Spring 1958).

7. "Interview with Roger Edens," *Sight & Sound* (Spring 1958).

8. Andre Sennwald, "The Screen," *New York Times,* September 19, 1935, 28.

9. Sennwald, "The Screen."

10. John R. Baldwin, "The Girl the Whole World Raves About," *Motion Picture,* January 1936.

11. Kobal, *People Will Talk.*

12. Kobal, *People Will Talk.*

13. Kobal, *People Will Talk.*

14. Kobal, *People Will Talk.*

15. Eleanor Powell, Private conversation with Lisa Royère, c. 1979.

16. John Hyde, William Morris Agency, to Harry Kaufman, July 8, 1935, Shubert Archive, New York, NY.

17. John Hyde to Harry Kaufman.

18. Philip K. Scheuer, "Eleanor Powell Done with New York for Keeps, Now," *Los Angeles Times,* May 24, 1936, 49.

19. Some sources state that Mankiewicz had also worked as an uncredited writer on *Broadway Melody of 1936,* but this could not be confirmed over various script versions. See, for example, "Joseph L. Mankiewicz," IMDb (website), https://www.imdb.com/name/nm0000581/.

20. Grace Wilcox, "The World's Greatest Feminine Hoofer," *Oakland Tribune,* September 15, 1935, 70.

8. Full Velocity

1. Mark Griffin, *A Hundred or More Hidden Things: The Life and Films of Vincente Minnelli* (Boston: Da Capo, 2010).

2. *Variety,* September 25, 1935, 72.

3. "Hollywood Longs for Eleanor Powell," *Boston Globe,* September 8, 1935, A41.

4. "Hollywood Longs for Eleanor Powell."

5. "Shubert Theatre At Home Abroad," *Boston Globe,* September 4, 1935, 22.

6. "Shubert Theatre At Home Abroad."

7. Brooks Atkinson, "Beatrice Lillie and Ethel Waters in a Musical Travelogue Entitled 'At Home Abroad,'" *New York Times,* September 20, 1935, 17.

8. Rowland Field, "Beatrice Lillie and Company Set Merry Pace in At Home Abroad, New Musical Hit Making its Debut at Winter Garden," *Brooklyn Times Union,* September 20, 1935, 7.

9. James Aswell, "My New York," *Times* (Hammond, IN), November 14, 1935.

10. J. Walter Thompson, "Shell Chateau," *Variety,* October 9, 1935, 35.

11. Jerry Ames and Jim Siegelman, *The Book of Tap: Recovering America's Long Lost Dance* (New York: D. McKay, 1977).

12. Eleanor Powell, interview by Jane Ardmore, October 29, 1975, Jane Ardmore Papers, Margaret Herrick Library, Academy of Motion Picture Arts and Sciences, Beverly Hills, CA.

13. Margie Schultz, *Eleanor Powell: A Bio-Bibliography* (Santa Barbara, CA: Greenwood, 1994).

14. "Review," *Variety,* November 20, 1935.

15. "World's Most Famous Tap Dancer Proud of New England Heritage," *Springfield Sunday Union and Republican,* December 29, 1935.

16. "Bea Lillie Ethel Waters 'At Home Abroad' Half Hour Radio Minnelli Live Cleaned," YouTube, last modified October 5, 2012, https://youtu.be/U2F0ME00Z54.

17. "Dancer Collapses," *Chicago Tribune,* January 24, 1936, 12.

18. "Miss Powell Quits Show," *New York Times,* January 24, 1936, 14.

19. Dr. Louis Morton to Lee Shubert, January 26, 1936, Shubert Archive, New York.

20. Edna Ferguson, "Powell Ill, Hint Snubs by Rest of Cast," *New York Daily News,* January 24, 1936, 239.

21. Edna Ferguson, "Powell Ill."

22. *Daily News,* February 8, 1936, 13.

23. *Detroit Tribune,* February 15, 1936, 6.

9. Born to Dance

1. Cole Porter, *The Letters of Cole Porter,* ed. Cliff Eisen and Dominic McHugh (New Haven: Yale University Press, 2019).

2. "Vast Crowd Lines Platform to Greet Super-Chief," *Daily Times-Press* (Streator, IL), May 13, 1936, 5.

3. "Crowds Greet New Super Chief: Famous Tap Dancer among Passengers," *Albuquerque Journal,* May 14, 1936, 3.

4. "Returns," *Illustrated Daily News* (Los Angeles), May 15, 1936, 23.

5. "New Eleanor Will Return to Films," *Tampa Times,* May 8, 1936, 1.

6. Interoffice communication to Mr. Hendrickson from Mr. Mayer's office, August 15, 1936, Legal Department Files, Metro-Goldwyn-Mayer Studios, Culver City, CA.

7. "Vogue for Dancing Sweeps Film Colony," *Salem News,* April 27, 1936, 5.

8. Robbin Coons, "Tap Dancing Craze Hits Picture Folk," *Hollywood Citizen-News,* April 22, 1936, 6.

9. Virginia Irwin, "Tap Dancers with and without Rhythm," *St. Louis Post-Dispatch,* March 27, 1936, 3F.

10. Porter, *Letters of Cole Porter.*

11. Lawrence J. Quirk, *James Stewart: Behind the Scenes of a Wonderful Life* (Lanham, MD: Applause, 1997).

12. Jay Rubin, "Jay Rubin Interviews Eleanor Powell," *Classic Film Collector,* March 1976.

13. Porter, *Letters of Cole Porter.*

14. Sidney Skolsky, "Watching Them Make Pictures," *Miami Tribune,* July 17, 1936, 13.

15. Rubin, "Jay Rubin Interviews Eleanor Powell."

16. Rubin, "Jay Rubin Interviews Eleanor Powell."

17. Ruth Tildesley, "Take-a-Chance Stewart," *Screenland,* May 1937.

18. Rubin, "Jay Rubin Interviews Eleanor Powell."

19. Rubin, "Jay Rubin Interviews Eleanor Powell."

20. Porter, *The Letters of Cole Porter.*

21. "Interview with Roger Edens," *Sight & Sound* (Spring 1958).

22. Kobal, *People Will Talk.*

23. "'Screen Genius' Death Stuns Industry's Heads," *Los Angeles Times,* September 15, 1936, 4.

24. Samuel Marx, *Mayer and Thalberg: The Make-Believe Saints* (New York: Random House, 1975).

25. "New York Critics Hail Biggest Musical," *New York Times,* December 11, 1936, 35.

26. "Capitol's 'Born to Dance' with Eleanor Powell Tapping to Cole Porter Tunes, Is Tops," *New York Times,* December 5, 1936.

10. "Feelin' Like a Million"

1. *Advance-News,* April 28, 1937, 10.

2. George Murphy and Victor Lasky, *"Say . . . Didn't You Used to be George Murphy?"* (New York: Bartholomew House, 1970).

3. Judy Garland prerecorded and filmed "Yours and Mine" and "Your Broadway and My Broadway," but both numbers were ultimately discarded from the final version of *Broadway Melody of 1938;* only the recordings survive. For her rendition of "Yours and Mine" (sung with Eloise Rawitzer and The St. Brendan's Boys Choir) *see* Just Judy Garland, "Judy Garland—'Yours and Mine,' Take 9," YouTube, October 20, 2022, https://youtu.be/TwxYE3VjzIg. For her version of "Your Broadway and My Broadway," *see* Just Judy Garland, "Judy Garland—'Your Broadway and My Broadway,' Take 7," YouTube, October 17.2022, https://youtu.be/lo-BeCgqKmQ.

4. Murphy and Lasky, *"Used to be George Murphy?"*

5. *Advance-News,* March 11, 1937, 11.

6. *Motion Picture Herald,* May 22, 1937.

7. Ralph Hadsell, interview by Paula Broussard, January 14, 1984.

8. "Film Previews: Broadway Melody of 1938," *Variety,* August 14, 1937.

9. Louella O. Parsons, "In Hollywood," *Lexington Kentucky Herald,* August 1, 1937.

10. Charles Darnton, "What Eleanor Powell Has Lost," *Screenland,* March 1938.

11. *Los Angeles Evening Herald and Express,* September 8, 1937.

12. George Cohen to Ross Hastings, September 10, 1937, Legal Department, Metro-Goldwyn-Mayer Studios, Culver City, CA.

13. Howard Gutner, *MGM Style: Cedric Gibbons and the Art of the Golden Age of Hollywood* (Lanham, MD: Rowman & Littlefield, 2019).

14. D. Scott Calhoun, "Eleanor Powell Talk Lightened," YouTube, July 26, 2022, video of lecture given at Variety Arts Theatre, Los Angeles, CA, 1981, https://youtu.be/D4ByUszL6Xo.

15. Kobal, *People Will Talk*.

16. Edith Lindeman, "A Night on a 'Colossal' Hollywood Set," *Richmond Times-Dispatch,* October 24, 1937, 4.

17. Kobal, *People Will Talk*.

18. "The Films That Got Away," The Judy Room (website), accessed November 20, 2022, https://www.thejudyroom.com/filmography/judy-garland-unfinished-films/. Judy Garland did not appear in *Rosalie,* but the MGM music department records note that she recorded this song for the film on August 27, 1937.

19. Sid Luft, *Judy & I: My Life with Judy Garland* (London: Omnibus, 2018).

20. *Hollywood Studio Magazine,* May 1985, 19.

21. May Mann, "Her Next Step, The Wedding March," *Albuquerque Journal,* May 26, 1940, 19.

22. Tommy "Butch" Bond and Ronald Genini, *Darn Right It's Butch: Memories of Our Gang, the Little Rascals* (Wayne, PA: Morgin, 1994).

23. "The Screen in Review," *New York Times,* December 31, 1937, 9.

24. Jay Carmody, "Rosalie Gives 'Colossal' Much Bigger Meaning," *Evening Star* (Washington, DC), December 25, 1937, B8.

25. Luft, *Judy & I*.

26. "Film Dancer's New Step May Replace Big Apple," *Waco (TX) News-Tribune,* January 12, 1938, 1.

27. "He-Men Secretaries Best, Says Eleanor Powell," *Pittsburgh Sun-Telegraph,* January 12, 1938, 9.

28. "Broadway," *New York Daily News,* January 17, 1938, 34.

29. Eleanor Roosevelt, "Film Folk I Have Known," *Photoplay,* January 1939.

30. Charles Darnton, "Roosevelts Merry as Marx Bros.!" *Screenland,* September 1938.

31. "'Unimpeachable Eleanor' Aids in Success of Birthday Ball," *Baltimore Sun,* January 30, 1938, 18.

32. Darnton, "Roosevelts Merry as Marx Bros.!"

33. Darnton, "Roosevelts Merry as Marx Bros.!"

11. Fulfilling Dreams

1. Louella O. Parsons, "Judy Garland Cast for Film Version in 'The Wizard of Oz,'" *Courier-Post* (Camden, NJ), February 24, 1938, 17.

2. Frederick C. Othman, "Eleanor Powell Demonstrates Hula as Reporter Watches Entranced," *Atlanta Constitution,* February 26, 1939.

3. "Star Used Prize-Ring Methods," *Times and Democrat* (Orangeburg, SC), April 28, 1939, 13.

4. *San Francisco Examiner,* December 1, 1938, 16.

5. "Robert Young Watches All of Powell's Scenes When Filming Honolulu," *Brooklyn Daily Eagle,* March 26, 1939.

6. Frederick C. Othman, "Learning the Hula No Snap, Eleanor Powell Points Out," *Detroit Free Press,* February 16, 1939.

7. Grace Wilcox, "For Women Only: Interview with a Dancing Star," *Detroit Free Press,* January 29, 1939, 10.

8. E. K. Titus, "Hula Shocks Hawaiians—It's Just a Tap Dance Shimmy, They Say," *Knoxville News-Sentinel,* February 23, 1939, 15.

9. Darnton, "What Eleanor Powell Has Lost."

10. "*Honolulu:* Burns and Allen Scene So Crazy It Can't Be Written," *MGM Studios News,* January 14, 1939.

11. "Girl Missing for 12 Hours, Returns with Five Stars' Autographs," *Evening Star* (Washington, DC), January 30, 1939.

12. "15,000 Dance Here to Help Fight on Polio," *Baltimore Sun,* January 31, 1939, 20.

13. Eleanor Powell, "Young Dancer: Eleanor Powell's Letter to the DTA," *Dance Magazine,* May 1939.

14. "Variety House Reviews," *Variety,* May 3, 1939, 44.

15. "Variety House Reviews," *Variety,* May 24, 1939, 37.

16. "1939: Custom Motors by Eleanor Powell, Styling by Alex Tremulis," Gyronaut X-1: World's Fastest Motorcycle (website), accessed October 5, 2021, https://www.gyronautx1.com/live-updates/1939-custom-motors-by-eleanor-powell-styling-by-alex-tremulis.

17. Luft, *Judy & I.*

12. King and Queen

1. David Tearle, "No Wonder She's Happy," *Silver Screen,* August 1939.

2. Paul Harrison, "When Rheumatism Sets In, Eleanor Powell Can Earn Her Keep as a Production Designer," *Pittsburgh Press,* January 15, 1940, 10.

3. Kaspar Monahan, "Boy Friends Second to Chicken Livers," *Pittsburgh Press,* May 22, 1939, 6.

4. Eleanor Powell, "I'll Never Dance with Astaire," *Picturegoer,* January 1, 1937.

5. Powell interview by Jane Ardmore.

6. Paul Walker, "Reviews and Previews," *Harrisburg (PA) Telegraph,* December 2, 1939, 9.

7. AFI's Oral History Collection Interviews with Norman Taurog © 1973, used courtesy of American Film Institute.

8. Norman Taurog interview.

9. Harrison, "When Rheumatism Sets In."

10. Paul Harrison, "Great Toscanini Weeps as Eleanor Powell Dances," *Idaho Evening Times,* December 28, 1939.

11. Kobal, *People Will Talk.*

12. Hedda Hopper, "Fred Astaire Knows How to Be Happy," *St. Louis Globe-Democrat,* August 17, 1952.

13. *Box Office Digest,* February 8, 1940, 10.

14. Louella O. Parsons, *Fresno Bee,* February 11, 1940, 12.

13. Love and Disappointment

1. Mayme Ober, "Eleanor Powell May Pick Hometown of Springfield for Her Marriage to Pye," *Boston Globe,* April 7, 1940, B13.

2. "Dancer Eleanor Powell Reveals Engagement to Film Art Director," *Democrat and Chronicle* (Rochester, NY), April 5, 1940, 1.

3. "'Ziegfeld' in Sept if Powell Better," *Hollywood Reporter,* July 10, 1940.

4. Tennessee Williams, *The Selected Letters of Tennessee Williams, 1920–1945* (New York: New Directions, 2000).

5. Eleanor Powell, "Young Dancer: Hollywood Letter," *Dance Magazine,* December 1940.

6. Jimmie Fidler, "Touring in Filmland," *Monrovia (CA) Daily News-Post,* January 24, 1941, 8.

7. Vincente Minnelli and Hector Arce, *I Remember It Well* (New York: Doubleday, 1974).

8. Colin Briggs, *Cordially Yours, Ann Sothern* (Albany, GA: Bear Manor Media, 2006).

9. Kobal, *People Will Talk.*

10. Jeffrey Spivak, *Buzz: The Life and Art of Busby Berkeley* (Lexington: University Press of Kentucky, 2010).

11. Spivak, *The Life and Art of Busby Berkeley.*

12. "At the Capitol," *New York Times,* September 19, 1941, 27.

14. Hollywood at War

1. Kobal, *People Will Talk.*

2. Harrison Carroll, "Behind the Scenes in Hollywood," *Jackson (TN) Sun,* December 9, 1941.

3. "MGM Dance News," *Kinematograph Weekly,* October 23, 1941, 28.

4. Lille Foster, *U. S. Army Life 1941–1945: In the Letters of Theodore Pattengill Foster* (Morrisville, NC: Lulu, 2018).

5. Louella O. Parsons, "Eyeing Hollywood," *Morning News* (Wilmington, DE), November 22, 1941, 19.

6. "'Prop Puns' Game Hollywood Pastime," *Detroit Evening Times,* January 31, 1942, 7.

7. Harrison, "When Rheumatism Sets In."

8. Kobal, *People Will Talk.*

9. Kobal, *People Will Talk.*

10. *Battle Creek Enquirer,* July 16, 1942, 19.

11. Bosley Crowther, The Screen, *New York Times,* June 26, 1942, 16.

12. "'Ship Ahoy' Tuneful Escape," *Hollywood Reporter,* April 17, 1942, 4.

13. *Los Angeles Daily News,* April 21, 1942.

14. "Rambling Reporter," *Hollywood Reporter,* May 7, 1942, 2.

15. Peter Ford, *Glenn Ford: A Life* (Madison: University of Wisconsin Press, 2011).

16. John Truesdell, "In Hollywood," *Des Moines Register,* July 2, 1942, 14.

17. Powell, "Young Dancer."

18. "Ford-Powell Engaged," *Los Angeles Daily News,* August 26, 1942, 28.

19. "Hollywood Real Scenes," *Johnson City Tennessee Chronicle,* September 1, 1942, 4.

15. Disillusion and Hope

1. Calhoun, "Eleanor Powell Talk Lightened."

2. Calhoun, "Eleanor Powell Talk Lightened."

3. Eleanor Powell to Douglas Ebersole, January 7, 1944. From the collection of Tom Young.

4. Emanuel Levy, *Vincente Minnelli: Hollywood's Dark Dreamer* (New York: St. Martin's, 2009).

5. Powell to Douglas Ebersole.

6. Powell to Douglas Ebersole.

7. "One-Man Comedy, the Same Being Red Skelton, with an Assist from Eleanor Powell, Opens at Paramount," *New York Times,* November 11, 1943.

8. "'I Dood It' Skelton Scream: Bows to Cummings for Riotous Musical," *Hollywood Reporter,* July 27, 1943, 4.

9. Albert Johnson, "The Films of Vincente Minnelli: Part I," *Film Quarterly* 12, no. 2 (1958): 21–35, https://doi:10.2307/3186050, accessed July 9, 2021.

10. "'I Dood It'," *Hollywood Reporter,* July 27, 1943, 4.

11. Sheila Graham, "Hollywood Women in Sudden Panic to Acquire Husbands," *Miami Daily News,* February 3, 1943, 17.

12. Louella O. Parsons, "Eleanor Powell Plans to Retire after She Marries Glenn Ford," *Sacramento Bee,* May 21, 1943, 17.

13. Powell to Douglas Ebersole.

16. Mizpah

1. Ford, *Glenn Ford: A Life.*

2. Powell to Doug Ebersole.

3. Harold Heffernan, "Hollywood Horizon," *Record* (Hackensack, NJ), November 30, 1943, 15.

4. "New Films," *Hartford Courant,* July 27, 1944, 6.

5. "Artists' 'Sensations of 1945' Smart Revue by Specialists," *San Francisco Examiner,* July 28, 1944, 9.

6. *San Fernando Valley Times,* May 11, 1944, 18.

7. Ford, *Glenn Ford: A Life.*

8. Powell interview by Ardmore.

9. Ford, *Glenn Ford: A Life.*

10. Neal Gabler, *An Empire of Their Own: How the Jews Invented Hollywood* (New York: Anchor, 2010).

17. Back on the Boards

1. Dora Albert, "How Are the Glenn Fords Doing?" *Screenland,* September 1946.

2. James R. Parish and Ronald L. Bowers, *The MGM Stock Company: The Golden Era* (Liverpool, UK: Outlet, 1972).

3. Albert, "How Are the Glenn Fords Doing?"

4. Earl Wilson, "Earl Wilson's Broadway Chatter," *Daily Independent* (Kannapolis, NC), March 12, 1947, 10.

5. Ford, *Glenn Ford: A Life.*

6. Ford, *Glenn Ford: A Life.*

7. Harry MacArthur, "After Dark," *Evening Star* (Washington, DC), October 30, 1947, 53.

8. MacArthur, "After Dark."

9. Ford, *Glenn Ford: A Life.*

10. Ruth Brigham, "Prettiest Gal in Movies?" *Miami Herald,* May 9, 1948, 95.

11. "Beverly Hills," *Cincinnati Enquirer,* December 4, 1948, 23.

12. "Taps to Debussy," *Guardian* (London, UK), March 23, 1949.

13. "The Palladium," *Stage,* March 24, 1949.

14. "Half-Hour on Her Toes," *Daily Herald* (London), March 22, 1949.

15. "Henry Will Show the Sights," *Evening Standard* (London, UK), April 12, 1949.

16. Bob Thomas, "Eleanor Powell Dancing after Long Film Absence," *Bakersfield Californian,* November 2, 1949, 14.

17. Esther Williams and Digby Diehl, *The Million Dollar Mermaid* (New York: Simon & Schuster, 1999).

18. Thomas, "Eleanor Powell Dancing."

19. Williams and Diehl, *The Million Dollar Mermaid.*

20. Harold V. Cohen, "The New Film," *Pittsburgh Post-Gazette,* July 21, 1950, 8.

21. *Los Angeles Mirror,* March 16, 1950, 44.

22. Hedda Hopper, *Los Angeles Times,* August 10, 1950, 36.

23. *Los Angeles Daily News,* May 17, 1950, 39.

24. Hedda Hopper, "A Two-Star Family Lives the Quiet Life," Hedda Hopper on Hollywood, *Baltimore Sun,* January 28, 1951, A8.

25. Hopper, "A Two-Star Family Lives the Quiet Life."

26. Louella O. Parsons, "Denise Darcel Will Take Western Role," *Bakersfield Californian,* March 9, 1951, 22.

27. "400 Attend Reception Honoring Ben Hogans," *Fort Worth Star-Telegram,* March 24, 1951, 9.

28. Ford, *Glenn Ford: A Life.*

29. Louella O. Parsons, "Gallico Story Next for Ford," *Cedar Rapids Gazette,* June 5, 1951, 10.

30. George Tashman, "Glenn Ford Is a Survivor," *Berkeley Gazette,* August 11, 1978, 11.

18. Walking through Fire

1. "20th to do Jimmy Durante Story," *Los Angeles Examiner,* January 17, 1952, 17.

2. Burt Reynolds, *My Life* (New York: Hyperion, 1994).

3. Schultz, *Eleanor Powell: A Bio-Bibliography.*

4. Harrison Carroll, "Behind the Scenes in Hollywood," *Fairfield (IA) Daily Ledger,* May 19, 1952, 5.

5. Louella O. Parsons, "Eleanor Powell Marriage Threatens to Break Up," *Philadelphia Inquirer,* June 21, 1952, 12.

6. "Glenn Fords Reunited," *San Francisco Examiner,* June 24, 1952, 3.

7. Ford, *Glenn Ford: A Life.*

8. In the course of researching Glenn's bisexual infidelities, several accounts came to light. Dancer Tom Knutson reported Eleanor's comments made to him during rehearsals for *The Hollywood Palace* television show to choreographer/writer Larry Billman. Billman later wrote of the conversations in a letter to author Margie Schultz dated May 1, 1992, during her research for *Eleanor Powell: A Bio-bibliography.* Knutson recalled conversations where Eleanor told of learning that Glenn had picked up boys and her constant fear that he might be caught. Though other sources revealed similar stories, we have chosen only to include information from Eleanor's own statements or from personal sources we could directly quote.

9. Raymond R. Sarlot and Fred E. Basten, *Life at the Marmont* (New York: Penguin, 1987).

10. Erskine Johnson, Hollywood, *Adirondack Daily Enterprise* (Saranac Lake, NY), September 15, 1952, 11.

11. Sheilah Graham, Hollywood Diary, *Evening Star* (Washington, DC), September 15, 1952, A14.

12. Ford, *Glenn Ford: A Life.*

13. "Ex-Dancer Tried Out on TV in a Bible Telling Program," *Provo Daily Herald,* October 14, 1954, 22.

14. Graham, Hollywood Diary, October 15, 1954, A32.

15. Louella O. Parsons, "Eleanor Powell and Glenn Ford Work Out Family Rule," *Cumberland (MD) Times,* April 10, 1955, 23.

16. Mark Knowles, *The Man Who Made the Jailhouse Rock: Alex Romero, Hollywood Choreographer* (Jefferson, NC: McFarland, 2013).

17. "Eleanor Powell Divorced from Actor Husband," *Valley Times* (North Hollywood, CA), November 23, 1959, 1.

18. Ford, *Glenn Ford: A Life.*

19. Ford, *Glenn Ford: A Life.*

20. Ford, *Glenn Ford: A Life.*

21. Ford, *Glenn Ford: A Life.*

22. Ford, *Glenn Ford: A Life.*

23. Louella O. Parsons, "Gene Tierney Has Breakdown Again," *Miami Herald,* October 29, 1956, 44.

24. Sheilah Graham, Hollywood Report, *Evening Star* (Washington, DC), September 30, 1956.

25. *Evening Independent* (Massillon, OH), July 18, 1956, 4.

26. Mike Connelly, "Mickey Rooney's Negotiating," *Palm Springs Desert Sun,* March 9, 1957, 4.

27. Shirley MacLaine, *My Lucky Stars: A Hollywood Memoir* (New York: Random House, 2011).

28. "Eleanor Powell: World's Greatest Tap Dancer Comes Back," *Long Beach Independent,* January 22, 1961, 131.

29. "Eleanor Powell: World's Greatest Tap Dancer Comes Back."

30. Hedda Hopper, "Eleanor Powell Tells of Divorce," *Los Angeles Times,* May 7, 1959.

31. Hopper, "Eleanor Powell Tells of Divorce."

32. Ford, *Glenn Ford: A Life.*

33. Maybin Hewes Sherman, telephone interview by Paula Broussard, January 3, 2022.

34. Hopper, "Eleanor Powell Tells of Divorce."

35. Raymond Strait, *Hollywood's Star Children* (New York: S.P.I., 1992).

36. Strait, *Hollywood's Star Children.*

37. "Eleanor Powell Divorced from Actor Husband," *Valley Times* (North Hollywood, CA), November 23, 1959, 1.

38. "Miss Powell, Glenn Ford Are Divorced," *Morning Call* (Paterson, NJ), November 24, 1959, 28.

39. "Eleanor Powell Says Marriage Long in Jeopardy," *Mitchell (SD) Daily Republic,* May 2, 1959.

40. Lloyd Shearer, "Eleanor Powell, World's Greatest Woman Tap Dancer Comes Back," *Pasadena (CA) Star-News,* January 22, 1961, 88.

19. The Phoenix

1. *Independent Star News* (Long Beach, CA), January 22, 1961, 88.

2. Hedda Hopper, "Looking at Hollywood," *Chicago Tribune,* November 27, 1959, 40.

3. Eleanor Powell Western Union Telegram to Hedda Hopper, November 27, 1959, Hedda Hopper Papers, Margaret Herrick Library, Academy of Motion Picture Arts and Sciences, Beverly Hills, CA.

4. "Eleanor Powell to Resume Dancing," *Wilkes-Barre (PA) Record,* January 25, 1961, 18.

5. Florabel Muir, "Eleanor Powell's Amazing," *Daily News* (New York, NY), February 12, 1961, 16.

6. "Thank You and You and You for Making It Possible," *Reno Evening Gazette,* November 22, 1961, 32.

7. Harrison Carroll, Behind the Scenes in Hollywood, *Brazil (IN) Daily Times,* May 12, 1959.

8. Emery Wister, "I Danced and Cried," *Charlotte News,* December 22, 1962.

9. Strait, *Hollywood's Star Children.*

10. Whitney Boulton, "Looking Sideways," *Clovis (NM) News-Journal,* February 9, 1961, 12.

11. Boulton, "Looking Sideways."

12. Gerald M. Healy, "Eleanor Powell Coming Home," *Springfield (MA) Sunday Republican,* May 17, 1964, 4D.

13. "Thank You and You and You for Making It Possible," *Reno Evening Gazette.*

14. "The Rebirth of Eleanor Powell," *Springfield (MA) Republican* March 19, 1961.

15. Walter Terry, "Hoofing Disappears from American Dancing," *Janesville (WI) Daily Gazette,* August 3, 1961, 18.

16. Harrison Carroll, Behind the Scenes in Hollywood, *Brazil (IN) Daily Times,* April 17, 1961, 12.

17. Earl Wilson, "Eleanor Flips Bracelet Back," Last Night, *Morning Call* (Allentown, PA), June 28, 1961, 30.

18. Dorothy Kilgallen, "Eleanor Powell about to Marry?" *Cincinnati Enquirer,* December 12, 1961.

19. Art Long, "Pete Filled the Years of Famed Dancer's Leave," *Reno Gazette-Journal,* November 18, 1961, 18.

20. Pat Mascola, "Eleanor Powell Puts on Stellar Show Despite Injured Leg," *Sun-Tattler* (Hollywood, FL), March 9, 1962, 14.

21. Herb Kelly, Show Scene, *Miami News,* March 10, 1962, 7.

22. "Eleanor Powell to be Married," *Gazette* (Cedar Rapids, IA), November 1, 1963, 21.

23. Tony Charmoli, *Stars in My Eyes* (Teaneck, NJ: TurningPointPress, 2016).

24. Charmoli, *Stars in My Eyes.*

25. Gene Tuttle, "Las Vegas' First Nighter," *Las Vegas Sun,* April 21, 1962, 4.

26. Ralph Pearl, Vegas Daze and Nights, *Las Vegas Sun,* April 23, 1962, 4.

27. Maybin Hewes Sherman telephone interview by Paula Broussard, January 3, 2022.

28. Roy Fitzell interview by Heather Castillo, December 22, 2008.

29. Ralph Pearl, Vegas Daze and Nights, *Las Vegas Sun,* July 30, 1962, 5.

30. Ford, *Glenn Ford: A Life.*

31. Long, "Pete Filled the Years."

32. Bob Thomas, "Eleanor Powell Has Fun in New Career," *Corpus Christi News,* December 20, 1962, 8C.

33. Powell interview by Jane Ardmore.

34. "Storm Washes Out Princess Grace's Gala," *Evening Standard* (London, UK), August 8, 1964, 4.

35. Eleanor Powell letter to Stanley Woodward, October 3, 1964, Stanley Woodward Papers, 1875–1970, Smithsonian Institution, Archives of American Art.

36. Eleanor Powell letter to Stanley Woodward, January 22, 1965, Stanley Woodward Papers, 1875–1970, Smithsonian Institution, Archives of American Art.

20. Winding Down

1. Eleanor Powell letter to Stanley Woodward, September 16, 1965, Stanley Woodward Papers, 1875–1970, Smithsonian Institution, Archives of American Art.

2. Eleanor Powell letter to Stanley Woodward, September 22, 1966, Stanley Woodward Papers, 1875–1970, Smithsonian Institution, Archives of American Art.

3. David Baumgarten, *The 14th Day of Christmas* (Scotts Valley, CA: CreateSpace, 2015).

4. Nadine M. Edwards, "New Repertory Company Bows," *Hollywood Citizen-News,* September 8, 1965.

5. Edwards, "New Repertory Company Bows."

6. Ford, *Glenn Ford: A Life.*

7. Alexander Roman, dir., *Peter Ford: A Little Prince,* 2012, documentary.

8. Ford, *Glenn Ford: A Life.*

9. Bob Thomas, "Fred Astaire Goes Back to Work at 75," *Boston Globe,* June 8, 1974, 11.

10. Powell interview by Jane Ardmore.

11. James Scott Bell, "The Greatest Dancer Who Ever Lived," *Killzone* (blog), last modified 2009, https://killzoneblog.com/2009/12/greatest-dancer-who-ever-lived.html.

12. Bell, "The Greatest Dancer Who Ever Lived."

13. Jeff Parker, "Eleanor Powell Born to Dance: With Loving Memories," *Hollywood Studio Magazine,* August 1982. Jack "Jeff" Parker passed away on July 7, 1984, at the age of fifty.

14. Private conversation with Lisa Royère.

15. Eleanor Powell letter to Lisa Royère, September 23, 1977. In author's possession.

16. Eleanor Powell letter to Lisa Royère, September 8, 1981. In author's possession.

Bibliography

Archives and Collections

Academy of Motion Picture Arts & Sciences
Academy Film Archive
Hollywood, CA

American Film Institute
Oral History Program in Motion Picture History
Louis B. Mayer Library
Los Angeles, CA

Institute of Jazz Studies
Rutgers University
New Brunswick, NJ
   Marshall Stearns Collection

Legal Department Files (accessed in 1984)
Metro-Goldwyn-Mayer Studios, Culver City, CA

Library of Congress
Moving Image Research Center
Washington, DC

Margaret Herrick Library,
Academy of Motion Picture Arts and Sciences,
Beverly Hills, CA
   Metro-Goldwyn-Mayer Collection
   Hedda Hopper Papers
   Jane Ardmore Papers

New York Public Library
Lincoln Center, New York, NY
   Billy Rose Performing Arts Collection

Bibliography

Shubert Archive
New York, NY

Smithsonian Institution,
Archives of American Art
Washington, DC
    Stanley Woodward Papers

University of Wyoming, American Heritage Center
Division of Rare Books and Special Collections
Laramie, WY
    Eleanor Powell Collection

USC Cinematic Arts Library
University of Southern California
Los Angeles, CA
    Arthur Freed Collection
    Andrew Stone Collection

Wood Museum of Springfield History
Springfield, MA

Published Works

Astaire, Fred. *Steps in Time.* New York: Harper & Brothers, 1959.

Basinger, Jeanine. *The Star Machine.* New York: Vintage, 2009.

Baumgarten, David. *The 14th Day of Christmas.* Scotts Valley, CA: CreateSpace, 2015.

Billman, Larry. *Film Choreographers and Dance Directors: An Illustrated Biographical Encyclopedia, with a History and Filmographies, 1893 through 1995.* Jefferson, NC: McFarland, 1997.

Blum, Daniel C. *A Pictorial History of the American Theatre, 1900–1950.* Toronto: Ambassador, 1950.

Bond, Tommy "Butch," and Ronald Genini. *Darn Right It's Butch: Memories of Our Gang, the Little Rascals.* Radnor, PA: Morgin, 1994.

Bordman, Gerald M. *American Musical Theatre: A Chronicle,* 3rd ed. New York: Oxford University Press, 1978.

Brideson, Cynthia, and Sara Brideson. *Ziegfeld and His Follies: A Biography of Broadway's Greatest Producer.* Lexington: University Press of Kentucky, 2015.

Briggs, Colin. *Cordially Yours, Ann Sothern.* Albany, GA: BearManor Media, 2006.

Charmoli, Tony. *Stars in My Eyes.* Teaneck, NJ: TurningPointPress, 2016.

Dietz, Dan. *The Complete Book of 1930s Broadway Musicals.* Lanham, MD: Rowman & Littlefield, 2018.

Ellenberger, Allan R., and Robert M. Paton. *Anita Page: A Career Chronicle and Biography.* Jefferson, NC: McFarland, 2021.

Ford, Peter. *Glenn Ford: A Life.* Madison: University of Wisconsin Press, 2011.

Foster, Lille. *U.S. Army Life 1941–1945: In the Letters of Theodore Pattengill Foster.* Morrisville, NC: Lulu, 2018.

Franceschina, John. *Duke Ellington's Music for the Theatre.* Jefferson, NC: McFarland, 2017.

Frankel, Noralee. *Stripping Gypsy: The Life of Gypsy Rose Lee.* New York: Oxford University Press, 2009.

Gabler, Neal. *An Empire of Their Own: How the Jews Invented Hollywood.* New York: Anchor, 2010.

Gordon, Jeff. *Foxy Lady: The Authorized Biography of Lynn Bari.* Albany, GA: BearManor Media, 2010.

Green, Stanley. *Ring Bells! Sing Songs!: Broadway Musicals of the 1930's.* New York: Galahad, 1971.

Griffin, Mark. *A Hundred or More Hidden Things: The Life and Films of Vincente Minnelli.* Boston: Da Capo, 2010.

Gutner, Howard. *MGM Style: Cedric Gibbons and the Art of the Golden Age of Hollywood.* Lanham, MD: Rowman & Littlefield, 2019.

Jason, Sybil. *Five Minutes More.* Albany, GA: BearManor Media, 2007.

Jones, Jan. *Billy Rose Presents: Casa Mañana.* Fort Worth: Texas Christian University Press, 1999.

Knowles, Mark. *The Man Who Made the Jailhouse Rock: Alex Romero, Hollywood Choreographer.* Jefferson, NC: McFarland, 2013.

Kobal, John. *People Will Talk.* New York: Alfred A. Knopf, 1985.

Leaming, Barbara. *If This Was Happiness: A Biography of Rita Hayworth.* New York: Viking, 1989.

Levin, Alice B. *Eleanor Powell: First Lady of Dance.* San Francisco, CA: Empire, 1997.

Levy, Emanuel. *Vincente Minnelli: Hollywood's Dark Dreamer.* New York: St. Martin's, 2009.

Liebman, Roy. *Vitaphone Films: A Catalogue of the Features and Shorts.* Jefferson, NC: McFarland, 2015.

Luft, Sid. *Judy & I: My Life with Judy Garland.* London: Omnibus, 2018.

Lulay, Gail. *Nelson Eddy: America's Favorite Baritone: An Authorized Biographical Tribute.* Wheeling, IL: Goldfleet, 1992.

MacLaine, Shirley. *My Lucky Stars: A Hollywood Memoir.* New York: Random House, 2011.

Marafioti, Pasqual M. *The New Vocal Art.* New York: Boni and Liveright, 1925.

Marmorstein, Gary. *A Ship without a Sail: The Life of Lorenz Hart.* New York: Simon & Schuster, 2013.

Marx, Samuel. *Mayer and Thalberg: The Make-Believe Saints.* New York: Random House, 1975.

Minnelli, Vincente, and Hector Arce. *I Remember It Well.* New York: Doubleday, 1974.

Murphy, George, and Victor Lasky. *"Say . . . Didn't You Used to be George Murphy?"* New York: Bartholomew House, 1970.

Nolan, Frederick. *Lorenz Hart: A Poet on Broadway.* New York: Oxford University Press, 1995.

Ohl, Vicki. *Fine and Dandy: The Life and Work of Kay Swift.* New Haven: Yale University Press, 2004.

Parish, James R., and Ronald L. Bowers. *The MGM Stock Company: The Golden Era.* Liverpool: Outlet, 1972.

Porter, Cole. *The Letters of Cole Porter.* Edited by Cliff Eisen and Dominic McHugh. New Haven: Yale University Press, 2019.

Quirk, Lawrence J. *James Stewart: Behind the Scenes of a Wonderful Life.* New York: Applause, 1997.

Reid, John. *Movies Magnificent: 150 Must-See Cinema Classics.* Morrisville, NC: Lulu, 2005.

Reynolds, Burt. *My Life.* New York: Hyperion, 1994.

Sarlot, Raymond R., and Fred E. Basten. *Life at the Marmont.* London: Penguin, 1987.

Savage, James A. *A Genealogical Dictionary of the First Settlers of New England: Showing Three Generations of Those Who Came before May, 1692, on the Basis of Farmer's Register.* Boston: Little, Brown, 1860.

Schultz, Margie. *Eleanor Powell: A Bio-Bibliography.* Santa Barbara, CA: Greenwood, 1994.

Shipman, David. *Judy Garland: The Secret Life of an American Legend.* New York: Hyperion, 1992.

Slide, Anthony. *The Encyclopedia of Vaudeville.* Jackson: University Press of Mississippi, 2012.

Spivak, Jeffrey. *Buzz: The Life and Art of Busby Berkeley.* Lexington: University Press of Kentucky, 2010.

Stearns, Marshall W., and Jean Stearns. *Jazz Dance: The Story of American Vernacular Dance.* New York: Macmillan, 1979.

Strait, Raymond. *Hollywood's Star Children.* New York: S.P.I., 1992.

Van Leuven, Holly. *Ray Bolger: More Than a Scarecrow.* New York: Oxford University Press, 2018.

Weber, Nicholas F. *Patron Saints: Five Rebels Who Opened America to a New Art, 1928–1943.* New Haven: Yale University Press, 1995.

Williams, Esther, and Digby Diehl. *The Million Dollar Mermaid.* New York: Simon & Schuster, 1999.

Williams, Tennessee. *The Selected Letters of Tennessee Williams, 1920–1945.* New York: New Directions, 2000.

Ziegfeld, Richard E., and Paulette Ziegfeld. *The Ziegfeld Touch: The Life and Times of Florenz Ziegfeld, Jr.* New York: Harry N. Abrams, 1992.

Index

Abbott and Costello, 163, 174

Academy Awards, 67, 106, 161

Ackerman, Jack, 159

Adrian (Gilbert Adrian), 73, 77, 177

Affair in Trinidad (film), 211–12

Ainley, Richard, 176

Aitchison, Andrew, 205

"All Ashore (I Am the Captain)" (song), 144, 149, 151

Allen, Gracie, 86, 128, 131–32, 134

Allen, Vera, 82

Allison, Tom, 233

Alton, Robert "Bob," 11, 53

Aly Khan, Prince, 212

Ambassador Hotel (Atlantic City), 14–15; Ambassador Recreation Club, 16; Canary Tea Room, 14; Pompeiian Grill, 15–16

Ambassador Hotel (Los Angeles), 174

American in Paris, An (film), 167, 211

Americano, The (film), 216

Amos 'n Andy, 45

Anchors Aweigh (film), 182

Anderson, John Murray, 52

Andrews Sisters, 173

Ankers, Evelyn, 173–74

Arden, Donn, 232–33, 235

Armstrong, Louis, 74, 87

Army and Navy Relief Society, 171

Arnaz, Desi, 163, 171, 249

Arnaz, Desi, Jr., 249

Arno, Judy (née Judith Powell), 243

Arnst, Bobbe, 24

Aronson, Wes, 135

Arturo Romero and his Magic Violins, 239

Astaire, Fred, 161, 240; AFI tribute to, 256; appearance, concern over, 149; as high standard for Eleanor, 120; *Broadway Melody of 1940* and, 139–40, 143–49; comparison of Eleanor to, 76, 89; considered for *Girl Crazy,* 177; considered for television special with Eleanor, 223; considered for *The Duchess of Idaho,* 206; *Dancing Lady* and, 67; disciplined approach to dance, 146; Fred Astaire Dance Studios and, 203; Grauman's Chinese Theatre footprint ceremony, 123; height and MGM's concern over, 139; *Hot-Cha!* and, 38; legal battle over rival drum dance for *A Damsel in Distress,* 119; partnership with Eleanor, end of, 151; refusal to introduce Eleanor, 241; star status retained with age, 182; studio search to find equivalent of, 70; *That's Entertainment* and, 252; *Top Hat* and, 80

Astaire, Fred and Adele, 23

Astor, Lady Nancy, 125

Astoria Studios, 56. *See also* Paramount Long Island Studio

Athena (film), 208

Atherton, Galen, 8, 16

At Home Abroad (radio), 90. *See also* radio appearances

At Home Abroad (show), 81–86, 88–90, 92, 96, 102, 141, 162, 178. *See also* stage career

Atkinson, Buddy, 135

Atlantic City, 14–19; Ambassador Hotel, 14–16; Ambassador Recreation Club,

281

Index

Index

Screen Classics

Screen Classics is a series of critical biographies, film histories, and analytical studies focusing on neglected filmmakers and important screen artists and subjects, from the era of silent cinema through the golden age of Hollywood to the international generation of today. Books in the Screen Classics series are intended for scholars and general readers alike. The contributing authors are established figures in their respective fields. This series also serves the purpose of advancing scholarship on film personalities and themes with ties to Kentucky.

Series Editor
Patrick McGilligan

Books in the Series

My Life in Focus: A Photographer's Journey with Elizabeth Taylor and the Hollywood Jet Set
  Gianni Bozzacchi with Joey Tayler
Hollywood Divided: The 1950 Screen Directors Guild Meeting and the Impact of the Blacklist
  Kevin Brianton
He's Got Rhythm: The Life and Career of Gene Kelly
  Cynthia Brideson and Sara Brideson
Ziegfeld and His Follies: A Biography of Broadway's Greatest Producer
  Cynthia Brideson and Sara Brideson
Eleanor Powell: Born to Dance
  Paula Broussard and Lisa Royère
The Marxist and the Movies: A Biography of Paul Jarrico
  Larry Ceplair
Dalton Trumbo: Blacklisted Hollywood Radical
  Larry Ceplair and Christopher Trumbo
Warren Oates: A Wild Life
  Susan Compo
Improvising Out Loud: My Life Teaching Hollywood How to Act
  Jeff Corey with Emily Corey
Crane: Sex, Celebrity, and My Father's Unsolved Murder
  Robert Crane and Christopher Fryer
Jack Nicholson: The Early Years
  Robert Crane and Christopher Fryer
Anne Bancroft: A Life
  Douglass K. Daniel
Being Hal Ashby: Life of a Hollywood Rebel
  Nick Dawson
Bruce Dern: A Memoir
  Bruce Dern with Christopher Fryer and Robert Crane
Intrepid Laughter: Preston Sturges and the Movies
  Andrew Dickos
The Woman Who Dared: The Life and Times of Pearl White, Queen of the Serials
  William M. Drew
Miriam Hopkins: Life and Films of a Hollywood Rebel
  Allan R. Ellenberger
Vitagraph: America's First Great Motion Picture Studio
  Andrew A. Erish
Jayne Mansfield: The Girl Couldn't Help It
  Eve Golden
John Gilbert: The Last of the Silent Film Stars
  Eve Golden
Strictly Dynamite: The Sensational Life of Lupe Velez
  Eve Golden
Stuntwomen: The Untold Hollywood Story
  Mollie Gregory
Jean Gabin: The Actor Who Was France
  Joseph Harriss
Otto Preminger: The Man Who Would Be King, updated edition
  Foster Hirsch
Saul Bass: Anatomy of Film Design
  Jan-Christopher Horak
Lawrence Tierney: Hollywood's Real-Life Tough Guy
  Burt Kearns

Milton Keynes UK
Ingram Content Group UK Ltd.
UKHW012059300823
427777UK00004B/74/J

9 780813 197883